❖

Hard Time

Understanding and Reforming the Prison

Third Edition

ROBERT JOHNSON
American University

WADSWORTH

★ ™

THOMSON LEARNING

Australia • Canada • Mexico • Singapore • Spain
United Kingdom • United States

For my mother, Kay, ever my most accepting reader
For my wife, Deirdra, always my most devoted reader
For my sons, Brian and Patrick, surely my most avid readers

Executive Editor, Criminal Justice:
Sabra Horne
Assistant Editor: Dawn Mesa
Editorial Assistant: Lee McCracken
Marketing Manager: Jennifer Somerville
Marketing Assistant: Karyl Davis
Project Manager, Editorial Production:
Erica Silverstein

Print/Media Buyer: Robert King
Permissions Editor: Joohee Lee
Production Service: Shepherd, Inc.
Copy Editor: Jeanne Patterson
Cover Designer: Yvo Riezebos
Cover Image: PhotoDisc
Text and Cover Printer: Webcom Limited
Compositor: Shepherd, Inc.

For permission to use material from this text, contact us by
Web: http://www.thomsonrights.com
Fax: 1-800-730-2215
Phone: 1-800-730-2214

Wadsworth/Thomson Learning
10 Davis Drive
Belmont, CA 94002-3098
USA

For more information about our products, contact us:
Thomson Learning Academic Resource Center
1-800-423-0563
http://www.wadsworth.com

International Headquarters
Thomson Learning
International Division
290 Harbor Drive, 2nd Floor
Stamford, CT 06902-7477
USA

UK/Europe/Middle East/South Africa
Thomson Learning
Berkshire House
168-173 High Holborn
London WC1V 7AA
United Kingdom

Asia
Thomson Learning
60 Albert Street, #15-01
Albert Complex
Singapore 189969

Canada
Nelson Thomson Learning
1120 Birchmount Road
Toronto, Ontario M1K 5G4
Canada

Library of Congress Cataloging-in-Publication Data
Johnson, Robert
    Hard Time : understanding and reforming the prison / Robert Johnson.—3rd ed.
        p. cm.
    Includes bibliographical references and index.
    ISBN 0-534-50717-4 (alk. paper)
    1. Prisons—United States. 2. Prison psychology. 3. Prison administration—United States. I. Title
HV9471 .J64 2001
365.7'0973—dc21
                                                                    2001039121

Contents

iii

II   LIVING AND WORKING IN PRISON

Foreword

As editor of the *Wadsworth Series on Contemporary Issues in Crime and Justice,* I am delighted to introduce this, the third edition of *Hard Time,* by Robert Johnson. The Wadsworth Series publishes books that address important issues in crime and justice in ways that go well beyond the coverage provided by typical classroom textbooks. It is the aim of this series to deepen students' understanding of important questions facing criminology and criminal justice. The series has, over the years, published some of the most important books on current topics of interest to the field.

Professor Robert Johnson's book, *Hard Time,* now in its third edition, is just such a book. Nobody has done a better job of presenting what it means to be locked up in today's prison system, a prospect few of us will face, but something that more and more Americans are encountering, as the U.S. prison system continues to grow. That is one of today's ironies: for nearly thirty years, the total number of prisoners locked up in prisons and jails has grown steadily—in times of rising crime and during times when crime rates dropped—to the point that today's prison population is about six times what it was in 1972.

Yet when the average American is asked about the penal system, as likely as not the answer will be that prisons are "soft" and punishment is "too lenient." Today, prison is a lot less rare than it has every been, and it is focused on minorities and the poor: about 7 percent of African American males are locked up on any given day (nearly one-third of all black males are expected to be imprisoned during their lifetimes). In some neighborhoods of poor people, it is hard to find a family that has not been touched by the prison through the incarceration of at least one family member. The prison, an original American invention, has been a part of American social control for nearly two centuries, but it has never been as prominent a social institution as it is today.

That is why it is so peculiar that the prison, this American invention of increasing prominence, is so poorly understood. Common thought has it that the prison system is not so bad, and prison time is pretty easy. Professor Johnson has written a book that shows how wrong it is to think of prisons as "easy" or prison time as inconsequential. It is true, of course, that prisons today are intended to be less cruel than prisons when they were first invented. Today, torture is illegal and brutality is forbidden as well (although there is plenty of evidence that it occurs in prisons anyway, though not incessantly). But that does not mean that incarceration is an experience without pain. In place of corporal suffering, the modern prison imposes losses that count more as spiritual and social deficits. The loss of freedom is significant, as is the loss of social status that comes with being a convict. On top of that, there is the pressure that doing time brings—simply a challenge to make it inside the walls, to adjust to an environment that is hostile to most of what we all would want. Professor Johnson tells us that imprisonment in a "disheartening and threatening" experience, no matter how "easy" it seems to be. There is stress and pressure on everyone, and they all have to figure out a way to cope with the grave prison environment.

This is a key idea in Professor Johnson's study of the prison: everybody in the prison has to figure out a way to cope with the stressful environment. For prisoners, this means there is a need to figure out how to make it in the context of a potentially hostile and even dangerous group of peers. But there is also a private adjustment—the prisoner who has figured out how to handle the social world of the prison must also find a way to counter its psychological meaning. The problem of being confined is not simply that of being locked up with a bunch of other prisoners, but it is also the difficulty of having one's self-esteem and identity bombarded as well, with the evidence of a failed life and a lesser human status. But the public-private challenge is not only a problem for the inmate but also a problem for those who guard the prisoner. Here, too, there is a social challenge of interacting on a daily basis with those who are confined, of managing authority in an ambiguous situation. There is also the personal issue: how can a person come to grips with being someone else's captor? What at first glance appears to be a relatively simple social function—the prison—upon investigation emerges as a complex social and psychological world, laden with challenges so profound that one's very own identity is at stake.

It is against these questions that the problem of prison reform faces its most serious challenges. How can we make prisons more humane environments, more reasonable places for some people to be confined and others to be employed as workers? Indeed, should we strive for this end? Is it possible, even worthy, as a goal? Professor Johnson engages these questions, and ends with a call for a program of "coping competence."

Almost everyone has an opinion about prison, but for most of us, it is an opinion formed on the basis of images rather than information, feelings rather than experiences. After reading this book, filled as it is with new and rich perspective on confinement, most of us will experience a change in our views. We will see the prison world in its greater complexity, and we will have a new respect for the challenges faced by those who live and work in these places.

I am delighted to introduce this new edition to the Series. *Hard Time,* by Robert Johnson, is a very good book on a fascinating topic. It gives a portrait of contemporary prison life better than any other book available today.

Todd R. Clear
New York City
May 9, 2001

Preface

Hard Time is a book about prisons. The focus is on men, but core concerns of women are considered as well. The book explores what I believe are basic human dimensions of prison life and adjustment, and closes with an inclusive, person-centered vision of prison reform. Firsthand testimony and observations drawn from people who live or work in prisons are highlighted and specially marked with black squares (■) throughout the book.

Most of the people we send to prison are men, roughly 94 percent. Most prisoners serve time in prisons that are, as living environments if not in terms of strict classification criteria, maximum-security institutions.[1] The maximum-security prison for men has served as the explicit or implicit model—the point of departure if not the template—for virtually all men's prisons and many women's prisons as well. Life in these prisons is depriving and painful. On that score at least, prisons vary in degree, not kind. The inhabitants of every prison serve hard time. Nothing can change this basic and enduring fact. That hard time can also be constructive time is, in my view, the key to understanding and reforming the prison.

The thesis of this book is simple. Prisoners serve hard time, as they are meant to, but typically learn little of value during their stint behind bars. They adapt to prison in immature and often destructive ways. As a result, they leave prison no better, and sometimes considerably worse, than when they went in. But mature coping is possible in prison, can be facilitated by staff and programs, and can result in the correction or rehabilitation of offenders. Prisons, then, can be decent, humane institutions; imprisonment can be a constructively painful experience. It is my contention that we can ask no more of our prisons, and should settle for no less.

Hard Time is divided into three parts. Part One reviews the history of prisons. In Chapter One, the earliest forms of incarceration are examined. Chapter Two covers modern prisons—prisons developed over the 19th and 20th centuries, notably the penitentiary, the reformatory, the Big House, the correctional institution, and briefly, the contemporary prison. The subject of Chapter Three is centrality of pain as a feature of life in confinement under

---

[1] Many prisoners serve time in institutions officially classified as medium security, but that label describes formal security procedures rather than living conditions. Medium-security prisons are virtually indistinguishable from maximum-security prisons in terms of the daily pressures of life and adjustment—the pains of imprisonment—they present to their inhabitants. This is particularly true in these days of crowded prisons, where offenders with serious felony records are shunted off to medium security institutions on a regular basis.

different penal regimes. First-person accounts of adaptation to prison by men and women are emphasized. In Part Two, patterns of adjustment to the pains of contemporary prisons are examined in detail. Here, too, the emphasis is on first-person accounts. Basic features of human adjustment to prison—that is, adjustments shared by men and women—as well as continuities in prison adjustment over time—from early to contemporary prisons—are noted and examined. The notion of mature coping, as evidenced by men and by women, is developed in Chapter Four and guides the reader through this section. The social adjustments of prisoners (Chapters Five and Six) and staff (Chapters Seven and Eight) are then considered in turn. Prospects for mature coping among prisoners, with support from the staff, are emphasized. In Part Three, the book concludes with a review of the latest developments in the management of prison environments (Chapter Nine) and prison programs (Chapter Ten). The book closes with a reform proposal in which mature coping adaptation to the pains of imprisonment, together with help in navigating the transition to the free world, are primary objectives of correctional work.

The third edition of *Hard Time* differs in important ways from its earlier incarnations. Most notably, the discussion has been broadened to explicitly include the concerns of women and minorities in the prison community. It has always been my goal to examine basic human dimensions of adaptation to prison. In this edition, I am able to highlight several aspects of prison adjustment (for example, the central role of niches in the prison adjustment process) that are widely shared by men and women, and by minority and nonminority inmates as well. The concepts of forgiveness and reconciliation, implicit in earlier editions, receive more attention. Similarly, the process of reintegration in the free community upon release from prison receives more coverage. Of course, the obligatory updating of materials has been done as well. This edition incorporates the latest statistics and research on the various issues broached in the text. As in earlier editions, I make explicit my contention that prisons are limited instruments of public policy that should be treated as scarce resources, to be used sparingly in our various campaigns to control crime. For the record, I do not advocate the use of prisons at the levels we see today or with all of the offender populations we see behind bars these days. On the other hand, there is little doubt that prisons are here to stay, and I continue to be committed to the constructive uses of prisons where and when this is possible.

Hard Time enters its third edition as we mark the thirtieth anniversary of the Attica prison riot. Attica is not a central topic of this book, nor are prison riots a primary concern. The Attica riot was, however, a momentous event in the history of modern prisons and its legacy may help us gain perspective on the state of American prisons today.

The Attica riot was the first event of its kind to secure extended prime-time television coverage. The riot was headline news from start to finish (it lasted four days). It was the first American prison riot that could be thought of as political, explicitly calling into question the legitimacy of the prison as an institution of criminal justice. The main participants were militant convicts, most of them

young black men who presented themselves to a watching world as revolutionaries rather than disgruntled or abused convicts, the more common poses
assumed by aggrieved prisoners before and after Attica. This riot was a kind of
war on the prison as an institution and an indictment of the society that
spawned such settings of repression, replete with hostages, a demilitarized zone
(in Attica's D Yard, where inmate and civilian negotiators congregated, under the
gaze of the media), political speeches by inmate leaders dressed in disguises that
were the prison equivalent of guerrilla warfare regalia, and of course a lengthy
list of demands.

Most of the inmate demands had to do with better daily living conditions,
including such mundane requests as better food and more showers, requirements that, modest as they may seem, have been and remain the staple of prison
riots. But the Attica rioters also insisted on a general amnesty (a correctional
officer had died of injuries sustained at the outset of the riot) and asylum in a
third world country where people of color might live in peace, free from the
pernicious racism they felt had shaped their lives and the lives of those before
them, going back centuries to the institution of slavery, the original sin of
American race relations. These latter requests—amnesty and asylum—proved
to be sticking points. It is unclear who might have the authority to grant them,
but in any event no one came forward to grant them. Negotiations stalled.
Soon, the prison was retaken by force, with forty people—twenty-nine inmates
and eleven staff—dying in the bloody process.

The tragic end to the riot seared Attica into our memories in a paradoxical way. For it was the violent retaking of the prison by officials that wrought
the bulk of the blood and the carnage, not the behavior of the inmates during
the taking or the retaking of the prison. Dead hostages and inmates were, with
the exception of the three inmates killed by their fellows during the course of
the riot, the victims of official violence—of shotgun wielding state police and
off-duty correctional officers who stormed the prison under the cover provided by tear-gas dropped from helicopters that hovered just above the prison
wall. A reign of terror followed the retaking of the prison that was nothing
short of criminal. Prisoners were beaten, first in the yard, then in the cell blocks
for some days to come. There were good guys and bad guys on display during
the Attica riot, in other words, but in the end it appeared that too many of the
good guys were inmates and too many of the bad guys were police or correctional officers. Lawsuits generated by the riot, and only recently come to
fruition, highlight the moral ambiguity of this riot. A civilian jury found in
favor of the relatives of inmates, awarding eight million dollars in damages.

What is the legacy of Attica? It would be an evasion to say that the significance of this event is to be found in the eyes of the beholder, but that answer
is not far from the truth. For the first years after Attica, prisons appeared to have
become more relaxed and less repressive, as if the authorities were chastened by
the awful violence of the riot and hesitant to enforce order. Soon, these loosely
run prisons became unworkable and dangerous, for staff and inmate alike.
Reluctant authorities could not, it would seem, effectively ride herd on angry
inmates who questioned the justice of their imprisonment, of the prison itself,

and of the larger society that built prisons and sanctioned the placement of convicts within their walls. The image of the prison was fast becoming one of an institution under siege.

Outside the correctional field, in a world rapidly turning from the liberalism of the sixties to the conservatism of the seventies and beyond, the lesson of Attica was not that the state could too easily abuse its power but that the state had been insufficiently resolute in the exercise of that power. Certainly the decline of order in prisons after Attica—a decline found in women's prisons as well as in men's prisons—would seem to back up this perception. Be that as it may, while some of the viewing public saw in the Attica riot a story of downtrodden humanity struggling to break free from the bonds of oppression, many others apparently saw chaos and the shameful consequences of official vacillation and cowardice. If there is a culture war afoot in America, with conservatives pushing a law-and-order and back-to-basics agenda as a reaction to the liberal, permissive sixties, the battle cry for the prison front of that larger war effort would be "Attica: Never Again." For most people, it would now seem, Attica was the problem—it had been weak, soft, an easy target. Prisons henceforth would be rigid and regimented. Hard time would get harder. Punishment would rule.

For corrections as a field, the first casualty of the culture war was indeterminate sentencing, which for most of the twentieth century had served as the bedrock of rehabilitation. The core notions underlying indeterminate sentences were that offenders could be reformed, and that they should be released when they were rehabilitated, not when they had served some arbitrary amount of time. But if one wants punishment with a conservative, even fundamentalist twist, sentences, like the Ten Commandments, must be set in stone. To this way of thinking, all criminals are equally bad and equally unregenerate. Sentences must be set for mandatory terms and must be calibrated to mete out suitably harsh punishments, including added penalties for repeat offenders—hence the mandatory minimum and various "two" and "three strike" laws that have proliferated since Attica.

Next came efforts to tighten prison conditions. If prisons were for punishment and not for rehabilitation, then the order of the day was deprivation rather than enrichment, oppression rather than correction. One might agree that prisons, even when focused on rehabilitation, meted out "hard time," but it was clear that one could make hard time harder still by limiting if not removing amenities, privileges, and, later, correctional programs. Why should prisoners have anything given to them? What did they truly deserve? Very little, it would seem. More and more, three hots and a cot—with that cot securely bolted to the floor of a cell—have come to sound like the basic components of a contemporary regime of penal confinement.

Some of the movement to make prisons more uncongenial than normal has proven to be political posturing. It is by no means clear, for example, that average prisoners in ordinary prisons find today that they can't lift weights or play handball anymore because some politician wanted to prove him or herself suitably tough on crime. But it does seem that a climate of constraint rather than facilitation has taken hold across much of the corrections field. Prisons today are, in the main, more limited and limiting, crowded and controlling, and finally, isolated and isolating. Modern technology allows us to reduce the number of staff and to deploy existing staff in roles that limit—and sometimes eliminate—social interaction with prisoners. We don't have prisons that are so impersonal that they are run entirely by computers. But the impetus of technology, particularly when linked to a profit motive (as seen in the growing movement to privatize prisons), suggests that prisons may become more cold and mechanical in the coming years.

No one knows how far technology will creep into our prisons, but supermax prisons, now present in some thirty-six states, suggest that the picture of technology at work in penal institutions may not be a pretty one, at least for the highest security prisoners—the ones we may not want to touch or talk with or even observe face-to-face. In supermax prisons, inmates virtually never leave their cells and have almost no contact with other human beings over the course of their confinement, which can last for years. These supermax prisons give the "hole"—traditional prison segregation—a good name! At least in the old-fashioned segregation units, the prisoner had some regular interaction with officers and even fellow inmates. In many supermax prisons, one only hears an officer's voice when he or she speaks to you over the intercom; the sound of authority comes to you in stereo, from speakers located conveniently in your cell, working in tandem with the television cameras that offer the prison staff candid views of you during your hours of seeming solitude. Likewise, the raw power of authority can be delivered by remote control. In supermax prisons, difficult inmates are fitted with "stun belts" that can be activated at a distance, reducing the prisoner to a quivering mass of pain and confusion at the mere push of a button. Alternatively, officers are equipped with electrical prods. At least in these extreme settings, then, we see the use of technology to make violence by officials easy and effective, and hence to widen the distance between staff and inmates.

Of course, supermax prisons are not typical prisons. Supermax prisons are prohibitively expensive, and the regime they offer staff as well as inmates is a grim and unrewarding one for normal human beings. In regular prisons for men and women, the topic of this book, control is less oppressive and technology less pervasive and intrusive. Some uses of technology in regular penal institutions, for example in routine surveillance, permit a safer social order to emerge. Our focus will be on standard prisons and, where possible, on the hopeful trends and possibilities they offer. But we must remember that the lure of repression, embodied in the supermax prison, lurks ominously below the surface of current correctional arrangements. An awareness of this fact may add to our resolve to work for decent prisons. The alternatives—indecent and oppressive prisons—are unworthy of the civilized society they would purport to serve.

ACKNOWLEDGMENTS

Over the fifteen years this book has been in print, I have had the good fortune to receive thoughtful reviews from a number of distinguished colleagues, including Melissa Benningfield, Robert Bing, Marianna Burt, Leo Carroll, Thomas Carroll, John Conrad, Francis T. Cullen, Robert Fosen, Gerald Garrett, Lynne Goodstein, Paul Leighton, Charles A. Lindquist, Robert Levinson, Lucien Lombardo, Norval Morris, Joann Morton, Barbara Owen, Alexander Pisciotta, Jeffrey Reiman, Martin Schwartz, Hans Toch, and Edward Zamble. My thanks to them all.

I have been the grateful beneficiary of several diligent and devoted graduate assistants, most recently Kate MacNamee and Paige Marie Harrison, two promising young scholars working their way through our graduate program. Other students who offered help and inspiration include Nina Chernoff, Chris Goode, Jennifer Stair, and Angela Vernet.

I offer a warm thanks to my versatile assistant, Brigid Moore, whose proficiency and unfailing good cheer has made my tenure as department chair a pleasure rather than a burden. Brigid runs a smooth office, with everything sorted and in its proper place. Academic issues come in for their fair share of distracting work, but Brigid never lets mundane administrative details distract me from my larger tasks, that of teaching and writing. Of course, all of this is possible and acceptable because we have a dean who values research and scholarship. I offer heartfelt thanks to Dean Walter D. Broadnax, himself a distinguished scholar and administrator, for extending to us the trust and autonomy we need to do our various jobs and to do them well.

ABOUT THE AUTHOR

Robert Johnson is a Professor of Justice, Law, and Society in the School of Public Affairs at American University in Washington, D.C. He holds a bachelor's degree in psychology from Fairfield University, and master's and doctoral degrees in criminal justice from the University at Albany, State University of New York. Dr. Johnson's books include *Culture and Crisis in Confinement, Condemned To Die: Life Under Sentence of Death,* and *Death Work: A Study of the Modern Execution Process.* (Now in its second edition, *Death Work* received the Academy of Criminal Justice Science's Outstanding Book Award.). Dr. Johnson coedited and contributed to *The Pains of Imprisonment* and *Crime and Punishment: Inside Views,* and has published numerous articles in professional journals and anthologies. Professor Johnson has testified before state and federal courts and the U.S. Congress, and has provided expert affidavits to the European Commission of Human Rights. He received the American University Award for Outstanding Scholarship and the American University Teacher/Scholar of the Year Award. Dr. Johnson is a faculty member (Honora Causa) of Phi Kappa Phi, and has been formally honored as a Distinguished Alumnus of the Nelson A. Rockefeller College of Public Affairs and Policy, University at Albany, State University of New York.

Prison time must be hard time, a metaphorical death,
a sustained, twilight condition of death-in-life . . .
Yet the little death of a prison sentence doesn't quite kill
the prisoner, because prisons, in spite of their ability
to make the inmate's life unbearable, can't kill time . . .
Life goes on and since it does, miracles occur.

JOHN EDGAR WIDEMAN
Brothers and Keepers

1

❖

The Roots of Imprisonment

t is hard to think of crime without also thinking of prison. To most of us, crime means street crime, especially violent street crime. The punishment of choice for such crime is prison, and our image of prison is largely formed by the Big House of Hollywood fame. Hard criminals are meant to serve hard time in hard places like Alcatraz, aptly nicknamed "the Rock." You do the crime, you do the time—hard time, behind prison walls.

For better or worse, prisons are a fact of modern life, as solid and imposing as the walls that surround and contain them. Individual prisons may come and go, but the institution of the prison endures. Unlike the Wall of Jericho or, more recently, the Berlin Wall, the prison edifice stands firm. Indeed, prisons are a more central feature of our criminal justice system than at any time in history. More than ever, prison is our punishment of first resort for serious crime (and for many crimes that are arguably less than serious).

The fit between crime and prison, then, would seem to be a good one, at least an easy one to live with for people who don't have to live in prisons. For the average citizen, who presumes him or herself a most unlikely candidate for confinement, prisons take on a kind of mythic quality that makes them recurring subjects of popular culture, from songs, books, and movies to cartoons and jokes. One of my favorite cartoons is a *Far Side* segment featuring two prisoners hanging by their wrists from a dungeon wall. Off in the corner, a third prisoner is tied to a rack. No one struggles; everyone is utterly defeated. On the wall is a plaque that reads, in bold letters, "Congratulations, Bob. Torturer of the Month."[1] For us, prison as a setting of punishment—though not torture, which is why the cartoon makes us laugh rather than cry—comes to mind with the same easy facility that earlier generations thought of corporal or capital punishment. Just as errant English children in centuries past were warned that they would "come to a bad end," meaning the end of the hangman's rope, or threatened with a "lick" from the vicious "cat" (the cat-o'-nine-tails, a nine-tailed whip), we caution our delinquents about the rigors of life in prison, hoping to scare them straight.

Prisons have a peculiar salience in American culture, though few of us have visited a prison or even laid eyes on one. Recently, *The New Yorker* featured a cartoon with a prisoner sitting silently in his neatly maintained cell, reading a magazine, surrounded by posters touting several well-known prisons such as Attica and Stateville, including a pennant for Sing Sing, the original Big House to which offenders were consigned when they were "sent up the river" (the Hudson River) to pay their debt to society by breaking rocks in the prison quarry. It is as if these famous (or infamous) prisons were choice vacation spots or *alma maters* for the criminal set, the poster announcing a kind of Ivy League travel itinerary to which ambitious offenders might aspire. What I find striking is the humorist's assumption that an educated reading audience will know—by reputation—the various specific prisons that are the subjects of the posters adorning the inmate's wall. Readers can laugh at this cartoon, I suspect, because they are outsiders to the prison world and have only a limited sense of what goes on inside the prison, other than the vague notion that prisons punish people who need punishing. That offenders might remember prisons fondly or advertise them proudly suggests a comforting complicity between a guilty criminal and a society that must (perhaps guiltily) impose harsh penal sanctions. There is also, of course, a perverse pride of accomplishment reflected in this cartoon. In some circles, surviving prison—perhaps especially a well-known prison—is a badge of courage and a mark of criminal distinction.

Few of us spend much time pondering the state of our prisons. As upright citizens, we believe prisons are necessary. Most of us can't imagine the world without them. We take prisons for granted—no one living today can remember a time before prisons were a staple of criminal justice—and we suppose that, being inevitable, prisons are more or less just. Yet we harbor doubts. When pressed, we may concede that prisons are expensive to build and to operate and that they are, at best, ponderous instruments of public policy. It doesn't take much imagination to realize that sending offenders to prison is at once to penalize (sometimes traumatize) their loved ones, especially their children, and to impose added financial burdens on society, which must support those left behind when the offender is taken away and, later, absorb ex-prisoners with sharply limited employment prospects.[2] And though our prisons are awesome to behold—seemingly worth their weight in deterrence—a thoughtful observer can't help but note that prison sentences, even savage prison sentences, seem unable to bring the crime problem to heel by scaring prisoners straight or by occasioning in offenders the kind of reflection that changes lives for the better. (Prisons do deter some offenders, but they also make others more committed to crime as a way of life[3]; the lion's share of any change in crime rates—whether an increase or a decrease—is less a product of penal policy than of economic and demographic forces.) Yet we persist in building and staffing prisons at exorbitant costs and in stocking them with remarkable alacrity. At last count, American prisons housed well over a million inmates, with a projected annual growth rate of over 5 percent per year. The annual tab for our prison archipelago runs to about $25 billion.[4]

A PREDILECTION FOR PRISONS

The human preference for imprisoning criminals is of long standing. Confining dangerous people is an old if not venerable practice that, though generally carried out on a small scale, dates back at least to biblical times. Like the death penalty, another ancient practice, prison can be considered a civilized punishment. One only finds prisons in comparatively developed societies, and imprisonment typically represents an instance of restrained (albeit sometimes barely restrained) vengeance. Unlike the death penalty, however, prison can also be a *civilizing* penalty.[5] Prisons can reflect Plato's dictum that a person subject to punishment should emerge "a better man, or failing that, less of a wretch."[6] That is, imprisonment is a punishment from which the offender, male or female, can learn something of value: how to deal with pain and loss in mature ways. Prisoners can at once pay their debt to society and learn to cope more responsibly with the many pressures and constraints found in prison and the free world alike.

Yet the prison has been a source of mostly gratuitous and destructive pain, offering not so much a lesson in civilization as an exercise in abuse and neglect. Most prisons have been anything but civilized, and their effects have been considerably less than civilizing. On the whole, this is not surprising. Confinement is, in essence, a way to expel criminals from the community, to get them out of sight. It is thus little more than a sophisticated version of banishment, which is "society's most primitive form of self-defense."[7] For prisons to be civilizing institutions, there must be a conscious effort to make them decent, humane settings of confinement.

Prisons affect more citizens than one might at first suppose. Some of us—inmates past and present—comprise prison's reluctant alumni. Certain groups, notably poor African Americans, have borne an especially heavy burden, suffering incarceration rates that are remarkably high and growing higher virtually by the day. Still, most Americans, perhaps all of us, pay for prisons in one way or another: with tax dollars, spent out to cover direct prison costs that now, as noted earlier, run into the billions on an annual basis; with loved ones lost to confinement, some permanently, most for varying periods of time, but all changed by prison, irrevocably; with the violation of our humane values, the silent casualties of the brutal excesses of some prisons and the excessive use of prisons with less serious offenders. It is common to think of prisons as necessary evils that must be stoically endured, but that is only partially true. Prisons are necessary, but they need not be evil. We can and must use prisons in just and color-blind ways, and we can and must make our prisons decent, humane institutions of social control.

In symbol and in practice, prisons will *always* be a central feature of crime control in modern societies. Whether we imprison too many criminals or too few, serving sentences too long or too short, under conditions too harsh or too lax, prisons will be with us. And we will use prisons with much the same array of offenders we do today and have done for centuries (though the rates at which we confine different sorts of offenders can and do vary, sometimes substantially). In the main, prisons house a motley crew of impulsive, inadequate, pathetic but often noxiously intrusive characters who tend to be drawn disproportionately from socially vulnerable groups, notably the poor and especially poor people of color. Their crimes, often fueled by drugs or alcohol or both, run the gamut from lesser property crimes like larceny, drunk driving, and handling stolen property to the more serious and threatening property crimes such as burglary and robbery, to the unambiguously violent crimes of rape and homicide.

Today's prisons hold a large and growing population of drug offenders. Contrary to impressions left by the media, these are not, with rare exceptions, mafia kingpins or Columbian druglords but small-time runners, dealers, and addicted users.[8] A disproportionate number of them are young black men, and many, including a fair number of first offenders, face long mandatory minimum sentences "that are comparable to the sentences for homicide."[9] (In at least one jurisdiction, sentences for cocaine sales are harsher than sentences for homicide.[10]) Some of these drug offenders, similar to offenders generally, lead impoverished and disorganized lives, eking out a precarious existence on the fringes of conventional society.[11] Many others, however, are more fully integrated into the larger society. As many as two-thirds have a high-school education; others have maintained reasonably stable employment histories. These are not, generally speaking, the down-and-out element of society but people with some social attachments and hence some prospects for a decent life.[12] For the most part, their crimes are neither violent nor predatory in any meaningful sense of those terms; they are small fish passed off to an angry and frightened public as big catches in a largely futile and highly selective War on Drugs.[13] It is, in my view, both unjust and unwise—and perhaps racist as well—to imprison such offenders at all, let alone for long sentences, when suitable community options abound.[14]

Today's prisons also hold a large and growing number of minorities, particularly poor blacks, a group whose situation I will consider at some length.[15] Statistics on the over-representation of African Americans in our prisons have recently reached startling proportions, but blacks have been overrepresented in prisons since the end of slavery following the Civil War. It is ironic that many Americans view prison as a "black problem" because they suppose crime is a "black problem." We may well have it backward. African Americans have had and continue to have a "prison problem," starting with the unjust incarceration that was slavery. Discriminatory uses of incarceration—beginning with slavery, which we might think of as the orginal incarceration of African Americans—have contributed to high rates of poverty and of serious crime, which in turn have produced high rates of imprisonment.

In America, it is a sad if not shameful fact that poverty and minority status often go hand in hand. Poverty, in turn, tends to breed garden-variety street crime, since this sort of crime is a common adaptation to blocked opportunities for assimilation into American society and achievement of the American Dream of material success.[16] The connection among poverty, minority status, and street crime unites virtually all immigrant groups in American history. African Americans form a unique group, however, because they did not choose to come to America but rather were captured and enslaved and, hence, given no opportunity whatsoever for participation in American society.

The enslavement of African Americans, long forgotten by many in white America, has had lasting consequences for the black community. One legacy of slavery—and of a host of subsequent racist institutions and practices—is that poverty has been, *for centuries,* much more common among blacks than among whites.[17] Black poverty has also been much more ecologically concentrated than white poverty, due to residential segregation and limited job opportunities.[18] Black ghettos in turn have typically been more deteriorated and disorganized than poor white neighborhoods.[19] Another legacy of slavery—and, again, of a host of subsequent racist institutions and practices—is that the experience of lawlessness and injustice at the hands of formal authorities has been, *for centuries,* much more common among blacks than among whites.[20] Many blacks have thus lived on the margins of the larger society, outside the mainstream economy and outside the law, effectively confined first on plantations, later in rural shanty towns, and today in urban ghettos, in each instance in settings marked by profound—and profoundly alienating—social isolation.[21] Variously characterized today as "truly disadvantaged" and comprising a hard-core "underclass,"[22] many African Americans in times past and even today see "little reason to respect the law or to look down upon those who were punished and sent to jail"[23] and much reason to view and treat authorities of the justice system with contempt.[24]

It is, then, fair to say that no other group in American history has faced such conditions of continuing deprivation and injustice, often under the authority of law—including laws that explicitly allowed slavery and, later, racial segregation.[25] It is also fair to say that no other group in American history has lived for so long under what can only be called criminogenic conditions. The predictable result is a high rate of street crime together with a high rate of incarceration of black men and women. High rates of imprisonment, in turn, promote more social isolation and more crime, leading to yet more incarceration.[26]

Statistics on race and imprisonment, as we shall see, reveal a compelling pattern of racial bias. Yet these numbers tell only a part of the story of crime and prison in the lives of African Americans. It is tragically the case that American prisons, in times past, have often confined poor people for whom simply *being* an African American was either their *only* crime or the *real* reason that their crimes were punished with incarceration rather than a lesser sanction.[27] We see what may well be vestigial manifestations of racist uses of prisons in today's massive and continuing war on drugs.[28]

Prisons are, then, notably flawed institutions, and they can be put to flagrantly unjust purposes, including social control and racial oppression.[29] But there is no escaping them. Prisons have a major role to play in the punishment of crime. On balance, prisons are better than the competing alternatives available to control predatory criminals. Many prisoners are violent or repeat offenders, and those who are violent repeat offenders make up a sizable minority. Society must be protected from the predations of these criminals. Incarceration, from which escape is rare, virtually guarantees such protection for the term of the sentence imposed by the court. No viable alternative sanction has a comparable track record of success at this basic mission of social protection.[30] Our sensibilities lead us to conclude that locking up predatory criminals is better than torturing or, except in extreme cases, killing them. Our common sense, backed by research, leads us to conclude that locking up predators is better than releasing them directly to community supervision, even intensive community supervision, where the opportunities to prey on innocent citizens are rife and, for many, seemingly irresistible.[31] The societal consensus with respect to predatory criminals is this: Prison comes first, then community sanctions; protect society, punish the offender, then take measured risks in the community, backed by the threat of further incarceration.

THE CASE FOR DECENT PRISONS

If there is no escaping prison, there is also no escaping the fact that we must reform our prisons if they are to be institutions of just punishment. One area of reform, beyond the scope of this book, is sentencing reform. There is no doubt that we have come to rely too readily and too heavily on prisons, particularly with less serious offenders who could be safely handled in the community. The disproportionate effect of the prison on the black community, historically and today, fairly cries out for a sentencing policy that explicitly aims to break the cycle of incarceration that has made the prison a rite of passage in the ghetto, comparable to high school for earlier generations of Americans.

More germane to this book is the sad fact that many of our prisons are fundamentally indecent, inhumane institutions that traffic in abuse or neglect. Perhaps the most obvious and serious problem is violence. Prisoners abuse one another, and sometimes the staff, quite viciously. This violence usually is the work of hard-core convicts who prowl the prison yard, making it a no-man's land for staff and inmate alike (see Chapter Five). Though prisons hold many violent offenders, comparatively few prisoners turn to violence when in prison. Those who do act in defiance of the peaceful social order that is sought by most members of the prison staff, supported by most inmates, and achieved in most sectors of contemporary prisons (see Chapter Six). Brutality on the part of guards also occurs in contemporary prisons. As we shall see in Chapter Seven, this brutality is sometimes disturbingly common. But these abuses, like their counterparts among the inmates, are usually perpetrated by a minority of the staff, and they always represent flagrant disregard of prison policy (see Chapter Eight). Thus, the contemporary prison, for all its short-comings, is often quite civilized: most of its officials and prisoners do what they can, with the resources at their disposal, to keep the pains of prison life to a minimum.

Violence is plain to see and easy to abhor. A less obvious problem is human warehousing. Many prisons today are all play and no work—few jobs, little schooling, limited training, anemic programs. If these prisons sent out brochures—of course, they do not; no prisons do—these "promotional" mate-rials would feature leisure activities, mostly sports. Inmates in sweat suits and jogging shoes, some running, others doing calisthenics, would grace the cover of our hypothetical prison brochure. In the background, we would see rows of bleachers with a complement of spectators, some working on their tans, others catching up on the latest prison gossip. But surface appearances to the contrary, these prisons are not country clubs: the guests are involuntary, the conditions generally Spartan, and the routine deadly dull. Little can be found in these insti-tutions to lift the human spirit or mend broken lives. Most prisoners spin out empty days—killing time napping in their cells, walking the yard with their buddies, exercising, or, most commonly, slouching semicomatose before inces-santly blaring televisions, which have become the babysitter of choice in many of our prisons.

The Maryland Penitentiary is a reasonably typical maximum-security state prison for men. The prisoners who choose not to work—fully two-thirds of the roughly one thousand there—have days filled with unstructured time that they devote to recreational pursuits of one sort or another. In the words of one Maryland prisoner:

> They can take showers, use the phones or go outside in the yard. They can run, play softball or football depending on the season, lift weights or engage in the boxing and basketball competitions that are organized in some form all year long. But as often as not you can find them before the TV, which goes all day long. In the unbearably lonely and empty life of an inmate, 'Oprah,' game shows and the soaps provide a powerful distraction and consolation.[32]

Free citizens imagine they would enjoy such a daily regimen. The very idea of inmates filling their days with sports and television makes taxpayers gnash their teeth. Indeed, over the past decade there has been a move afoot in a num-ber of state legislatures to cut out television and sports in prison, with the explicit aim of "making hard time harder."[33] Few of these reforms have been put into policy or law, and in a sense they are entirely superfluous. Even with these modest amenities, as our Maryland inmate makes clear, prison offers an "unbearably lonely and empty life," punctuated on occasion with violence emanating from fellow inmates or, less often, from staff.

In the absence of other reforms, simply making prison conditions more restrictive is apt to promote gratuitous pain and pointless suffering. "I don't see how they can make this place any worse," observed one inmate of a notably austere and often violent Florida state prison. "I guess they could beat us."[34] This inmate's comments are prophetic. Prisons that offer nothing but restricted confinement tend to have high levels of violence, including violence used by staff as part of last-ditch efforts at social control.[35] A troubling case in point is the supermax prison, a kind of high-tech dungeon reserved for prisoners who are thought to be unmanageable in normal, maximum security prisons. These settings feature a regime of near solitary confinement. Amenities are few, and the staff, working behind a wall of technology (not to mentions walls of shatterproof plexiglass), have little human contact with their charges. Officers and inmates remain strangers to one another, and abusive encounters appear to be disturbingly common.[36] Though supermax prisons are a growing—and troubling—penal trend, to date only about two thousand prisoners (a tiny fraction of the total prison population) are housed in thirty-six supermax facilities across the country.

Warehouse prisons, with or without occasional creature comforts, are empty enterprises. Mostly, they squander human potential. The intentions of the officials who manage these prisons may well be benign, but the effects are not. For example, staff who defend supermax prisons argue that these institutions remove dangerous inmates from regular institutions, making those prisons safer for staff and prisoner alike. They see the severe restrictions of supermax prisons as necessary to protect disruptive inmates from one another and to protect staff from abusive inmates.[37] However one may assess these claims, the fact remains that human beings are not meant to be warehoused, whether that warehouse offers a regime of meaningless recreation or empty cell time. Warehouse prisons offer an existence, not a life. Their inhabitants survive rather than live. Warehouse prisons are our modern-day houses of the dead, to draw on Dostoyevsky, not because of brutality but because of inertia. They may provide some comforts, but they are not comfortable. They offer high levels of security, but no one feels secure. They don't instruct or correct. They merely contain. Apathy, that most destructive of sentiments, reigns supreme. In a modern-day gesture reminiscent of Marie Antoinette, we in effect say, "Let them have cake . . . and (maybe) basketball and (almost certainly) TV." Anything to keep the natives quiet in their cages. The empty lives such prison regimes offer are themselves a kind of violence, the violence of neglect.

Prisons too often become human warehouses because prisons hold people who don't count for much in our eyes—poor people and especially (in the American context) poor people of color, notably African Americans. Poverty is itself something of a stigma in America. We think of poverty as a personal failing, and we think of the poor as a morally impaired and undeserving lot. When poor people turn to crime, they are doubly stigmatized. We are apt to think of poor and especially poor black offenders in stereotypical terms, as if they were all inveterate, remorseless, predatory career criminals, a class of modern urban monsters stalking our streets. These hard-core offenders, we suppose, are a breed apart. Their behavior is inexplicable to us; we imagine that human beings simply don't behave this way. We find them unforgivable—because forgiveness implies a shared humanity, and we don't acknowledge a shared humanity with criminals. One might look at criminals and say, with humility, "There but for the grace of God go I," but few of us do.[38] We don't imagine that we could ever be in the shoes of criminals. For most people, criminals are alien; it is Us versus Them, Good versus Bad. We, the good citizens, are innocent of crime, pure of motive; they, the bad criminals, are guilty of crime, moved by malevolence. In a curious tautology, we assume that crime is what criminals do because they are and always will be criminals. Once captured and confined, criminals are easily discounted and just as easily forgotten. Few of us lose sleep at night worrying about the plight of our nation's convicts.

Many of us seem unreceptive to the simple and yet profoundly humanistic notion that the vast majority of criminals are ordinary and unremarkable people in difficult circumstances. Shouldering the burden of poverty and often of racism as well, people who turn to crime are not cheerful sadists but rather imperfect human beings who have struggled with hard lives; made bad choices; done stupid, even mean and occasionally violent things but still care about their lives and their loved ones and hope to one day make something of themselves. Now it is true that a minority of criminals are frighteningly and persistently violent, and some are no doubt sadistic. Their crimes are monstrous even if they are not monsters. Harsh lives helped form these ugly predilections, but we are not inclined to view the development of criminals in human terms or to try to understand the forces that shaped and ultimately warped their lives. That sort of thinking implicates society in the genesis of crime. It is easier—comforting, even—to believe in monsters, for whom (or for which) no one is responsible.

Yet the evidence clearly indicates that the large bulk of poor offenders are far from any vision of the malevolent hard-core criminal. Rather, they are disorganized, bumbling, somewhat pathetic characters. Immaturity rather than malevolence is the guiding theme of their lives and their crimes. Some of their crimes are serious—badly managed lives can back people into desperate situations, where impulsive violence can result—but mostly the crimes of these offenders are small time, sporadic, spur of the moment misadventures that land them behind bars time and again. There is little success at crime and, for the vast majority, little commitment to crime as a way of life. Naively, touchingly, most offenders still hope to turn things around. That is how they enter prison—chastened but hopeful. They soon discover that penal institutions too often have little or nothing to offer them.[39]

It is instructive to note that our animus against street criminals does not extend to white collar offenders. We often try to understand and even forgive the criminal behavior of these offenders, who are people like us. We are apt to give weight to the pressures and constraints under which white-collar criminals act, for example, and to write laws that impose comparatively mild sentences for these crimes. We understand, and we can empathize if not sympathize. Regrettably, there is much truth to the cynical notion, perhaps best expressed by the folksinger Woodie Guthrie, that the best way to rob a bank is to own one. As a general matter, the chances of apprehension for white-collar crime are low; if caught, the chances a white-collar offender will be sent to prison at all, let alone for a lengthy term, are even lower. (Penal institutions reserved for white-collar offenders are, moreover, much more accommodating than those reserved for street criminals.) Yet neither empathy nor tolerance nor lenient sentences are extended to run-of-the-mill street criminals. Their crimes come in for long sentences, often with substantial mandatory minimum terms—meaning that, no matter what the personal circumstances or situational pressures, these offenders go to prison for a long time if not a lifetime.

One look at our prisons, moreover, suggests that we carry a profound prejudice against their inhabitants. We act as if all prisoners were alike, were primitive creatures suitable for containment in the monotonous cells and cell blocks we house them in for years and even decades on end. We tolerate incredibly poor conditions when it comes to penal institutions. A recent assessment of the District of Columbia jail revealed that

> Inmates routinely resort to washing their underwear, jumpsuits and sheets in cell toilets because the laundry machines have been broken for 10 months. . . . Vermin are rampant in cellblocks and in kitchen areas. Insects breed in puddles of water, the fault of leaky, decrepit plumbing. There is little air movement in critical areas of the building because vents are clogged with dust and grime, creating a potential trap for airborne diseases and at times pushing room temperatures hazardously high. Some inmates have endured days wearing only underwear because of a shortage of jumpsuits, and at least 29 nurses worked at the jail last year without any record that they underwent screening for tuberculosis—a condition of employment there.[40]

Half-naked inmates, wearing clothes cleaned in toilets, surrounded by insects and vermin, sweltering in close quarters, and attended by nurses who may be infected with tuberculosis! And this in the District of Columbia, our nation's capitol, not some rural backwater town! The District's prison, Lorton Correctional Facility, has been criticized for similar abuses. Lorton is slated to be closed in the next year or so, but primitive, almost medieval conditions, though by no means the norm, can be found in more American penal institutions than one would imagine.

Our prisons today are typically called correctional institutions, which implies that the rehabilitation of prisoners is their main agenda. The label is misleading. Many Americans endorse the idea that prisons should rehabilitate offenders, at least in the abstract, but we as a society don't put much money behind this laudable goal. (There is a parallel here with health care for the uninsured. We are for it in principle but won't pay for it in practice.) Nor do we hold people accountable for failure to run prisons that correct offenders. Wardens are not fired when treatment programs falter or when conditions of confinement deteriorate. Wardens are fired because of escapes and because of scandals that point to lapses in security that might plausibly promote escapes. We put our money and our trust in security: *E Pluribus Unum Carceris*—out of

many (inmates), one prison (regime). Our money purchases massive buildings surrounded by imposing walls of concrete or concertina wire; prison officers, sometimes dressed like soldiers and increasingly trained following a military model of organization and deportment; and technology deployed in service of surveillance and control. More money is spent on control technology, such as cameras and stun belts, than on correctional programs or treatment personnel. Programs require relationships, particularly relationships of trust, which take time and care. Technology offers a quick fix: cameras that allow us to watch prisoners without having to interact with them or enter their world; stun belts that permit us to threaten or use painful electric shocks to gain control over prisoners through raw fear, without having to establish the respect on which authority is built.

As a practical matter, the bottom line for prisons today is incapacitation, the simple holding of prisoners for the duration of their sentences. A bigger system, from this vantage point, is a better system. A big system that runs smoothly is the best system of all. Incapacitation is, to be sure, a modest goal, even a negative goal. We hold prisoners because we believe they will offend if we let them out of our sight. We run our prisons as though we expect prisoners to fail. We expect them to behave badly in prison unless monitored constantly and punished harshly. We expect them to return to crime upon release, so we impose restrictive parole policies and send them back to prison (where we imagine they belong) for even minor transgressions of regulations. Aftercare is now little more than an afterthought. Instead of services, we offer surveillance. Parole as a helping enterprise is dead. The value of punishment these days is found in secure containment. Quality of life—a concern for basic decency—is secondary.[41]

Some critics of the prison applaud these trends. Their skeptical view is that a decent prison is an oxymoron, a contradiction in terms. For them, prisons are inherently corrupt and unregenerate institutions. Of course, some prisons are miserable, brutal places that traffic in violence on a daily basis; others feature neglect, offering leisure time pursuits as a substitute for productive activity. Many prisons prove stubbornly resistant to reform. But prisons are not inherently good or bad. Prisons are human institutions, and as such they are as good or bad as we make them. Decent prisons are possible because they are simply prisons that are adequate for human habitation. As human institutions, prisons can be arranged to support human life—to allow inmates to *live as human beings* during the course of their confinement. In decent prisons, inmates are not treated like so many objects or animals to be stored or caged, neglected or abused. A limited human life unfolds behind the walls of decent prisons, but it is a human life all the same. If a society can be judged by the quality of its prisons, as Fyodor Dostoyevsky maintained, a civilized society must strive to house its criminals in decent prisons. It stands to reason that civilized prisons are likely to prove civilizing as well, to the benefit of us all.

Prisons hold criminals, and criminals are perhaps the least deserving and indeed least civilized members of any society. Why should our treatment of criminals reflect on our civilization? Criminals violate the basic tenets of civilization by preying on others, making innocent citizens unsafe and insecure in their persons and in their property. Criminals are a blight on society. We lock them up so that we can go about the business of enjoying the fruits of our civilization. As a general rule, we don't care about the prisons they live in, as long as they are suitably grim. Our gut reaction is that criminals deserve criminal treatment (though we are unwilling to acknowledge that this would make criminals of us all!) At least, we seem willing to tolerate what may amount to criminal conditions of confinement, as long as we don't have to face and defend them. Long before former President Clinton devised his "don't ask, don't tell" policy for gays in the military, we as a society invoked a "don't ask, don't tell" approach to prisons—we as a society don't ask about our prisons and our officials don't tell us about them.

But Dostoyevsky had an important point. A civilized society is one in which citizens treat one another decently—with civility and courtesy—because civilized people know that other human beings are people like themselves, possessed of dignity and worth. To treat other people like people may be the hallmark of civilization. The more people we treat as fellow human beings—women as well as men, rich as well as poor, minority as well as majority races and cultures, conformist as well as nonconformist—the more civilized we are. Appreciating the range and diversity of humanity is important, because it is easy to be civilized with people like ourselves, who share our values and way of life. Those people make us feel good about ourselves, and it is natural to reciprocate and make them feel welcome when among us. Criminals are a different matter. They don't affirm our values, they test them. They don't make us feel welcome; they threaten and frighten us. Crime is a provocation to anger, even rage, and an invitation to abuse criminals in the name of revenge. Yet whatever criminals do—and criminals do some terrible things—they remain human beings, however miserable or flawed. Crime is a human failing. The criminal, at large and in the prison cell, is ever and always a human being and must be treated as such. Prisons, then, pose difficult tests of our values because the conditions of our prisons are a measure of our capacity to recognize and respect the humanity of offenders, people we fear and hate.

Other critics question whether offenders deserve decent treatment in a world in which some free and innocent people suffer indecent conditions on a daily basis.[42] This is called the less eligibility principle. Criminals, the undeserving, are said to deserve less than any noncriminal member of society. Stated in general terms, this principle is deceptively appealing. Why should *any* criminal live better than *any* law-abiding citizen? Mustn't virtue have its rewards, crime its punishment? Yet in practice, the principle of less eligibility leads us to endorse the untenable proposition that a society can take full and complete control over prisoners and hence be responsible for them and then can, perhaps even should, *purposely* subject those prisoners to brutal and unjust conditions merely because brutality and injustice exist in the free world. The proposition fails because citizens and prisoners cannot be directly compared in this way. Free citizens have control over their own lives and are, as a result, responsible for them. Society, through its agent, the prison, assumes control over the lives of prisoners and hence becomes responsible for the quality of life in prison. To run indecent prisons for the sake of some abstract notion of equity is barbaric and, if you will, an injustice to criminals and the larger society to which they will one day return, further inured to violence.[43]

Decent Prisons and Mature Coping

Decent prisons are possible and defensible. They are merely "good enough" institutions—prisons good enough for the job of housing offenders under humane conditions. Many people define humaneness to mean comfort and, hence, to infer that a humane prison is a materially plush and comfortable one. Nothing could be further from the truth. Such a prison would be as indecent as a prison marred by violence or neglect. Prisoners do not have a right to an easy or comfortable time behind bars. Nor do they have a right to a life of penal leisure, even under physically barren or otherwise uninviting conditions. Prisoners must serve hard time. This is both just, since criminals deserve to suffer for the harms they have done to others, and inevitable, since prisons are inherently painful.

But hard time can also be constructive time: prisoners can learn something worthwhile during their confinement. The most valuable lessons that prisoners can learn are those that enable them to cope maturely with the pains of imprisonment. As I define *mature coping,* it means: (1) dealing directly with one's problems, using the resources legitimately at one's disposal; (2) refusing to employ deceit or violence other than in self-defense; and (3) building mutual and supportive relationships with others. Inmates who cope maturely come to grips with problems in prison living, and they do so without violating the rights of others to be safe in their person and in their property. More generally, they treat others, staff and inmate alike, as fellow human beings who are possessed of dignity and worth. These inmates are the solid citizens of the prison community.

It goes without saying that mature coping comes hard for the veteran criminals who fill our prisons. Most criminals cope immaturely with life's problems, which is in large measure why they find themselves in prison. Often, they deny problems rather than deal with them directly. When they confront problems—often because those problems are looking them squarely in the face—they do so impulsively, with little thought or reflection. Their thinking, moreover, often is distorted and self-defeating. Many see themselves exclusively as pawns of life and victims of injustice, with little or no appreciation for the poor choices they have made and the injustices they have inflicted on others. For them, life is a Darwinian struggle. They live by the preemptive strike, turning the Golden Rule on its head. Their motto: Do unto others before they do unto you. Ultimately, might makes right—because it works, at least in the short run.

All prisoners were outlaws in the free world, and some of them remain outlaws behind bars. Most inmates, it is true, bemoan the primitive dangers of the prison yard; they prefer to live more civilly in relatively sheltered environments, squirreling themselves away in their cells or spending most of their time in one form of recreation or another. Their goal, however, is merely to avoid the more unruly members of the community of criminals who populate prison. They do not cope with their problems; they avoid them. Nor do they build constructive ties to others. They simply want to do their own time in prison as safely and comfortably as possible. We can only suppose that upon release they will take up once again the disorganized and essentially purposeless lives that led them to crime and ultimately to prison.

Yet some prisoners, admittedly a minority, learn to cope maturely. They live and work in what I call *constructive niches* or *sanctuaries* (see Chapter Six); often, they are supported in their adjustment efforts by concerned correctional officers (see Chapter Eight). These inmates use niches not merely as havens from prison violence but as arenas for responsible living and personal reform. They honor the obligations of prison citizenship. With appropriate policy reforms (developed in Chapter Nine), other prisoners could be placed in supportive prison environments and encouraged to live as citizens of the prison community. As a natural result of their enhanced self-confidence and emerging commitment to conventional values, they could also be encouraged to develop the educational and vocational skills that are essential to their successful adjustment upon release from prison.

Lessons in mature living learned in prison are of more general value than one might first suppose. Though it may not be obvious, there are parallels, sometimes striking parallels, between the pains of prison and the pains of life in general. These similarities can be exploited for correctional purposes. Prison citizenship can serve as a rehearsal for citizenship in other harsh environments, most notably the low-income, high-crime (and distinctly prison-like) milieus from which most prisoners are drawn and to which the vast majority of them will return. Paradoxically, then, the pains of imprisonment, properly managed by officials and adapted to maturely by inmates, can be the primary source of the prison's correctional agenda.

Decent Prisons as a Human Right

Prisoners, all prisoners, retain a right to conditions of confinement that show consideration and respect for their humanity. Prisoners are in varying degrees responsible for their crimes, and they deserve to suffer for the harms they have done to others. This means that, first and foremost, offenders must be treated as persons who deserve to suffer the deprivation of freedom inherent in imprisonment, as well as the loss or attenuation of many of the comforts and privileges that attach to freedom in our society. Our modern understanding of this arrangement is that offenders are sent to prison *as* punishment—loss of freedom—not *for* any additional punishment that might be given out behind bars. Earlier prisons were settings of punishment, notably corporal punishment, which was meted out with some regularity. Modern prisons are settings of deprivation.

A decent prison, then, has a bare-bones, severe quality to it. The regime is one that is short on amenities but long, so far as is possible, on autonomy. For an austere regime need not entail the elimination of choice. The hallmark of personhood is self-determination, which brings with it the capacity for personal growth and, potentially, self-actualization.[44] Note that self-determination requires that a person deal directly with problems, the first element of mature coping. No just punishment—and hence no decent prison—can abrogate the prisoner's capacity for self-determination. Persons have the moral right to make choices that influence their lives and the moral obligation to bear responsibility for the consequences of those choices. In a sense, prisoners have chosen the punishment of prison as a consequence of their crimes, but prison need not be a human wasteland. To the maximum extent feasible, prisons must promote autonomy even as they limit freedom. Certainly prisoners are not free to leave the prison or even free to move about within the prison at will. They are not free to exploit or abuse others or to commit crimes behind bars. But prisoners should be free to make choices within the prison world that have meaningful implications for the quality and character of the lives they will lead behind bars and, ultimately, upon release.

Self-determination develops best and operates most effectively in a secure, stable environment. In a stable world, people can plan and direct their lives in accordance with their choices, producing more or less anticipated consequences for which they can be readily held accountable. In an insecure and unstable world, unpredictable contingencies tend to shape existence. Essentially random events, or events over which one has no reasonable control, overshadow individual choice. Hence, one's choices bear little relationship to the consequences one suffers or to the larger contours of one's life. In such a world, impulsive, present-centered behavior comes to dominate individual adjustment; social relations become less stable and planning less likely to bear fruit. A sense of irresponsibility reigns, which can produce resignation or, as in the case of criminals, license. The world is unfair, says the criminal, so I will do anything I can to get what I want. I am an innocent victim, so I am entitled to victimize others in turn. Life is hard, so I will be harder, more unfeeling, more brutal.

Decent prisons must offer an alternative to the predatory world of the street criminal. They must be secure institutions, settings in which individuals are safe from the predations of others and hence free, if they so choose, to live without resort to deception or violence in their dealings with others. Free, in other words, to deal with one another in a mature fashion. Free, if they wish, to arrange their lives in accordance with choices made upon reflection and not under duress. In such a world, prisoners can learn to anticipate and accept the consequences of personal choices.

Human beings are, by nature, social animals. As Allman has succinctly observed, "The key to understanding our evolutionary success, as well as the unique combination of everyday behaviors that set us apart from every other living thing today, is our unique talents as social beings."[45] All human environments have a social component to them. We are reared in families, live in communities, and work and play in groups. Even when we are alone, our minds are populated by thoughts of others and by experiences drawn from the world of people. Though we enter and leave the world alone, most of us—and perhaps at some level, all of us—are possessed of an appetite, a genuine hunger, for relations with others. We must cope with life. For most people most of the time, that means we must cope with other human beings. Our choices often are about how (and not whether) we will relate to others, even if, as with criminals, those choices often feature destructive relations with others.

A decent prison, then, must feature a secure *social* world in which offenders have open to them the opportunity to develop constructive interpersonal relations with one another, with staff, and with people from the free world.[46] Stated differently, the social world of a decent prison is built on mature social relations. Such relations are the bedrock upon which our "moral sense" is built.[47] Our basic notions of right and wrong, in other words, are premised on our capacity to feel for and relate to other human beings, to take their interests seriously and, moreover, to take the needs and concerns of others into account when we fashion our own lives. The goal in a decent prison is for the prisoners to adapt to life behind bars in healthy and responsible ways and from such adaptations to develop a mature coping strategy for life in the free world as well. Note that supermax prisons are inherently indecent—unless they are used sparingly and as bridges back to more normal prison environments. On their own, supermax prisons offer nothing but solitary captivity and profound insecurity, which cannot prepare a person for a life of responsible freedom in the company of others.

PRISON AMERICA

Prisons today are a booming industry and indeed are filled in record numbers. At year-end 1999, the most recent date for which complete figures are available, federal and state prison populations reached a record high of over one million inmates—1,366,721 to be exact.[48] (Note that this and subsequent figures do not include jail inmates or inmates in juvenile correctional facilities.) The year-end 1999 population figures represent a phenomenal fourfold increase from 1980, when the prison population, then considered large, stood at 329,821. Another measure of the remarkable growth in the use of prison over the last decade is found in incarceration rates. As of year-end 1999, the overall rate of incarceration in the United States was a record 476 sentenced inmates per 100,000 residents, a dramatic increase since 1980, when the rate was 139 per 100,000.[49] Prison growth patterns have proven persistent and robust. Since 1991, the *rate* at which the prison population has increased—not merely the absolute number of prisoners—has continued to rise each year, from 6.7 percent to 7.4 percent.[50]

Overall incarceration rates help us track dominant trends, yet they mask important variations in the use of incarceration. One source of variation is by region. Incarceration rates per 100,000 are substantially higher in the South (543) and the West (421) than in the Midwest (367) and the Northeast (330).[51] Incarceration rates also vary greatly by gender and race. Rates of confinement are much greater for men than for women. For men, figures from year-end 1999 reveal a confinement rate of 913 per 100,000; for women, the comparable rate was 59 per 100,000. The male incarceration rate is thus about sixteen times higher than the female rate, though rates of confinement for women are growing at a higher pace than that for men.[52] (Note that the female prisoner population has actually more than doubled in number since 1990, from 44,065 to 90,668, for an average annual increase of 8.3 percent from 1990 to 1999.[53]) Overall, men account for 93.4 percent of the total prison population, while women comprise only 6.6 percent.

Incarceration rate differences by race are dramatic, and these differences hold for men and women and for prisoners of different age groups. For black males, the 1999 incarceration rate was 3,408 per 100,000, which represents a 179 percent increase from the 1,899 per 100,000 rate in 1980 and is fully eight times the incarceration rate of white males (417 per 100,000). Human Rights Watch reports that, following a state by state analysis, the "highest rate of white male incarceration (1,151) is lower than the lowest rate of black male incarceration (1,195). . . . [I]f current rates of incarceration remain unchanged, 28.5 percent of black men will be confined in prison at least once during their lifetime, a figure six times greater than that for white men."[54] The absolute figures are lower for women, but the same racial disparities prevail. Thus, the incarceration rate for black women is 212 per 100,000; for white women, the rate is 27 per 100,000. Looking at the intersection of race and age, we see some especially disturbing trends. Figures for 1999, the most recent year available for age and race, document incarceration rates for black men between the ages of 20 and 35—the prime years of life—that average 8,374 per 100,000. For white men, the incarceration rates for ages 20 to 35 average 2,271 per 100,000.[55] It is notable—and deeply troubling—that black men and women make up only 13 percent of the nation's population but account for 30 percent of arrestees, 41 percent of jail inmates, and fully 49 percent of our prison population.[56]

The composition of contemporary prisons differs markedly from the prisons of 1980. Stated simply, our prisons hold more drug offenders and more black offenders. Drug offenders made up about 7.5 percent of our state and federal prisoners in 1980; by 1998, that figure had more than tripled, rising to 24 percent. Federal prisons hold relatively more drug offenders than state prisons: in 1980, drug offenders made up 25 percent of federal prisoners (viz 6 percent of state prisoners); in 1998, drug offenders made up a remarkable 58 percent of federal prisoners (viz 21 percent of state prisoners). The growing prevalence of drug offenders in our prisons produces the ironic result that persons convicted of serious offenses of violence—murder, sexual assault, robbery, and aggravated assault—represent a substantially reduced percentage of our state and federal prison populations, dropping from 57 percent in 1980 to 44.6 percent in 1998. It is astonishing to note that in 1998, violent offenders made up a mere 12 percent of our nation's federal prisons, down from 34 percent in 1980.

The growth in our state and federal prison populations also reflects particularly dramatic increases in incarceration rates for black men, especially young black men, as already noted. Much of the growth in the black incarceration rate can be traced to our war on drugs; the rate of incarceration for drug offenses has been estimated to be thirteen times greater for black men than for white men.[57] Incarceration rates in America for offenders generally—and for black offenders in particular—are quite high by international standards and, indeed, may be the highest in the world.[58] These figures are for prisons only and do not include people in other settings of punitive confinement or in the community but still under control of the correctional system. Others held in confinement in 1999 include 18,394 in territorial prisons; 605,943 in local jails; 7,675 in Immigration and Naturalization Services (INS) facilities; 2,279 in military facilities; 1,621 in jails on Indian reservations; and upwards of 100,000 youth in juvenile facilities.[59]

Prisons house a virtual nation of convicts. It is a nation most of us wish to forget, comprised primarily of poor men and, especially, poor young black men. A case can be made that we use prison too freely and in ways that are essentially racist. We will return to these important points in the final chapter of this book when we place prison reform in a broader social and political context. For now, it is sufficient to stress that, whatever the size of our prisons and independent of the types of offenders they contain, it is unconscionable for society to relegate prisoners to a human junk heap, to sentence them to endure pain without any redeeming social benefit or purpose. People punished in this futile and demeaning way will leave prison no better, and sometimes much worse, than when they went in. Instead, prison policy must be fashioned to promote mature adjustment to the inevitable pains of confinement. The goal is citizen building, first in decent prisons, later in the free world. This is an altogether appropriate correctional endeavor. For prisons must promote the virtues of citizenship even as they confine and punish our most wayward citizens. They must be instruments of punishment that are in fact both civilized and civilizing.

To place today's prisons in perspective and to help us develop a realistic agenda for prison reform, we examine the history of prisons (Chapters Two and Three). We focus on the evolution of prisons as social environments—as places where people live and work. Our aim is to assess prisons over time in terms of their decency, that is, the extent to which prison regimes permit or encourage self-determination among the inmates and their keepers. We see in our examination of contemporary prisons (Chapters Four through Eight) that it is only in the last generation or so that prisons have achieved a social order and management structure that allow staff, potentially if not often in practice, to hold out to prisoners the prospect of developing as human beings during their confinement. We conclude (Chapter Nine and Ten) with a reform agenda that spells out the contours of a decent prison in terms of its organizational structure, social environment, and program opportunities.

PRISON AS A NATURAL MEANS OF PUNISHMENT

The claim made earlier in this book, that prisons have been around for centuries, may surprise some readers. The fact is however, that confining people who harm or threaten us is an old practice because it is a natural thing to do, perhaps even as natural as striking out and physically hurting our enemies and then banishing them from our midst. Better, it is natural to hurt our enemies physically and then lock them up for good measure—to keep them under control and hence subject to further injury, including execution or banishment.

As a system of punitive control, prison beats hands down the competing alternatives of execution and banishment. There is, afterall, a limit to the number of executions a society can carry out; no regime in human history has had sufficient appetite for blood to execute all or even most of its offenders. And banishment, though simple and appealing in principle as a means to rid society of undesirables, is apt to be seen as too easy or too unreliable. The banished person is set free in a new world, a fate that is not always or obviously a punishment. The plain fact is that many offenders have welcomed this sanction and the freedom it confers.[60] Others have returned to the scenes of their original crimes after completion of their sentences, only to take up once again their predatory activities.[61] An added difficulty with banishment is that one must have a place to which prisoner can be exiled, and the availability of such settings is never assured. With prison, at least, there is the assurance of punitive restraints and control of the deviant for the time and purpose set by the relevant authorities.

To be sure, early prisons were self-consciously punitive and controlling; their internal regimes were intentionally inhumane. No warden of an early prison cared about decency. No thought whatsoever was given to allowing self-determination to prisoners. Constructive manifestations of autonomy, security, and relatedness to others were nowhere in evidence. The earliest prisons were haphazardly arranged, inflicting pain without purpose or, put another way, meting out pain for pain's sake. The Mamertine Prison, probably the first formal and enduring prison, was built under the sewers of Rome in 64 B.C. and contained dungeons in which "prisoners were confined in what were basically cages."[62] It is evident that this institution was built (under a primitive sewer!) for no other purpose than causing prisoners to suffer great discomfort while confined there. Its internal environs have been described as "repulsive and fearful, because of the neglect, the darkness and the stench."[63] It is as if the Fathers of Rome saw the threats to public health posed by human waste and by human deviance as equivalent and opted to expel both from the sight and consciousness of the Roman citizenry. As it turns out, their thinking, though not the organization of their prisons, anticipated the preoccupation with contamination and infection that gave impetus to the modern penitentiary.

Punishments formally expressed in the loss of liberty over time, like contemporary prison sentences of so many years duration, are a modern phenomenon.[64] But the use of prison to produce pain is not new. Nor are the pains of prison subtle or hard to understand, especially in the crude form in which confinement was originally practiced. People thrown into a cage, and perhaps tied or chained to a wall for good measure, suffer obvious deprivations (obvious enough to be the subject of slightly perverse cartoon humor, as noted earlier). Isolated and immobilized, they are reduced to the status of children or even infants who are, to quote Willard Gaylin, at once "helpless and unloved."[65] They are forced to enter what Gaylin describes as "the matrix of disaster," a situation of primal and extreme vulnerability in which they are subject to indiscriminate physical and emotional abuse. Their fate is in some respects "comparable to death" because we are social beings whose very nature requires relationships with others.[66] Incarceration strains and often sunders vital social bonds. No alternative society or subculture within the prison can fully restore or replace them. Indeed, it is hard to envision inmates in early prisons as anything other than "the living dead," physically alive but forgotten by the world outside the prison walls. Those who built and used the first prisons to achieve this mass burial no doubt had some idea what they were creating.

Early prisons served retributive functions. Imprisonment was part of the harm intentionally visited upon offenders to pay them back for the harm done to their victims. Confinement may have been only a small part of this retribution. After all, other punishments, featuring burned or torn or mutilated flesh, were considerably more dramatic and painful. As real and obvious as it is, the pain of confinement in itself can be discounted or minimized; it leaves no visible traces, no bodily testimony in the form of welts or scars. Moreover, the pain of isolation is never spectacular, and early punishments often relied on the spectacle of pain to frighten the masses and hence secure their obedience to the sovereign.[67]

Still, prison could and no doubt did serve as an adjunct to the public punishment of the body, reinforcing and extending its message. Imprisonment is an intimidating, even terrifying, experience, a reason in itself to avoid crime. The prospect of a stint beneath the sewers of Rome could reasonably be expected to deter some criminals. Even more obvious is the role confinement plays in the incapacitation of convicted offenders. Criminals in cells don't commit crimes against the free citizenry. And this effect can be envisioned without the aid of a statistical projection. It is easy to anticipate, since the restraint of confinement is a simple elaboration of wrestling someone into submission. Confinement simply extends the period of submissive immobility.

Imprisonment is thus a punishment that can reasonably be expected to hurt, deter, and incapacitate offenders, as well as to hold them for other punishments. It is also easy and inexpensive to confine people, at least on a small scale and for short periods of time. Building a few cages or simply fencing a common area is no more difficult or costly than constructing a whipping post or a gallows. In each instance, criminals can be set to work building the agency of their punishment, and each of these instruments of punishment can be used over and over again. Prisoners have to be fed and otherwise maintained, and this might sometimes prove costly, but it was not uncommon for prisoners, including those condemned to die, to pay their own keep in money, goods, or labor.[68] Prison made revenge simple and sweet, like the various corporal punishments used throughout history, both in and out of prison.

The logic of confining dangerous people is so basic and compelling that one is tempted to see the act of imprisoning as an instinctive response—like fight or flight—to a kind of adversity. In this view, the notion of confinement (as distinct from its embodiment in any particular institution) would derive from reactions to recurring experiences in nature, particularly those that posed threats to the survival of the species. The original threat that resulted in confinement was probably contagious disease.

PRISON AS A NATURAL MEANS OF QUARANTINE

Some type of expulsion from the community, backed by restraint and confinement, would be a natural means of isolating diseased persons from the community and would prevent their returning to infect the healthy. It would be preferable to fighting or attacking diseased people and thus risking contamination or to fleeing from them and therefore forfeiting one's property and means of livelihood. Confinement would ensure the absence of the diseased people, who are presumably a source of anxiety, fear, and perhaps even dread, particularly if the disease produced disfiguring symptoms. At the same time, confinement would punish the infected people for their impurity in a way that is poignantly symbolic. As pariahs, persons physically and, supposedly, morally contaminated, they had placed themselves outside the human community and hence are fit subjects of abandonment by their fellows. They would be guarded by other pariahs, drawn from their own or from equally disreputable ranks, and would be eligible for other punishments, such as stoning, which could be inflicted from a distance.

The earliest and most notable connection between disease and confinement has to do with leprosy, which has ancient origins and gave rise to a number of practices of exclusion, among which were leper colonies. It is "the image of the leper," states Foucault, "cut off from all human contact, [that] underlies projects of exclusion." One of the more ambitious "projects of exclusion" is the prison.[69] Prisons were meant to be painful, and early settings of confinement were suitably miserable. The Roman Mamertine Prison, described earlier, is a telling case in point. Later prisons were little better. Prisoners were variously stored in sulphur pits, mines, stone quarries, and the hulls of ships.[70] The famous *gaols,* predecessors of today's local jails, were at best human warehouses in which men, women, and children—and sometimes animals as well—were confined in public rooms with little or nothing constructive to do.[71] These penal institutions were typically filthy, disease-ridden, and marked by chronic violence. Promiscuity and even prostitution were routine. One imagines that rape, too, was routine, as no attempt was made to separate the sexes or to control "the ample supply of cheap alcohol" available in these prisons.[72]

Prisoners, seen as polluted creatures beyond the reach of care or compassion, were free to abuse one another at will—and to die, mostly from disease and often at high rates, making a public death within the prison's congregate wards a common spectacle. William Fennor, jailed in 1616 for assault, provides this account of death in an English gaol:

  ■ In this place a man shall not look about him but some poor soul or other lies groaning and labouring under the burden of some dangerous disease;

the child weeping over his dying father, the mother over her sick child; one friend over another, who can no sooner rise from him, but he is ready to stumble over another in as miserable a plight as him he but newly took leave of. So that if a man come thither he at first will think himself in some churchyard that hath been fattened with some great plague, for they lie together like so many graves.[73] ■

Geffray Mynshul portrayed King's Bench prison in 1617 as "a grave to bury men alive." The social environment that developed in this and other funereal prisons, he contended, was a microcosm of suffering or, in Mynshul's words, "a Microcosmoos, a little world of woe, . . . a mappe of misery."[74] Penal settings such as these, whenever and wherever they emerge, may indeed trace their lineage to the leper colony.

One can find a limited but telling contemporary parallel to this situation in segregation units reserved for inmates with HIV/AIDS. At Alabama's infamous Thunderdorm, for example, infected inmates are kept at arm's length. Officials wear rubber gloves and want nothing to do with the prisoners. The prisoners, in turn, are admonished to care for the dying among them, since no one in authority will reach out to touch and help them. Thunderdorm is, indeed, a modern-day "mappe of misery," exploring the limited terrain allotted to these inmates with HIV/AIDS, who are treated as modern-day lepers. The Supreme Court, on January 19, 2000, "left intact a lower court's ruling permitting Alabama prisons to segregate hundreds of HIV-positive inmates and keep them from educational programs and even from religious services where they might mix with other prisoners."[75] Reforms in the management of HIV-positive inmates are discussed in Chapter Nine.

In later centuries, and particularly during the Middle Ages, some prisons took on a more disciplined cast and added reformation of the wayward to their objectives. These settings were less reminiscent of amorphous, static colonies and more like organized societies with a job to do. That job was penance, and the object of penance was spiritual purity. This reflected the influence of the monastery on the prison, and indeed as early as the fourth century there is evidence of cells in monasteries reserved for persons consigned to years of solitary penance.[76] It was not until the thirteenth century, during the Inquisition, however, that prisons began to feature a regime of solitary reflection.[77] Religious "criminals" (heretics) were to plumb their consciences in dungeon cells and repent their sins; 600 years later, at the turn of the nineteenth century, common criminals in penitentiaries were expected to expiate their crimes.[78] The sinner and the criminal were to be cleansed of their impurities. In pursuing their rehabilitation through solitary reflection, they were following a purifying routine of solitude that "has been recommended, both by practice and precept of holy men, in all ages, sometimes to retire from scenes of public concourse, for the purpose of communing with our own hearts, and meditating on heaven."[79]

The connection between solitude and purity, seen first in monasteries and later in prisons, may also originate with the problem of contagious disease. One lesson drawn from the management of sick people is simply that the impure can be excluded from society at large but allowed to intermingle freely and further contaminate one another. This is the lesson embodied in the leper colony and related "projects of exclusion." A different lesson may be learned about the preservation of those who are well: isolation can protect health by preventing exposure to disease. And if the sick are isolated (quarantined) from each other, health may be restored. The good (healthy) or reformed (cured) person leads a pure existence, and this is measured in solitude and good thoughts rather than in fellowship and good works. In social isolation there is purity and life; in sociability there is danger of contamination, soiling, illness, and death. Reform, for those deemed worthy, requires the pristine sterility of solitary confinement and the inner purification of reflection and penance. It is in this disciplined silence that the sinner is reclaimed for God, the criminal for society.

THE PLAGUE AND THE PENITENTIARY

Quarantines were a fact of life during the plague, but it was no easy matter to put a quarantine in place.[80] One had to move fast, since plague victims typically died in a matter of days and in numbers that are almost incomprehensible. In the three-year period between 1348 and 1351, for example, some twenty-four million people, fully one-third of Europe's population, died of plague.[81] It is hard to imagine the sense of vulnerability produced by the plague. Disease and death were everywhere. People were, literally, afraid to breathe. On the one hand, some people were warned by doctors against breathing too much "bad" air. Others, following medical advice, spent "their wakeful hours inhaling the stench from human waste" to avoid taking in too much "good" air.[82] Contagion was considered a risk of every possible human encounter. "It was thought that the breath, clothing, bedding, or even stare of an infected individual could pass on the deadly plague."[83] Moreover, the symptoms of plague in its early stage (sores around the groin or underarm, discreetly hidden by clothing) were sufficiently subtle to render everyone a potential agent of infection.

The challenge, then, was to isolate the healthy not only from the sick but, more importantly, from the *possibly* sick. In a very real sense, *anyone* could be classified as possibly sick. Under these conditions, no one could feel safe around anyone else. One response, naturally enough, was to abandon hope for the future and live each moment as if it were one's last. This was frequently done, and there is a body of literature and art that testifies to the prevalence of unrestrained hedonism during this era.[84] Another course of action was to place entire towns under strict and comprehensive quarantines. Those plague-stricken towns that imposed total quarantines in effect turned themselves into disciplined prisons to ensure the safety of their citizens.

A medieval town-as-prison, described vividly by Foucault, predates by centuries the first formal disciplinary prison, yet within its confines we see the essential ingredients of the penitentiary: isolation, regimentation, organized surveillance, custodial maintenance, and, no doubt, prayer and penance as well. We behold the natural development of a total institution:

> First, a strict spatial partitioning: the closing of the town and its outlying districts, a prohibition to leave the town on pain of death, the killing of all stray animals; the division of the town into distinct quarters, each governed by an intendant. Each street is placed under the authority of a syndic, who keeps it under surveillance; if he leaves the street, he will be condemned to death. On the appointed day, everyone is ordered to stay indoors: it is forbidden to leave on pain of death. The syndic himself comes to lock the door of each house from the outside; he takes the key with him and hands it over to the intendant of the quarter; the intendant keeps it until the end of the quarantine. Each family will have made its own provisions; but, for bread and wine, small wooden canals are set up between the street and the interior of the houses, thus allowing each person to receive his ration without communicating with the suppliers and other residents; meat, fish and herbs will be hoisted up into the house with pulleys and baskets. If it is absolutely necessary to leave the house, it will be done in turn, avoiding any meeting. Only the intendants, syndics and guards will move about the streets and also, between the infected houses, from one corpse to another, the "crows," who can be left to die: these are "people of little substance who carry the sick, bury the dead, clean and do many vile and abject offices." It is segmented, immobile, frozen space. Each individual is fixed in his place. And, if he moves he does so at the risk of life, contagion or punishment.
>
> Inspection functions ceaselessly. The gaze is alert everywhere: "A considerable body of militia, commanded by good officers and men of substance," guards at the gates, at the town hall and in every quarter to ensure the prompt obedience of the people and the most absolute authority of the magistrates, "as also to observe all disorder, theft and extortion." At each of the town gates there will be an observation post; at the end of each street sentinels. Every day, the intendant visits the quarter in his charge, inquires whether the syndics have carried out their tasks, whether the inhabitants have anything to complain of; they "observe their actions." Every day, too, the syndic goes into the street for which he is responsible; stops before each house; gets all the inhabitants to appear at the windows (those who live overlooking the courtyard will be allocated a window looking onto the street at which no one but they may show themselves); he calls each of them by name; informs himself as to the state of each and every one of them— "in which respect the inhabitants will be compelled to speak the truth under pain of death"; if someone does not appear at the window, the syndic must ask why: "In this way he will find out easily enough whether dead or sick are being concealed." Everyone locked up in his cage, everyone at his window, answering to his

name and showing himself when asked—it is the great review of the living and the dead.[85]

Most medieval towns did not respond to the plague in this way, though quarantines of a lesser order were quite common.[86] But some towns did resort to total quarantines and in doing so foreshadowed the modern prison. Foucault may well be correct when he maintains that "the plague gave rise to disciplinary projects. . . . Underlying disciplinary projects the image of the plague stands for all forms of confusion and disorder."[87] The first of these disciplinary projects was the prison-town constructed to stem the "confusion and disorder" of the plague. A descendant of this curious town is the penitentiary, a disciplined and orderly response to the confusion and disorder of life in the New World.

NOTES

1. My colleagues promptly altered my copy of the cartoon, replacing *Bob* with *Rob*, which is what my friends call me. Who said academics were a humorless lot?

2. Hagan and Dinovitz (1999).

3. A recent meta-analysis of fifty recidivism studies by Gendreau and Goggin (2000: 24) indicates that "recidivism rates were higher among offenders sent to prison when compared to those sentenced to probation/parole, and higher among inmates who served longer versus shorter prison sentences." *Criminal Justice Research Reports*.

4. This figure is for fiscal year 1996, the most recent year available. See Stephan (1999).

5. I am indebted to my colleague Jeffrey H. Reiman, William Fraser McDowell Professor of Philosophy at American University, for the notion that punishment should be both civilized and civilizing.

6. Plato did in fact support the death penalty but for reasons that are irrelevant today. He saw crime as a kind of disease that contaminated and tortured its host; the serious and incurable criminal would be released from his earthly bondage by execution, a punishment that was presumed to make him less of a wretch. Philippe Aries (1982) tells us that other

notions of death prevalent before the twentieth century, particularly those associated with a forgiving God and a congenial afterlife, made a foreseen death a tame and desirable arrangement. Here, too, execution might be conceived of as a blessing of sorts, allowing the criminal to come to terms with his Maker. In our secular age, where people are neither believed possessed by criminal demons of one sort or another nor the confident beneficiaries of a guaranteed afterlife, the benefits of death cannot be invoked to defend the death penalty (see Johnson, 1998:234–239). For more on Plato's views on punishment, see Mackenzie (1981).

7. Sherman and Hawkins (1981:55).

8. See Tonry (1995). A recent Human Rights Watch Report (May, 2000) offers compelling evidence on the flaws and biases of our War on Drugs:

People are sent to prison for both drug possession and sales-related conduct. In 1996, the simple possession of drugs (excluding possession with intent to sell) was the most serious conviction offense for 28 percent of all drug offenders admitted to state prison (Table 12). Fifty-six percent of drug offender admissions were for drug sales, and the rest for other drug-related offenses (e.g., fraudulent prescriptions and unlawful possession of syringes). In nine states (Alabama, Colorado,

Georgia, Minnesota, Mississippi, South Dakota, Texas, Utah, and Virginia) more than 50 percent of drug offenders sent to prison were convicted of simple possession.

Whether convicted on possession or sales charges, relatively few of the drug offender prison admissions over the past two decades have been high-profile drug traffickers, "kingpins," or persons occupying high level positions within sophisticated drug dealing enterprises. Available research indicates that most incarcerated drug offenders are bit players in the drug trade, such as small-time dealers selling to customers on the streets, addicts trying to support their habit, "mules" or couriers trying to earn some extra cash, and women pressed into occasional service by drug dealing boyfriends.

9. Blumstein (1994:399).

10. In Georgia, for example, an offender could be sentenced to life without parole for a drug offense but not for murder. "It's a quirk in the law that you can get more time for selling cocaine than you can for killing somebody," observed a judge. "Maybe one of these days they'll straighten this madness out." See Nation in Brief (2000: A6).

11. See Austin and Irwin (2000).

12. See Lynch and Sabol (1994).

13. See Reiman (1997).

14. See Tonry (1995); Clear and Braga (1994); see generally Morris and Tonry (1990).

15. Other minorities, notably Hispanics and American Indians, are overrepresented in our prisons, but the biases at work in the case of African Americans are arguably more profound, affect more people, and are of longer duration.

16. See Messner and Rosenfeld (1997).

17. Mandel (1978 & 1992).

18. Massey and Denton (1993).

19. Wilson (1987); Sampson and Wilson (1995).

20. Sellin (1928 & 1935); Wolfgang and Cohen (1970); Hagan and Peterson (1995).

21. Sampson and Wilson (1995); Mann (1995).

22. Wilson (1987).

23. Oshinsky (1996: 131–32).

24. Hagan and Peterson (1995).

25. See Litwack (1998).

26. See Sabol and Lynch (1998).

27. See Oshinsky (1996).

28. See Tonry (1995); Mauer (1999).

29. For a fuller discussion of this problem, Johnson (2000).

30. Garland (1990).

31. See Petersilia and Turner (1990, 1993).

32. Bratt (1993:C2).

33. Nossiter (1994).

34. Booth (1994:A1 & A8).

35. See Kauffman (1998); Austin and Irwin (2000).

36. Human Rights Watch (February, 2000).

37. Human Rights Watch (February, 2000).

38. This quote has been attributed to a number of saints, including Saint Paul.

39. Austin and Irwin (2000).

40. Kovaleski (2000:A1)

41. Austin and Irwin (2000).

42. See Logan and Gaes (1993).

43. See Conrad (1988).

44. Maslow (1966).

45. *Allman (1994:20).*

46. People from the outside world would include those who enter the prison as volunteers, usually associated with community programs, as well as visitors and others from the outside world with whom inmates come in contact over their terms.

47. See Wilson (1993).

48. Beck (2000)

49. See Beck and Bonczar (1994:1); Gilliard and Beck (1994:1).

50. Gilliard and Beck (1994:1). It should be noted, however, that between year-end 1998 and year-end 1999, the prison population rose only 3.4 percent, less than the 6.5 percent average annual growth since 1990. This was "the lowest rate since 1979 and had the smallest absolute increase since 1988" (Beck, 2000:1).

51. See Beck (2000:3).

52. See Beck (2000:5).

53. Beck (2000:5).

54. Human Rights Watch (May, 2000).

55. See Beck (2000).

56. See *Punishment and Prejudice,* III.

57. See *Punishment and Prejudice,* Table 14.

58. Lynch (1993); Mauer (1999).

59. Beck (2000:1).

60. See Stern (1987:10).

61. See McLynn (1989:76).

62. The name "Mamertine" is of medieval origin. In the classical period, this prison was referred to as the Tullianum (Peck, 1922:278). It was the site of both executions and punitive confinement (Lanciani, 1900:285–86). The date of its origin is in dispute. The 1983 ACA document dates the construction of the prison at 64 B.C., and I have adopted their figure because it is a source easily available to criminologists and penologists (ACA, 1983:3). However, the building "in part at least, is as old as any structure in the city" of Rome (Platner, 1904:240), which means that it could have originated as early as 753 B.C. That is unlikely, but the building's "construction is so old," in the words of one historian, "that it points to a time when the arch was not used in Roman architecture" (Peck, 1922:278). There also is some dispute as to the prison's size. The ACA document refers to it as "vast," but other accounts suggest that it may have comprised only a few dungeons (Peck, 1922:279). There is, finally, some dispute as to whether this structure was originally built to serve as a prison or was initially a spring-house or an ancient tomb that was later used as a prison (Plat-

ner, 1904:242). In any event, it is the view of Platner (1904:242), an authority on Roman history and topography, that "there is no doubt that this was the Carcer of the republic," which would delimit its point of origin to 527–509 B.C. There were other, lesser prisons during the republican period as well, including one (the Lautumiae) built in a stone quarry (Peck, 1922:279).

63. Peck (1922:279).

64. The historical conditions that made such sentences possible mark the birth of the prison as a major institution of punishment. These conditions are explored in the next chapter. For now, it is sufficient to note, in the words of Melossi and Pavarini (1981:3), that

The transition from private vendetta to retributive punishment, that is, the transition from an almost "biological" phenomenon to a juridical category, requires as a necessary precondition the cultural dominance of the concept of equivalents based on exchange value . . . "[F]or it to be possible for the idea to emerge that one could make recompense for an offense with a piece of abstract freedom determined in advance, it was necessary for all concrete forms of social wealth to be reduced to the most abstract and simple form, to human labour measured in time." Thus, under a socioeconomic system such as feudalism—in which the historic development of "human labour measured in time" (read: wage labour) was still incomplete—retributive punishment, determined by an exchange value, was not in a position to find in the privation of time the equivalent of the crime. Instead, the equivalent of the injury produced by the crime was realised in the privation of assets socially valued at that time: life, physical wholeness, money, loss of status.

In this context, Melossi and Pavarini (1981:2) make the claim that "in precapitalist societies prison as a form of punishment did not exist. This can be seen to be the case historically so long as we bear in mind that it was not so much the prison institution that was unknown . . . [as] the penalty of confinement as a deprivation of liberty."

65. Gaylin (1978:19).

66. Gaylin (1978:22).

67. Foucault (1977).

68. McConville (1981).

69. In addition to the prison, projects of exclusion include capital punishment and deportation. Each such punishment can be considered a kind of social and/or physical death sentence. See Sherman and Hawkins (1981:55).

70. ACA (1983).

71. McConville (1981); Byrne (1989).

72. Byrne (1989:25).

73. Quoted in Byrne (1989:49).

74. Quoted in Byrne (1989:106).

75. See Greenhouse (2000): The quarantined housing for inmates with HIV/AIDS at Alabama's Thunderdorm (Limestone Prison) amounts to "a new kind of death row, one that houses every male prisoner in the state who carries the AIDS virus. Hemmed in by double chain-link fences topped by razor ribbon, and forbidden to have contact with other, uninfected prisoners or perform ordinary prison jobs, the 130 residents of the Thunderdorm form one of America's first AIDS colonies" (Whitman, 1990:21). The name *Thunderdorm* is "derived from the so-called Thunderdome, a brutal arena where gladiators fight to the death in a 'Mad Max' film" (Whitman, 1990:21). The number of male prisoners in Alabama's Thunderdorm has grown to nearly two hundred; currently two dorms are set aside for male inmates with HIV/AIDS. Alabama runs a separate segregation unit for female prisoners with HIV/AIDS at the Julia Tutwiler Prison for Women (see Thrush, 1994). Conditions are essentially the same as those for men. In Alabama and Mississippi, inmates who test positive for HIV "are shut out of work-release programs, vocational training, sex-

offender treatment, assignments in prison factories, workshops and farms, sports and fitness facilities, even menial jobs in the prison cafeteria and laundry" (Thrush, 1994:85).

In the mid-eighties, at the height of the AIDS scare, segregation of infected inmates was common (Whitman, 1990). Today, only the Alabama, Mississippi, and South Carolina prison systems house HIV/AIDS inmates in segregation units. All other prison systems, state and federal, integrate or mainstream these prisoners in varying degrees.

76. ACA (1983:3); McConille (1981:31).

77. Newman (1978).

78. The first penitentiaries "were in a sense monastic prisons where penance replaced civic punishments" (Norris, l985:23). The link between penance and punishment is implied in the term "penitentiary," which comes from "the Latin word for 'penitence' and 'repentance,'" and shares "the same root as the words for punishment, pain, and revenge" (Norris, 1985:75).

79. Hirsch (1982:1209).

80. Gottfried (1983).

81. Gottfried (1983:77).

82. DiBacco (1994:15).

83. Gottfried (1983:113).

84. Chaucer's ribald and occasionally bawdy *Canterbury Tales* is one of the best known testimonials to this lifestyle. So, too, is Boccacio's *Decameron,* which is more explicitly concerned with life in the shadow of the Black Death.

85. Foucault (1977:195–96).

86. Gottfried (1983).

87. Foucault (1977:198).

REFERENCES

Allman, W. F. *The Stone Age Present: How Evolution Has Shaped Modern Life—From Sex, Violence, and Language to Emotions, Morals, and Communities.* New York: & Schuster, 1994.

American Correctional Association (ACA). *The American Prison: From the Beginning . . .* ACA Publishers, 1983.

Aries, P. *The Hour of Our Death.* New York: Vintage, 1982.

Austin, J. "Correctional options: An overview." *Corrections Today* (February 1995) (Article not paginated in journal).

Austin, J., and J. Irwin. *It's About Time: America's Imprisonment Binge.* Belmont, CA: Wadsworth, 2000.

Beck, A. J. "Prisoners in 1999." *BJS Bulletin* (August 2000). Washington, DC: U.S. Department of Justice, Office of Justice Programs, Bureau of Justice Statistics.

Beck, A. J., and T. P. Bonczar. "State and federal prison population tops one million." *Bureau of Justice Advance Report* (October 27, 1994):1–6.

Blumstein, A. "Prisons." In J. Q. Wilson and J. Petersilia (eds.). *Crime.* San Francisco: ICS Press, 1994:387–420.

Blumstein, A., and A. J. Beck. "Factors contributing to the growth in U.S. prison populations." In M. Tonry and J. Petersilia (eds.). University of Chicago Press, Chicago: *Prisons.* 1999:17–61.

Booth, W. "Without the 'rock,' Florida inmates get the hard place." *The Washington Post* (October 30, 1994): A1, A8.

Bratt, L. "Menace II the mind: For a generation of black men in prison, television is the dangerous drug of choice." *The Washington Post* (July 11, 1993):C1, C2.

Bureau of Justice Statistics. "The prevalence of imprisonment." *Special Report.* July, 1985.

Byrne, R. *Prisons and Punishments of London.* London: Harrap, 1989.

Clear, T. R., and A. A. Braga. "Community corrections." In J. Q. Wilson and J. Petersilia (eds.). *Crime.* San Francisco: ICS Press, 1994:421–44.

Conrad, J. P. "What do the undeserving deserve?" In R. Johnson and H. Toch (eds.). *The Pains of Imprisonment.* Prospect Heights, IL.: Waveland Press, 1988:313–30.

DiBacco, T. V. "The dark history of the 'black death.'" *The Washington Post* (October 4, 1994) Health section:13, 15.

Foucault, M. *Discipline and Punish: The Birth of the Prison.* New York: Pantheon, 1977.

Garland, D. *Punishment and Modern Society: A Study in Social Theory.* Chicago: University of Chicago Press, 1990.

Gaylin, W. "In the beginning." In Gaylin et al. (eds.). *Doing Good: The Limits of Benevolence.* New York: Pantheon, 1978.

Gendreau, P. and C. Coggins. "Prisons may increase rather than reduce recidivism: The effect of prison sentences on recidivism." *Criminal Justice Research Reports* Nov/Dec 2000:34.

Gilliard, D. K., and A. J. Beck. *Prisoners in 1993.* Bulletin, Bureau of Justice Statistics, 1994:1–10.

Gottfried, R. *The Black Death: Natural and Human Disaster in Medieval Europe.* New York: Free Press, 1983.

Greenhouse, P. "Supreme Court roundup: Justices allow segregation of inmates with HIV." *New York Times,* January 19, 2000.

Hagan J., and R. Dinovitz. "Collateral consequences of imprisonment for children, communities, and prisoners." In M. Tonry and J. Petersilia (eds.). *Prisons.* Chicago: University of Chicago Press, 1999:121–62.

Hagan, J., and R. D. Peterson. "Criminal inequality in America: Patterns and consequences." In J. Hagan and R. D. Peterson (eds). *Crime and Inequality.* Stanford: Stanford University Press, 1995:14–36.

Hibbard, G. R. (ed.). *Three Elizabethan Pamphlets*. London: George G. Harrap & Co., 1951.

Hirsch, A. J. "From pillory to penitentiary: The rise of criminal incarceration in early Massachusetts." *Michigan Law Review,* 80 (1982).

Human Rights Watch Report, *Out of Sight Super-Maximum Securtiy Confinement in the United States*. February, 2000.

Human Rights Watch Report, *Punishment and Prejudice: Racial Disparities in the War on Drugs*. May, 2000.

Irwin, J. I. , and J. Austin. *It's About Time: America's Imprisonment Binge*. Belmont, CA.: Wadsworth, 1994.

Johnson, R. *Death Work: A Study of the Modern Execution Process*. Belmont, CA: Wadsworth, 1990. 2nd ed. 1998.

Johnson R. "American Prisons and the African-American Experience: A History of Social Control and Racial Oppression," *Corrections Compendium* 25 (9) September, 2000: 6–10 & 28–30.

Kauffman, K. *Prison Officers and Their World*. Cambridge: Harvard University Press, 1988.

Kovaleski, S. F. "D.C. finds danger in ailing jail." *The Washington Post,* Sunday, Septmember 17, 2001:A1.

Lanciani, R. A. *The Ruins and Excavations of Ancient Rome*. Boston: Houghton Mifflin, 1900.

Lawes, L. L. *Twenty Thousand Years in Sing Sing*. New York: Ray Long & Richard R. Smith, 1932.

Litwack, L. F. *Trouble in Mind: Black Southerners in the Age of Jim Crow*. New York: Knopf, 1998.

Logan, C. H., and G. G. Gaes. "Meta-analysis and the rehabilitation of punishment." *Justice Quarterly* 10 (2) 1993:245–63.

Lynch, J. P. "A cross-national comparison of length of custodial sentences for serious crimes." *Justice Quarterly* 10 (4) 1993:639–60.

Lynch, J. P., and W. J. Sabol. "The use of coercive social control and changes in the race and class composition of U.S. prison populations." Paper presented at the 1994 Annual Meeting of the American Society of Crimonology, Miami, November 9, 1994.

Mackenzie, M. M. *Plato on Punishment*. Berkeley: University of California Press, 1981.

Mandell, J. R. *The Roots of Black Poverty: The Southern Plantation Economy After the Civil War*. Durham: Duke University Press, 1978.

Mandell, J. R. *Not Slave, Not Free: The African American Economic Experience Since the Civil War*. Durham: Duke University Press, 1992.

Mann, C. R. "The contribution of institutionalized racism to minority crime." In D. F. Hawkins (ed.). *Ethnicity, Race and Crime: Perspective Across Time and Place*. Albany: State University of New York at Albany Press, 1995:259–80.

Maslow, A. *Eupsychian Management*. Homewood, IL: Irwin, 1966.

Massey, D. S., and N. A. Denton. *American Apartheid: Segregation and the Making of the Underclass*. Cambridge: Harvard University Press, 1993.

Mauer, M. "America behind bars." A report of *The Sentencing Project*. February 1992, 20 pages.

Mauer, M. *Race to Incarcerate*. New York: New Press, 1999.

McConville, S. *A History of English Prison Administration*. London: Routledge & Kegan Paul, 1981.

McLynn, F. *Crime and Punishment in 18th Century England*. London: Routledge, 1989.

Melossi, D., and M. Pavarini. *The Prison and the Factory: Origins of the Penitentiary System*. Translated by G. Cousin. Totowa, NJ: Barnes & Noble, 1981.

Messner, S. F., and R. Rosenfeld. *Crime and the American Dream*. Belmont, CA: Wadsworth, 1997.

Morris, N., and M. Tonry. *Between Prison and Probation: Intermediate Punishments in a Rational Sentencing System*. New York: Oxford, 1990.

Nation in Brief, entry on Columbus, Ga., *The Washington Post,* Monday, October 23, 2000:A6.

Newman, G. *The Punishment Response.* Philadelphia: Lippincott, 1978.

Norris, R. L. *Prison Reformers and Penitential Publicists in France, England, and the United States, 1774–1847.* Unpublished dissertation: The American University, 1985.

Nossiter, A. "Making hard time harder: States cut jail TV and sports." *The New York Times* (September 17, 1994):1, 11.

Oshinsky, D. M. *"Worse Than Slavery" Parchman Farm and the Ordeal of Jim Crow Justice.* New York: Free Press, 1996.

Peck, H. T. (ed.). *Harper's Dictionary of Classical Literature and Antiquity.* New York: American Book, 1922.

Petersilia, J., and S. Turner. "Comparing intensive and regular supervision for high-risk probationers: Early results from an experiment in California. *Crime & Delinquency* 36 (1) 1990:87–111.

Petersilia, J., and S. Turner. "Intensive probation and parole." In M. H. Tonry (ed.). *Crime and Justice: A Review of Research.* Chicago: University of Chicago Press, 1993.

Platner, S. B. *The Topography and Monuments of Ancient Rome.* Norwood, MA: Norwood Press, 1904.

Reiman, J. H. *The Rich Get Richer and the Poor Get Prison,* 5th ed. New York: Allyn & Bacon, 1997.

Rosen, G. "Public health." *Encyclopedia Americana* Book 22, 1967:759–67.

Sabol, W. J., and J. P. Lynch. "Assessing the Longer-Run Consequences of Incarceration." Paper presented at the Annual Research Conference of the Association for Public Policy and Management, New York, October 30, 1998.

Sampson, R. J., and W. J. Wilson. "Toward a theory of race, crime, and urban inequality." In J. Hagan and R. D. Peterson (eds.). *Crime and Inequality.* Stanford: Stanford University Press, 1995:37–54.

Sellin, T. "The negro criminal: A statistical note." *Annals of the American Academy of Political and Social Science* 140, 1928:52–64.

Sellin, T. "Race prejudice in the administration of justice." *American Journal of Sociology* 41, 1935:312–17.

Sherman, M. E., and G. Hawkins. *Imprisonment in America: Choosing the Future.* Chicago: University of Chicago Press, 1981.

Stephan, J. J. *State Prison Expenditures, 1996.* Washington, D.C.: U.S. Department of Justice, Office of Justice Programs, Bureau of Justice Statistics.

Stern, V. *Bricks of Shame: Britain's Prisons.* New York: Viking Penguin, 1987.

Thrush, G. "AIDS: Words from the front." *Spin* (June 1994):85–86.

Tonry, M. *Malign Neglect: Race, Crime, and Punishment in America.* New York: Oxford University Press, 1995.

Whitman, D. "Inside an AIDS colony." *U.S. News & World Report* (January 29, 1990):20–26.

Wilson, J. Q. *The Moral Sense.* New York: Free Press, 1993.

Wilson, W. J. *The Truly Disadvantaged: The Inner City, the Underclass, and Public Policy.* Chicago: Chicago University Press, 1987.

Wolfgang, M., and B. Cohen. *Crime and Race: Conceptions and Misconceptions.* New York: Institute of Human Relations Press, 1970.

2

❖

Modern Prisons
in Historical Context

PENITENTIARIES

Life in the penitentiary was marked by disciplined isolation, much like life in Foucault's plague town. The purpose of this strict regime was twofold: to protect prisoners from moral contamination and to restore them to habits of correct living. The penitentiary was a plague town, if you will, in which the object was both to protect health and improve character. Prisoners were to leave their confinement not only untouched by the confusion and disorder—the criminogenic plague—that had pursued them to the walls of their prison home but also at peace with themselves, their God, and their society. Penitentiary prisoners would keep a lonely and ascetic vigil, and their reward would be to emerge as new, reformed human beings.[1]

The penitentiary was meant to be a grand and even noble experiment in prison reform. Although, in practice, this institution proved to be an exercise in organized brutality, the ideal of reform through discipline captured the American imagination. Americans thought of the penitentiary as nothing less than a new and enlightened punishment for a new and enlightened world. They embraced it with what the French penal authorities Tocqueville and Beaumont termed a *monomanie*—a monomania or obsession shared by no other nation. (Astute readers will note that our passion for prisons is still very much with us, though our faith in the reformative powers of these institutions has waned.)

The penitentiary was the first truly modern prison. It was the template or model from which most if not all subsequent prisons were cast. In the most general sense, the penitentiary was meant to be the perfect prison—a separate, self-contained, pure moral universe dedicated to the reclamation of wayward men and women. It would isolate criminals from a corrupt and corrupting world; and it would reshape their characters through the imposition of a strict routine of solitude, work, and worship.

American Prisons before the Penitentiary

Though Americans may claim the penitentiary as their own, it did not exist in the colonial period. Then, criminals were not confined for purposes of personal reform or even, until late in the colonial period, for a sentence of punishment. American colonists "took a pessimistic view of humankind: man was a depraved creature cursed by original sin. There was no hope of 'correcting' or 'rehabilitating' the offender. An inscrutable God controlled the fate of the individual."[2] Accordingly, the penitentiary had no place in the Puritan world.

The Puritan view of crime and punishment was, on the whole, a harsh one. Still, the notion of who was an offender under God's inscrutable control was applied with considerable compassion, at least in the early days of the colonial experience. Then, towns were small communities and those who turned to deviance were seen as wayward citizens—fallen neighbors rather than evil criminals. Early Puritans maintained that criminality, like disease, was treatable if it was caught in time.[3] When a person's transgressions were few or minor and, hence, criminality was seen as in its early stages, the Puritans saw punishment as a vehicle of healing and reintegration. "The first impulse of all concerned," notes Hirsch, "was to heal the wounds as best they could."[4] The pillory and stocks, for example, at least as originally used in Puritan villages, were meant to admonish offenders and to draw them back into the fold. Miscreants were placed on a wooden frame or platform with holes into which head and hands (and in the stocks, stocking feet, hence the name stocks) were locked securely. Often, a sign or placard would indicate the offenses in question. Passersby were invited to express their contempt for the behavior of offenders. The message embodied in this punishment was, in essence, "Shame on you; you know better; change your ways while you still can." Exclusionary punishments, like banishment, mutilation, and the death penalty, marked a person as permanently beyond the protection of the community. They were used only as a last resort in the colonies, especially the Massachusetts Colony.[5]

But times change, and with them the meaning of crime and punishment changes as well. As the population of the Massachusetts Colony grew during the eighteenth century, the various communities making up the colony became less stable; residents were more transient, communities less tight-knit. Offenders were, in fact as well as perception, more often strangers than neighbors. As strangers who made trouble for the good people of the town, they were seen as evil. Typically, they were depicted as members of "an antagonistic subculture" and as villains pure and simple.[6] In this context, the old ways of public punishment backfired. A reprimand from a neighbor may move one to repent; censure from an authority will likely harden and embitter. The pillory and stocks, which came to include whipping, became occasions of alienating humiliation rather than exercises in moral reeducation. Such punishments "destroyed the fear of shame," noted a social commentator in 1784, "and produce[d] a desire of revenge, which serve[d] to stimulate their vicious inclination."[7]

Angry, shameless criminals rather than errant but contrite neighbors came to dominate the ranks of the deviant. It is against this backdrop, in what can be described as the comparatively impersonal communities of eighteenth-century colonial America, that incarceration as a formal banishment became more common. At this juncture, it would be fair to say that colonists began to punish offenders with a growing vengeance because they saw them as out-and-out criminals rather than misguided people, and because God's will demanded that crime be avenged. The underlying notion was that all laws "were ultimately God's laws and to fail to enforce them would compound the ill by offending against Him."[8] Punishment at this point in history was expected to produce few social benefits. Perhaps fittingly, little was expected of the prisons of this day other than incapacitation.[9]

Colonial prisons, like most if not all early prisons, were not personal communities but impersonal institutions marked by brutality and neglect. These prisons offered few comforts. With the exception of brief and misguided efforts at public punishment and moral instruction—undertaken in the prison yard and featuring stocks and pillories—these institutions made no pretense at reform or rehabilitation.[10] The grim quality of life within their environs is captured in the very term *jail* or, in its English variant, *gaol* (which has the same pronunciation). As Hirsch has observed, "The Latin root of the word 'jail' (or 'gaol') is 'gaviola,' which means cage or hole." As Hirsch wryly notes, "This probably indicates the earliest form of this familiar institution."[11]

Even the first American prisons, built after the Revolution in the closing decades of the eighteenth century, were not meant to be penitentiaries—places of correction—but were erected as specters of punishment and deterrence.[12] They were forbidding in appearance, and their internal policies of punishment were notoriously harsh. Few believed or even "imagined that life inside the prison might rehabilitate the criminal. . . . A repulsion from the gallows rather than any faith in the penitentiary spurred the late eighteenth century [prison] construction."[13] These prisons were, by all accounts, deplorable. Their counterparts in England were known by the telling designation *Squalor Carceris*—squalid, filthy cages—which could have applied with equal force to the American institutions.[14]

The first American prison reform group, established in the latter part of the eighteenth century, set for itself the task of "alleviating the miseries of public prisons," which were by all accounts legion.[15] The most notable of these problems was the prevalence of contagious diseases. "Early prison reformers," Norris reminds us, "had good reason to suspect that gaol fever killed more inmates than the death penalty."[16] One observer characterized the prisons of this day as less healthy than a "pest house in times of plague."[17] London's Newgate Prison provides a telling case in point. It was, noted Byrne, "a prison whose stench in warm weather forced neighboring shops to close, a prison which no doctor would visit, a 'tomb for the living.'"[18] Though repellent and life-threatening—in a word, squalid—Newgate was an altogether unremarkable institution in its day.

Among the earliest prison reforms in both England and America was the separation of prisoners, where possible, into cells or some other form of relatively isolated quarters. (As we noted in Chapter One, before the advent of penitentiary reforms, prisoners lived like lepers, often in groups mixing men, women, children, and even animals.) Separation was accepted as a penological principle because it prevented or at least reduced the spread of disease among the prisoners and those who associated with them, primarily their keepers and the agents of the court. The excesses of *Squalor Carceris* were originally moderated, then, not for humanitarian reasons but because the diseases bred by such confinement "came to be seen as a threat to the well-being of society."[19] It took some time before separation was also seen as a means of preventing moral contamination and ultimately as a vehicle for reforming the prisoner.[20] Only gradually, then, were reformers able to "make our prisons Penitentiary Houses and places of correction" rather than stark and disease-infested human warehouses.[21]

An American Plague of Deviance: An Enlightened Quarantine

From the outset, penitentiaries were meant to be experiments in rational, disciplined living that combined punishment and personal reform. The emergence of the penitentiary in America was the result of many social forces at work at the turn of the nineteenth century. In particular, the penitentiary was affected by a number of trends that made the resolution of such social problems as poverty, mental illness, and crime appear to be within easy reach. The most general of these was the spirit of the Enlightenment, perhaps best captured in Locke's assertion, widely endorsed in intellectual circles at the time, that the mind is at birth a tabula rasa or "blank slate" upon which nature, following laws that can be studied, fashioned a person's character and predilections. This was taken by American reformers to mean that one could understand deviance as a worldly problem, specifically an environmental problem, and do something about it. A penitentiary—a prison that provided a healthy environment and hence reformed criminals—was possible.

Yet the New Republic was a tumultuous place, for with an open future came an unstable present. As the nineteenth century unfolded, America was an increasingly impersonal capitalist nation with growing urban centers of production. Small-town agrarian America, the America of cozy colonies with village artisans and small farms, was on the decline. The old folkways were gradually breaking down or at least seemed fragile and easily corrupted in this new environment. Crime and other social ills were on the rise, including the emergence of urban mobs and occasional riots, sometimes associated with public executions.[22] Neither family nor church nor school seemed able to hold the line against the forces of disorder that were sweeping over the young American cities. To the growing middle class, from which much support for the penitentiary was drawn, these various signs of social decay were especially repugnant. This group, Mazur observes, "dreaded vice, craved order, advocated self-control, and valued social privacy."[23] Public punishments were seen by this elite as crass and brutalizing and as invitations to unruly mob behavior. Private punishments—notably indoor executions (held within prison walls) and the use of the penitentiary—offered the hope of civilized sanctions that might shield offenders from these sources of corruption and move them to repent.[24]

The New Republic was indeed a different place from its colonial predecessor, and, at least in terms of the quality of community life, most of the differences seemed bad. Rothman tells us that during this period, biographies of criminals painted "a dismal picture . . . of a society filled with a myriad of temptations" awaiting the person who ventured out into its crowded, corrupt places.

> It was almost as if the town, in a nightmarish image, was made up of a number of households, frail and huddled together, facing the sturdy and wide doors of the tavern, the gaudy opening into a house of prostitution or theater filled with dissipated customers; all the while, thieves and drunkards milled the streets, introducing the unwary youngster to vice and corruption. Every family was under siege, surrounded by enemies ready to take advantage of any misstep. The honest citizen was like a vigilant soldier, well trained to guard against temptation. Should he relax for a moment, the results would be disastrous. Once, observers believed, neighbors had disciplined neighbors. Now it seemed that rowdies corrupted rowdies. Rothman, (1971:70–71)

Moreover, one's neighbors, rowdy or not, were less likely to take responsibility for their fellows, especially their marginal and troublesome fellows. For in a burgeoning capitalist economy, the web of community relations inexorably gave way to impersonal wage relations[25] and greater personal freedoms.[26] Those unable to cope on their own—orphans, the poor, the mentally ill—were a burden that individuals increasingly passed along to the state, which was fast becoming the new "community" and indeed even the new "parent" in modern society.[27] Criminals, whose adjustment problems were thought to overlap quite a bit with the dependent classes, also became the province of the state. A panoply of state institutions—orphanages, poor houses, insane asylums, and penitentiaries—originated or proliferated at this time and quickly became the option of first resort for the management of delinquents.[28] Their shared mission was to instill in wayward citizens the discipline and self-control essential to a productive existence in the changing social order that would culminate, within a scant few decades, in the Industrial Revolution.[29]

Models of Reformative Penitentiary Quarantine

The Separate System   The separate system originated in Philadelphia at the Walnut Street jail, opened in 1790, and is sometimes called the Philadelphia or Pennsylvania system. The regime was one of solitary confinement and manual labor, a simple monastic existence in which the prisoners were kept separate from one another as well as from the outside world. Describing this system, Beaumont and Tocqueville observed that its advocates

> have thought that absolute separation of the criminals can alone protect them from mutual pollution, and they have adopted the principle of separation in all its rigor. According to this system, the convict, once thrown into his cell, remains there without interruption, until the expiration of his punishment. He is separated from the whole world; and the penitentiaries, full of malefactors like himself, but every one of them entirely isolated, do not present to him even a society in the prison. If it is true that in establishments of this nature, all evil originates from the intercourse of the prisoners among themselves, we are obliged to acknowledge that nowhere is this vice avoided with greater safety than at Philadelphia, where the prisoners find themselves utterly unable to communicate with each other; and it is incontestable that this perfect isolation secures the prisoner from all fatal contamination.[30]

Prisoners served time in a manner reminiscent of the monks of antiquity or the heretics of the early Middle Ages. Sentences were measured in loss of freedom, but the aim of punishment was penance resulting in purity and personal reform. At issue was a fundamental change of character, a conversion. Here the penitentiary was a place of penance in the full sense of the word. Even the prisoners' labors, essentially craft work, were intended to focus their minds on the simple things of nature and hence to bring ever to their thoughts the image of their Maker. For the prisoners of the separate system, there was to be no escape from reflection and, in theory, repentance.

The Congregate System The congregate system was first introduced at Auburn Prison beginning in 1821 and is often called simply the Auburn System. Prisoners of this system slept in solitary cells. Though they congregated for work and meals, only their bodies mingled. Silence reigned throughout the prison. "They are united," observed Beaumont and Tocqueville, "but no moral connection exists among them. They see without knowing each other. They are in society without [social] intercourse."[31] There was no communication and hence no contamination. Prisoners left their cells for the greater part of each day, primarily for work and sometimes also for meals. But they carried within themselves the sharp strictures of this silent prison regime. For in the congregate penitentiary, "everything passes," in the words of Beaumont and Tocqueville,

> in the most profound silence, and nothing is heard in the whole prison but the steps of those who march, or sounds proceeding from the workshops. But when the day is finished, and the prisoners have retired to their cells, the silence within these vast walls, which contain so many prisoners, is like that of death. We have often trod during night those monotonous and dumb galleries, where a lamp is always burning: we felt

as if we traversed catacombs; there were a thousand living beings, and yet it was a desert solitude.[32]

Here, too, penance and purity were sought; solitary penance by night, pure labor by day, silence broken only by the sound of machines and tools. Throughout, prisoners have time to reflect and repent. The congregate system retained the monastic features of the separate system in its solitary cells and silent labor but blended them with a more contemporary lifestyle. A monastery at night; by day, a quasi-military organization of activities (all scheduled), movement (in unison and in lockstep), eating (backs straight, at attention) and work (long hours, usually at rote factory labor). The aim of this system was to produce docile, obedient inmates. Accordingly, regimentation was the cornerstone of congregate prison life. As is made abundantly clear in Beaumont and Tocqueville's description of the daily routine at Auburn, "The order of one day is that of the whole year. Thus, one hour of the convict follows with overwhelming uniformity the other, from the moment of . . . entry into the prison to the expiration of . . . punishment."[33]

The merits of these competing penitentiary systems were debated hotly and at great length. In the end, however, the details of the penitentiary regime and the practical definition of rehabilitation were determined as much by financial matters as by the merits of either penological perspective. Thus, the congregate system became the model for the American penitentiary at least in part because workers were in short supply in nineteenth-century America and, hence, the deployment of prisoners at factory labor provided an affordable quarantine against the dangers and corruptions of the larger world. Elsewhere, notably in Europe, workers were in greater supply. With no appreciable demand for prison labor, the solitary system was hailed in Europe as a more pure implementation of the penitentiary ideal and became the dominant form of the penitentiary.

Women and Minorities in the Penitentiary For the most part, women and blacks were excluded from the presumed benefits of the penitentiary. Women sentenced to penitentiaries were few in number. Even fewer were exposed to the penitentiary regime. Those who were confined to penitentiaries often were warehoused, relegated to the unsupervised attics and kitchens and back rooms of these institutions.

> When the penitentiaries came into vogue, women, too, were sent to these institutions, but the level of their care dropped below that accorded to men. There were few female convicts. Sometimes there were but one or two, and in any case they were vastly outnumbered by men. To administrators, women were a great nuisance. They had to be isolated to prevent sexual mischief, but there were too few women to fill a wing of cells. Therefore officials locked them in large rooms above the guardhouse or messhall. To these officials, it seemed extravagant to hire a matron to supervise a small number of women. These prisoners were thus often left entirely on their own, vulnerable to attacks by one another and male

guards. Secluded from the main population, women had less access than men to the physician and chaplain. Unlike men, they were not marched to workshops, messhalls, or exercise yards. Food and needlework were brought to their quarters, where the women remained, day in and day out, for the years of their sentences.[34]

In these barren environments, women were allowed to intermingle and contaminate one another in the time-honored tradition of neglect characteristic of prisons before the advent of the penitentiary.

The early penitentiaries held few African Americans since most blacks were essentially incarcerated on slave plantations. Exact figures are unavailable, since the early prison census figures did not even include a category for blacks.[35] Beaumont and Tocqueville note that "in those states in which there exists one negro to thirty whites, the prisons contain one negro to four white persons."[36] Though black prisoners were overrepresented in prisons, they were, in the main, housed in regular, mass confinement prisons, which made no effort at reforming prisoners and served merely to warehouse them until release.

Paradoxically, the case can be made that women and African Americans were inadvertently spared the considerable indignities of the penitentiary. For, as a practical matter, putting rhetoric and intention to one side, penitentiaries offered at best only a deceptive facade of humanity. Pain, both physical and psychological, was a central feature of the penitentiary regime. Penitentiary prisoners often went hungry; firsthand accounts report prisoners begging for food from the prison kitchen and being punished for their temerity. Diseases ran rampant among poorly nourished prisoners. Even for the healthy and well-fed, life in the penitentiary was lonely and depressing and left no room whatsoever for adult autonomy. There was also the crucible of fear, for penitentiaries from the outset were maintained by threat and practice of violence. Strict rules were routinely enforced with harsh punishments, including whippings and confinement to dark cells for weeks on end. Looked at from the inside, as seen by the prisoners and not the reformers, the penitentiary was a profoundly inhumane institution.

Penitentiaries were born in a period of optimism about the prospects of reforming criminals. They reflected the Enlightenment faith that people entered the world as "blank slates" upon which environments, including reformative prison environments, would trace individual characters. This optimism persisted for decades, even as experience proved penitentiaries to be unworkable. Indeed, from early on, there was evidence that penitentiaries brutalized their charges. Gradually, in the face of continuing signs of failure together with the influx of ethnic and racial minorities, faith in the penitentiary waned and these institutions took on a purely custodial form, with little or no pretense at personal reform.

To be sure, the men's reformatory movement, best exemplified in the famous Elmira Reformatory, dating from 1870, kept a version of the reform-oriented prison alive after the passing of the penitentiary as a setting of rehabilitation. But this was true only for young white men and only briefly, in the context of some twenty institutions developed and devoted to the discipline and rehabilitation of wayward young men. The reformatory movement thrived on gender stereotypes as applied to white men and women. For men, military drills formed a key feature of the reformatory regime, which sought to produce disciplined "Christian gentlemen."[37] For women, domestic pursuits were at the heart of the reformatory regime, which in this instance sought to produce Christian gentlewomen. (Note that black men and women were still primarily in the South; the vast majority of black offenders were subject to plantation prison discipline, discussed subsequently, and, hence, were ineligible for placement in reformatories.) Ironically, the men's reformatory as a prison type proved, at bottom, to be a brutal, punitive penal institution, an exercise in "benevolent repression" very much like the penitentiary and no more likely to reform its inhabitants.[38] The rhetoric of the young men's reformatory, promising differential classification and treatment but delivering heavy-handed and often brutal control, had no discernible impact on the main lines of evolution followed by prisons for men, other than to confirm the general tendency of penal institutions to degenerate into custodial enterprises in the absence of sustained efforts at reform.

Prisons opened at the turn of the twentieth century reflected the demise of the penitentiary. They were seen as industrial prisons in which inmates labored to defray operating costs and to fill idle time. Little or no attention was given to the notion of personal reform. In effect, these "fallen penitentiaries" were settings of purposeless, gratuitous pain. Increasingly, they were filled with devalued minorities, including African Americans who had recently migrated from the South. These prisons, which simply carried on the custodial warehousing agenda of the earliest prisons in a disciplined and regimented fashion, came to be known as Big Houses.

THE BIG HOUSE

For much of this century, maximum-security prisons outside the south were colloquially known as Big Houses. (Their counterparts in the South were known as plantation prisons or simply penal farms.) If one were to think of prisons as having genealogical lines of descent, one would say that the Big House was the primary descendant and heir apparent of the penitentiary.[39] In these prisons, a disciplined and often silent routine prevailed. Prisoners worked, originally in factories where productivity and profit were sought and later at such empty enterprises as the infamous stone quarries, in which axe-wielding men broke rocks for no other reason than to show their submission to the prison authorities. The Big House prison reflected no grand correctional scheme or purpose; neither penance nor reformation was sought. Routines were harsh and often intentionally empty. Activities served little purpose other than to maintain order.

The quintessential Big House, at least in the eyes of the public, was Alcatraz, though Alcatraz was unique in its day in that its regime was marked by exceptionally tight security. It is a matter of historical record that Big Houses, like Alcatraz, Sing Sing, and Stateville, to name a few better-known institutions, offered virtually no remedial programs to their inmates and, on the whole, "were places of pervasive brutality."[40] As in the penitentiaries that the Big Houses seemed to mimic, with but a passing nod to the ideals of progressive penology, pain was at the heart of the confinement experience.

The Big House, though harsh and repressive by contemporary standards, was a modest step forward in the evolution of prisons. Humanitarian reforms helped to shape its inner world, though these had to do with reducing deprivations and discomforts rather than establishing a correctional agenda or purpose. Thus, whereas the penitentiary offered a life essentially devoid of amenity or even distraction, the Big House routine was the culmination of a series of humanitarian milestones that made these prisons marginally more accommodating. (Yet again, it should be kept in mind that most of the beneficiaries of reforms in the Big House were white. For the first half of the twentieth century, most black prisoners were to be found in southern plantation prisons, remarkably harsh penal settings that are discussed later.)

The first humanitarian advance was the introduction of tobacco, which was greeted by the prisoners with great relief. Officials report, without a hint of irony, that a calm settled over the prison once the "soothing syrup" of tobacco was given to the formerly irritable and rambunctious prisoners.[41] (Ironically, many prisoners today report great relief at the restrictions upon smoking introduced in more and more prisons, though there can be little doubt that inmates who smoke must chaff under these new policies.) The second reform milestone was the abolition of corporal punishment. In Sing Sing, a fairly typical prison of its day, corporal punishment was abolished in 1871. Prior to that time, upwards of 60 percent of the prisoners would be subjected to the whip on an annual basis.[42] Among prisons outside the South, whippings and other physical sanctions became an underground, unauthorized activity by the turn of the twentieth century. Tragically, regimes of corporal punishment, official and unofficial, remained in place in many southern prisons for much of the century.

The emergence of significant internal freedoms comprises the third and final reform milestone. These freedoms came in the wake of the lockstep march, a hallmark of the penitentiary, which was abolished in Sing Sing in 1900. The daily humiliations of constrained movement implied in this shameful march soon gave way to freedom of movement in the recreation yard, first on Sundays (beginning in Sing Sing in 1912) and then, gradually over the early decades of the twentieth century, each day of the week.[43]

There is no doubt that the Big House was more humane than the penitentiary, but similarities between these institutions are apparent. As in the penitentiary, order in the Big House was the result of the threat and use of force, including, in the early decades of this century, clubs and guns, which were carried by line officers as they went about their duties. As in the penitentiaries, rules of silence prevailed in the Big House. Silence was both a cause and a consequence of order in the Big House and a profound symbol of the authority of the keepers. This silence was, in the words of Lewis Lawes, a famous prison warden of the day, "the hush of repression."[44]

Though more comfortable than their counterparts in the penitentiary, prisoners of the Big House led bleak lives. Cells were cramped and barren; possessions were limited to bare essentials. Food was generally in good supply but was utterly uninspiring and was, in the eyes of the prisoners, mere fuel for reluctant bodies and nothing more. If the dominant theme of the penitentiary was terror, the dominant theme of the Big House was boredom bred by an endlessly monotonous routine. "Every minute of the day," said Victor Nelson, a prisoner, "all the year round, the most dominant tone is one of monotony."[45] In the extreme, the Big House could be described as a world populated by people seemingly more dead than alive, shuffling mindlessly through each day, heading nowhere, slowly, for there is nothing of any consequence for them to do. In Nelson's words, "All about me was living death: anemic bodies, starved souls, hatred and misery: a world of wants and wishes, hungers and lusts. . ."[46] In the Big House, then, as in the penitentiary, the prison was in essence a world circumscribed by human suffering.

Big House prisons came to contain a sizable representation and eventually an overrepresentation of minorities, though no sociological accounts describe the distinctive experience and adjustment of minority prisoners in these highly structured milieus. Certainly Big House prisons were racially segregated, as was the larger society, by policy in the early years and later by custom. Ethnic segregation of a voluntary sort was no doubt quite extreme, just as it was—and to some degree still is—in and out of prison today.[47] Descriptions of the social life of northern Big House prisons proceed as if African American prisoners did not exist at all within their walls, though of course that is entirely untrue.

Black prisoners, seemingly invisible to white social scientists and even to white convicts, must have formed a world of their own, apart from that of white prisoners and white officials. Fictional accounts, written by black convicts, suggest that black inmates of Big House prisons led a more materially impoverished life than their white contemporaries. In one story, a white prisoner stumbles on an enclave of black prisoners far from the mainline prison living area in a setting called "Black Bottom." In the story, it is as if the black prisoners are buried within the prison, settling at its bottom, left to suffer greatly in isolation from the larger white prison society.[48] In the typical Big House prison, as in the outside world at this time, it is whites who rise to positions of influence and even comfort due to their connections with the white power structure; few if any blacks have such an opportunity. Material from southern prisons, which during this era were of the plantation type, suggests that the harshest and most restrictive conditions within these prisons, particularly relating to labor, were reserved for blacks.

The Plantation Prison—A Southern Big House

Many southern states bypassed the penitentiary entirely and developed an agrarian variant of the Big House known as the plantation prison, which traces its origins to the slave plantation.[49] Life on plantation prisons was marked by disciplined field labor of the most servile, back-breaking sort. These regimes could be profitable, or at least self-supporting, but their distinctive feature was oppression. Correctional goals like penance or personal reform were never given a second thought.

Plantation prisons contained a gross overrepresentation of black prisoners, both men and women. After the Civil War, newly emancipated African Americans would be incarcerated on the flimsiest pretexts and then put to hard labor in the fields of these prisons, often in chain gangs. Shackled groups of prisoners were also deployed to build various public works, notably roads and railroads. Other newly freed slaves would become indebted to white land owners and would be forced to work as peons to pay off debts or would have to sign restrictive contracts so that they could obtain food and housing. Blacks who resisted or rebelled had ample reason to fear for their lives. Lynchings of "uppity" blacks who "didn't know their place" occurred on a weekly basis and featured grotesque violence, including public immolations and mutilations. Even lawful executions often reflected profound racial bias and indeed could be thought of as little more than "legal lynchings."[50] In these various ways, vast numbers of blacks were subjected to prison or prison-like work regimes that drew their inspiration from slavery and offered none of the hope, however illusory, associated with the penitentiary and none of the humanitarian reforms, however modest, associated with the Big House.[51]

Mississippi's Parchman prison, like all plantation prisons, "resembled an antebellum plantation with convicts in place of slaves."[52] The work was the same in both settings: farm labor done in groups following disciplined routines and set to rhythmic chants, with men working in unison for long hours in the open fields. So, too, was there a rigid caste system on both the plantation and the plantation prison, with the warden or master and his overseers or officers in complete control of the work and living experiences of the captive laborers. Yet, in what is a cruel historical irony, plantation prisons and other forms of forced convict labor "perpetuated the worst features of slavery"[53] and offered a regime of punishment that was, almost unbelievably, "worse than slavery."[54]

On the antebellum slave plantation, the master had a vested interest in the slaves, who were a valuable economic commodity—comparable, as Frederick Douglass's *Narrative* makes clear, to livestock.[55] As a result, the master was likely to maintain physically decent working and living conditions to preserve his investment.[56] In plantation prisons, however, as well as in the various convict leasing camps that held prisoners sentenced to hard labor, individual convicts were commodities of little or no intrinsic value because they were easily replaced, at low or even no cost, when they became ill or died. "Before the war we owned the negroes," observed one employer of leased convicts in 1883. "If a man had a good nigger, he could afford to take care of him; if he was sick get a doctor. He might even put gold plugs in his teeth. But these convicts: we don't own 'em. One dies, get another."[57]

As a result of what might be called "no-cost brutality," conditions on plantation prisons and convict labor camps *typically* sunk to abysmal levels.[58] Plantation prisoners would be worked or even beaten to death on a regular basis; starvation and disease would claim the lives of others. The brutality and callous indifference of officials are, by modern standards, almost incomprehensible:

> The fields were shadeless and sunstroke was a leading cause of death. Prisoners were beaten for breaking the rules, for falling behind in their work, or sometimes for the pleasure of the guards. In the 1870s, neighboring farmers complained that the groans and screams "of the convicts at night [are] often so absolutely heart rending as to prevent sleeping." Camp officials responded by gagging the prisoners to muffle their cries.[59]

It is telling that the life span of a prisoner serving time in a Texas prison at the turn of the century was around six or seven years. Remarkably, we learn that "ten years . . . is the utmost length of time that a convict can be expected to remain alive in a Georgia penitentiary" of this time.[60] In Mississippi in the 1880s, "Not a single leased convict ever lived long enough to serve a sentence of ten years or more."[61] A sentence to a plantation prison was, more often than we would like to remember, a sentence of death.

Black prisoners in chains—individually or in gangs—were a central feature of the southern penal system. Prisoners could be chained in the fields within the prison compound; they could be chained in work gangs sent out to build roads or clear land. "Originally," noted Sellin, "the chain gang was apparently a punishment reserved for ex-slaves or their descendants who committed crimes."[62] During the heyday of the chain gang, African Americans comprised the vast bulk of southern prisoners—upwards of 90 percent.[63] Most of these prisoners were men but there was a fair number of women as well.[64] Black women, moreover, would be subjected to the same harsh regime as the men. Rafter reports the following exchange, which took place during an 1870 Georgia investigation of the use of prisoners leased to chain gangs:

Q. [Assemblyman Virgil Hillyer]—Were there any women working on the Brunswick Railroad?

A. [prisoner witness]—Yes, I think there were 19 or 20. They belonged both to the chain-gang and the Penitentiary.

Q. Did you see any of them whipped?

A. Yes.

Q. Were they whipped on the bare skin?

A. Yes; I saw their bare skin myself.

Q. On what part of the body were they whipped?

A. On the butt.

Q. Were they whipped in the presence of the men?

A. Yes.

Q. How many licks did they receive?

A. About 20.

Q. Were they kept in separate stockades?

A. In the same stockade, but in separate rooms.

Q. Out on the works, were they required to wait on the calls of nature in the presence of the men?

A. Yes; they were required to do their business right in the cuts where they worked, the same as the men did. It was taken out in the wheelbarrows and carts.

Q. [Mr. Turner, another assemblyman]—Were the white and colored women mixed together?

A. There were no white women there. One started there, and I heard Mr. Alexander [the lessee] say he turned her loose. He was talking to the guard; I was working in the cut. He said his wife was a white woman, and he could not stand it to see a white woman worked in such places.[65]

Work on the chain gang and at hard field labor was generally reserved for blacks and much less often meted out to whites. Comparatively few white men, and virtually no white women, were exposed to these brutal work regimes.[66]

Plantation prisons for men proved to be enduring institutions. Accounts of life in a Texas unit for black prisoners, from roughly 1950 through 1970, reveal an institution that had changed little from the plantation prisons of a century earlier. Crushing labor and raw brutality remained the norm. Prisoners were tortured for misbehavior; they were beaten or even shot for lagging behind in their work.[67] A hint of such conditions is provided in the following excerpt, describing how slow field workers would be *hung up by their hands overnight,* a routine torture on a modern plantation prison that would drive some offenders to suicidal behavior:

■ When my turn came, Cap'n Smooth took my right wrist and clamped the cuff on—tight. Then he backed me up against the iron bars that separated the messhall from the inner hall. With one cuff clamped on my right wrist and my back against the bars, he took the unclosed cuff and looped it through the bars above my head while he clamped on the other cuff. When he finished, I was left hanging with my toes barely touching the floor. . . . Along about hour six, one of the hangers began moaning louder and louder, violently, jerking and pulling against his cuffs. He frantically wiggled and twisted his body around until he was facing the bars. Using his foot to push against them, he reared back, pitching, straining, and pulling as hard as he could. Realizing he couldn't get loose, he bit his wrists as if they were two chocolate eclairs, growling and gnawing away like a coon with its foot caught in a steel trap.

The blood-splattered con hanging next to him pulled as far away as he could, hollered and yelled for the picket boss.

Looking down from his perch, the picket boss ordered the turnkey, "Run git a bucket an dash sum water on them two crazy nigguhs down on the end." The dousing worked; he quit mutilating his wrists and contented himself to moaning and groaning out the night like the rest of us.

Finally, the dim lights were turned back to bright. The picket guard handed down the cuff keys to the turnkey, who unlocked us from the bars. After the cuffs were removed, my swollen wrists throbbed like a bad toothache.[68] ■

Sample and the other inmates, including the man who savagely ripped his own flesh with his teeth, were then fed and sent off to work in the fields under the hot sun.

After 1970, federal court holdings tamed the excesses of plantation prisons, though it took a full two decades in some cases.[69] But even today, as we enter the new millennium, settings like Louisiana's Angola Prison retain the aura if not reality of a plantation run with docile slaves. To visit Angola today is to go back in time to an earlier penal existence, shorn only of its worst physical excesses.[70]

Varieties of Twentieth-Century Women's Prisons

Big House and plantation prisons have in common a focus on custody rather than care. Custodial prisons existed for women as well as for men. The origins of Big House prisons for women, like that of their male counterparts, can be traced to the penitentiary. As the numbers of women penitentiary prisoners grew, separate units within men's penitentiaries were developed for women. Eventually, these units were moved off the men's prison grounds to become completely separate and autonomous institutions. Most of these new separate institutions for women were run on a custodial model, which Rafter convincingly argues is an inherently masculine model of imprisonment.

The custodial model of the prison as applied to women featured "retributive purpose, high-security architecture, a male-dominated authority structure, programs that stressed earnings, and harsh discipline"; in essence, "women's custodial institutions treated inmates like men."[71] Confinement in custodial regimes—whether of the Big House or plantation prison type—was hard on the women, who were uniquely vulnerable in such settings. "Probably lonelier and certainly more vulnerable to sexual exploitation, easier to ignore because so few in number, and viewed with distaste by prison officials, women in custodial units were treated as the dregs of the state prisoner population."[72]

Women in Custodial (Big House) Prisons Accounts by inmates of women's custodial or Big House prisons highlight the diversity of populations within these institutions (similar to the diversity within men's prisons). This 1930 description of entry into a women's prison offers a glimpse of a motley and diverse crew of women—petty thieves, addicts, prostitutes of varying ages and nationalities—lockstepping to meet a warden:

■ Directly behind Red-Frotz [the matron] walked Laura, the Candy Kid, seventeen year old shoplifter, prostitute and drug-addict, an inveterate thief, pretty as a picture.

Then Rebecca, thirty year old Jewess, diseased, heavily sentenced after a fourth offence at shoplifting.

Next Old Lady Cuno, eighty-seven, arrested for begging, always swearing in German and smelling like a fish factory.

Following her, Stephanie, the Czechoslovakian girl, with swarthy complexion and large black eyes, with her deep guttural voice, an all-around crook and shoplifter.

Then back of her, Dora Conignsby, drug-addict and prostitute, with the needle pocked body. Next, Big Bertha, a burly dark-complexioned drug-addict, with her mottled hair in curlers and skirts above her bare knees.

Then Pauline, the most beautiful girl in the prison, kleptomaniac, graduate of Vassar, with the background of a fine family, up the second time for cashing bad checks.

Behind her, Lillian Johnson, six feet tall, pretty but a badly diseased prostitute. Then the Kid from Georgia, a nineteen year old girl taken from a sailor's dive, very badly diseased with red spots all over her body.

After her Rachel Endress, whose husband had framed her, then myself, followed by Ethel Kingsley, morose murderess, who had killed her husband in a row about another woman, and at the end of the rogue's gallery line Joan Barnum, bootleg queen, up for ten years for shooting a policeman.

Thus we lock-stepped down the iron stairs to the warden's office.[73]

The warden proceeds to fondle the women as a part of their orientation to his prison regime, warning them that those who do not submit to their superiors will be punished:

"The first law of this prison," he continued, putting his hand on my shoulder, and gradually running it down my side, a smirk of sensual pleasure playing upon his leather-like countenance . . . is to obey at all times to obey your superiors to fit in to your surroundings without fault-finding or complaint . . . " His hand had now progressed below my skirt, and he was pressing and patting my naked thigh . . . "because unruly prisoners are not wanted here and they are apt to get into trouble . . . "[74]

Sexual abuse was disturbingly common in custodial prisons for women that were run by men. Women inmates might well be fondled at intake, as in the preceding excerpt, and later raped in their cells by their male keepers. On other occasions, guards would make sport of their sexual encounters with their female captives.[75] The impression one gains from this literature is that the women relegated to custodial institutions, from the penitentiary onward, had little or no choice but to submit to the predations of their keepers. In the harsh assessment of a nineteenth-century observer, criminal women were "if possible, more depraved than the men; they have less reason, more passion and no shame. Collected generally, from the vitiated sewer of venality, they are schooled in its depravity, and practised in its impudence."[76] Coffey's views, to be sure, were shared by many early twentieth-century observers as well, at least through the period when custodial prisons for women were run by men. As outright moral pariahs, women offenders in these prisons were presumed to be spoiled goods, there for the taking by their male keepers. It is regrettably the case that the problem of sexual abuse of female inmates by their male keepers remains a problem to this day, though the incidents are fewer and less egregious.[77]

Parenthetically, sexual abuse has been a salient issue in men's prisons as well. In many penitentiaries, and in a fair number of modern prisons, especially in the South, where corporal punishment remained a licit or illicit practice until as recently as the 1970s, physical punishment of half-naked men had arguably sexual connotations. "Throughout the prison literature," Franklin observes, "we are constantly confronting the spectacle of guards and other prison officials making male prisoners take off their pants to be flogged."[78] One of the worst beatings the infamous Captain Billy Sanders administers is to Jack, a kind of handsome-sailor convict toward whom the Captain felt some "friendship":

■ I know there was something twisted in Billy Sanders' emotional life. There were so many occasions in which he prefaced a flogging by announcing that his wife hadn't given him sexual satisfaction the night before, and he was going to make up for it now, that theories about sadism came back to my mind when I saw the results of Jack's beating and I wondered whether it wasn't Jack's hard luck that night that Sanders had always expressed a liking for him. Something more than punishment or even vengeance entered into that beating.[79] ■

Indications are that the frequency of sexual abuse of male prisoners by officials was comparatively rare and is, one would expect, virtually absent today, with the passing of corporal punishment from the prison scene. Rape of one prisoner by another, however, was distressingly common in some men's prisons, though protective custody offers a safe harbor for most prisoners these days. Coerced sexual relations among prisoners have been and remain a fact of life in virtually all men's prisons. Rape of one inmate by another is rare in women's prisons, though coerced relations, where the weapon is psychological pressure, no doubt occur with some regularity.[80]

Women's Reformatories A notable departure from the masculine model of imprisonment for women was the reformatory. The women's reformatory movement, analyzed with great insight by Rafter, lasted from roughly 1860 to 1935 and produced approximately twenty-one institutions.[81] Reformatories, patterned on home or domestic environments, were an explicit rejection of the male custodial model of imprisonment.

Unwalled institutions, women's reformatories architecturally expressed their founders' belief that women, because more tractable, required fewer constraints than men. Rejecting large congregate buildings, women reformatories came to adopt the 'cottage' plan, holding groups of twenty or so inmates in small buildings where they could live with a motherly matron in a familial setting.[82] The philosophy of rehabilitation that guided women's reformatories, again rejecting the male model, was premised on domestic training:

> Inmates were taught to cook, clean, and wait on table; at parole, they
> were sent to middle class homes to work as servants. Whereas men's
> reformatories sought to inculcate 'manliness,' women's reformatories
> encouraged femininity—sexual restraint, genteel demeanor, and
> domesticity. When women were disciplined, they might be scolded and
> sent, like children, to their 'rooms.' Indeed, the entire regimen was
> designed to induce a childlike submissiveness.[83]

Perhaps the most distinctive feature of women's reformatories was their "emphasis, on propriety and decorum—on preparing women to lead the 'true good womanly life.' " Rafter draws attention to "the Thursday evening exercise and entertainment" offered at the Detroit House of Shelter in the early 1870s:

> On this evening the whole family dress in their neatest and best attire. All
> assemble in our parlor . . . and enjoy themselves in conversation and
> needlework, awaiting the friend who week by week on Thursday
> evening, never failing, comes at half past seven o'clock to read aloud an
> hour of entertaining stories and poetry carefully selected and explained.
> After exchange of salutations between the 'young ladies' and madam and
> the visitor, and after the reading, tea and simple refreshments are served in
> form and manner the same as in refined society.[84]

Here we see what became "the hallmarks of the reformatory program: replication of the rituals of genteel society, faith in the reforming power of middle-class role models, and insistence that inmates behave like ladies."[85] (One found nothing of the sort in institutions for boys or men. As already noted, the men's reformatories were modeled on the military and not on the home.) Ironically, women from custodial institutions might well find domestic reformatory regimes unappealing. One such group of female felons, after being ostensibly saved from a corrupt institution run by men, were reportedly "indignant when . . . they found they could no longer trade 'certain favors' for liquor and tobacco."[86] These offenders clearly preferred the old, custodial regime, where they could trade sex for privileges, to the new reformatory program, with its genteel teas and ladylike sociability.

Women's reformatories were designed for young, minor offenders, especially those whose behavior contravened strict standards of sexual propriety.[87] The prototypical reformatory inmate would be a young white girl of working-class background. Her crime might entail little more than sexual autonomy, though this would be viewed as the earmark of prostitution. Young black women, who "often constituted larger proportions within female state prisoner populations than did black men within male prisoner groups,"[88] were essentially excluded from the women's reformatory movement. They were seen by reformers as undeveloped morally and as too much like men to be fully adapted to the domestic model that undergirded the women's reformatory. Black female offenders were sent to custodial prisons, including plantation prisons, in large numbers. In these settings, African American women were often treated as brutally as their male contemporaries. Reformatories were meant for novices in crime whose characters were presumed ripe for redemption. The same can be said for the original penitentiaries, whose clients were "the good boy turned bad, the amateur in the trade."[89] The object in both of these reform institutions was to save those deemed valuable enough to warrant an investment of resources, not to reclaim hardened and essentially worthless criminals.

Reformatories were expensive institutions to run. By the 1930s, states found them to be unaffordable. "The stock market crash of 1929 and ensuing Great Depression play a major role: states simply could no longer afford to operate institutions that held petty offenders for long periods of moral retraining."[90] Reformatories were subsequently filled with common felons and returned, in varying degrees, to the (male) custodial model of imprisonment. It should be noted that custodial institutions for women "were more numerous [than reformatories] even after the reformatory movement had come to fruition."[91] These custodial institutions for women, much like custodial institutions for men, "were hardly touched by the reformatory movement. They continued along lines laid down in the early nineteenth century, slowly growing and in some cases developing into fully separate prisons."[92] Certainly it is the custodial prison, shorn of any correctional aspirations, that has been the main prison reserved for minorities, both men and women.

THE CORRECTIONAL INSTITUTION

The correctional institution emerged gradually from the Big House prison, with the first stirrings of this new prison type manifesting themselves in the 1940s and 50s. The daily regimes at correctional institutions were typically more relaxed and accommodating than that of the Big House; correctional programs were available, though often more in name than in substance. The benefits of correctional institutions, however, are easily exaggerated. The main differences between Big Houses and correctional institutions are of degree rather than kind. Correctional institutions did not correct, even if there were now some staff members who took corrections as their goal. Nor did correctional institutions abolish the pains of imprisonment. Correctional institutions were, at bottom, simply more tolerable human warehouses than the Big Houses they supplanted, less a departure than a toned-down imitation. Often, correctional institutions occupied the same physical plants as the Big Houses. Indeed, one might classify most of these prisons as Big Houses "gone soft."

Correctional institutions were marked by a less intrusive discipline than was the case at the Big Houses. They offered more yard and recreational privileges; more liberal mail and visitation policies; more amenities, including an occasional movie or concert; and more educational, vocational, and therapeutic programs, though these various remedial efforts seemed to be thrown in as window dressing. These changes made life in prison less oppressive. Even so, prisoners spent most of their time in their cells or engaged in some type of menial work. They soon discovered that free time could be "dead" time; like prisoners of the Big Houses before them, prisoners in correctional institutions often milled about the yard with nothing constructive to do. Boredom prevailed, though it was not the grinding boredom born of regimentation as in the Big House. Gradually, considerable resentment developed; officials had promised rehabilitation programs but not delivered them. The difficulty was that officials, however well intended they might have been, simply did not know how to conduct a correctional enterprise. Nor did they have the resources or staff to make a serious attempt at that task. The correctional institution, like the penitentiary before it, promised to transform people, but mostly these institutions simply left prisoners more or less on their own.

In the 1950s, Trenton State Prison in New Jersey was a fairly typical correctional institution for men, merging the disciplined and harsh climate of the Big House with a smattering of educational, vocational, and treatment programs. Gresham Sykes's classic study, *The Society of Captives,* describes Trenton State Prison. Significantly, Sykes describes the dominant reality at Trenton as one of pain. "The inmates are agreed," he emphasized, "that life in the maximum security prison is depriving or frustrating in the extreme."[93] To survive, the prisoner turned not to programs or officials but to peers. In essence, Sykes concluded that the prisoners must reject the larger society and embrace the society of captives if they are to survive psychologically. The prison society, however, promoted an exploitative view of the world. Weaker inmates were fair game for the strong. At best, prisoners are admonished to "do their own time," to use an old prison phrase, and leave others to their predations, turning a deaf ear to the cries of victims.

Trenton State contained a substantial overrepresentation of minority offenders, no doubt a source of some conflict in the prison community. This salient fact is only mentioned in passing by Sykes, who observes, "the inmate population is shot through with a variety of ethnic and social cleavages" that keep prisoners from acting in concert or maintaining a high degree of solidarity.[94] Similarly, Irwin makes clear that Soledad prison during the 1950s, also a correctional institution, was populated by groups called *tips* or *cliques,* which were largely defined in racial and ethnic terms.[95] There, conflict simmered below the surface of daily life, erupting only occasionally, suppressed in large measure out of a vain hope that all inmates might benefit from correctional programs. In fact, however, treatment and the prospect of mature interpersonal relations were at best a footnote to the Darwinian ebb and flow of daily life in the prison yard of the correctional institution. The violence would come later, after the demise of the correctional institution.

Life in Trenton State Prison, though grim, was altogether unremarkable. The plain fact is that prisons—all prisons—are built for punishment and hence are meant to be painful. The theme of punishment is nowhere more evident than in the massive walls that keep prisoners both out of sight and out of circulation. As Rothman has observed:

> The image that captures the essence of the American prison is not one of inmates exercising in the yard or attending classes or taking psychometric tests, but of the physical presence of the walls. And the walls were incredible, rising twenty to thirty feet above the ground and going down another five to twenty feet below the ground, with anywhere from five to fifteen towers jutting out above them. The occasional legislator who questioned the enormous expense of erecting these structures was told in no uncertain terms that thirty feet was better than twenty-five feet for preventing inmates from scaling the walls, and that every extra foot below the ground was a necessary safeguard against their tunneling out. In the end, reformers, with their grand hopes of transforming the institution, were up against the wall.[96]

Many of our contemporary prisons are built without those imposing grey walls, though these institutions usually feature barbed wire, and this wire, ironically, is often a shade of grey. Almost all prisons feature an interior environment that is a dull grey or some related drab color:

■ Everything is a shade of grey. That's the color of prison.
   The sky is grey. The walls are sand-grey. The yard is grey-black asphalt, and the inmates' uniforms, which appear green, are really a shade of grey.
   Grey as a color is neutral; as a controlling force it is repressive; and debilitating as a life influence.
   Grey controls all. It gets into the mood, the spirit, and even the food has a grey-bland taste.
   It is no accident that grey is chosen color. An integral part of any controller's plan is the color scheme.
   In prison, grey dominates.[97] ■

Colorful prisons—so-called "pastel prisons," some built to resemble college dormitories—are few in number and are reserved for prisoners adjudged to pose little threat to one another, to staff, and to the public. To the extent that such pastel prisons exist, they are likely to house women.[98] Women's penal institutions more often resemble college campuses than prison compounds. Dorm rooms often replace cells; it is not uncommon to find vases of flowers in the rooms of confined female felons. The grounds may be lovingly landscaped by inmates, with help from the staff. Connecticut's Niantic Prison, known as The Farm, is a case in point. Niantic contains many high-security areas with social climates that resemble comparable male institutions, but it also has areas that are distinctively feminine:

That summer Katie and Lori landscape the front of the cottage by planting rows and clumps of red salvia, snapdragons, and impatiens. To give it some symmetry, they collect dozens of medium-sized rocks, paint them white, and use them to form borders for the flower gardens. Both women work quietly each day, digging, hoeing, and planting like monks lost in prayer. When people walk by to admire their work, they simply smile and return to their task. . . . After they finish landscaping the cottage, Katie begins eyeing a shaded patch across the road and decide it would make a perfect spot for a meditation garden, something the residents and staff can appreciate and use. She and Lori circulate the word to COs and the green house supervisor that they need herbs and shade-loving plants. Then she sits down to design the garden. Before long, the plants begin arriving and the small patch is transformed into a beautiful blanket of herbs and perennials. One CO brings in three pine chairs he has built to place at the center of the garden. . .[99]

Yet the ostensible comforts of women's prisons (or at least of subenvironments within some women's prisons) are belied by the custodial realities of daily life in these institutions, which are experienced by their inhabitants as regimens of repression marked by too many rules and too few program opportunities. Those programs that exist, moreover, still follow stereotypical gender lines, focusing on domestic skills rather than job skills. Indeed, correctional institutions for women are of a piece with earlier women's prisons. The continuing theme is one of sexism and neglect. It is telling that the garden just described was appended to a unit known as "Sleepy Hollow," a place for lifers that was expressly considered a sanctuary or niche by its inhabitants. Younger inmates serving shorter sentences typically found themselves in units with names like Calcutta, which gives a good idea of the social climate of these living environments.

Contemporary Prisons

Most of today's prisons are formally known as correctional institutions, but few of them are guided by a correctional mission or ideology. As far as I and most other criminologists are concerned, the correctional institution as a type has largely passed from the prison scene. From the mid-1960s to the present, a new prison type has emerged. It is defined by the climate of violence and predation on the part of the prisoners that often marks its yards and other public areas. Known simply as the "violent prison,"[100] it has been aptly described as a "human warehouse with a junglelike underground."[101]

With the passing of the disciplined and controlling routines of penitentiaries and Big Houses, today's prisons are marked by more inmate violence than at any time since the advent of the penitentiary. This is most apparent in men's prisons. Prison uprisings, though not on the scale of the infamous Attica and Santa Fe prison riots, occur with disturbing regularity in men's prisons. So, too, are inmate-on-inmate and inmate-on-staff violence more common today than was the case in earlier prisons, and here I would include women's prisons as well as prisons for men. Gangs and the requisite culture of toughness are alive and well in women's prisons these days.[102] While staff still abuse inmates, there is little doubt that this grossly unprofessional behavior is, in the main, considerably less in evidence in today's prisons than in earlier prisons, where staff-on-inmate violence was once a routine feature of daily life.

To be sure, our violent prisons are not monolithic milieus, whether they house self-described hard men or tough women. Inmates typically are allowed a wide range of possessions in their cells. There are also many freedoms allowed to prisoners. In particular, internal freedom of movement is readily available in many if not most contemporary prisons.[103] Resources and mobility combine to create a remarkable ecological diversity, with the result that these prisons have a range of internal environments marked by differing social climates. Indeed, an underlife of niches and sanctuaries develops to shelter men and women from the violence or simply the intrusiveness of their peers. The ecology of today's prisons is strikingly parallel to that of our dangerous and yet highly differentiated urban slums. Still, drawing attention to the distinctive prevalence of inmate violence in contemporary prisons reminds us that these prisons are different from their immediate predecessors in this century. The evolution of the twentieth-century prison, from a stable if oppressive Big House, through a brief flirtation with corrections, to what now often amounts to a contained but turbulent ghetto, tells much about the character of life and adjustment in the contemporary prison. This evolution, discussed at length in Chapter Five, highlights the enduring reality of prison's pains, as well as the distinctive configuration those pains assume in today's maximum-security penal institutions.

NOTES

1. Rothman (1971); Ignatieff (1978).

2. Walker (1980:47).

3. Hirsch (1982:1222–23).

4. Hirsch (1982:1223–24).

5. As Hirsch (1982:1228) has observed,

There remained one last set of punishments designed, not to reintegrate the offender into the community, but to cast him out of it once and for all. Banishment served as the ordinary mechanism whereby Massachusetts communities rid themselves of undesirables. Less common, but equally effective, were branding and mutilation, punishments that fixed upon the offenders an indelible "mark of infamy," to warn community members to keep their distance. Recourse to the gallows also took the offender out of the community, though this most final of all punishments was applied only in extraordinary cases.

6. Hirsch (1982:1240).

7. Quoted in Hirsch (1982:1233).

8. Sherman and Hawkins (1981:81).

9. Ironically, public punishments lingered for a brief time in colonial prisons, the very institutions that had arisen to take the place of now-defunct community punishments. Here, it was presumed, a community of sorts still existed (Hirsch, 1982:1242). As it turned out, these prisons, in Massachusetts and elsewhere in the Colonies, did not house communities in any meaningful sense of the term. Public prison punishment died out quickly, in

part because the practice was seen by the convicts as raw abuse rather than moral education. As had occurred in the free world, prisoners subjected to these public punishments were alienated rather than reclaimed by this treatment.

Likewise, efforts to place admonitory placards and signs strategically about the prison compound, drafted from the practices of Puritan villages as a means to instruct and chastise wayward convicts, proved short-lived. Coffey, writing in 1823 about the New York State Prison, describes these signs, most calling prominently for repentance, as utterly ridiculous in the eyes of the prisoners:

The Inspectors, grasp at every opportunity of shewing a reformation in the convicts, through their, immediate means. They state in their report, to the Legislature, that on the 24th of April, 1822, "they placed boards in different parts of the prison yard, on which are sentences of admonition; such as reminding the prisoner of the evil consequences of transgression, and the folly of being self tormentors; which has operated powerfully upon the minds of many" . . . *When they were affixed in the prison yard, the convicts were perfectly surprised at the imbecility that had suggested them. Some of them most wittily paraphrased several of the inscriptions; many ridiculed and laughed them to scorn; and others openly pitied the impotency of the Inspectors. (Coffey, 1823:194)*

10. See Coffey (1823:194), and Hirsch (1982:1242).

11. See Hirsch (1982:1180).

12. The first of these was Connecticut's "mine prison," whose dank and desolate environs harken back to the early Roman prisons (most notably the Mamertine prison, which was discussed in Chapter One, and the Lautumiae prison, mentioned in Note 62 of that chapter) (ACA, 1983:26–27).

13. Rothman (1971:54); see also Mazur (1989).

14. These institutions reflected the thinking of the "classical" criminological scholars, notably Beccaria and Bentham. According to John Conrad, they saw prisons "as a means of rationalizing the

processes of punishment"; for them, "the sentence of imprisonment implied a system of punishment rather than the exercise of vengeance by the state" (personal communication). The object of this system of prison punishment was "maximum general deterrence" (McConville, 1981:xi). Deplorable prison conditions were thought to be humane in the sense that they sacrificed only a few lives but saved many others by deterring would-be criminals (McConville, 1981:62).

15. Norris (1985:82).

16. Norris (1985:82).

17. Norris (1985:82).

18. Byrne (1989:25).

19. McConville (1981:86).

20. McConville (1981:98).

21. ACA (1983:14).

22. See Lane (1979 & 1980). Similar forces were at work in England, which was undergoing "a period of tumultuous economic and social change" during the period when penitentiaries were introduced (Ignatieff, 1978:211).

23. See Mazur (1989:8).

24. See Mazur (1989).

25. Scull (1977:2425).

26. Ignatieff (1978:212).

27. Kittrie (1971).

28. Rothman (1971).

29. Rusche and Kirchheimer (1939); Foucault (1977); Ignatieff (1978); Dobash (1983).

30. Beaumont and Tocqueville (1833/1964:57).

31. Beaumont and Tocqueville (1833/1964:58).

32. Beaumont and Tocqueville (1833/1964:65).

33. Beaumont and Tocqueville (1833/1964:65–66).

34. Rafter (1990, xxvi).

35. Cahalan (1979).

36. Beaumont and Tocqueville (1833-1964:61).

37. Pisciotta (1983 & 1994).

38. See Pisciotta (1994).

39. For at least the first three decades of this century, penitentiary-like discipline (and sometimes hard labor) was maintained in prisons for the sake of custody alone. According to the authoritative *Survey of Release Procedures,*

Imprisonment in 1900–1935 was substantially what it had been one hundred years earlier: custody, punishment, and hard labor. By the end of the period in many prisons it reverted to just custody and punishment. (Quoted in Barnes & Teeters, 1952:556)

40. Rothman (1980:152).

41. Elgar (1886:12).

42. Lawes (1932).

43. Lawes (1932).

44. Lawes (1932:34).

45. Nelson (1936:15).

46. Nelson (1936:4).

47. See Carroll (1988) and Johnson (2000).

48. See Himes (1934).

49. See Oshinsky (1996); Crouch and Marquart (1989).

50. See Tolnay and Beck (1995).

51. See Franklin (1989); Sellin (1976).

52. Oshinsky (1996:139).

53. Sellin (1976:134).

54. Oshinsky (1996).

55. Douglass (1845/1968:44).

56. See David and Fogel (1976).

57. Oshinsky (1996:55).

58. See Franklin (1989); Sellin (1976); Oshinsky (1996).

59. Oshinsky (1996:61).

60. Oshinsky (1996:61 & 63).

61. Oshinsky (1996:46).

62. Sellin (1976:163).

63. Sellin (1976:146).

64. See Rafter (1990:150–51).

65. Rafter (1990:150–51).

66. See Oshinsky (1996).

67. See Sample (1984).

68. Sample (1984:147–48).

69. See Crouch and Marquart (1989).

70. See Bergner (1998).

71. Rafter (1990:21).

72. Rafter (1990:21).

73. O'Brien (1938:80–81), quoted in Franklin (1989:171–72).

74. O'Brien, quoted in Franklin (1989:171–72).

75. See, for example, Anonymous (1871).

76. Coffey (1823:61).

77. See Human Rights Watch *World Report* (1998).

78. Franklin (1989:175).

79. Quoted in Franklin (1989:175).

80. See Conover (2000).

81. Rafter (1990).

82. Rafter (1990: xxvii–xxviii).

83. Rafter (1990: xxviii).

84. Quoted in Rafter (1990: 27).

85. Rafter (1990:27).

86. Rafter (1990: 32).

87. Rafter (1990).

88. Rafter (1990: 141).

89. Rothman (1971:247).

90. Rafter (1990:82).

91. Rafter (1990:83).

92. Rafter (1990:83).

93. Sykes (1958/1966:63).

94. Sykes (1958/1966:81).

95. Irwin (1970).

96. Rothman (1980:157–58).

97. Washington (1981:5).

98. See Rafter (1990); Rierden (1997).

99. Rierden (1997:152).

100. See Irwin (1980).

101. Toch (1988:41).

102. See, generally, Braswell, Montgomery, and Lombardo (1994); for women's prisons, see Rierden (1997) and Owen (1998).

103. Supermax prisons are a probable exception to this observation, though I am aware of no study in which the ecology of such institutions has been studied.

REFERENCES

American Correctional Association (ACA). *The American Prison: From the Beginning . . .* ACA Publishers, 1983.

Anonymous. *An Illustrated History and Description of State Prison Life, By One Who Has Been There. Written by a Convict in a Convict's Cell.* Globe Publishing, 1871.

Barnes, H. E., and N. K. Teeters. *New Horizons in Criminology.* New York: Prentice-Hall, 1952.

Beaumont, G. D., and A. D. Tocqueville. *On the Penitentiary System in the United States and Its Application in France.* Carbondale: Southern Illinois University Press, 1833/1964.

Bergner, Daniel. *God of the Rodeo.* Westminster, MD Crown Pub, 1998.

Braswell, M. C., R. H. Montgomery, and L. X. Lombardo (eds.). *Prison Violence in America.* Cincinnati, OH: Anderson, 1994.

Byrne, R. *Prisons and Punishments of London.* London: Harrap, 1989.

Cahalan, M. "Trends in incarceration in the United States since 1880." *Crime & Delinquency* 25 (1) 1979: 9–41.

Carroll, L. "Race, ethnicity and the social order of the prison." In R. Johnson and H. Toch (eds.). *The Pains of Imprisonment.* Prospect Heights, IL: Waveland Press, 1988: 181–203.

Coffey, W. A. *Inside Out: Or, An Interior View of the New York State Prison; Together With Bibliographic Sketches of the Lives of Several of the Convicts.* New York: Printed for the author, 1823.

Conover, T. *Newjack: Guarding Sing Sing.* New York: Random House, 2000.

Crouch, B. M., and J. W. Marquart. *An Appeal to Justice: Litigated Reform of Texas Prisons.* Austin: University of Texas Press, 1989.

David, P. A., and D. W. Fogel. *Time on the Cross.* New York: Oxford, 1976.

Dobash, R. P. "Labour and discipline in Scottish and English prisons: Moral correction, punishment and useful toil." *Sociology* 17 91(1) 1983: 1–25.

Douglass, F. *Narrative of the Life of Frederick Douglass, An American Slave, Written by Himself.* New York: Signet, 1945/1968.

Elgar, T. (Convict No. 6179). *Convict Life; or, Penitentiary Citizenship in the Illinois State Pen.* Rochester, NY: 1886.

Foucault, M. *Discipline and Punishment: The Birth of the Prison.* New York: Pantheon, 1977.

Franklin, H. B. *Prison Literature in America.* New York: Oxford University Press, 1989.

Himes, C. "To what red hell?" *Esquire* 2 (October) 1934: 100–101, 122, 127.

Hirsch, A. J. "From pillory to penitentiary: The rise of criminal incarceration in early Massachusetts." *Michigan Law Review* 80 (1982).

Human Rights Watch *World Report,* 1998.

Ignatieff, M. *A Just Measure of Pain: The Penitentiary in the Industrial Revolution, 1750–1850.* New York: Pantheon, 1978.

Irwin, J. *The Felon.* Englewood Cliffs, NJ: Prentice-Hall, 1970.

Irwin, J. *Prisons in Turmoil.* Boston: Little, Brown, 1980.

Johnson, R. "American prisons and the African-American experience: A history of social control and racial oppression." *Corrections Compendium* 25 (9) September 2000: 6–10 & 28–30.

Kittrie, N. M. *The Right to Be Different.* Baltimore: The Johns Hopkins Press, 1971.

Lane, R. *Violent Death in the City: Suicide, Accident, and Murder in Nineteenth-Century Philadelphia.* Cambridge: Harvard University Press, 1979.

Lane, R. "Urban police and crime in nineteenth-century America." In N. Morris and M. Tonry (eds.). *Crime and Justice: An Annual Review of Research.* Chicago: University of Chicago Press, 1980.

Lawes L. E. *Twenty Thousand Years in Sing Sing.* New York: Ray Long & Richard R. Smith, Inc., 1932.

Mazur, L. P. *Rites of Execution: Capital Punishment and the Transformation of American Culture, 1776–1865.* New York: Oxford University Press, 1989.

McConville, S. *A History of English Prison Administration.* London: Routledge & Kegan Paul, 1981.

Nelson, V. F. *Prison Days and Nights.* New York: Garden City Publishing Co., Inc., 1936.

Norris, R. L. *Prison Reformers and Penitential Publicists in France, England, and the United States, 1774–1847.* Unpublished dissertation: American University, 1985.

O'Brien, E. *So I Went To Prison.* New York: 1938.

Oshinsky, D. M. *Worse Than Slavery: Parchman Farm and the Ordeal of Jim Crow Justice.* Detroit: Free Press, 1996.

Owen, B. *"In the Mix": Struggle and Survival in a Women's Prison.* Albany, NY: State University of New York Press, 1998.

Pisciotta, A. W. *Benevolent Repression: Social Control and the American Reformatory Prison Movement.* New York: New York University Press, 1994.

Rafter, N. H. *Partial Justice: Women, Prisons, and Social Control.* (2nd ed.) Newark, NJ Transaction, 1990.

Rierden, A. *The Farm: Life Inside a Women's Prison.* Amherst, MA: University of Massachusetts Press, 1997.

Rothman, D. J. *The Discovery of the Asylum: Social Order and Disorder in the New Republic.* Boston: Little, Brown, 1971 & 1990.

Rothman, D. J. *Conscience and Convenience: The Asylum and Its Alternatives in Progressive America.* Boston: Little, Brown, 1980.

Rusche, G., and O. Kirchheimer. *Punishment and Social Structure.* New York: Columbia University Press, 1939.

Sample, A. R. *Racehoss: Big Emma's Boy.* New York: Ballantine Books, 1984.

Scull, A. T. *Decarceration: Community Treatment and the Deviant—A Radical View.* Englewood Cliffs, NJ: Prentice-Hall, 1977.

Sellin, J. T. *Slavery and the Penal System.* New York: Elsevier, 1976.

Sherman, M. E., and G. Hawkins. *Imprisonment in America: Choosing the Future.* Chicago: University of Chicago Press, 1981.

Sykes, G. *The Society of Captives.* New Jersey: Princeton University Press, 1958.

Toch, H. "Study and reducing stress." In R. Johnson and H. Toch (eds.). *The Pains of Imprisonment.* Prospect Heights, IL: Waveland Press, 1988: 25–44.

Tolnay, S. E., and E. M. Beck. *A Festival of Violence: An Analysis of Southern Lynchings, 1882–1930.* Carbondale University of Illinois Press, 1995.

Walker, S. *Popular Justice: A History of American Criminal Justice.* New York: Oxford University Press, 1980.

Washington, J. *A Bright Spot in the Yard: Notes and Stories From a Prison Journal.* Trumansburg, NY: Crossing Press, 1981.

3

❖

The Pains of Modern
Imprisonment

Prisons present a simple exterior to the world but they are hard places to understand and change. One difficulty is that there is a distinctly utopian bias to the work of many prison reformers. The prison has been cast in terms of one Grand Scheme or another, not assessed as an entity in its own right that must be appreciated on its own terms. Prisons are nothing if not painful, yet the implications of this stark fact have never been fully appreciated by reformers.

In particular, there has been a tendency to romanticize the disciplined isolation that prisoners find so painful, as though solitary captivity were really an asset, even a blessing. Many reformers would have it that the prison exists as a separate and pure world, free from the corruptions and constraints of society and unencumbered by any special liabilities of its own. Here, in this neutral environment—this pallid but pure community—offenders would not so much suffer fruitlessly in solitude as be reborn or reconstituted. Upon release, they would emerge as reformed sinners ready to resist the temptations of free society, as docile laborers ripe for conscription in the workforce or, more recently, as men and women primed by one correctional program or another to embrace middle-class values.

Thoroughgoing utopianism of this sort has been less common in the twentieth century. Stateville Prison from the 1930s to the early 1960s was, however, one notable instance. Though the prisoners, almost to a man, found Stateville to be an oppressively rigid environment, its very regularity and discipline were thought by officials to set Stateville apart from the mundane considerations of life in free society. "Stateville was Joseph Ragen's answer to Walden Two," we learn from a thoughtful commentator on that well-known prison.[1] One would not normally think of a prison, any prison, in the same breadth as a pastoral community of idealists, yet it is true, as Jacobs notes, that at Stateville, as at Walden Two,

> Every person and every object had its place. From the award-winning gardens to the clocklike regularity of the movement of prisoners in precise formations from assignment to assignment, the prison reflected its warden's zeal for order and harmony. Indeed, Ragen and the organization's elite looked on the prison as morally superior to the outside society with its petty politics and debilitating corruption.[2]

Here, as in the penitentiary, a regime of discipline was meant to reform the prisoners. And here, as in the penitentiary, it is as if the prison and the prisoner were, like Rorschach's famous inkblot figures, infinitely adaptable to the ideals of reformers. Reduced to mere props, the prisoners were depersonalized and viewed as being both congenially oblivious to pain and ever open to the prospect of change.

The converse of this utopianism is the tendency of critics to see prison as a malevolent monstrosity that brutalizes all it touches, in which pain is not minimized or denied but exaggerated to the point where prisoners could not survive without compromising their humanity. We are told that subterranean beatings of hapless prisoners by brutal guards are the norm, and that at best a mere gloss of humanity covers and distorts the surface of prison life.[3] In this scenario, which is more commonly adopted by those who wish to abolish rather than merely to reform the prison, only contact with the community can cure the prison's ills. The paradox is that the prison is capable of the extremes envisioned by reformers and critics—prisons can offer both human community and dehumanizing violence—but the dominant reality falls between them on an ecological continuum that we examine later in this book.

Those who wish to avoid imposing their own ideals on the prison—ideals that may well blind them to the nature of prison life—must operate inductively, from the ground up. They must develop an agenda for prison reform based on what the prison really does to the various people, staff as well as inmates, who inhabit it. This is genuine humanism. It does not impute motives or values but finds them in the experiences of the people under study. From this point of view, there is a constant theme in prison history: prisons have offered painful experiences and been hard places in which to live and work with dignity. Let us then begin the task of understanding and reforming today's prisons by acknowledging that the prisons we inherit are settings of pain. We must define our correctional goals in light of this enduring reality.

THE CIVILIZATION OF PUNISHMENT

Pain, though it is as permanent and obdurate as the fortress walls that enclose most prisons, is not countenanced in the language of the justice system. Talk of pain seems crude, uncivilized. Instead, the justice system takes refuge in the deceptive claims of rehabilitation or in the neutral tongue of bureaucracy. No pain is meted out: "measures" and "interventions" and "treatments" are undertaken. The high drama of inflicting pain by imprisoning criminals (because we are angry and the offender deserves to suffer) is reduced to the "delivery of a commodity." Nils Christie's observations on this matter are blunt and to the point:

> [T]he basic law should be called a "pain-law." . . . The penal law professors do most definitely not like to be designated "pain-law" professors. The judges do not like to sentence people to pain. Their preference is to sentence them to various "measures." The receiving institutions do not like to be regarded, or to regard themselves, as "pain-inflicting" institutions. Still, such a terminology would actually present a very precise message: punishment as administered by the penal law system is the conscious inflicting of pain. Those who are punished are supposed to suffer. If they by and large enjoyed it, we would change the method. It is intended within penal institutions that those at the receiving end shall get something that makes them unhappy, something that hurts. . . .
>
> Pain delivery is the concept for what in our time has developed into a calm, efficient, hygienic operation. Seen from the perspective of those delivering the service, it is not first and foremost drama, tragedy, intense sufferings. Infliction of pain is in dissonance with some major ideals, but can be carried out in an innocent, somnambulistic insulation from the value conflict. The pains of punishments are left to the receivers. Through the choice of words, working routines, division of labour and repetition, the whole thing has become the delivery of a commodity.[4]

At first blush, the failure of the justice system to acknowledge the use of pain would appear to be a clear-cut case of hypocrisy. Pain that is denied in policy or hidden behind prison walls remains pain nonetheless. As Christie reminds us, it is simply "left to the receivers" to bear while the rest of us go about our daily lives in blissful ignorance. However, the deeper reality may be that we fail to emphasize pain not because we are lying to ourselves but because we are increasingly ambivalent about it. I made this point in the first two editions of this book, and it has been reiterated by Clear.[5] Clear, however, uses the word *harm* rather than *pain* or *suffering* at the center of his analysis, as when he observes, "Professionals in the field of corrections are loath to admit that they are bureaucrats whose jobs it is to implement judicially decreed harms."[6] There is much value in Clear's book, but it is, in my view, misleading to say that we as a society seek to harm or damage offenders when we punish them. Pain and suffering need not produce damage and, indeed, can be a source of moral education (see Chapter One). Moreover, the general thrust of modern prison practice is to minimize pain and suffering and in my view, to avoid inflicting damage on offenders. Pain has become, in other words, a necessary evil we aim to minimize, not a policy of choice.

Pain is an inevitable and, within limits, a just feature of imprisonment, but we no longer freely inflict pain in order to make prisons work. We recognize that pain can create more prison management problems than it solves. When pain becomes excessive, prisons become hard to operate. Now it is always possible, in principle, to escalate pain and break the will of the prisoners—to resort, in other words, to outright brutality and run the prison on raw fear. This method may have been more useful in the past—occasionally in the not-so-distant past, especially in southern plantation prisons—but it exacted a great cost from inmate and keeper alike. Even a cursory historical review offers testimony to the abysmal quality of life (and by implication, work) in the first prisons and in the penitentiaries. Rule by terror—both living under terror and being agents of terror—would seem to have even more obvious drawbacks today. Such a regime is flagrantly illegal and likely to be successfully litigated, those violent southern prisons being good cases in point.[7] It is also sorely out of step with the times and utterly indefensible in terms of our current values.

More often than intentionally promoting pain, genuine efforts are made by prison officials and others in the justice system to reduce suffering and to keep the pains of imprisonment within tolerable limits. As Toch and I have observed, "To create pain is not what administrators do intentionally. . . . Pain and stress are the undesired ingredients of prison life the official must live with. As constraints (such as crowding) increase the harshness of imprisonment, ameliorating stress becomes a new and salient goal."[8] The contemporary prison, then, is not only a pain-delivering institution but also a pain-limiting institution. As such, it reflects a larger historical trend away from inflicting excessive pain on criminals, a trend that may be at the very heart of what we mean by civilization. As John Stuart Mill observed, "One of the effects of civilization (not to say one of the ingredients in it) is, that the spectacle, and even the very idea of pain, is more and more kept out of the sight of those classes who enjoy in their fullness the benefits of civilization."[9]

Civilization means a growth in knowledge, which, Reiman reminds us, "brings increased power to prevent or reduce pain."[10] Civilization also means an increase in our ability to communicate with others outside our immediate environment, and this "extends the circle of people with whom we empathize."[11] As a result, "progress in civilization is characterized by a lower tolerance for one's own pain and that suffered by others."[12] This means that "the spectacle, and even the very idea of pain" that so troubled John Stuart Mill must be hidden from more and more people. Ultimately, it must seem to disappear from punishment itself. By this growing unwillingness to administer pain do we measure our civilization, notes Reiman, and "by our example, continue the work of civilizing."[13]

The Amelioration of Pain: Three Stages

The civilization of punishment, if you will, has passed through three stages. First, punishment was removed from the public view, hidden within prisons. This permitted certain types of abuses, but it eliminated the spectacle of public corporal punishment and the orgies of violence sometimes associated with it.[14] Public floggings and executions, in particular, had a nasty tendency to degenerate into carnivals or mob scenes, neither of which were notably civilized.[15] It is one thing to run penitentiaries, however violent or even torturous they may be; it is another to parade torturous practices in the public square, for all to see.

Next, physical pain (that is to say, tangible, bodily pain) was eliminated as a permissible part of punishment. Prisoners can no longer be subjected to corporal punishment. Even such infamous settings as Alcatraz and Marion, aptly described by Ward as "standard setters for maximum custody and maximum punishment" from the 1930s through to the 1990s, "have accomplished their missions without employing regimes that involve physical punishment."[16] The same is true for Pelican Bay and other contemporary supermax prisons. To the extent that convicts in modern prisons are subjected to physical punishment by guards, it is *always* a violation of official policy. Today, this prohibition of painful assaults on the body applies even to capital punishment. As Foucault has observed,

> Physical pain, the pain of the body itself, is no longer the constituent element of the penalty . . . If it is still necessary for the law to reach and manipulate the body of the convict, it will be at a distance, in the proper way, according to strict rules. . . . Today a doctor must watch over those condemned to death, right up to the last moment—thus juxtaposing himself as the agent of welfare, as the alleviator of pain, with the official whose task it is to end life. . . . [Thus] the modern rituals of execution attest to . . . the disappearance of the spectacle [of punishment] and the elimination of pain.[17]

Death by lethal injection is the purest case of an execution ostensibly free of drama and physical pain.[18] The condemned lies on a gurney and is anesthetized before his or her life is taken, which is indeed a far cry from being drawn and quartered. The more general point, however, is that each of the modern methods of execution—the electric chair, the gas chamber, and lethal injection—was developed with the explicit goal of reducing both the spectacle and the physical pain of capital punishment.[19]

Finally, our notion of what is permissible psychological pain has been circumscribed. The seminal discussion of the psychological pains of imprisonment is provided by Sykes in his book, *Society of Captives*. Sykes argues that imprisonment, by its very nature, deprives liberty, limits goods and services, deprives or at least sharply reduces access to heterosexual relations, and limits both autonomy and security. These deprivations are inherent in imprisonment, whether in a penitentiary or in any other prison and whether the offenders are men or women, young or old. Of course, in early prisons and in penitentiaries, there were physical punishments as well. For today's prisons, the pains of confinement are *limited* to these psychological deprivations, except where failures of policy allow physical brutality to flourish in the form of extralegal, illegitimate punishments.

Living with Deprivation

Loss of Liberty The first deprivation of imprisonment is the loss of liberty. For the prisoner, states Sykes, "loss of liberty is a double one—first, by confinement to the institution and second, by confinement within the institution."[20]

The significance of this loss goes beyond limitations of movement, however frustrating these may be. A deeper loss is found in "the involuntary seclusion of the outlaw" from the larger society and all that entails in terms of lost contact with loved ones and one's former way of life.[21] Deeper still is the pain of moral rejection implied in confinement. For confinement represents, and has always represented, a statement by society that the prisoner is no longer a person to be trusted or respected to move freely among his or her fellow citizens.[22]

Inmates are society's pariahs. They know it, and the rejection hurts. As one female inmate put it, reflecting on the assembly line procedure she encountered on entering the prison, "You go in there, you weren't a person anymore, you weren't human anymore, they could care less."[23] Her concerns about impersonality—that as an inmate one is not even a person, let alone a person to be trusted or cared for—resonate with male inmates as well. In one male inmate's words, "Like an ancient tree—gnarled and wizened by time and nature's elements—my heart has grown rugged and callused. A price extracted by the unfeeling environment I'm forced to survive in."[24]

The central, coercive fact of confinement is captivity, the loss of freedom. By some reckonings, the deprivation of liberty is the most basic and profound suffering inflicted by imprisonment—the root or essential problem from which all other difficulties and losses inexorably flow.[25]

Deprivation of Goods and Services The second deprivation is that of goods and services. Prisons consign inmates to conditions of relative poverty. In the early prisons and in the penitentiaries, there was abject poverty and, sometimes, life-threatening shortages of medicine and food. In the Big House, a spartan regime provided adequate food and shelter but few amenities. Today's prisons, as we have noted, are more accommodating; amenities are more common (especially in women's prisons), and recreation is seen as a daily right rather than, as in the Big House, an occasional privilege. There was, of course, no recreation whatsoever in the penitentiaries.

One can imagine a prison that deprived only liberty and left prisoners to idle away their time in luxurious conditions, and indeed many prison critics claim that "country club prisons" offer just such regimes. But this has never been the fate of regular criminals and only rarely the fate of individual prisoners with unique political or economic circumstances. For the typical criminal, loss of liberty means loss of access to a range of goods and services one might have been able to earn or otherwise acquire were one free.

Many offenders have led miserable lives outside, and, as a result, they may find the objective material conditions of prison to be as good as, or even better than, those they faced in the free world. This observation may well hold for prisons of all types, from the Mamertine Prison onward. Still, prisoners are apt to *believe* they could do better in the free world and hence conclude that prison conditions are "painfully depriving."[26] Prison conditions are thus likely to be seen as symbolically inadequate even if they are sufficient for a decent material existence. As Sykes has cogently observed,

A standard of living can be hopelessly inadequate, from the individual's viewpoint, because it bores him to death or fails to provide those subtle symbolic overtones which we invest in the world of possessions. And this is the core of the prisoner's problem in the area of goods and services. He wants—or needs, if you will—not just the so-called necessities of life but also the amenities: cigarettes and liquor as well as calories, interesting foods as well as sheer bulk, individual clothing as well as adequate clothing, individual furnishings for his living quarters as well as shelter, privacy as well as space.[27]

Hence it is that, even in a prison world seen by outsiders as perfectly adequate, it is a natural human tendency for the prisoners to feel aggrieved and to see the prison's "present material impoverishment as a painful loss."[28]

The pain of this material loss, moreover, runs deeper than daily discomfort. For citizens of the nineteenth and twentieth centuries, at least, material goods are taken to be an index of one's worth as a human being. To be poor is to be a failure as a human being. Thus it is that

impoverishment remains as one of the most bitter attacks on the individual's self-image that our society has to offer and prisoners cannot ignore the implication of their straitened circumstances. Whatever the discomforts and irritations of the prisoner's Spartan existence may be, they must carry the additional burden of social definitions which equate their material deprivation with personal inadequacy.[29]

The connection between material goods and personal worth is almost certainly a special burden to the poor. With few achievements to fall back on, material things become a central measure of one's value. As Jean Harris observed, "The women at Bedford want all the good things as much, or possibly more, than you do. *They measure their own self-worth, not by what's inside, but what's outside, what shows.*"[30] [emphasis added]. There is no reason to doubt the applicability of this statement to male offenders, who periodically fight to the death over name-brand tennis shoes and starter jackets. In both men's and women's prisons, elaborate underground economies provide access to various types of contraband, including special food, clothing, and even drugs, which is thought to lessen some of the impact of the loss of goods and services.

Deprivation of Heterosexual Contact   Sexual deprivation is the third pain of imprisonment. "If the inmate, then, is rejected and impoverished by the facts of his imprisonment," states Sykes, "he is also figuratively castrated by his involuntary celibacy."[31] (For female inmates, the parallel metaphor presumably would involve figurative imposition of a chastity belt.) Until quite recently, with the spread of home furloughs and conjugal visits, heterosexual celibacy among prisoners was complete and the deprivation of heterosexual contact was essentially total.

Sykes notes that the pains of heterosexual frustration go beyond physical discomfort and entail psychological pains that call into doubt the gender identity of the lonely convict. (Sykes is speaking of men only, but in my view his points have general applicability.) Two salient problems emerge. One is pressure toward homosexual satisfaction of one's sexual needs, which provokes anxiety in many prisoners. The other is the tendency for traditionally male personality traits such as toughness to become exaggerated in the absence of the moderating effect of persons of the opposite sex (women in men's prison, men in women's prisons), thus distorting in psychologically painful ways the image of manliness (in the men's prison) and womanliness (in the women's prison). Given the hard realities of a lonely prison life, it is perhaps unsurprising that toughness becomes highly valued in all major groups—men and women, adolescents and adults—exposed to confinement.

Some readers may doubt the salience of concerns for toughness in women's prisons. I offer the following excerpt from a woman doing time in a woman's maximum security prison. Her concerns on the issue of toughness, shared by many of her sisters in confinement, are *indistinguishable* from those of her male counterparts in men's prisons:

■ After being in prison for so many years, you get to carry a reputation. You (learn you) can mess more with this person, you can't mess with that one. You can run over this one—take her fucking shit and make her look like shit, make her look like a punk bitch. But this one over here you can't mess with because she ain't going to let you punk her out like this one over here. Like I walk up to a broad and say, "Hey motherfucker, I want that watch," and she gets all scared and I take it and say, "Thank you, you fucking punk bitch."[32] ■

Men may decline to say "thank you" to their victims, but the rest of the encounter is all too familiar to observers of male prison culture. If anything, concerns for toughness reach even greater extremes in high-security penal institutions for adolescent boys and girls, where identity concerns are more salient and where abuse of others, including overt sexual abuse, may become a staple of daily life. As one girl in a training school observed, describing social norms adopted by training school boys as well, "all the girls, you know, we go around with masks on . . . We can never be natural when we are here. Coz' if you're natural, then you are weak and you'll get taken down, and you're not worth shit"[33] A culture of victimization may sometimes emerge with the collaboration of staff, who control the more predatory prisoners by sacrificing the weaker ones.[34]

Relatively few prisoners have written about the sexual deprivations of prison life. Those who have done so are men, and they provide accounts that bear out Sykes's claims. If anything, prisoners who discuss sexual deprivation see this loss as uniquely cruel. As Nelson, a prisoner of a Big House in the 1920s and 30s, observed:

■ The imprisoned man is essentially the man isolated from the woman. It is in this respect that he differs most sharply from the man in the free world. If the imprisoned man endures hardships in the way of poverty, mal-nourishment, paucity of entertainment, recreation, and the like, so also does the average man in the free world. But the free man, regardless of his financial, personal, social and other limitations, can and does—legally or illegally—have access to the woman. The imprisoned man is completely and utterly cut off from her. . . .[35] ◾

The prisoner thus deprived, Nelson assures us, suffers nothing less than sexual starvation. Sexual starvation is unique. Unlike starvation for food, which ends in death, sexual starvation can persist for great periods of time:

◾ For of all the possible forms of starvation, surely none is more demoralizing than sexual starvation. If one becomes sufficiently hungry or thirsty, one naturally suffers a great deal; but usually only for a comparatively brief time. Relief is always in sight—even if it come in the desperate form of death. But to be starved for month after weary month, year after endless year, in a place where "every day is like a year, a year whose days are long," for sexual satisfaction which, in the case of a lifer, may never come, this is the secret quintessence of human misery.[36] ◾

The fantasies of sexually starved prisoners, to borrow Nelson's metaphor, tend to be overtly erotic. Contemporary prisoners have reported ongoing love affairs with centerfolds displayed prominently on cell walls. George Mosby Jr., a prison poet, writes lovingly "of an old con" with just such a love object:

◾ he has grown in love
with the nude brown centerfold
on the wall above his bunk
her breasts are too big for her thin body
and the page has worn sheer
where he touches her
before he sleeps to dream each night
imagining the fragrance of her womb
he knows her eyes
as a man knows the eyes of a woman
he's spent a life-time with: they're branded
in his mind.
he licks his lips sometimes
as if imagining her kisses
her tongue wet and slippery as spinach
in his mouth
(dazed as stone) he sits
and whips himself with thoughts of her
whispering to her: in twenty years
no-one has ever heard him promise her anything
other than all the love he can muster
and all the man he can be.[37] ◾

Other convicts describe imaginative dummies constructed to highlight anatomically appealing features of the female form. It is also probably true that sexual hunger pushes some men into homosexual encounters about which they are anxious or uncomfortable. The larger point though, made in the abstract by Sykes and drawn from real life in Nelson's case, is that sexual hunger is not only a physical yearning but a cry for the companionship of women. "By sexual hunger I mean a hunger not only for sexual intercourse, but a hunger for the voice, the touch, the laugh, the tears of Woman; a hunger for Woman Herself."[38]

There is no doubt that sexual hunger afflicts women prisoners, though little has been written about this phenomenon. It is wise to remember that for much of human history, women were perceived as more sexual than men—as more rapacious in sexual appetite and therefore more likely to experience hunger in the absence of sexual outlets. (Remember that Coffey, writing in 1823, described women prisoners as more depraved, more enslaved to passion, and less subject to shame than their male counterparts. These statements were utterly unremarkable in his day. See Chapter 2.) Ironically, the modern era has seen the characterization of women as less sexual than men, as weak and vulnerable rather than lusty and strong, though this may be changing as we enter the Millennium.[39] Be that as it may, in today's prisons, opportunities for emotional and sexual intimacy appear to be more readily available in women's prisons than in men's prisons. Women's prisons are often populated by intimate couples (called "homosexual dyads" in the cold language of the social sciences) and by supportive extended inmate families. Inmate marriages appear to be more common in women's prisons.[40] Sexual behavior in women's prisons seems at least as salient, and on occasion perhaps even more public, than is the case in men's prisons. "They have no shame," stated one inmate, referring to couples who have sex in the cell blocks in broad daylight. " 'No, it was no big deal,' one of the girls said, `You can watch, I don't care.' And it was like, it didn't mean anything to them, it was no big deal."[41]

One factor in the apparently enhanced sexuality of women prisoners may be environmental: many women's prisons feature dormitories, which are conducive to liaisons. Jean Harris, who served time in Bedford Hills Prison in New York, argues that dormitories, though described by many as a humane advance in the management of prisons, actually takes us back to premodern prisons like Newgate, an eighteenth-century prison mixing men, women, and children, where sexual promiscuity ran rampant:

> To put two hundred women into dormitories where anyone can go in or out of anyone's cubicle, or in and out of shared showers and toilets, is to invite a sexual orgy that won't stop. The women know which C.O.s on night duty fall asleep at what time and which C.O.s play the street games with them, and nightlife is lived around them. There are women there who would give their souls to be moved and some who think it's the best ticket in town. Prison dormitories are a step back toward Newgate and anyone in the prison business knows it.[42]

Bedford is no Newgate, Harris acknowledges, but then wryly observes: "It was not uncommon for a woman [in Newgate] to have to give herself sexually in order to get her daily food. Obviously, that's no longer required, but I'm told it's still one way to get a really good meal."[43]

In the main, male and female prisoners today probably suffer less sexual hunger than their counterparts from earlier years. Furloughs and conjugal visits, increasingly available since the mid-1970s, allow some access to members of the opposite sex. Visiting rooms are settings that are fairly regularly exploited for *sub rosa* heterosexual trysts.[44] Homosexual outlets, too, are more readily available, partly because prisoners can move about fairly freely in many of today's prisons and because the stigma associated with such conduct has been sharply reduced in society and in the prison. Thus, a contemporary prisoner at Lompoc, a federal prison, told one researcher that "most dudes with homosexuals are married [to them]."[45] Such marriages may involve formal ceremonies of sorts; this is true in men's and women's prisons, including such unlikely settings as plantation prisons.[46] When separation or divorce occurs, personal crises may ensue.[47] Fleisher describes a flamboyantly homosexual prisoner at Lompoc who would make the nightly rounds of the cell blocks looking for sex partners. It would seem that no official of Lompoc prison attempted to thwart him in these endeavors. Nor is there any concerted effort to curb the sexual appetites of the estimated 10 percent of his fellow inmates who were "actively engaged in sex" during the period of Fleisher's study.[48] As noted earlier, such public promiscuity may be, if anything, more common in women's prisons.

Still, for most prisoners today, men and women, homosexual outlets are unavailable, and others who seek such relationships may be unable to secure satisfying arrangements. Furloughs and conjugal visits must be earned; not all prisoners are eligible, and those who are must often wait years for the privilege. Writing of prison life in the 1970s, and having had the benefit of a furlough, McCall could observe with obvious feeling that "Sometimes sexual tension got so heavy in my chest that I felt I might just explode, blow up in a puff of smoke."[49] McCall was not alone in this reaction. "You're in a place," he notes, "where everybody's got the same problem; everybody feels like Superman with a helluva hump on his back."[50] This sorry state of affairs is readily apparent to correctional officers. As Conover has noted, speaking of his work at Sing Sing as a correctional officer:

■ With raucous sounds and smells of sweat and threat, B-block virtually seethed with testosterone. Some of it was channeled into bodybuilding; much more found its outlet in masturbation. Jerking off is the main sexual activity in any prison. Sometimes you'd catch a glimpse; occasionally you'd catch a whiff. The cumulative daily output of these 636 men was probably huge, a sad symbol of their thwarted energies.[51] ■

Masturbation, the only sure sexual outlet and apparently the most common sexual practice behind bars, is surely unsatisfying to most prisoners, who appear to crave personal relationships as well as physical release. The pains of sexual deprivation thus remain substantial for today's Superman and, perhaps to a lesser degree, for today's Superwoman as well.

Deprivation of Autonomy   The loss of autonomy is the fourth deprivation suffered by prisoners. In all prisons, the inmate is under the control of officials and hence is in varying degrees dependent upon them and vulnerable to mistreatment at their hands. Brutal punishments reigned in early prisons. Autonomy was not even a consideration of the dealings of keepers and the kept, though poor surveillance in the early prisons allowed subterranean areas of human freedoms. In the penitentiary and in the Big House, the prisoner "is subjected to a vast body of rules and commands which are designed to control his behavior in minute detail."[52] Rules are, moreover, nonnegotiable and beyond dispute. Staff need not give reasons; inmates need only obey. In essence, prisoners have been forcibly returned to the helpless, dependent status of children. "Of the many threats which may confront the individual," observes Sykes, "either in or out of prison, there are few better calculated to arouse acute anxieties than the attempt to reimpose the subservience of youth."[53]

It should be apparent that concern for autonomy is a human trait, and hence this concern is shared by women as well as men. Indeed, there is some evidence that the daily impingements of rules and regulations chaff even more painfully against the sensibilities of female prisoners, who appear to feel a greater need to know the reasons for these restrictions and appear to be more frustrated when such reasons are not forthcoming or are not satisfactory.[54] As one staff member at a women's prison observed, "Women inmates will ask 'why' all day long. The word 'why' is out of their mouth before you even answer their question."[55] One is left with the impression that staff see this concern for reasons as childish. This is ironic, since the underlying motive when one questions authority is for recognition of one's adult autonomy in the face of demands for blind—childish—obedience.

On the other hand, a blanket commitment to violate any and all rules is indeed childish. Nelson found this attitude common among Big House prisoners. He describes prisoners' attitudes toward rules as similar to children's, with no sense of their larger purpose and only a self-centered resentment of the restrictions the rules entail. "There is," he states,

■ simply no respect for laws and rules as necessary adjuncts to civilization and social organization. The prisoner feels that the rules have been made merely in order to prevent him from doing the things he wants to do, and thus he resents them very strongly and breaks them when he can.[56] ■

Harris makes this same point for contemporary women inmates at Bedford Hills, where she maintains that disrespect for rules and for authority can reach remarkable levels:

■ Many of the women refused to do anything asked of them for the sheer pleasure of starting something. They were children with adult desires and criminal experiences. A woman called "Peachy" on my floor regularly yells, "I do what I wanna do. I'm running this show. I'm the king." Another one, looking straight at a C.O. said, "I can do anything I fuckin' please."[57] ■

In what turns out to be a prophetic observation, Nelson argues that the word of the guard on matters of rule violations is always taken over that of the convict, and that this must be so if the system of discipline is to endure:

> The word of a prison guard naturally outweighs that of a convict—and this gives the guard power which he quickly learns to employ against the prisoners who displease him. They know that whatever the guard says, when reporting them for violating rules, will be believed by the warden. It must be believed, otherwise the whole system of discipline within the prison is shattered.[58]

Some thirty-five years later the word of the guard would be given less weight by correctional officials, as due process and other concerns reduced the officer's authority in the 1960s, 1970s, and early 1980s in prisons for men and women. Rules would become less rigid; enforcement would become lax. Explanations would be expected, indeed demanded, by restive convicts. One result of this change in the meaning of rules in prison was, at least for a time, the virtual collapse of discipline, with a resulting surge in inmate violence in men's prisons (see Chapter Five) and perhaps women's prisons as well.[59]

Rules still exist, of course, and they irk and restrain most prisoners—women more than men, by all accounts. But some respect for the prisoner's autonomy is afforded in today's rule enforcement context in prisons for men as well as for women, which makes this pain of imprisonment less potent than in times past. Men may not ask "why" as often as women, but they do ask and they do expect—and typically receive—a plausible answer. And both men and women break some rules, some of the time, with impunity. States Harris, "I watch some of the women jerk C.O.s around like puppets on a string."[60] Open disrespect for the admonitions of officers is certainly reprehensible; some defiance of one's keepers is probably to be preferred to utter and slavish submission to their authority, which bespeaks a regime of terror.

Deprivation of Security   Loss of security is described by Sykes as the fifth and final deprivation of imprisonment. In early prisons, from the Mamertine prison through penitentiaries and industrial prisons, the main source of insecurity was the officers, who wielded nearly total power over the prisoners. Officials were feared figures in plantation prisons and in the Big House, to be sure, as they are in some contemporary prisons, where abuses by staff can become rampant. But whenever freedom of movement emerged in prison, one's fellow convicts came to represent potent threats to personal security. This occurred in some early prisons, where poor supervision and congregate confinement allowed the community of lepers, if you will, to prey on one another. This occurred in some penitentiaries, when regimes of solitude and silence broke down, allowing convicts to corrupt and debase one another. Prisoners became a progressively more potent threat to one another in the Big House, where sufficient free time and loosely supervised recreation in the yard allowed a full-blown prisoner society to evolve. In such a setting, states Sykes, the individual prisoner is thrown into prolonged intimacy with other men who in many cases have a long history of violent, aggressive behavior. It is a situation which can prove to be anxiety-provoking even for the hardened recidivist and it is in this light that we can understand the comment of an inmate of the New Jersey State Prison who said, "The worst thing about prison is you have to live with other prisoners."[61]

By today's standards, Big Houses were well controlled and the prison society operated within sharp constraints. Still, "outlaws" emerged among the prisoners and could wreak havoc among their fellows. "There are," states Sykes,

> a sufficient number of outlaws within this group of outlaws to deprive the average prisoner of that sense of security which comes from living among men who can be reasonably expected to abide by the rules of society. While it is true that every prisoner does not live in the constant fear of being robbed or beaten, the constant companionship of thieves, rapists, murderers, and aggressive homosexuals is far from reassuring.[62]

Accordingly, the prisoner of the Big House can never feel completely safe in the prison. His physical security and psychological integrity are always potentially at risk:

> His expectations concerning the conforming behavior of others destroyed, unable and unwilling to rely on the officials for protection, uncertain of whether or not today's joke will be tomorrow's bitter insult, the prison inmate can never feel safe. And at a deeper level lies the anxiety about his reactions to this unstable world, for then his manhood will be evaluated in the public view.[63]

Women prisoners, too, can never feel safe, for their worth can all too readily "be evaluated in the public view." Though the physical safety concerns of women are less salient than those of men, they are present. Convict women advertise their toughness, and some are—or appear to be—sexual predators. As one inmate at Connecticut's Niantic Prison, known as The Farm, stated, "My biggest fear is that some bitch will force me to become gay . . . She'll sneak into my room some night and there won't be nothin' I can do about it."[64] Ego concerns—concerns for being humiliated and belittled—appear at least as salient among women as among men. As another women at The Farm observed,

> ■ In confined spaces like this, someone puts you down, it can bring you to tears in a heart beat. Everything can hurt you here. And that is sad, because on the streets you can take just about everything and walk away. But you can't walk away in here. You have to take it and listen to what they have to say about you, even if it is not true.[65] ■

Concerns for security may explain why relatively more women than men appear to spend their time alone or in small groups, away from the public areas of the prison where trouble in its many forms is apt to take place. "The majority of [female] prisoners," notes Owen, "opt out of any public life and begin to retreat into the concentric levels of privacy afforded through institutional structure, daily routine, and individual effort."[66] In the words of one female prisoner, "You might as well call us hermits because we are in our room every chance we get. I go to work. I come home. There is nothing for me out in the yard."[67]

With the demise of the discipline of the Big House, which is discussed at length in Chapter Five, there was a period of some fifteen to twenty years— from roughly the mid-1960s until the mid- to late 1980s—when prisoner violence among men was at a high point in many if not most prisons in the nation. Conrad could look back on the "repressive but reasonably safe" Big House with nostalgia, arguing persuasively that the loss of security was greater for convicts during this period than at any time in recent prison history.[68] Conrad was, in my opinion, correct in this assertion. Meanwhile, however, internal reforms have reduced violence considerably in contemporary prisons, to the point where even this deprivation may be reduced relative to prisons of earlier eras. This matter is discussed at some length in the final chapter of this book, where we take up the matter of prison reform.

It is Sykes's view that the various psychological deprivations of modern prisons represent harms that are equivalent to the physical maltreatment found in prisons of earlier days, notably the penitentiaries. He states,

> These deprivations or frustrations of the modern prison may indeed be the acceptable or unavoidable implications of imprisonment, but we must recognize the fact that they can be just as painful as the physical maltreatment which they have replaced. . . . Such attacks on the psychological level are less easily seen than a sadistic beating, a pair of shackles in the floor, or the caged man on a treadmill, but the destruction of the psyche is no less fearful than bodily affliction. . . .[69]

The destruction of the human personality, which lies at the heart of dehumanization, is indeed a fearful thing, but Sykes overstates the relative magnitude of this harm. Corporal punishments were themselves assaults on the psyche or person as well as on the body of the prisoner. To be whipped in public, often while half-naked, is both humiliating and painful. Harms flowing from the terrifying physical abuse of a whipping would entail psychological as well as physical mutilations. Such practices are both physically brutal and profoundly degrading to the prisoners as persons. To be spared physical abuse is to be spared a great deal of human suffering.

Today's psychological pains of imprisonment are formidable in themselves, to be sure, but they are, I contend, considerably less substantial and hurtful than the pains of life in earlier prisons.[70] The utter indifference and brutality of the ancient prisons, typified in *Squalor Carceris* and the officially orchestrated terror so integral to the running of the penitentiary, are things of the past. The prisoner mortality rate in southern plantation prisons at the turn of the twentieth century would be intolerable today, at least in part because of the racial bias so prominently displayed. Mortality rates for black prisoners in Mississippi in the

1880s were especially high, in some cases approaching 20 percent. (The rate for white prisoners was much lower, often around 2 percent, a figure that nevertheless is quite high by contemporary standards.) Plantation prisoners were virtually all black. "Whites," Oshinsky tells us with characteristic understatement, "rarely left the penitentiary walls."[71]

In contrast, the comparatively mild emotion of shame occasioned by psychological assaults on the self, present in the penitentiary but subservient to fear, has become the primary source of coercive control in modern "total institutions" such as the prison, where the life expectancy of prisoners, black and white, may surpass that of their free world counterparts.[72] Significantly, these institutions now provide something approximating a total world for their inmates, not in the sense that they feel utterly vulnerable and must obey out of raw fear (as in all premodern prisons), but because they are dependent upon the institution for basic resources, feel personally shamed and inadequate under those conditions, and hence can be manipulated or persuaded to follow the dictates of an authority that at once both sustains and demeans them.

The link between dependency and shame, which can be exploited for the sake of punishment, is a modern one. In Sennett's words,

> In aristocratic or other traditional societies, weakness was not *per se* a shameful fact. One inherited one's weakness in society; it was not of one's own making. The master inherited his strengths; they too were impersonal. Thus in documents of the old regime we often find the plainest speaking of servants to their masters. Man and position were distinct . . . it is not under these conditions humiliating to be dependent.[73]

Nor was it shameful to be dependent according to the philosophy of the Enlightenment. One inherited one's environment, which in turn shaped one's character. Once again, "man and position were distinct." Dependency did not connote shame or subjugation.

This equilibrium gradually shifted during the nineteenth century in response to the rampant uncertainty of social relations under industrial capitalism. Dependency came to be seen as a failing and, hence, as a cause for shame. As Sennett has observed,

> The market made positions of dependence unstable. You could rise, you could fall. The most powerful impact ideologically of this instability was that people began to feel personally responsible for their place in the world; they viewed their success or failure in struggling for existence as a matter of personal strength or weakness. . . . Shame about being dependent is the legacy of the 19th century industrial society to our own.[74]

Increasingly, persons in authority were able to punish and control their subordinates by inflicting shame. The result is that "shame has taken the place of violence as a routine form of punishment in Western societies. The reason is simple and perverse. The shame an autonomous person can arouse in subordinates is an implicit control."[75]

The various degradations of life in total institutions like the prison are prime examples of this phenomenon. Gradually the prison, like the larger society, came to rely more on shame and less on violence as a means of social control. Penitentiary inmates were meant to suffer shame in the form of the remorse, though the daily regime of the penitentiary was not expressly organized to promote and accentuate shame as a means of social control (as distinct from repentance). Over time, shaven heads and ill-fitting uniforms were intentionally inflicted to express the dependent and shameful state of the prisoners and to use those disabilities to gain control over their behavior. Bereft of a personal identity—or at least denied respect for what identity he or she maintained—the confined offender increasingly was expected to adopt the *social role* of the inmate and to fall into the prison routine. Brutality became increasingly superfluous and even counterproductive as a source of daily control of prison life. Surveillance, the gaze of authority that lay at the heart of the disciplinary regime, as vividly revealed in the panoptical version of the penitentiary, gradually became the backbone of prison discipline.[76] Where surveillance failed, cooptation of rebellious inmates neutralized discontent. Compliance rather than overt coercion became the preferred mechanism of control.

Yet, even in regard to the infliction of the comparatively tame emotion of shame, prisons have become less total, prisoners less dependent on their keepers. In Goffman's terms, today's prisoners suffer fewer "mortifications, debasements, and profanations of self."[77] They have more autonomy than their predecessors of only a generation ago; they have more control over their appearance and over the routine that makes up their prison day. They have more possessions and more freedoms, big and small. They are less closely watched. The ambiance of their prisons more closely resembles the modern urban slum street corner than the nineteenth-century penitentiary or the twentieth-century Big House.[78] Shame remains a salient feature of prison life, as it does in the slums, but these days shame is apt to evoke defensiveness and anger, even rage, rather than docility.[79] Order is more likely to be negotiated by the prisoners and the staff, though prisoners must bargain from a position of weakness. The notion that staff and inmates can share a constructive agenda—that they might work together in service of a prison community that promotes mature coping and responsible citizenship—looms as a distinct possibility for perhaps the first time in prison history.

CIVILIZED PRISONS: PAIN DELIMITED

We live in a time of tame punishments relative to practices in centuries past. Our present-day conception of "bloodthirsty" punishment does not call for blood or even for physical pain: our worst murderers face bloodless and, we hope, physically painless executions.[80] Nor does our notion of harsh punishment encompass the use of calculated psychological abuse of those we confine. Our worst version of prison punishment is captured in the (modern) proverbial notion of "locking the door and throwing away the key." We relegate serious criminals to years of neglect, which is, to be sure, a terrible thing in itself, but it is significant that we do not expect criminals to experience overt physical or psychological abuse as a planned feature of their confinement. It is for these reasons that prisons of only a century ago seem flagrantly inhumane, even barbaric, by contemporary standards.

Solitary confinement is a case in point. In prisons past, notably the penitentiary, the plantation prison, and the Big House, solitary confinement meant complete physical isolation in barren cells, including dark cells. There were no exercise periods. Visits were not allowed. Bread and water diets were standard fare. No one today would seriously consider such confinement as anything other than torture. Even regimes of confinement that roughly approximate true solitary confinement—death row and supermax prisons—are apt to be seen as torturous.[81] Nor is brutal corporal punishment, once standard fare in prison, practiced in any contemporary penal institution. In fact, it is widely believed today by prison officials that "no aim of prison—including retributive punishment—is served by arbitrary, gratuitous, ill-distributed distress."[82] Abuses do occur in today's prisons, and they sometimes take the form of lengthy solitary confinement and staff brutality (the latter practice being a variant of corporal punishment).[83] But such treatment is no longer the norm. It is fair to say that, with a limited array of psychological stresses as the most horrible punishment we are willing to inflict upon our criminals, we are becoming both more civilized and more potentially civilizing in our punishments.

Prisons are still in the pain business but with well-defined limits. Prisoners may well deserve to suffer for the harm they have done to others, but prison officials are not eager to punish them and have no desire whatsoever to harm or damage them. Officials supervise the administration of painful experiences but do not consciously or systematically inflict pain to make prisoners suffer. Indeed, some of the worst pains of today's prisons are the product of the officials' inability to control the more violent prisoners; prison's slum communities, like their counterparts in the free world, are notoriously hard to police. Prisons can be brutal and degrading, but this, with rare exceptions, is neither intended nor passively countenanced. Certainly brutality is no longer defended by officials as a necessary component of prison discipline! The brutal prison in today's world reflects a failure of policy, a triumph of convenience over conscience, and a challenge to responsible prison administrators.

NOTES

1. Jacobs (1977:31).

2. Jacobs (1977:31). A less pure and somewhat paradoxical case of modern correctional utopianism was provided by some political prisoners during the 1960s and 1970s, most notably George Jackson (see

Dorin & Johnson, 1979). Prisoners like Jackson acted as though they held the misguided view that the rigors of prison made it an ideal milieu for political recruitment and foment.

3. Hamm and his associates, for example, maintain that today's prisons are systematically abusive, making them indistinguishable from earlier prisons (see Hamm, Coupez, Hose, & Weinstein, 1994). This study is, in my view, short on method and long on ideology. It exhibits at least two salient flaws. First, the complex notion of humaneness is used as a foil, as though humaneness were limited to matters of discipline and did not encompass the general habitability of prisons. The prison literature is reviewed selectively and with no sense of history. There are, if you will, no shades of grey in the prison world: guards are hacks who prey on innocent inmate victims; prisons are settings of brutality featuring daily violence and abuse. Things are today as they always have been in prison, which is to say, uniformly awful and degrading. Anyone who argues or presents evidence to the contrary is uninformed and painfully naive. All of this makes good rhetoric but poor social science. Second, the empirical survey of prison discipline practices that forms the heart of the study is profoundly flawed. The sample of respondents returning prison discipline questionnaires is tiny (10 percent), self-selected (drawn primarily from prisoners who were members of prisoners' rights or advocacy groups), and disproportionately made up of long-term maximum security inmates; no effort is made to establish that this group is representative of long-termers in general, let alone prisoners in general. Responses to this questionnaire paint a picture of the prison much like that provided by Jack Abbott (see Chapter Five), a deeply alienated man who has a penchant for exaggerating prison abuses and minimizing his own role in degenerating encounters with prison staff and officials. Taking the posture of the innocent and aggrieved victim, Abbott offered what is essentially a caricature of the contemporary prison. The respondents in this study appear to do the same. The result is that we are asked to

reject a "myth" of humane imprisonment and accept in its place the view that today's prisons are settings of undiluted abuse and inhumanity where the victims are the morally upright (jailhouse lawyers and "those who exhibit personal integrity") and the spiritually downtrodden (prisoners with mental handicaps), and the victimizers—the hacks—are essentially felons in uniform.

4. Christie (1981:16 & 19).

5. See Clear (1994:4–5).

6. Clear (1994:5).

7. See Johnson (1975).

8. Johnson and Toch (1988:14–15).

9. John Stuart Mill (1977:136).

10. Reiman (1985:135).

11. Reiman (1985:135).

12. Reiman (1985:135).

13. Reiman (1985:136).

14. See Spierenburg (1984).

15. Foucault (1977); Newman (1978).

16. Ward (1994:92).

17. Foucault (1977:11).

18. I say ostensibly because, in point of fact, anesthesiologists "can find no scientific support for believing the methods being used [for lethal injection] are effective for quick and painless execution" (Capron, 1984:A23). Descriptions of other methods of execution suggest that, at least on some occasions, condemned prisoners experience pain, even if for only brief periods of time (see, for example, Denno, 1994). There is, of course, no way of knowing for sure, since no one has survived an execution to tell about it, except following equipment failure, which of course changes fundamentally the experience of execution (see, for example, Miller & Bowman, 1988).

19. Accounts by prison officials assigned to carry out executions during this century attest to this observation. See, for example, former San Quentin warden Duffy's (1962) impassioned plea for the humanity of using the gas chamber

instead of hanging. More generally, see my discussion of the taming of the execution process over the course of Western history (Johnson, 1998).

20. Sykes (1966:65).

21. Sykes (1966:65).

22. Sykes (1966:65).

23. Owen (1998:77).

24. Hairgrove, in Johnson and Toch (2000:147).

25. Bondeson (1989:31 and 157).

26. Sykes (1966:67–68).

27. Sykes (1966:68).

28. Sykes (1966:68).

29. Sykes (1966:70).

30. Harris (1988:207).

31. Sykes (1966:70).

32. Owen (1988:151).

33. Bondeson (1989:105).

34. See Bartollas, Miller, and Dinitz (1976); Abbott (1991); and Hume (1996). Problems of victimization appear to be less pronounced in lower security institutions for juveniles. See Maitland and Sluder (1998).

35. Nelson (1936:141–42).

36. Nelson (1936:143).

37. In Bruchac (1984:237).

38. Nelson (1936:143).

39. "Throughout antiquity and the Middle Ages . . . it was widely accepted that women were the lustier of the sexes; Tiresias' maxim that women take nine-tenths of the pleasure in lovemaking was common wisdom." This view changed with the Enlightenment, in which the woman was cast as "the domestic angel, whose only longings were for motherhood and submissive wifedom" (Mead, 2000:147). Mead is commenting on Carol Groneman's book, *Nymphomania: A History* (2000).

40. Owen (1998:147).

41. Owen (1998:142).

42. Harris (1988:216).

43. Harris (1988:41).

44. See Fishman (1990).

45. Fleisher (1989:162).

46. See, for example, Sample (1984:190–91).

47. Fleisher (1989:163).

48. Fleisher (1989:157).

49. McCall (1995:200).

50. McCall (1995:191).

51. Conover (2000:261).

52. Sykes (1966:73).

53. Sykes (1966:76).

54. James Fox (1992) found that this was a central concern of women who mutilated themselves in prison.

55. Owen (1998: 165).

56. Nelson (1936:125).

57. Harris (1988:94).

58. Nelson (1936:125–26).

59. A reading of Harris (1988) and Rierden (1996) certainly leaves the distinct impression that the weakened power of correctional officers permitted the growth of individual and gang violence in the women's prisons they lived in (Harris) and studied (Rierden).

60. Harris (1988:152).

61. Sykes (1966:77).

62. Sykes (1966:77).

63. Sykes (1966:78).

64. Rierden (1997:39).

65. Rierden (1997:172).

66. Owen (1998:89).

67. Owen (1998:89).

68. Conrad (1988:320).

69. Sykes (1966:64). I discuss this matter in some detail in Johnson (1998, Chapter Eight).

70. This point is obvious to some, and I believe it is correct, but the issue is not as

decisively resolved as one would at first suppose. Certainly today's prisons are less objectively painful and depriving than prisons past, and this is an important index of progress. Data on subjective pain—the experience of suffering in prison—would provide another measure of progress. Are modern prisons less subjectively painful than their counterparts in early times, as measured by the suffering of the respective inhabitants? Regrettably, we have no way of knowing whether the *relative suffering* experienced by prisoners today is less than that of their counterparts in earlier times, because we have no way of quantifying perceptions of the pains of imprisonment while at the same time holding constant the level of pain seen as normal or acceptable in life at different stages of history. How painful was a medieval dungeon relative to daily life in the Middle Ages? How painful was Trenton State Prison relative to life in America in the 1950s? How painful are today's prisons relative to daily life in our now violence-infested, drug-suffused slums? The data one would need to pose the question of relative suffering today, let alone for times past, are quite complex. I am aware of no studies that have broached this area of inquiry, though some promising leads may be found in the emerging field of panetics (see Siu, 1988).

71. Oshinsky (1996:46).

72. See Goffman (1961) for the seminal discussion of the total institution. Aging in prison is explored in Rothman, Dunlop, and Entzel (200).

73. Sennett (1981:46).

74. Sennett (1981:46).

75. Sennett (1981:95). The retreat from physical pain as a major part of punishment is the result of a complex historical process. It is not the product of a failure of memory or nerve, as Newman (1983:3 & 25) has suggested in his treatise urging us to return to the primordial (not to say manly) practice of corporal punishment.

76. See Foucault (1977).

77. Goffman (1961:43–48).

78. Carroll (1988:182).

79. Carmichael and Hamilton (1967); Grier and Cobbs (1968).

80. Johnson (1998); Spierenburg (1984). Today's executions may in fact be painful, but this is unintended pain of relatively short duration. It is wise to remember that executions for most of human history were extended spectacles featuring extraordinary painful punishments of the body of the condemned.

81. Death row confinement typically takes the form of extended solitary confinement unbroken by any substantial labor or recreation. I have argued that this is indeed a contemporary instance of torture (Johnson, 1989 & 1998). Supermax prisons, many of which impose extended periods of solitary confinement, are periodically identified by groups like Amnesty International as settings of torture.

82. Johnson and Toch (1988:15).

83. These abuses are cataloged in Bowker (1980) and in Braswell, Montgomery, and Lombardo (1994).

REFERENCES

Abbott, D. E. *I Cried, You Didn't Listen: A Survivor's Expose of the California Youth Authority.* Los Angeles: Feral House, 1991.

Bartollas, C., S. J. Miller, and S. Dinitz. *Juvenile Victimization: The Institutional Paradox.* New York: Halstead Press, 1976.

Bondeson, U.V., *Prisoners in Prison Societies* (NJ: Transaction Publishers, 1989:31 & 157).

Bondeson, 1989:105.

Bowker, L. *Prison Victimization.* New York: Elsevier, 1980.

Braswell, M. C., R. H. Montgomery, and L. X. Lombardo (eds.). *Prison Violence in America.* Cincinnati, OH: Anderson, 1994.

Bruchac, J. *The Light From Another Country: Poetry From American Prisons.*

Greenfield Center, NY: Greenfield Review Press, 1984.

Capron, A. M. "Should doctors help execute prisoners?" *The Washington Post* (December 6, 1984):A23.

Carmichael, S., and C. Hamilton. *Black Power.* New York: Random House, 1967.

Carroll, L. "Race, ethnicity, and the social order of the prison." In R. Johnson and H. Toch (eds.). *The Pains of Imprisonment.* Prospect Heights, IL: Waveland Press, 1988:181–203.

Christie, N. *Limits to Pain.* Oxford: Martin Robertson, 1981.

Clear, T. R. *Harm in American Penology: Offenders, Victims, and Their Communities.* Albany: State University of New York Press, 1994.

Conover, T. *Newjack: Guarding Sing Sing.* New York: Random House, 2000.

Conrad, J. P. "What do the undeserving deserve?" In R. Johnson and H. Toch (eds.). *The Pains of Imprisonment.* Prospect Heights, IL: Waveland Press, 1988:313–30.

Denno, D. W. "Is electrocution an unconstitutional method of execution? The engineering of death over the century." *William and Mary Law Review* 35 (2) 1994: 551–692.

Dorin, D., and R. Johnson. "The premature dragon: George Jackson as a model for the new militant inmate." *Contemporary Crises* 3 (1979):295–315.

Duffy, C. T., with A. Hirshbert. *88 Men and 2 Women.* New York: Doubleday, 1962.

Fishman, L. T. *Women at the Wall: A Study of Prisoners' Wives Doing Time on the Outside.* Albany, NY: State University of New York Press, 1990.

Fleisher, M. S. *Warehousing Violence.* Newbury Park, CA: Sage, 1989.

Foucault, M. *Discipline and Punish: The Birth of the Prison.* New York: Pantheon, 1977.

Fox, J. "Women in crisis." In H. Toch. *Mosaic of Despair: Human Breakdowns in Prison.* Washington, DC: American Psychological Association Press, 1992:181–204.

Goffman, E. *Asylums.* New York: Anchor Books, 1961.

Grier, W., and P. Cobbs. *Black Rage.* New York: Basic Books, 1968.

Groneman, C. *Nymphomania: A History.* New York: Norton, 2000.

Hairgrove, D. D. "A single unheard voice." In R. Johnson and H. Toch (eds.). *Crime and Punishment: Inside Views.* Los Angeles: Roxbury Publishing Company, 2000:147–49.

Hamm, M. S., T. Coupez, F. E. Hoze, and C. Weinstein. "The myth of humane imprisonment: A critical analysis of severe discipline in U.S. maximum security prisons, 1945–1990." In M. C. Braswell, R. H. Montgomery, and L. X. Lombardo (eds.). *Prison Violence in America.* Cincinnati, OH: Anderson, 1994:167–200.

Harris, J. *They Always Call Us Ladies: Stories From Prison.* New York: Kensington Publishing, 1988.

Hume, E. *No Matter How Loud I Shout: A Year in the Life of Juvenile Court.* New York: Touchstone, 1996.

Jacobs, J. B. *Stateville: The Penitentiary in Mass Society.* Chicago: University of Chicago Press, 1977.

Johnson, Hon. F. M. "Memorandum of opinion." In *Pugh v. Locke,* January 13, 1975.

Johnson, R. *Condemned to Die: Life Under Sentence of Death.* Prospect Heights, IL: Waveland Press, 1989.

Johnson, R. *Death Work: A Study of the Modern Execution Process.* Belmont Grove, CA: Wadsworth, 1998.

Johnson, R., and H. Toch. "Introduction." In R. Johnson and H. Toch (eds.). *The Pains of Imprisonment.* Prospect Heights, IL: Waveland, 1988:13–21.

Maitland, A. S., and R. D. Sluder. "Victimization and youthful prison inmates: An empirical analysis." *The Prison Journal* 78 (1) March 1998:55–73.

McCall, N. *Makes Me Wanna Holler: A Young Black Man in America.* New York: Vintage, 1995.

Mead, R. "Sex and sensibility: The histories of nymphomania and celibacy." *The New Yorker* (September 18, 2000):146–48.

Mill, J. S. "Civilization: Essay on politics and society." *Collected Work of John Stuart Mill,* vol. 18. Toronto: University of Toronto Press, 1977:119–47.

Miller, A. S., and J. H. Bowman. *Death by Installments: The Ordeal of Willie Francis.* New York: Greenwood Press, 1988.

Nelson, V. F. *Prison Days and Nights.* Garden City, NY: Garden City Publishing, 1936.

Newman, G. *The Punishment Response.* Philadelphia: Lippincott, 1978.

Newman, G. *Just and Painful: A Case for the Corporal Punishment of Criminals.* London: Collier Macmillan, 1983.

Oshinsky, D. M. *Worse Than Slavery: Parchman Farm and the Ordeal of Jim Crow Justice.* New York: Free Press, 1996.

Owen, B. *"In the Mix": Struggle and Survival in a Women's Prison.* Albany: State University of New York Press, 1998.

Reiman, J. H. "Civilization and the death penalty: Answering van den Haag." *Philosophy and Public Affairs* 14 (2) 1985:115–48.

Rierden, A. *The Farm: A Life Inside a Women's Prison.* Amherst, MA: University of Massachusetts Press, 1996.

Rothman, M. B. Dunlop, B. D. and Entzel, P. (Eds.) *Elders, Crime, and the Criminal Justice System: Myths, Perceptions and Reality in the 21st Century.* New York: Springer Publishing Company, 2000.

Sample, A. R. Racehoss: Big Emma's Boy. New York: Ballentine Books, 1984.

Sennett, R. *Authority.* New York: Vintage Books, 1981.

Siu, R. G. H. "Panetics: The study of the infliction of suffering." *Journal of Humanistic Psychology* 28 (3) 1988:6–22.

Spierenburg, P. *The Spectacle of Suffering: Executions and the Evolution of Repression: From a Preindustrial Metropolis to the European Experience.* Cambridge: Cambridge University Press, 1984.

Sykes, G. M. *The Society of Captives: A Study of a Maximum Security Prison.* New York: Atheneum, 1966.

Ward, D. A. "Alcatraz and Marion: Confinement in super maximum security." In J. R. Roberts (ed.). *Escaping Prison Myths: Selected Topics in the History of Federal Corrections.* Washington, DC: The American University Press, 1994:81–93.

4

❖

Mature Coping

The Challenge of Adjustment in Contemporary Prisons

Prisons today are meant to be less painful than their predecessors. We do not intentionally impose physical, mental, or emotional suffering on inmates. The pains experienced in contemporary prisons, for all intents and purposes, originate in psychological stresses. And though these stresses can be quite substantial, today's prisons offer more opportunities for constructive adaptation than did earlier prisons. Still, although contemporary prisons may be comparatively civilized and potentially civilizing, adjustment to prison is always a challenge. We must understand this challenge in the larger context of the offender's adjustment to life, and work to facilitate mature adjustment both in and out of prison.

The pains of life in contemporary prisons are real. There is no point in denying them. Nor does it make sense to see pain merely as an obstacle to correctional work, for it is an obstacle that can never be circumvented. Pain is an enduring feature of the correctional enterprise. We must accept this hard reality and quite explicitly attempt to promote growth through adversity. This is a genuine correctional agenda. For people who cope maturely with prison, I will argue, are people who have grown as human beings and been rehabilitated in the process.

"Imprisonment," as I have observed elsewhere, "is a disheartening and threatening experience" for most men and women.[1] Typically, prisoners find their careers disrupted, their relationships suspended, their hopes and dreams gone sour. Few inmates have "experienced comparable stress in the free world, or have developed coping strategies or perspectives that shield them from prison problems. Although prisoners differ from each other, and may feel the pressures of confinement somewhat differently, they concur on the extraordinarily stressful nature of life in maximum security penal institutions."[2] Moreover, for many inmates—male, as well as female—the stresses of imprisonment are aggravated because they cope with prison in immature and ultimately destructive ways. All too often, this is compounded by the immature actions of the staff. Tough, rebellious inmates and callous, insensitive guards may well be the public models of deportment commonly seen on prison yards (as we shall see in Chapters Five and Seven, respectively), but they are not models for mature problem solving. The hard stoicism of the prisoner who can "take it" without flinching and "dish it out" without remorse is particularly destructive in today's overcrowded prisons, where close and often abrasive contact calls for tact, diplomacy, and the ability to transcend stereotypical roles and relationships. Chronic tension and violence are testimonials to failures of adjustment under these conditions.[3]

Of course, living in prison has never been easy, and it never will be. This holds true whether prisons are crowded or sparsely populated and whether prisoners are veterans or novices. And simply to survive is not enough. Prisoners must cope maturely with the demands of prison life; if they do not, the prison experience will simply add to their catalog of failure and defeat. Mature coping, in fact, does more than prevent one's prison life from becoming yet another series of personal setbacks. Mature coping is at the core of what we mean by correction or rehabilitation and, thus, creates the possibility of a more constructive life after release from prison.[4]

Let me now examine the three major attributes of mature coping, show that much of what passes for adjustment among persistent felons falls short of this goal, and explain why men and women who respond maturely to prison stress are likely to become reformed citizens. In doing so, I will introduce a number of themes that will be developed in subsequent chapters.

MATURE COPING

In Chapter One, we defined human nature as featuring self-determination or autonomy, which develops most fully in secure social environments that permit and indeed encourage human relationships. Mature coping means, in essence, dealing with life's problems like a responsive and responsible human being, one who seeks autonomy without violating the rights of others, security without resort to deception or violence, and relatedness to others as the finest and fullest expression of human identity. It is of course true that most inmates have not been fully or even largely habilitated—equipped or trained—to behave in these ways; thus, to speak of their need for *re*habilitation is, in a sense, to put the cart before the horse.[5] But like all people, prisoners have some natural inclinations toward autonomy, security, and relatedness to others, and the experience of prison can build on those inclinations.

The result, in my view, can be said to comprise their personal rehabilitation or correction.

Dealing with Problems and Achieving Autonomy

Mature coping means, first, dealing with problems: meeting problems head-on, using all resources legitimately at one's disposal. This aspect of mature coping involves "assertiveness," a sense of "personal efficacy," and an "internal locus of control" with respect to one's immediate environment.[6] It is certainly true that "persons who expect to exert control"—who are confident enough to behave assertively and believe that self-directed efforts will pay off—"can find ways to do so even when opportunities for control are severely limited."[7] They follow the sage advice of Pulitzer Prize winning African American poet Gwendolyn Brooks: "When handed a lemon, make lemonade."[8] Even better, some people blame fate for the lemons they receive and take full credit for the lemonade![9] Such persons are more autonomous and optimistic than their passive, pessimistic counterparts.

Autonomy is, in general, a profoundly rewarding experience. "Both people and animals are happier, healthier, more active, solve problems better, and feel less stress when they are given choice and control."[10] There is some specific evidence that prisoners with a sense of control over their lives adjust better to prison and to life on the outside. Such persons are more goal-directed in their adjustment, more involved in prison programs, experience less conflict with authorities and other inmates, and violate fewer prison rules; they experience less emotional distress and fewer symptoms of physical illness in their daily prison lives.[11] There is preliminary evidence suggesting that these prisoners may recidivate—return to crime on release—at lower levels than other inmates.[12] This finding is important, because the issue is not exclusively what works in the matter of adjustment but what facilitates adjustment within the constraints of legitimate society. Some predators, we know, "assert" themselves in service of internally orchestrated adjustment goals and skillfully elude the authorities, but they do not cope maturely.

In effect, mature coping is doing the best you can with what is rightfully yours. But persistent and serious criminals, who regularly become prison inmates, don't settle for what is rightfully theirs. They have been described, aptly, as "hasty hedonists" and "jungle cats" who live by a preemptive version of the Golden Rule: "do unto others as they would do unto you . . . only do it first."[13] The flamboyant posturing often characteristic of this lifestyle is captured in the following statement by a man who is currently serving time for a murder he committed while making a drug deal to support himself "in the life":

■ Straight people don't understand. I mean, they think dudes is after the things straight people got. It ain't that at all. People in the life ain't looking for no home and grass in the yard. . . . We the show people. The glamour people. Come on the set with the finest car, the finest women, the finest vines. Hear people talking about you. Hear the bar get quiet when you walk in the door. Throw down a yard and tell everybody drink up. See. It's rep. It's glamour. That's what it's about. What else a dude gon do in this . . . world. You make something out of nothing.[14] ■

People like this can be masters at making something out of nothing. They are possessed of "delinquent egos"[15] that help them to "make hay in the few moments the sun is shining" on their slum street corners and associated hot spots,[16] and they are ready to do so at the expense of others. Persistent offenders (especially persistent violent offenders) often have an inflated—though precarious—sense of their personal worth, which makes ordinary people mere fodder for their criminal exploits.[17] Note that Robbie Widerman unapologetically refers to himself and his peers as "the show people. The glamour people." As the elite of sorts, men (and women) like Robbie see themselves as superior to regular folk and, ultimately, above the law. Ordinary life is simply too dull for them. The high point of their lives is apt to be found in acts of impulsivity, where the thrill of living on the raw edge of emotion gives meaning, however passing, to an existence devoid of lasting achievement. At times, crime has not only adventurous but almost sensuous connotations.[18] In the words of one such man,

■ If I could keep only one memory or moment in my life and that was it—all the rest would be erased—I think the one moment that I would keep is the shootout with the police in Glendale. The experience of shooting it out with that cop was absolutely, totally, the most beautiful experience in my life. I'm not crazy. *It was beautiful!* . . . The truth is, I've always liked living on the edge of madness, being the one out there—the one that they are trying to catch—the lone warrior who does his own thing, who answers only to himself.[19] ■

This impulsive and often predatory hedonism is adaptive in the short run.[20] Jungle cats may survive and even prosper in prisons and ghettos, settings where persons with "middle class egos"—that "sell immediacy short" and are "other directed"—would be "pounced upon and consumed."[21]

But many, perhaps even most, chronic felons are by no means masters of the criminal arts or even adept hedonists. Crime for them is not a lifestyle to which they aspired as a result of planning and choice. It is a way of life they selected by default. Many are bumbling, ineffectual people of limited intelligence.[22] Some—no one knows how many—appear to be saddled with a host of biomedical deficits that, often in conjunction with low IQ, limit their ability to cope with life in conventional ways.[23] These offenders are inept at virtually everything they do, including crime. Zamble, Porporino, and Kalotay underscore this point:

[M]ost of our subjects had a great deal of trouble coping with life outside of prison. . . . In general, they had an inadequate repertoire of possible coping responses, especially those involving higher-level strategies. . . . [O]ne might have predicted that some sort of major maladaptive consequences were almost inevitable for many of them: if they had not been imprisoned, some other calamitous events would have occurred.[24]

Most offenders, whether due to personal or social deficits, or both, are not "able to analyze situations rationally or to make choices that facilitate their desires."[25] For most offenders, then, "coping difficulties are a central cause of the maintenance and repetition of criminal acts, if not their origin."[26] The problems they confront in life are fairly typical, centering on interpersonal and financial difficulties, but their coping efforts are unsystematic, unsustained, and, at best, ineffectual. Too often, their coping efforts *aggravate* the very problems they are intended to solve, making matters worse rather than better:

> Rarely did [their coping efforts] include any consistent attempts at developing some deliberate, persistent, or systematic approach to a situation, a conscious strategy of self-control or other cognitive technique, or any sort of planning and organization. . . . Roughly 70% did things that would be likely to exacerbate at least one of the three situations that inmates identified as their most serious problems, even when the risks were rated conservatively. We repeatedly heard how subjects had reacted to pressure from an employer by sabotaging the job, how they responded to difficulties with their wives by philandering, or how they dealt with the anxiety of money problems by spending all available funds on drugs.[27]

These offenders are better characterized as troubled and troublesome people rather than devil-may-care rogues. They lead lives of pain and inflict pain on others in response to their own inadequacy. For male convicts, relations with women can be destructive and controlling in the extreme. As one convict observed, absolutely without remorse or shame, women are ready candidates for abuse. "I cracked her a good one," he related in an interview with Earley,

■ because she had it coming. Now, I don't believe in beating up women, but if my old lady is talking to some man, she's gonna get knocked to the floor every time because I know old ladies are good for three things: giving pussy, cooking, and taking care of kids, and if I see her talking to another man, I know she ain't cooking, I know she ain't taking care of his kids, so she and him must be talking about pussy.[28] ■

There is joy in crime for men such as this, including the crime of wife-beating, but that joy tends to be short-lived. Their lives are deeply unsatisfying.

Some women are abusive and controlling in their relations with men or other women and seem to take pleasure in dominating and demeaning their mates.[29] More often, women are the victims rather than the victimizers in these unhealthy relationships, which they find traumatic. In Owen's words, "Physical and sexual abuse is a defining feature in the lives of many women in prison."[30] It is common for women in prison to talk about relations with controlling and abusive men as the key factor in their insecurity, promiscuity, and drug use.[31]

For men and women who have self-esteem problems, limited cognitive and interpersonal skills, and few conventional opportunities for success, crime can be quite attractive. As Halleck has observed, "If favorable opportunities for altering the internal or external environment are not available, criminal action looms as a seductive antidote to an unbearable feeling of helplessness."[32] Robbie Wideman expressed this helplessness quite eloquently, if a bit melodramatically, when he observed, "We see what's going down. We supposed to die. Take our little welfare checks and be quiet and die."[33] In contrast to the menial occupation and anonymous existence of the unskilled laborer, a life that looks like death to the average felon, crime offers a "moment of autonomy," high excitement, and a chance for camaraderie with peers.[34] (The increasing use of guns these days no doubt adds a special intensity to the moments of autonomy offered by crime, providing an "adrenaline rush" to armed felons who believe they are invincible.)[35] There is also an element of hope for the future, born of the sense that one is attacking one's problems directly by taking what one cannot properly lay claim to.[36] Fittingly, criminals see themselves as rebels serving the cause of their own self-aggrandizement.

Some criminals commit crimes sporadically and without any discernible pattern. Others adopt crime as way of life. For this latter group, known as chronic or lifestyle criminals, "Crime can be understood as a lifestyle characterized by a global sense of irresponsibility, self-indulgent interests, an intrusive approach to interpersonal relationships, and chronic violation of societal rules, laws, and mores."[37] Lifestyle criminals exempt themselves from the constraints of law-abiding lives; neither laws nor conventional jobs are suitable for them. Only crime, "with its accompanying irresponsibility and self-indulgence," meets their needs.[38] Prison doesn't deter them because they know they can survive prison.[39] Conventional adjustments, on the other hand, have little going for them. They offer both the meager rewards of a middle-class life, which is seen as "exceedingly boring and something to avoid at all cost."[40] They are also discouraged by the threat of failure at conventional living; for them, fear of failure can be great, as they have been repeatedly bruised by failures in living throughout their lives. A conventional life is thus seen as a high-cost, low-reward proposition. Naturally, these chronic offenders do what comes easily, what they enjoy, and what they do best: crime.

The difficulty is that crime offers only illusory benefits. Appearances to the contrary, crime is bad business practice and a miserable way to make a living. The plain fact is that "street crime . . . doesn't pay. It's quite irrational by sound business standards. . . . [T]he criminal stands a 78% chance of winding up in jail before attaining even [the] minimal goal" of a poverty-level income.[41] It is, of course, hard to come by reliable estimates of earnings from crime, at least in part because criminals routinely overestimate their take from crime. Even so, there is absolutely no evidence for the common belief that many street criminals get rich as a result of their criminal exploits. As a general rule, earnings from crime are at best modest and "below the earnings these criminals could make at work."[42] The proficient predators—the cream of the criminal crop, notably more sophisticated drug dealers, organized car thieves and some high-priced prostitutes—may do somewhat better in material terms, but even they pay a high price for what amounts to short-term pleasures and conquests.

The rewards of crime, meager and evanescent as they are, do little to mollify the anger that propels criminals to destructive (and self-destructive) behavior. Like their less adroit colleagues, even the best street criminals are possessed of a deeply rooted hostility that seems almost to feed upon itself, touching everyone and everything in its path. As Nettler has said, "If our nurturing is defective—unappreciative, inconsistent, lax, harsh, and careless—we grow up hostile, and the hostility seems as much turned inward as turned outward. The nurturing environments that produce this denigration of self and others are the same ones that breed criminality."[43] Many male offenders and most female offenders report histories of abuse, including sexual abuse, in their formative years.[44] Lives formed in cold and rejecting criminogenic environments are predictably turbulent and unrewarding. Virtually all chronic felons experience degenerating relations with friends and family (who may too often double as victims), failed work careers and downward social mobility (which add to pressures to prey on others), and a haunting sense that theirs is a pointless, dead-end existence.[45]

Chronic felons often complicate already badly managed lives by denying rather than facing and resolving their problems. They may successfully resist efforts by loved ones to discipline and control them, displaying "a maddening disregard for the inevitable consequences" of their destructive actions.[46] They are deeply immersed in the street life, a life in which one lives from moment to moment, anesthetized by drugs and insulated from concerns about the future. "[T]he average pattern" among felons while in the free world, for example, has been described as

> one of casual unplanned days, with greater dependence on friends than family or work, and little focus or goals. . . . [T]his way of spending time was also accompanied by a constant high level of alcohol and drug use. Many subjects must have gone through their days in a haze, and it is not surprising that there was little planning and few efforts at changing anything.[47]

The various elements of this lifestyle "all act to channel the effects of inadequate coping ability into violent and antisocial actions."[48] They make it easy to deny one's own problems as well as the damage done to others by one's self-serving forays.

Denial is a coping strategy that, when used to excess, always backfires. Problems denied simply do not disappear. Chronic offenders know this—or should know this—but they ignore its implications for their lives and go about business as usual. They act as if they are invulnerable. "In much the same way as a young child contemplates his invulnerability while donning a Superman costume, the lifestyle criminal is unrealistic in how he appraises himself, his attributes, and his chances of avoiding the consequences of his antisocial actions."[49] The very nature of antisocial actions may be distorted in the minds of felons. Criminals regularly minimize the seriousness of their crimes and the degree to which they are culpable for their crimes.[50] They may, for example, convince themselves that their crimes, even crimes of violence, are mere games:

■ Ain't nobody gon get killed. You just into cowboy and Indin shit like in the movies. You the gangsters but you the good guys too. No problem. . . . That's the way we was. Stone gangsters. Robbing people. Waving guns in people's face. Serious shit. But it was like playing too. A game. A big game and we was just big kids having fun. Guns wasn't real. Bullets wasn't real. Wasn't planning on hurting nobody. Pow. Pow. You know. Fall over. I got you. No, you didn't. You missed. Pow. Pow. I got you. You lying. I got you first. Cowboy and Indin shit like the old days. . . .[51] ■

Chronic offenders tend to let situations deteriorate until they become unmanageable, often ignoring repeated warnings that their criminal exploits are leading to disaster or that relationships or jobs are in trouble. When failure inevitably materializes—when, for example, criminal games result in apprehension and confinement—they react with bitter fatalism, as if the cards were always stacked against them.[52] Alternatively, impulses reign; the chronic offenders strike out blindly at the immediate cause of frustration (such as the boss who fires them or the police officer who arrests them) and do not analyze the deeper sources of their problems.[53] Tragically, crime victims often bear the brunt of their impotent anger.

Chronic felons combine poor self-control with limited insight into the dynamics of their adjustment. They are, in Walters' observations, "lazy" in thought and behavior and, moreover, "overly accepting" of their own half-baked ideas about life and adjustment.[54] Remember that Jean Harris saw her fellow female inmates as "children with adult desires and criminal experiences."[55] This view has been expressed by noted reformers, including Katherine Davis, an early warden of Bedford Hills, who observed: "They are not like bad girls. They are bad girls. They are strong individualists. So are children. Social consciousness is asleep in the criminal as it is in the child. In both it must be awakened, and after it is awakened, trained."[56] Unsurprisingly, these children in adult bodies act as pawns of what they take to be an arbitrary fate, juxtaposing passivity and impulsivity where informed and modulated action are called for. This immature behavior is promoted, even extolled, in prison culture where the whim of the moment often rules. Ironically, what is touted on the prison yard as strength or toughness amounts to nothing more than a posture of psychological denial that is leavened, to personal taste, with short-run hedonism and resentment of authority. Behind bars, such a stance may have a romantic side. As is shown in Chapter Five, it pits innocent and aggrieved cons against gratuitously emasculating hacks. But adopting an identity of this sort virtually ensures failure at conventional living in the free world.

Security Without Deception or Violence

The second characteristic of mature coping is addressing problems without resort to deception or violence, except when necessary for self-defense. Deception and violence are primitive behaviors. Except when engaged in to prevent immediate physical harm—itself a primitive self-defense situation[57]—deception and violence represent gross and reprehensible violations of the integrity of other human beings. Regrettably, deception and violence flourish in dangerous and unstable environments, where there is a chronic absence of trust in oneself and others, and preemptive strikes—hurting someone first and asking questions later—masquerade under the mantle of practical wisdom. Thus, in prisons and on slum streets, deception and violence are a regular feature of daily life and adjustment and, indeed, are seen as normal, even desirable behaviors.

Deception in one's dealings with others is, of course, a possibility in any social circumstance. It is apparently the case that the prospect of deception, which greatly complicates human social interaction, has been an important force in the evolution of the human psyche. The psyche must be attuned not only to peoples' words and deeds but also to the thoughts behind those words and deeds: to the thoughts people have about how others think as interactions unfold.[58] To be sure, deception is a possibility in any interaction; and, in some cases, unlike violence, deception can be harmless—as when one passes along false compliments meant to put someone at ease. But, as a general rule, deception of others is a destructive force because it impedes cooperation and undermines solidarity. It is therefore of crucial significance that deception is a *central* feature of prison culture.[59] Indeed, Empey reminds us, "deception is the name of the game" in prison; "[a]mong officials as well as among inmates, it will be the most skillful manipulator who most often gets what he wants"[60]—or what she wants. In women's prisons, manipulation is a preeminent consideration as well, particularly in the dealings of women inmates with male staff. "The danger here," noted Owen, "is getting manipulated. The men who try to game you will give up. Women will continue over a much longer time; they are more patient, will work on you a little bit at a time."[61]

To be sure, manipulation is also "the name of the game" on slum streets and in other areas marked by poverty and crime. In these settings, as in prisons, cooperation is comparatively rare, and, hence, honesty has limited adaptive value in public social encounters.[62] (Here, as in prisons, people are expected, at the very least, to be cagey. Telling the truth as a matter of course implies gross naïveté and may be the equivalent of revealing one's hand in a game of poker before the game is over.) Violence, moreover, is met with explicit approbation in these same milieus and is considered a hallmark, if not *the* hallmark, of toughness and respect.[63] "All my life," said one female inmate, "I wanted to look hard, to look mean," echoing sentiments common in men's prisons as well.[64] Tough cons, male or female, revel in their power and are admired—or at least feared—in the prison world.

The operating premise on slum streets as well as prison yards would appear to be that lying to and physically harming others are but behavioral cousins on a continuum of adaptive abuse. Whether on slum streets or in prison, the world is populated by victimizers who exploit others and a host of prospective victims variously known as "punks, chumps, pigeons, or fags."[65] Even one's friends are presumed to be less than fully trustworthy and thus are potential candidates for exploitation.[66] Since others are devalued, they become fair game. The authorities (police or guards) are seen as impotent and irrelevant; people are on their own, forced to make their own way.[67] In what amounts to a social jungle, it is the weak versus the strong, with no holds barred.[68] Bonds of trust built on words have little value. Small wonder so many people arm themselves in these environments. For them, a knife (in prison) or a gun (on the streets) is "like an American Express card . . . you don't leave home without it."[69]

The primitive quality of prison life comes across clearly in the comments of a prisoner in Leavenworth, a prison noted for a hard-core convict culture of violence. "I don't respect the law," this convict explained to Earley,

> because laws are for people who are weak and need them. If someone comes into my house and takes something, I'm not going to call a cop, I'm going to deal with it, and if I'm not man enough to get it back, then that guy has a right to take whatever he wants because I don't really deserve to own it. That's how society should be. If justice needs to be applied, I will apply it, and the reason that I have a right to apply it is because I have the power to do it. Having the power gives me permission.[70]

Indeed, not to take advantage of others is to show a kind of moral weakness, to advertise a potentially fateful failure of nerve in a social jungle. Correspondingly, not to be ready for violence at any time is a fateful—and often deadly—departure from prison norms:

> The first day I was in prison, two dudes busted in on this guy in the cell next to mine and stuck him twenty-six times with shanks. He was sitting on the crapper when they killed him, and he couldn't fight back because his pants were wrapped around his legs. Stupid bastard. Anyone who don't know better than to take a leg out of his pants in prison before he sits down on a toilet deserves to die. Something you learn in here.[71]

Recall the female convict who spoke with evident contempt for the "punk motherfuckers" she sarcastically thanked for giving in to her abuse (see Chapter Three). In her view, the victim deserved her fate because she was unable to protect herself. As this female convict put it, "This is prison. What you want is not what you get. If you don't like the combination, then you should not come to prison."[72]

This cynical and ultimately adolescent view of life—where there are no shades of grey, no tempered emotions, no feelings of concern or sadness for the "stupid bastard" butchered in the cell next door or the "punk motherfucker" ripped off with impunity—is common on slum streets. It is at the very heart of prison culture, however, in which anger and fear are the dominant emotions.[73] In one prisoner's words,

■ when you're in the joint you deal with people different than you do on the street. I mean your language and your actions. You just take a more aggressive posture. It's all body language. You learn to deal with people in jail. You learn to spot weakness there and you learn to hide it. . . . [Y]ou can do anything you want to a guy who's not ready to stand up by himself and fight for it. . . .

In jail you blow up more. You're not scared to blow up. If you bump into someone in jail, you can turn around and say, "Watch out, goof, or I'll tear your face off." But if you say that to someone on the street, you've got a good chance of the guy callin' the cops.[74] ■

Perceptions of this sort are perhaps the major reason why the prison is, to quote Gresham Sykes, "a gigantic playground—a place where blustering and brawling push life in the direction of a state of anomy."[75] In prison, anomy translates into a lack of norms dictating that one must help others in need. Here, perhaps for the first time in one's life, the person is very much on his own. Explains prison psychologist Glenn Walters,

■ Most of us are never pushed into a corner during our lives. . . . When you are small and need help, you run to your parents. When you get older, you run to a priest, a minister, a psychologist. If you have a legal problem, you hire an attorney. If someone threatens you, you call a cop. In prison there is no one to turn to, no one to solve your problems for you. If you go to the guards, you will be known as a snitch and that can get you killed. So you are on your own, perhaps for the first time in your life, and you are forced to deal with your own problems. Believe me, the guy demanding that you drop your drawers isn't going to be a good sport and simply let you walk away. You must either be willing to fight or you must give in.[76] ■

Regrettably, even those who fight may not be left alone. Though the evidence is anecdotal, it would appear that, at least in some prisons, rapes are becoming more brutal. In extreme cases, those who resist may be beaten to death by gangs of would-be rapists.[77]

The result of living on these terms is tragically predictable: "Prison's survivors become tougher, more pugnacious, and less able to feel for themselves or others, while its nonsurvivors become weaker, more susceptible, and less able to control their lives."[78] The loss of empathy is noted by Dannie Martin as he reflects on a violent incident he observed in prison that produced no feelings at all in him or his companions:

■ A man was stabbed in the chest in a noisy mess hall as we ate lunch one day in Lompoc penitentiary in California. He ran by the table where I was eating with three other men. Dark arterial blood was pumping out of his chest and splashing onto the floor within three feet of our table.

We watched him leave the dining room and then finished our lunch. After the meal, I remarked to one of the cons I'd been eating with that it seemed to me we should at least have lost our appetite.

"I don't see why we should've," he replied. "It was his problem, not ours."

I had been in prison for seven years at that time, and I began to realize that something drastic had happened to me. I had divorced my feelings from the things I could see about me, and my senses had withdrawn to a world that had nothing much to do with my environment.

As I pass the nine-year mark this month, I wonder how wide the chasm between my vision and my senses will be in two years, when I am due to be paroled.

It isn't a reassuring line of thought. But I also understand that while living in a crowded cage awash a sea of noise, I must acquire a caged mentality or I won't survive.[79] ■

Martin worries about who he is becoming in prison, and for good reason. Other offenders worry, too. As time passes in prison, prisoners discover that fellow human beings are apt to be seen in increaingly dehumanized terms. One result is that others may be seen as mere fodder for unbridled fantasies of aggression. In the words of another prisoner,

■ Being in here gets to you, day after day after day. Sometimes, I think about what it would be like to just go into a bank and blow the head off the first teller I see. I know that I am capable of that; I mean, any criminal is capable of that . . . you are around the dregs so much and for so long that you forget the worth of a human life.[80] ■

For this man, civilians are mere "cartoon characters" who people his violent fantasies.[80] The "caged mentality" these and other prisoners share graphically reinforces the general observation that neither the winners nor the losers leave the prison's playground better prepared for adult civilian life.

Caring for Self and Others: Self-Actualization
Through Human Relationships

The third characteristic of mature coping is making an effort to empathize with and assist others in need, to act as though we are indeed members of a human community who can work together to create a more secure and gratifying existence. The point is that one can achieve autonomy and security—that is, control of one's life—through relatedness to others. "Deep individual connections to others and the experience of benevolent persons and institutions result in feelings of safety and trust."[82] With trust in ourselves and in the world, "both individuals and groups can acquire confidence in their ability to gain security and fulfill essential motives through connection and cooperation."[83]

One such essential motive is control. Trust, in other words, can replace power as a mode of problem solving. Generally, power strategies operate destructively; power expresses itself in manipulation, deception, and violence, which in turn spawn division and dissension. Trust allows people to feel secure enough to relate to others openly and honestly and to cooperate with them in the resolution of difficulties. Ultimately, such cooperative relations hold out the prospect of self-actualization. As Staub makes clear, self-actualization can occur "in relationship to other people, as part of a community."[84] Self-actualization, then, need not be a solitary feat. Indeed, Staub maintains, "The full evolution of the self, the full use of the human potential, *requires* relationships and the development of deep connections and community."[85] Prison poet Henry Johnson makes a similar point: "To live unloved, makes us cold; cruel; remote."[86] We need to think of ourselves—of our *selves,* if you will—as persons-in-a-social-context, never fully alone, never fully submerged in the group, loved, ideally, but not suffocated by others. In the balancing of self and relations to others is to be found the most harmonious route to personal development.

Relatedness is not some idealistic panacea. At issue here is neither romantic love nor pure altruism. The notion of a selfless community of human beings is hopelessly romantic, particularly for people who have led hard lives. Nor is calculated relationship, in which one aims to establish a debt, sufficient to engender community. Rather, what is needed is "altruistic egotism," in which the objective is to help others, with the selfish *and* selfless motive of "*deserving* their help in return."[87] In prison and in hardscrabble environments like urban ghettos, those who deserve and receive support feel well loved.

Life would be implacably combative and unstable without altruistic egotism. Pure egotists, the selfish, hasty hedonists who seek their own gratification at the expense of others, are planting the seeds of their own destruction. They are breeding anger and ill-will in others, who will merely bide their time until they have the opportunity to pay them back. This is why such persons can never really trust others. They live in a world of enemies, people who have it in for them. Since they must always be on the defensive, they turn the Golden Rule on its head and hurt others as a matter of course.

> The person who follows the dictates of altruistic egotism, in contrast, admits to being self-centered and acts primarily for his own good; he greedily collects a fortune to assure his personal freedom and capacity for survival under the most satisfying conditions, but he does so through *amassing an army of friends.* No one will make personal enemies if his egotism . . . manifests itself only by inciting love, goodwill, gratitude, respect, and all other positive feelings that render him useful and often indispensable to his neighbors.[88]

One of the more touching manifestations of altruistic egotism is revealed in the "gift relationship," particularly when such vital gifts as food and clothing are given to those who are destitute and vulnerable.[89] The gift relationship was a fundamental social institution among concentration camp inmates. Here, as in the general case, the goal "is not to bribe or acquire, but to establish relations."[89] The result is that "self-interest turns to goodwill, and the gift relation becomes one of the constitutive structures of social being."[90]

Altruistic egotists are generous, but they are not saints. They take other people seriously and hold them accountable for their conduct. If gifts are repeatedly spurned, for example, altruistic egotists are not constrained to continue acting charitably toward an ungrateful neighbor. Nor are they impelled to love a neighbor who regularly abuses them. In practice, they follow a strategy of living that closely resembles the computer game strategy of "tit for tat." Tit for tat is the "strategy of starting with cooperation, and thereafter doing what the other player [person] did on the previous move [encounter]."[92] This strategy, particularly when the notion of "starting with cooperation" is generously construed, is ideally suited for cultivating cooperation. The other person is given at least one chance to behave cooperatively; if he persists in behaving abusively, he is treated abusively in turn. (In this context, deception and violence are species of justified self-defense. Even nice guys have to be tough when the situations call for it.[93]) If the other person reconsiders and then offers to cooperate, prior offenses are forgiven and the errant person is met with cooperation. Commonly, mutual cooperation emerges as the most sensible strategy of living. It becomes apparent that one's egotistical needs are best satisfied by altruistic endeavors.

Tit for tat's success in generating cooperation, notes Axelrod, "is due to being nice, provokable, forgiving, and clear." Elaborating, Axelrod observes that tit for tat's

> niceness means that it is never the first to [act uncooperatively], and this property prevents it from getting into unnecessary trouble. Its retaliation discourages the other side from persisting whenever [uncooperative action] is tried. Its forgiveness helps restore mutual cooperation. And its clarity makes its behavioral pattern easy to recognize; and once recognized, it is easy to perceive that the best way of dealing with tit for tat is to cooperate with it.[94]

Tit for tat is not so much a strategy for winning as it is a strategy for better living. The person need not retaliate exactly in kind against an uncooperative opponent, for example, for doing so, although justifiable on ethical grounds, might escalate tensions. Retaliation need only approximate the original injury. The objective of retaliation in a tit-for-tat scenario is twofold: to communicate that one is not a pushover and to open the door for interactions that further downplay hostility. The person following a tit-for-tat strategy is advised to be quick to anger when abused—so that he or she will be taken seriously—yet quick to forgive, so that cooperative relations may be established.[95] The tit-for-tat strategy is the peacemaker's strategy; reconciliation is a valued goal. It is crucial to appreciate that "tit for tat succeeds without doing better than anyone with whom it interacts. It succeeds by eliciting cooperation from others, not by defeating them."[96]

The tit-for-tat strategy can prove successful even in an environment filled with predators. The key is for the altruistic types to "selectively interact with each other," in effect forming niches within otherwise hostile milieus that both shelter them from harm and offer safe havens to predators who want to "defect" from violent relations and embrace cooperation.[97] In computer simulations, at least, the eventual result is that cooperation often spreads gradually throughout an environment, setting up new norms of conduct for entire populations. There is some evidence that organizational reforms—like the introduction of functional units, discussed at length in Chapters Nine and Ten—can create formal niches in which climates of cooperation and nonviolence permeate prisons, or at least portions of prisons.[98]

Prisoners generally are admonished to live by a predatory code of ethics and to avoid cooperation other than in the conduct of illicit activities. They are enjoined not to cultivate generosity, connectedness, and cooperation but to suppress these attributes by being cold, unfeeling, and hedonistically self-centered in their dealings with others, both in the free world and in the prison. They do not take people seriously but instead treat them as objects to be used to further their own ends. (More often than not, gifts are the opening gambit in a seduction or ruse; the person who offers to cooperate is taken to be an easy mark.) Their code of ethics is a product of inconsistent, harsh, and even defective nurturing. Bonds to others are, as a result, weak and unreliable.

For some inmates, social ties seem to be missing altogether from prison life. They see staff as distant and aloof. Fellow prisoners, they feel, are closed off to others. In the words of Diane Hamill Metzter, a women serving a life sentence,

No one in prison really cares. . . It's a chilling feeling to realize that no one's life here would be significantly changed if I were to die tomorrow. Loneliness breeds and thrives in the belly of the monster known as prison. It strikes constantly and insidiously and it never goes away.[99]

For some inmates, it would seem, the existential reality of prison life is that they are very much alone in a cold and rejecting world.

Yet relationships are always possible. We come into this world with an innate capacity to develop a conscience and hence to establish responsible social relationships.[100] This capacity may, for genetic reasons, be less pronounced in some of us than in others.[101] But it is present in some degree in all of us, and can be promoted or retarded by environmental forces. Warm, supportive environments promote the development of conscience. Such environments feature affection, responsiveness to feelings and concerns, the use of reasoning to resolve conflicts, inculcation of moral standards, and, above all, an explicit concern for helping others in need. Morality, in other words, is learned by precept, example, and action—by doing good.[102] Doing good, in turn, makes us feel good about ourselves and others. Forgoing the pleasures of the moment for a future good—which generally means taking into account the welfare of others—is part and parcel of what it means to have a conscience. Were it not for guilt and anxiety, the hallmarks of conscience, we would all live selfishly in the present.[103]

Harsh, repressive environments, in contrast, suppress the development of conscience and promote selfish, short-run hedonism. "Without nurturing," Nettler reminds us, the human animal grows up wild. It behaves violently. It destroys what it has not been trained to appreciate. It does not understand "right and wrong" except as greater and lesser might. As a consequence, what offends the conscience of socialized persons cannot offend the conscience of the unsocialized. There is nothing to offend.[104]

For those who grow up wild, conscience is a code word for weakness and a senseless limitation on the power they are ready to wield at a moment's notice.

Harsh environments may not merely be devoid of nurturance; there may be active attempts to inculcate guilt-free violence. As one Scottish life-sentence prisoner observed, "The only rule in our home was fear: fear of pain and violence. It was just endless. Endless and senseless."[105] In such homes, violence is the normal thing. Violence, even brutal violence, is

■   taken for granted, part and parcel of everyday life. It's normal: what would be abnormal would be if violence wasn't in your life. . . . I was brought up with it, I was brought up to it. My father carried a knife, my brothers carried knives, everyone: you wore a shirt and trousers and shoes, and a knife. You weren't properly dressed without one.[106] ■

This man, together with his brothers and father, shared the status of "hard men," which is to say, men who could mete out violence casually, as if it were natural. To be such a man made his father proud. "That was the greatest thing in the world you could be."[107] Family outings featured forays from pub to pub, looking for people to assault.

The parallel case for women is provided by the mother who allows or even encourages her young daughter to take up with the local biker gang, who in turn predictably passes her around like so much sexual property, paving the way for a life of drug abuse—to kill the pain—and prostitution—to pay for the drugs, and because prostitution is all she thinks she's good for. The young prostitute, in turn, predictably becomes a poor parent and a predator in her own right, using manipulation and sometimes violence in her dealings with others.[108] Rierden offers a case in point:

> [S]he never knew her father. Her mother was a stripper in a local
> nightclub and used to store drugs inside her house for the local
> motorcycle gangs. Tina got involved with the gangs at an early age. To be
> initiated, she had to sleep with gang members and strip at their parties.
> That led her to working the streets, because she figured she would at least
> get paid for having sex.[109]

This woman became addicted to drugs and was a negligent parent, with a daughter living in detention and a son who is "a professional car thief." "When he was younger, she recalls, he used to hold her back from johns who came to pick her up at their house. 'Then I'd break away from him and hop in the car with the trick and I'd look out the back and see my son chasing after us.' "[110]

Conscience is not the only victim of defective socialization. Without nurturing, the development of empathy is also stunted. Empathy, like conscience, appears to be promoted by "relatively benign, nonpunitive socialization experiences."[111] This is particularly true of those socialization experiences that stress role taking, so one is encouraged to see the other person's point of view; and affection, so one's own needs are satisfied and, thus, do not interfere with one's seeing and acting on the needs of others.

Single-parent homes have long been known to be a source of delinquency and other social disabilities.[112] More such homes are found in inner-city slums, especially black ghettos, than elsewhere in America, but the criminogenic dynamics operating in such homes are universal. In any case, single-parent, low-income, disorganized homes are becoming more prevalent in white communities as well.[113] Recently, attention has been focused on the prevalence of neglect and abuse among low-income families, particularly those run by single parents. In New York City, for example, Legal Aid Society figures indicate that abuse and neglect cases have increased by a factor of eight—from roughly 3,000 to 24,000—in the five-year period from 1984 to 1989.[114] The probable culprit: crack cocaine, which "produces volatility, or stupor, that causes loss of emotional contact with children."[115] The crack epidemic has passed, but there is no evidence that the damage it has caused to poor families has been undone. Though only a tiny fraction of our nation's children grow up in abusive homes, these homes are the formative environments for many chronic offenders, especially chronic violent offenders.[116]

Children raised in abusive homes are treated like commodities. They are often abandoned to the television set as youngsters, allowed to watch enormous amounts of violent programming because it holds their attention. Heavy exposure to television may not affect normal children adversely, but, among already-troubled children, a diet of television violence may increase propensities to violence, even if viewing habits change later in life. (Adult viewing habits do not appear to influence violent behavior. For better or worse, this makes the television a benign distraction in the prison.) Children of the poor are especially prone to watch excessive amounts of television, especially violence-oriented television. For poor children more than for other children, the television is in effect a substitute parent that models and reinforces violence as a normal and even preferred way of relating to others. Cross-cultural research suggests that the coming of age of the first "television generations" here and abroad may have been a factor in the phenomenal growth of violence in so many contemporary societies.[117]

These children are also treated like commodities in the sense that their parents or guardians store them like so many parcels rather than care for them like human beings who crave loving attention. "What strikes me is how many of our young black men were never held as babies," states Jasper Ormond, a drug treatment counselor for the D.C. Department of Corrections who was interviewed by Courtland Milloy, a columnist with *The Washington Post*.[118] Ormand goes on:

> So many of them never bonded to another human being. When they
> put a gun to somebody's head and pull the trigger, they don't see the

victims as people. They don't even see themselves as part of the human family.[119]

Fewer women may put guns to the heads of others, but they, too, are unloved creatures in these dysfunctional homes. These children, Ormand concludes, "are being socialized as pure individuals, with no empathy for others. What is missing is love, and what has emerged is a tremendous amount of self-hate."[120] These children see no future, no hope. They live each day in a state of psychological trauma. The pain and isolation of daily life are such that they would rather face death, which promises escape, than disrespect and the endless humiliation it entails.[120]

Lives devoid of love and contaminated by anger virtually drive people into crime. (Is anyone really surprised when a girl exposed to gang rape by her mother becomes a prostitute later in life on the premise that unwanted sex with men is inevitable so one might as well get paid?) If conscience and empathy somehow survive in the face of harsh and punitive socialization experiences, such as those decried by Ormond, they are too impoverished to exercise any moral restraints on self-serving conduct.[122] Thus, whether by outright lack of human morality or by facile rationalization, others are seen and treated as so many objects to be used for one's selfish purposes.

In the free world, poor social bonds are expressed in a routine distrust of others, especially strangers. But even the worst slum has room for civility and relationships. There is, in other words, a "social order" that has its roots in the expectation of minimal standards of conscience and community.[123] That social order is less robust these days, given the inroads made by guns and violence in low-income areas, including in inner-city schools, but it remains the case that the "decent" people still outnumber the "street" people and hold out to each other and their children the prospect of a civil life in slum communities.[124]

In prison, by contrast, men and women are explicitly and almost unanimously encouraged to be uncivil and amoral, that is, " 'to do their own time' and ignore the suffering and inhumanity that surround them."[125] (For women, the admonition "to do your own time" is expressed as "mind your own business."[125]) To be sure, there are a few permissible exceptions. One may have relationships with one's "main man" or fellow convicts or gang members; one may take care of one's prison lover or family, though these and other such arrangements seem at least in part to reflect calculated efforts to assure one's personal protection and perhaps further one's criminal objectives.[127] Certainly these relationships are typically impermanent. "Niantic love comes and goes," one inmate told Rierden, referring to the instability of "homosexual dyads" or love relationships in that women's prison. "Most women just like to play house."[128] Presumably, others "play" at being family—though the relationships are no doubt important while they last. Be this as it may, the prison's version of decorum typically calls for restraint in matters of affection and concern for others in the prison world, whatever one's true feelings might be. (This is readily apparent in most men's prisons,[129] as well as in women's prisons when one focuses on the convict world. There, toughness is prized and the "culture demands sharp survival skills and a quick eye for the ever-shifting hierarchy" of power.[130]) There are, as a result, few real friendships in prison. There are even fewer Good Samaritans (who surely would deserve "an army of friends") and fewer still who will own up to this rather egregious lapse from manliness or toughness. In the words of one prisoner, "You've got to keep in mind that [another person's problem] doesn't concern you . . . You want to help the guy, but prison is no place to be a Good Samaritan if you want to come out in one piece."[131]

The prison community is quite different from any free world community. Relations there are distinctly calculating and transient. "In prison," notes Seymour,

> there are no primary ties, few alliances that extend beyond the immediate situation, and few norms that transcend the bounds of one's immediate relationships. Adjusting means the ability to survive and cope with each other's company. Membership in groups is temporary and artificial, and where groups may be friendly, there are few friends. Mutual aid is given, but with an emphasis on reciprocity, not altruism. Cultural dissension is part of a perceived war of prisoners against each other, and sitting out the war is a major goal.[131]

To "make it" as an inmate, one must live in the present, ever suspicious and alert to the depredations and betrayals of others, drawing what little sustenance one can from the meager and often exploitive emotional ties available in the prison community.[132] Our prisons are moral cesspools, then, as much because of the callous disregard for others they promote as for the overt abuse that takes place there. Naturally, to the extent prisoners are permitted (by officials) and encouraged (by their peers) to treat others in need with indifference and even contempt, the greater will be their willingness to victimize others when it suits their interests.

PRISON ADJUSTMENT AND PERSONAL REFORM: RECONCILING PUBLIC AND PRIVATE CULTURES

Mature coping contradicts standard cultural prescriptions about appropriate prisoner deportment. The public culture of the prison has norms that dictate behavior "on the yard" and in other public areas of the prison such as mess halls, gyms, and the larger program and work sites. This culture emphasizes an almost automatic use of hostility and manipulation in one's relations with fellow inmates and especially with the staff and makes friendly and caring behavior—again, especially with respect to the staff, look servile and silly.

Thus, it is not surprising that prisoners often value roles that are, from the point of view of the larger society, distinctly antisocial. Goodstein's research, for example, reveals that most male inmates (43.5 percent of the maximum-security prisoners in her sample) would like to think of themselves as tough and rebellious in their dealings with staff, as "right guys" who take no guff from the "wrong guys," their keepers. Another 34.7 percent claim to value deception in their relations with staff, which they view as a legitimate, even mandatory, tactic in winning ealy release from confinement. A few prisoners (5.4 percent) take pride in being institutionalized; they punctuate leisure time with work at easy, high-status prison jobs, all the while studiously avoiding programs and other activities that might have rehabilitative value upon their release from prison. Only 16.3 percent expressly attempt to maintain a "generally positive attitude toward [their] environment."[134] This type of inmate "accepts the authority of the prison's official social system but maintains his commitment to life outside the institution."[135] While many inmates privately value this adjustment,[136] the only men who publicly admit to these beliefs are the much-maligned "square johns" no self-respecting convict would be caught dead with on the yard.

Square johns, whether male or female, are a minority of a typical prison, though this adaptation appears to be more common in women's prisons than in men's prisons. As Owen has noted,

> A significant minority of women at CCWF . . . maintain an identity that is not embedded in the prison culture. Members of this minority, made up of short-termers, middle-class women with little investment in a criminal identity, and those who have moved away from participation in the prison culture, may have little connection to "familying" and emotional relationships with other women.[137]

Square johns, male or female, tend to endorse or aspire to conventional values. They also tend to have stable family ties, which gives them something to fall back on during difficult periods of confinement and something to look forward to at the end of their prison terms. Their generally solid social skills and good behavior make them excellent candidates for higher-level prison jobs, particularly in women's prisons, and their commitment to getting back out to their families gives them an added reason to avoid trouble in the prison community. Put differently, they have a stake in the world of the prison officials rather than in the world of the convicts. From the perspective of the larger free community, these offenders are advantaged. Yet the very fact of confinement is a considerable stigma in the middle-class circles they hail from or wish to enter. And to make it in prison, where they tend to be pariahs, they must scrupulously avoid the convict world. They typically adjust in the manner of lifers—taking one day at a time, carefully apprising the risks and benefits of their actions, and trying above all to avoid trouble, which would jeopardize the prison life they have built for themselves.[138]

Some inmates adjust better than others, but there are few success stories in prison, few real winners. The predatory convicts who dominate the prison yard are stereotypes of adolescent immaturity. They have been described (by means of psychological tests) as "individuals who adhere to procriminal attitudes, who are self-centered, exploitive of others, easily led [by peers], and anxious to please [peers]; they recidivate at high rates,[139] particularly when the prison experience has boosted their self-esteem, (by proving how tough they are)[140] and when their exploitive behavior features violence[141]—when they have become, in other words, hardened criminals.[142] Their recidivism is sometimes obscured by the fact that they may appear to make the transition back to civilian life fairly well.[143] Like Goffman's prisoners who follow an "intransigent line," they attempt to deny the reality of prison and behave behind bars as though they are not really subject to the rules and restrictions of the prison.[144] For example, they break institutional rules with regularity[145] and are openly hostile to the authorities and the prison the authorities represent.[146] When they leave prison, they can pick up civilian life fairly readily since they live in a way that is, psychologically speaking, a continuation of their prison adjustment.

Before long, however, their proclivity to victimize others as a routine feature of daily life gets them in trouble with the law. Free citizens, known derisively as *square johns,* do not play prison games. On release, hard-core convicts find that ploys that work in the prison fail miserably in the free world. In the words of one such predatory convict interviewed by Earley:

> "I can walk into any prison in this country, any prison, and know immediately what's happening. I can deal with this crazy prison environment, with the so-called worst of the worst convicts in Marion and the so-called prison predators and all that baloney," he explained. "But in the outside world, I'm always getting tripped up. Every time I mess with a Square John, I end up getting fucked because you people have no concept of jailhouse respect and absolutely no honor. . . . You see," he continued, "in here, I know how to play all the games and play them well, but out on the streets, the deck always seems to be stacked against me."[147]

Such encounters may imperil the precarious and often inflated sense of self that many convicts develop from their criminal exploits, adding urgency to the need to dominate and control the ebb and flow of prison life. Given the significance of predatory convicts in today's prisons, their adjustments are discussed in detail in Chapter Six.

Some convicts mellow over time and become "institutionalized," or, in Goffman's terms, "colonized." They serve many prison sentences, and eventually come to make the prison their "home away from home." One finds evidence for this adjustment in all types of prisons, including early penitentiaries. "To many," states one penitentiary inmate, "there is no place so *natural* and so much like home as a prison."[148] States another penitentiary prisoner, "They find themselves naturally, at home, in a prison—and they cannot conceal their perfect acquaintance with its habits, and their familiarity with the incidents of a prison life."[149] One result is that levity rather than long-faced suffering was the order of the day among the more institutionalized convicts of the penitentiary.

> It was always to my mind a horrid place, and I naturally expected to find every visage sad, every eye sunk, every cheek pale, and every heart among convicts, uncommonly depressed. The severity of punishment—the

solitude of adversity—the bleakness of their prospects—the agony of their destitution—the horrid result of their crimes—I assuredly thought, were fully calculated to produce such appearance. But I was entirely mistaken. There was nothing to be seen, but unbounded levity. Cheerfulness and contentment played upon their cheeks; quietude of mind was visible in their actions.[150] ▮

Contemporary prison accounts surface their fair share of institutionalized convicts. Fleisher found a number of Lompoc inmates who had adopted an institutionalized adjustment. For these men, captivity is the norm, freedom the anomaly. They prefer prison to the free world because they have found, through hard experience, that freedom "means freedom to be out of work, freedom to be out of money, freedom to be without clean clothes, freedom to be without an apartment, and freedom to resume an alcohol or drug dependency, or both."[151] Prison, in contrast, means relative security. A similar picture emerges for female convicts. For many such women, as Owen observes, "prison is a better and safer place than their disrupted and disruptive lives on the streets."[152] One's needs are taken care of, and one's reputation as a tough character is assured by a history of prison survival. Institutionalized prisoners can assume menacing postures and may flaunt their indifference to the pains of imprisonment, but they are, in the final analysis, pathetic figures whose self-doubt and personal inadequacy consign them to a life of prison.[153] This pathos may be more apparent with women who "don't have nothing to go home to." As one such woman observed,

▮ I don't know my younger boy at all. I don't know what he looks like. I have never lived with my seven-year-old. I have seen him only once. *Convicts have always been my family* [emphasis added]. My heart's desire is to have someone close to me who is blood, rather than just convicts as family.[154] ▮

Like their more combative comrades, institutionalized male and female convicts win their battle with the prison but lose the larger war of survival in the free world. Since institutionalized prisoners are veterans of the prison, they "know the ropes" and can "play the angles"; after years of hard experience, they have enough sense to "keep their noses clean." They lead a manipulative and calculating existence and usually have what is, by prison standards, a materially comfortable life behind bars. They are "model prisoners," not in the sense that they exemplify the staff's version of the ideal prisoner—they do not—but because being a prisoner is what they do best. Where the predatory convicts simmer with hostility and yearn for freedom, these prisoners have become so acclimated to the prison routine that they become dependent upon it for a sense of security and self-esteem. This dependency is a double-edged sword, however, because it entails a loss of personal control that in turn promotes "higher levels of stress" than experienced by inmates who adapt to prison on their own terms.[155] The central legacy of institutional dependency is the reduced ability to cope in situations where one must rely on one's own initiative. Accordingly, institutionalized prisoners find it very difficult to make the transition to the free world, which has become alien, a place that swallows up fellow prisoners rather than offers an opportunity for a new life. "When somebody leaves here," said one female inmate, "those of us stuck here know that unless they come back, they're most likely out of our life for good. It's a great big black hole out there, and you just learn to accept that."[156] Because institutionalized offenders cannot rely on the dictates of authorities, on an explicit code of conduct, and on preordained schedules, they recidivate almost immediately.[157]

In terms of the norms and mores that make up the public culture of the prison, the undisputed losers of prison games are known as "inmates," a term that in this context is meant to set the run-of-the-mill prisoners—the "masses"—apart from the more savvy convicts.[158] Yet most inmates get by; they are neither victims (of the convicts) nor victimizers (like the convicts). Some of the more sophisticated ones become institutionalized, usually by carving out a narrow but safe round of life in conformity with the officials' view of prison decorum. (It is these prisoners, as is shown in Chapter Six, who are the prison's model inmates.) But from the larger population of inmates are drawn such low-status types as "punks," "dings," "scapegoats," and offenders who are—or who become—flagrantly mentally ill. These inmates are often devastated psychologically by the prison experience. Bowker provides a melancholy catalog of their fate in prison.[159] Quay demonstrates that the more dependent among these prisoners are unusually prone to recidivate.[160] These men and women are impaired for the purposes of adjustment in the free world and prone to escalating traumas in the prison.[161]

Kupers provides a composite picture of a mentally disordered inmate: "He or she suffered massive and repeated traumas early in life, had a great difficulty coping with the stress of harsh prison conditions, and then acted out and was sent to a punitive segregation unit where the isolation and idleness aggravated the mental disorder."[162] These offenders are difficult to understand and manage. As a result, they get into trouble repeatedly and then are placed in high-security and supermax prisons, which overcome their limited coping skills. As one such inmate at Pelican Bay, a supermax prison, told Kupers:

Sometimes I feel overwhelmed. I get trepidations, nervous, agitated, I go off the deep end. I don't really hear voices, just get to feeling like I can't breathe, the cell is getting smaller. Panic! It feels closed in, my heart pounds, these symptoms build up over days. . . It's the SHU [Special Housing Unit] that's making me this nervous. There's nothing like this at other prisons. Here I feel like I'm in a kennel, closed off from life itself. I feel like I live in a coffin, like a tomb."[163]

Such comments reveal extreme stress but were not uncommon. Indeed, these sentiments were shared by most of the mentally ill offenders interviewed by Kupers. "A majority of the inmates I have interviewed in super-maximum control units talk about their inability to concentrate, their heightened anxiety, their intermittent disorientation and confusion, their experience of unreality, and their tendency to strike out at the nearest person when they reach their 'breaking point.'"[164] These mentally ill inmates, sometimes released directly from supermax prisons into the free world, recidivate at rates considerably above more typical offenders.[165]

Poor coping is disturbingly common in prison. Yet mature behavior and, hence, the prospect of successful adjustment upon release can be found in prison on a more regular basis than might first be supposed. One reason is that "the actions available to inmates are constrained, and many of the ineffective, diversionary, or destructive actions they might take on the outside are precluded."[166] In prison, one cannot normally turn to hard drugs or heavy drinking to escape one's problems; nor can one beat one's spouse or children to let off steam. It is also much harder to deny problems:

> While an inmate can still . . . deal with [a problem] ineffectively, it is difficult to avoid dealing with it in some fashion, because the institutional world is so confined and restricted. An inmate's problems are inevitably part of his daily life, and they must be encountered regularly.[166]

Confinement also promotes an increase in introspection and critical examination of one's actions.[168] As one Canadian prisoner aptly observed, with perhaps a hint of irony, "I'm glad to be here because I had the opportunity to think a lot. You are alone and you learn about yourself. When I'm outside, I haven't the time for that. I'm too busy."[169] It can thus be the case that "the constraints of imprisonment can paradoxically make it easier for inmates to cope relatively more effectively with problems," at least with respect to the daily adjustment difficulties that surface behind bars.[170]

The adjustment of lifers (life-sentence prisoners) often reflects the legacy of improved coping created by the constraints of prison. Ethnographic accounts of prison adjustment among lifers, from the penitentiary to contemporary prisons and for men as well as women, emphasize that they tend to see prison as a home—an involuntary one, to be sure—but still a domestic world in which they have an investment; they care about such things as the level of cleanliness, the quality of the food, the variety of activities, and even relations with their keepers.[170] In contrast, these concerned citizens of the prison community see their short-sentence counterparts as rude visitors or disruptive tourists who have nothing to lose. Lifers, who feel they have everything to lose since prison is all they have, strive to make the most of the resources available in prison. As a result, they obey the rules and generally stay out of trouble, secure good jobs, participate in programs, involve themselves in organized clubs and recreation, and generally fill their days with structured activities—all so that they might live fully in the present and give as little thought as possible to the world they left behind. "I have to focus day to day," one female lifer told Owen. "If I think about the time that I have, it will drive me insane."[172]

A recent longitudinal study by Zamble reinforces these observations and traces the emergence of improved coping among a sample of twenty-five male Canadian long-termers over a seven-year study period. Zamble documents that these long-termers did not suffer "generalized emotional damage" as was speculated by some early penologists and critics of the prison.[173] Confirming early ethnographic studies, Zamble found that these long-termers tended to fill their days with "structured activities and regular routines, such as those of pre-ferred institutional employment."[174] They were correspondingly "less interested in the unstructured or aimless activities that typify institutional socialization."[175]

Those "unstructured or aimless activities" avoided by long-termers are often at the heart of the prison's public culture. It is this life in the prison yard that often pushed prisoners into destructive activities and, ultimately, con-tributed to high rates of recidivism.[176] Lifers saw clearly that trouble would reduce the quality of their prison lives:

> Unlike the very weak contingencies between behavior and consequences that the system presents to most prisoners, long-term inmates learn that misbehavior results in tangible diminution of the quality of their lives. Even if the contingencies are only inconsistently enforced, over a period of years the consequences of maladaptive behaviors are sure to be triggered.[177]

Lifers shared the perception that "short-termers were irresponsible and rowdy, and that mixing with them was likely to lead to trouble."[178] Short-termers had little to lose, and the link between their behavior and deprivations while in prison was weak. Lifers had much to lose, and over time this became quite clear to them. In general, they learned that they had to be more careful and controlled about prison living.

Zamble's long-termers, unlike short-termers, exploited constraints avail-able in the prison community so that they could lead structured, controlled, and ultimately autonomous lives. For example, they explicitly and consciously chose the cell over the yard as the main arena for their daily life in prison. They did this because they could control the routine in the cell. Life in the sheltered confines of the cell was more autonomous than life elsewhere in the prison:

> [W]hen they had the choice of whether to go out onto the range [yard] or stay in their cells, they increasingly chose the latter. . . . The most frequent reason given for this was the choice of activities that could be done better in their cell, such as studying, hobbycraft, or watching television. . . . Thus, over time subjects' lives had become more regulated by routines of their own choice and devising.[179]

Life in the cell and away from the yard offered a sensible withdrawal from the myriad emotional and interpersonal problems, and resulting problems with authorities, that present themselves in the public world of prison. The prison-ers developed a few relationships with others facing long terms, for support and protection, but they consciously held themselves back from involvement in the regular prison social life, which featured "confusion and uncertainties" and, in general, trouble.[180]

The majority of subjects largely withdrew from much of the diffuse and casual social networks that are typical of inmate interactions. Instead, they spent much of their discretionary time in their cells, and when they did socialize it was primarily with one or two close friends. Their socialization was centered more on these interactions, or on relationships with people on the outside, than on involvement with inmate social networks.[181]

Here we see, then, a healthy and constructive focus on relations with others as they are available within the constraints of the prison world.

None of Zamble's long-sentence prisoners mentioned concerns about their personal safety, even though they were directly queried on this point. It would appear that the prison under study was relatively safe and that, perhaps more importantly, they had been able to successfully remove themselves from the predatory relations that exist in all prisons to some degree. "In effect," states Zamble, "they sometimes seemed to be living within a world of their own, inside the prison but separate and apart from its ordinary discourse."[182] Their orientation was not to the present, as represented in the prison yard, but to the future, as captured in educational and other programs that would help them gain release and, in their view, successful readjustment in the outside world. Once again, we see these prisoners using prison resources, notably educational programs, to constrain and direct their behavior.

Consistently, Zamble's lifers showed improvements in coping competence as their sentences unfolded. Their behavior became more controlled and more reflective. They were more likely to seek social support and to deal with problems rather than avoid them:

> The changes in coping modes are generally in the direction toward more normal and mature ways. . . . Thus, in general, there seems to have been some improvement in subjects' coping abilities over time in prison. . . . [T]hey were working more at controlling their behavior in problem situations, seeking solace and advice from others more than before, and were less likely to avoid dealing with problems. Although the statistical evidence is weak, more of them may also have been monitoring, analyzing, and planning their responses. As a result, their efforts seemed more effective in dealing with problems, with lower risk of exacerbation.[183]

Better coping produced a host of benefits. There was, for example, an increase in prosocial attitudes[184] and a decrease in disciplinary problems over time.[185] Prisoners suffered less distress, as revealed in "a decrease over time in stress-related medical symptomology," including a decrease in anxiety and depression, as well as "some improvement in measures of general health."[186] Daily emotions tied to situational pressures within the prison remained constant since the pressures themselves were unchanged. Hence, emotional states like anger, boredom, or loneliness were unaffected by improved coping skills. Nor did the prisoners see themselves as happy or beset with fewer problems.[187]

They coped better, then, and suffered fewer impairments, but prison life remained difficult.

One reason prisoners cope better over time is that the stresses of prison life, though high at the outset, tend to level out as time passes. Prison life then becomes fairly predictable. Continuity of prison conditions is largely assured because prison offers a life marked by routines; prison thus offers many opportunities for acclimatization and adjustment. As a result, almost all prisoners, though especially long-termers, cope better over time with the problems and pressures of imprisonment. That is, they become acclimated to the prison environment.[188] These inmates learn to live with predictable constraints. Accordingly, they lead "compromise existences in which they achieve compromise goals, operating within available constraints" that are fixed by recurrent features of prison life.[189]

Some of the constraints on behavior imposed by prison can be circumvented, and this, in turn, can undermine constructive efforts at coping. The public prison culture might be seen as a means of doing just that, under the guise of ameliorating the pains of imprisonment.[190] The "right guy," for example, can readily obtain contraband, sometimes including hard drugs. Moreover, as the putative model of prison deportment, the right guy would seem by definition to be free of the need for critical introspection. Certainly the right guy lives on the yard, in the middle of the prison fray, not sequestered in his cell. He scorns programs as the refuge of the weak or effeminate. Nevertheless, most inmates are not right guys and, judging by what they do as distinct from what they say, they do not aspire to that role. (As we have seen, most female inmates do not adopt convict roles, either.) Instead, they disavow the mainline prison culture and the destructive behavior it promotes. These inmates may or may not subscribe, on a verbal level, to the convict code; they may or may not claim that "doing time" and "sticking together against the screws" are the wellsprings of prison life. What is important is that they show, through their actions, that they wish to avoid contact with the so-called prison community. For men and women, desire to avoid the mainline prison culture appears in some instances to be a source of deterrence and presumably can be converted to a motive for personal reform.[191]

Disaffection from the public prison culture is not unexpected. The values so saliently reflected in this culture landed these men and women in prison, a setting that has been known to give many a hasty hedonist a moment's pause. Moreover, most inmates see the dominant or public prison culture as causing more problems than it solves in the here-and-now world of the prison, a direct and immediate relationship between behavior and consequences that even the hastiest and least reflective of hedonists can appreciate.[192] As a result, most prisoners, and not only lifers, want to shelter themselves from this culture, not immerse themselves in its adolescent games.[193] This often means passing for a convict in one's public dealings with prisoners and staff (which one judiciously attempts to minimize) but evolving a markedly different lifestyle in one's private prison life.

The actual "day-to-day concerns" of the typical prisoner, whether male or female, "do not revolve around status, power, or honor in the prison world."[194] As Toch's research has made abundantly clear, most male prisoners attempt to carve out a private prison world composed of niches or sanctuaries, offering sheltered settings and benign activities that insulate them from the mainline prison.[195] Owen has made this same point quite effectively in her study of women in prison. "Women manage their prison sentences by carving out a life that provides for some measure of privacy and safety, a range of activity, a satisfying program, a living situation that is fairly comfortable, and a degree of material comforts."[196] Lifers, both male and female, seem especially likely to secure niches. Too, prisoners characterized by an internal locus of control and a corresponding sense of self-efficacy seem to "hold the advantage in obtaining, and maintaining, niches."[197] The larger point, however, is that the adjustment efforts of virtually all prisoners reveal a range of ecological options that support life "off the yard," in the relative privacy of the cell or, more exotically, in the physical and social settings that form the backwaters and byways of penal institutions.

The maximum-security prison, in other words, is not a monolith. (Even the penitentiary, which was in many respects monolithic, afforded some sanctuaries for harried prisoners.[198]) Today's prisons, moreover, provide substantial ecological diversity in the form of "varying degrees of privacy from irritants such as noise or crowding, safety from insult or attack, structure and consistency of procedures, support services that facilitate self-improvement, feedback or emotional support, activity to fill time, and freedom from circumscription of one's autonomy."[199] This observation, drawn from research in men's prisons, applies equally to penal institutions for women, which offer striking ecological diversity across living units. "Each of the cottages has its own particular culture," Rierden is told by an experienced officer at Niantic, a women's prison. Some settings, Rierden learns, "are as different as night from day."[200] Prisoners, male or female, who use the environmental diversity of prisons to create niches live not as role types or stereotypes parading about the prison yard but as individuals within small and manageable worlds, often, as with Zamble's lifers, built around their private cell activities. (Note that female lifers, like their male counterparts, establish for themselves "the homiest and most peaceful of all the cottages" where privacy is valued; the inmates treat the cottage "like home.")[201] Moreover, these prisoners, male as well as female, treat their peers and officers, some of whom have helped them in their adjustment efforts, as specific individuals who in some instances deserve a measure of respect and even affection, not as anonymous "cons" or "hacks" who are, by definition, candidates for abuse.[202]

Those prisoners who live outside the mainstream of prison culture have created for themselves a mosaic of prison worlds and adjustments in which stress is reduced and in which mature coping is possible. One option is to use niches as sanctuaries from stress and nothing more; in effect, to take prison life one day at a time and go about business as usual. This is probably the most common mode of prison adjustment, especially among those serving short sentences, but it has obvious drawbacks. "If inmates anesthetize themselves against the pains of imprisonment—or of life—by narrowing their vision, they are truly taking a short-sighted approach. In helping to deal with the present they are cutting themselves off from most of the possibilities of future improvement."[203] A better strategy is to use niches as arenas for constructive social learning, that is, as places where one feels secure enough to respond maturely to stress instead of avoiding it. It is reasonable to suppose that prisoners who adapt in this fashion, like those studied by Zamble, may be more likely to handle general life stresses in mature ways when they leave prison. They may be able, in other words, to honor the minimal obligations of citizenship, which amount to navigating life's difficulties without preying upon or otherwise exploiting others.[204] A central correctional task, then, to which we return when we consider the matter of prison reform in Chapters Nine and Ten, is to arrange prison environments that promote mature coping as an exercise in citizenship and as a desirable alternative to the immature response fostered by the public inmate culture.

GENERAL DYNAMICS OF ADJUSTMENT

At first blush, it sounds painfully naive to postulate a direct and positive link between prison adjustment and subsequent adjustment in the free world. To use the language of formal psychology, the "behavior contingencies" of prisons and the free world are markedly different. What one learns in prison should have little direct relevance to free-world situations "where one must structure one's own life, conditions are more varied, choices are required, and the range of possible behaviors is greatly enlarged."[205] Still, contingencies or "reinforcement schedules" in prisons can be altered to more closely approximate those in the free community. (Reforms of this sort are discussed in Chapter Nine.) Such reforms would increase the usefulness of specific coping lessons learned in prison, reinforced in formal correctional programs (the subject of Chapter 10) and later applied in the free world.

Independent of such reforms, however, there is and always has been a general similarity between the adjustment problems posed in prison and those in the outside world; for there is an important sense in which prison life and life in general are related. Prison problems are essentially exaggerated—though sometimes greatly exaggerated—versions of problems experienced in normal life. As a former inmate once observed, "The pain of imprisonment is offset by the discovery that you are strong enough to take it."[206] And, because essentially "the same system of pain and reward" operates both in prison and "in the outside world, you realize that you can succeed there, too."[207]

Imprisonment is painful because it deprives one of liberty, goods and services, heterosexual contacts, autonomy, and security.[208] It also puts an enormous strain on personal relationships with loved ones outside the walls (including children, a special concern of inmate mothers) and suspends or even ruins any notion of a conventional occupational career.[209] Yet all of us suffer these pains to some degree. None of us is as free as we would like, has all the goods and services we would like, is completely satisfied by our sexual outlets, or is as autonomous or secure as we would like. None of us is free from strain in our personal and family lives or in our jobs or careers. It is also true that all of us must cope with time:

> [T]ime transcends the conventional social order. Prisoners can be snatched from that order but not from time. Time imprisons us all. When the prisoner returns to society after serving his time, in an important sense he's never been away.[210]

Certainly the correspondence between general life problems and prison problems is especially salient for the lower-class men and women who make up the vast bulk of our prison populations. Indeed, we know that many of these people come from urban slums that are, in some respects at least, as harsh and depriving as the prisons they wind up in! "Doing time" in one ghetto or another is a familiar if uncongenial experience in their lives.

Thus, it can plausibly be argued that inmates who learns to cope maturely with the stresses posed by confinement are learning to cope maturely with the stresses of life.[211] Moreover, while immature coping typically complicates problems (even the most proficient predator must contemplate the army of enemies he is cultivating), mature coping enables one to solve problems or at least make them more manageable. These successes in coping are apt to build self-confidence and encourage more ambitious behavior, such as taking on new challenges, learning new skills, and generally engaging the world rather than running from opportunities or exploding when pressure mounts.[212] At this juncture, prisoners are no longer embroiled full-time in a dog-eat-dog fight for survival or trapped in a cycle of personal failure and defeat. They are thus more likely to sample traditional correctional programs in an effort to remedy personal deficiencies. More generally, they are ready to tackle the hard job of rebuilding their lives.

Central to this thesis is the notion that healthy self-esteem mediates coping behavior in any environment and must be enhanced if mature behavior is to occur.[213] (Healthy self-esteem features a positive of sense of one's worth that is realistic and stable, as distinct from the exaggerated, groundless, and unstable self-regard that characterizes egotists.) The psychological sequence underlying this adaptive process has been identified by Toch and can be paraphrased as follows:

1. Mature problem-solving efforts are likely to succeed and this builds healthy self-esteem and encourages more mature behavior.

2. A history of successful mature coping efforts produces a confident, resilient person who can learn from occasional failures rather than be demoralized or even traumatized by them; in short, success breeds success and makes failure manageable.

3. Immature behavior generally produces failure, which, in turn, lowers self-esteem and further inhibits effective problem solving.

4. A history of failure produces chronically low self-esteem, with the result that the person spends more time nursing hurt feelings and less time attending to the environment; stated differently, failure breeds failure and, eventually, crippling self-doubt.

Given this sequence, we cannot "engage in stress amelioration without being involved in rehabilitating people (inmates) or in developing them (staff)."[214] We find, in Zamble's words, "a self-reinforcing cycle of improvement" that sparks continuing efforts at "monitoring and controlling" dysfunctional behavior.[215]

The easy logical flow of this psychological sequence should not lead us to believe that building healthy self-esteem is, in practice, a simple business. Bandura reminds us that people sometimes go to great lengths to defend their self-images and to discount the implications of successful experiences at new ways of living.[216] Persistent offenders often resist change because they take pride in their criminal exploits, including the considerable feat of prison survival. For them, life has been a matter of repeated and painful experiences of failure at conventional living; their only successes, modest as they may be in objective terms, have been at criminal activities. A self image as a serious criminal—as a lone warrior set apart from an unjust world, as many male convicts like to see themselves—may well be inflated and unstable but it helps to reduce the pains of rejection by the larger society and is something an offender will cling to until a viable alternative is found.[217] Nevertheless, a history of successes at conventional activities, though it may be slow in coming, is necessary for healthy self-esteem and improved coping competence to develop.

Stress management and personal reform, then, are linked in direct if sometimes complicated ways. This connection forms the core of the correctional agenda; for stress, more than any other aspect of the prison experience, defines the quality of life and adjustment behind bars. As Toch and I have noted,

> Stress is an important feature of prison life, and indeed may be the central feature of prison life as it is experienced by the prisoners themselves. Stress can contaminate programs, undermine adjustment efforts, and leave a residue of bitterness and resentment among inmates. It can make the prison a destructive and debilitating institution; to ignore stress is to relegate prisons to the business of warehousing spoiled (and spoiling) human resources. Stress must be controlled if prisons are to become environments in which the work of corrections, in any sense of the word, can take place.[218]

Ultimately, the prison itself must deal competently, meaning *maturely,* with stress. Porporino and Zamble are surely correct when they maintain that

> there is a general consensus that imprisonment should not be damaging. Prisons should not change individuals for the worse. Social objectives [of

imprisonment] are not met to the extent that imprisonment serves to exacerbate psychological vulnerabilities and emotional difficulties, reinforce pro-criminal attitudes and aggressive behavior patterns, or curtail the development of coping skills needed to function in the outside world.[219]

Stated positively, prisons must be "resilient environments, settings orchestrated by line and managerial staff to meet the adjustment needs of prisoners."[220] The premise is that "even environments of stress such as prisons can become settings for survival and milieus for personal growth."[221] Even maximum-security prisons, in other words, can promote mature adjustment, and they must do just that if they are to play a viable role in the correctional process.

To make informed policy suggestions based on the connection between prison adjustment and personal reform, we must understand in detail how prisoners (Chapters Five and Six) and their keepers (Chapters Seven and Eight) come to terms with life in the contemporary prison world. It is to these matters that we next turn. In the final chapters of the book (Chapters Nine and Ten), we examine a correctional agenda that adapts the social realities of prison life to the demands of mature coping and personal reform.

NOTES

1. Johnson (1976:1–2).

2. Johnson (1976:1–2).

3. The various adjustment difficulties promoted by crowding in prison are addressed in the following: Lombardo (1988), riots in men's prisons; Smith (1988) and Johnson (1992), general stresses in prisons for men and women; Owens (1998), interpersonal tensions in a women's prison; and Kuper (1999), special problems of mentally ill male and female inmates.

4. Johnson and Toch, (1988:19–20); Toch (1988:36–39).

5. See Hawkins and Alpert (1989:184).

6. For assertiveness, see Howard and Scott (1965); for personal efficacy, see White (1959) and Bandura (1977); and for internal locus of control, see Rotter (1966).

7. See Goodstein, Mackenzie, and Shotland (1984:352) and MacKenzie, Goodstein, and Blouin (1987:65). In some situations, in normal life as well as in prison, opportunities for control are entirely

absent. Problems cannot be met directly because they are out of one's control. Examples include patients facing life-or-death surgery or advanced terminal illness. In both instances, patients can only await their fate. Given their objective and complete helplessness, "[d]istorted perceptions of reality through denial and rationalization" can be quite effective as strategies of adjustment (Porporino & Zamble, 1984:411).

8. Cited in McCall (1995:177). See also Brooks (1994).

9. As Maruna (2001:147) points out, "the peculiar combination of making excuses for past failures [the lemons life hands out] and yet taking responsibility for present and future accomplishments [the lemonade we make] is a well-established characteristic of another group of interest to social psychologists—healthy adults." Healthy adults look at life with an optimistic bias that insulates them from many of the stresses of life (Bandura 1989:1176; Seligman 1991:110).

10. Toch and Adams (1989:272).

11. See Goodstein and Wright (1989:24–45); Wooldredge (1999:244–45). Osgood, Gruber, Archer, and Newcomb (1985:76), reporting on a study "conducted at four correctional institutions for adolescents in a large Midwestern state" housing "males between the ages of 13 and 18," emphasized the value of autonomy in the constructive adjustment of the young offenders. Findings revealed that reduced autonomy among inmates led to increased support for the inmate subculture, much as Sykes has suggested; these boys stood in more or less unified opposition to the staff and the programs the staff offered and generally made trouble for the institution. In contrast, enhanced autonomy led to increased support for institutional goals. Of particular note, young offenders granted autonomy felt more secure and were more willing to participate in rehabilitation programs. Overall, enhanced autonomy produced "a more orderly and humane setting" (Osgood et al., 1985:87).

12. Zamble (1990:143).

13. Nettler (1984:209); Schwendinger and Schwendinger (1967:98).

14. Wideman (1984:131).

15. Aichhorn (1955).

16. Toch (1971:390).

17. Baumeister, 2001.

18. See Katz (1988).

19. Earley (1992:382–83).

20. The adaptive qualities of ghetto lifestyles are not usually captured in psychological measurements, which tend to draw upon an implicitly middle-class view of the world and the kind of ego it supports (Toch, 1971). For example, the most popular means of measuring sense of control over one's world, Rotter's (1966) Internal/External Locus of Control Scale, does not reliably assess the ego strengths of low-income persons and prisoners. Rotter's scale items feature a number of general statements about whether one perceives one's place and experience in the world as subject to internal (personal) or external (impersonal) control. For slum dwellers and prisoners, many of these items refer to outcomes that for them are in large measure objectively determined by external forces and are hence only partly subject to their personal control. The implications of the test scores are not adjusted to reflect the accuracy of perceptions.

Rotter's scale also focuses on narrowly middle-class concerns, such as the equity of academic grades or the rationality of politics, concerns that are largely irrelevant to more needy populations (see Miller, 1958; Toch, 1971). It is not at all clear how these items are read by respondents with respect to their own environments. Do prisoners who see an ambiguous and unresponsive larger society also see urban street corners and prison yards as alien and beyond their control? Even if they do—and surely many do not—the test tells us nothing about their perception of their own competency to cope in these environments. As Bandura (1977:204) has noted, "Rotter's conceptual scheme is primarily concerned with causal beliefs about action-outcome contingencies rather than with personal efficacy. Perceived self-efficacy and beliefs about the locus of causality must be distinguished. . . ."

21. Toch (1971:390).

22. Herrnstein (1994).

23. See Brennan, Mednick, and Volavka (1994).

24. Zamble, Porporino, and Kalotay (1984:64). This 1984 monograph was expanded and subsequently published as a book. The book, *Coping, Behavior, and Adaptation in Prison Inmates* (Zamble & Porporino, 1988) is highly recommended. Since I read the original monograph with some care, I have retained my references to that work in this book.

25. Zamble (1990:138).

26. Zamble and Porporino (1990:56).

27. Zamble and Porporino (1990:57–58).

28. Earley (1992:416–17).

29. For revealing case studies of abusive women, see Pearson (1997).

30. Owen (1998:42).

31. A number of women wrote chapters about these matters in Johnson and Toch (2000). The statistical link between abuse and criminality, including criminal violence, has been established for women as well as for men (Widom and Maxfield, 2001). The contours of personal trauma as they operate to promote criminality among women is thoughtfully explored in Girshick (1999).

32. Halleck (1967:72).

33. Wideman (1984:132).

34. Halleck (1967:77).

35. See McCall (1995:68 & 72), and Canada (1996).

36. Halleck (1967:76–83).

37. Walters (1990:71).

38. Walters (1990:106).

39. Walters (1990:107).

40. Walters (1990:109).

41. Mueller (1985:18).

42. Freeman (1994:190).

43. Nettler (1984:313).

44. Ditton (1999:1).

45. See Wideman (1984) and Maruna 2001.

46. Wideman (1984:66).

47. Zamble, Porporino, and Kalotay (1984:58).

48. Zamble, Porporino, and Kalotay (1984:128).

49. Walters (1990:88).

50. One pitfall of ethnographic work with criminals is taking their stories about crime at face value. On the one hand, criminals in prison often tell inflated tales of bloodthirsty violence to impress others with their machismo. Toch (1990:581) has suggested that Fleisher, in his ethnographic study of Lompoc prison, may well have fallen for such tall tales. On the other hand, criminals on the streets often adopt

the pose of persons unjustly arrested and confined for behavior of little consequence. In my view, Irwin and Austin appear to accept without question such statements by their interviewees (see Irwin & Austin 1994:40–49).

One interviewee, for example, related to Irwin and Austin that police questioned him because he resembled a suspected offender. "The police asked what was I doing over there. I wrestled with him and his gun fell out of his holster. I kicked it and ran. They got me later." The interviewee expressed a sense of injustice that he was charged for "taking [the officer's] gun." How the encounter with the police officer went from the officer asking questions to the interviewee wrestling with him and at least dislodging the officer's gun is never broached, though it is possible, even likely, that the interviewee committed some species of assault. Irwin and Austin discuss this case as an instance of someone ending up in prison simply because he was "around crime" and had not himself committed a crime. I do not wish to entirely discount their larger point—that the behavior of offenders is often less heinous than offense labels would imply—but the accounts of offenders often err in the other direction, minimizing the seriousness of the behavior that has landed them in trouble. Minimizing one's personal responsibility is one of a number of strategies of rationalization people can use to prevent themselves from facing and resolving serious personal problems.

51. Wideman (1984:145).

52. See Walters (1990); Yochelson and Samenow (1976).

53. See Walters (1990); Yochelson and Samenow (1976).

54. Walters (1990:88–89).

55. Harris (1988:94).

56. Quoted in Harris (1988:291).

57. Some people will take exception to my use of the term *primitive* in this way, but substantial anthropological evidence bears me out. The work of Lawrence Keeley, for example, makes it clear that violent

death rates were, at a minimum, more than fifty times higher among ancient peoples than among people in the modern world. Some very ancient societies had violent death rates thousands of times higher than current violent death rates. Violent death rates drop as societies become more civilized, Keeley observes, because less violent means of dispute resolution become institutionalized (Keeley, 1995).

58. Deception requires what Allman has termed "a theory of mind about others" so that one can try to manipulate what others are thinking and hence deceive them. "The human ability to develop a theory of mind about others appears to be a specialized feature of the brain that operates independently of other mental activities typically associated with intelligence." See Allman (1994:67).

59. See Clemmer (1940).

60. Empey (1982:25).

61. Owen (1998:170).

62. Suttles (1968); Hannerz (1969); Anderson (1994).

63. See Anderson (1994); Earley (1992).

64. Owen (1998:58).

65. Schwendinger and Schwendinger (1967:98).

66. Nettler (1984:209).

67. See Earley (1992); Anderson (1994).

68. Walters (1990:86–87); Anderson (1994).

69. Montgomery (1994:A4). Montgomery is quoting defense attorney Bill Lane, one of the lawyers arguing the "urban survival" theory in defense of Daimion Osby, a black man who shot two other black men who were menacing him. The defense for Osby's violence: " 'the fear that black people have of other black people' in the nation's most dangerous urban areas" (Montgomery, 1994:A4), a fear so great it leaves no alternative but to use preemptive violence when confronted with problems involving young black men, described by one expert at the trial as "the most dangerous people in America" (Montgomery, 1994:A4). The

fears are often real enough and, presumably, are greatly enhanced in prison, which gathers together the most dangerous felons in one environment. Nevertheless, the notion that the legally recognized remedy to this situation can be summary violence on the streets or in prisons would only make matters worse in these already troubled environments. See, generally, Canada (1996).

70. Earley (1992:211).

71. Earley (1992:50).

72. Owen (1998:151).

73. See Walters, in Earley (1992:50).

74. *Liaison* (1984:8).

75. Sykes (1966:105).

76. Walters (1990:68).

77. Hallinan (2001).

78. Johnson and Toch (1988:19–20).

79. Martin and Sussman, (1993: 193–94).

80. Earley (1992:25).

81. Earley (1992:25).

82. Staub (1989:265).

83. Staub (1989:265).

84. Staub (1989:269).

85. Staub (1989:269) [emphasis added].

86. In Bruchac (1984:149).

87. Selye (1975:72) [emphasis added].

88. Selye (1975:120) [emphasis added].

89. Mauss (1969).

90. Des Pres (1977:163).

91. Des Pres (1977:163).

92. Axelrod (1984:viii).

93. See Allman (1994).

94. Axelrod (1984:176).

95. See Allman (1994:82–83).

96. Axelrod (1984:189–90).

97. See Allman (1994:91).

98. See, for example, Toch (1977); Herrick (1989:8). A more visible if not more

common problem, however, is for a per-version of tit-for-tat logic to run amuck in already dangerous environments, such as slum communities marked by a robust drug trade. Here, the violence of the drug trade spreads outward into the commu-nity, raising the ante in encounters featur-ing conflict. We see graphic evidence for this in many inner-city communities, especially from 1985 to 1994, during which time there has been a tremendous growth of gun-related homicides among ghetto youths. As Blumstein (1994:412–13) has observed,

The nature of the [drug] industry has made guns a necessary tool of the trade for those who participate in it, and use of violence a standard means of dispute resolution as well as self-defense. Since that industry is often quite pervasive in many communities, it is inevitable that others in those communities will also arm themselves, at least as a self-defensive measure, and possibly also as a means of enhancing their status among their peers. The presence of violence in that industry . . . undoubtedly sets a tone in the community, undoubtedly generates a greater inurement to violence generally, and so stimulates violence by others. This leads to an escalation of violence. . . .

The District of Columbia provides a telling case in point. As US Attorney Eric H. Holder Jr. has observed, the drug trade in the District fueled an explosion of violence that has persisted, indeed grown worse, even as drug activities have declined. Holder's point, paraphrased by *Washington Post* reporter Lewis, was that

[W]hen drug-dealing began to decline [in D.C.], the guns remained. Instead of protecting drug supplies and prime sales locations . . . the guns were used to rob the remaining drug dealers and, more recently, to rob random victims. (Lewis, 1994:A24)

The guns not only remained but prolifer-ated in the District, at least among the young, as Blumstein would have pre-dicted. It is significant that youths in the District "are piling up gun charges at three times the rate of their adult coun-terparts and are arming themselves at twice the pace they did five years ago," when the drug trade in the District was at a high point (Lewis, 1995:A1). A cul-

ture of gun violence, initially given sig-nificant impetus by the drug trade, has now become a functionally autonomous phenomenon. See, generally, Canada (1996).

99. Metzger, in Johnson and Toch (2000:139).

100. Hoffman (1981); Nettler (1984).

101. See Wilson and Herrnstein (1985).

102. See Staub (1989:280).

103. Allman (1994:97–99).

104. Nettler (1984:289).

105. Parker (1990:84).

106. Parker (1990:86–87).

107. Parker (1990:87).

108. Some prostitutes take pleasure in degrading and even physically abusing their "Johns," who expect sex but get vio-lence instead. See Pearson (1997).

109. Rierden (1997:114).

110. Rierden (1997:114).

111. Hoffman (1982:306).

112. See Hirschi (1994); McLanahan and Sandefur (1995).

113. Since 1960, there have been dramatic increases in the rates at which children are born to unmarried mothers, particularly among low-income whites. "Back then," notes Samuelson (1994:A23), 22 percent of all black births and only 2 percent of all white births were to unmarried mothers; by 1991, those figures were 68 percent and 22 percent." Most of these children born of out wedlock to poor mothers are raised in single-parent homes and supported by welfare. Children in such homes are more likely to be abused, and this in turn pro-motes crime and, particularly, violent crime. Perhaps unsurprisingly, Samuelson (1994:A23) reminds us that since 1960 and coincident with the growth of "out-of-wedlock births and welfare dependency," the murder rate in America has more than doubled.

114. Will (1994:C7).

115. Will (1994:C7).

116. Though millions of American children live in poverty, estimates are that only "about one-half of 1 percent of all kids in this country grow up in circumstances where neither parents nor other adults adequately care for them. Many of these children are severely abused and neglected by deviant, delinquent, or criminal adults, including their biological parents" (DiIulio, 1995:C2). The "cycle of violence" often perpetuated in such environments has been well documented. As Widom and Maxfield's research has revealed, "being abused or neglected as a child increased the likelihood of arrest as a juvenile by 59 percent, as an adult by 28 percent, and for a violent crime by 30 percent" (2001:2). These effects are long-lasting, and appear operate affect black children more dramatically than white children: "white abused and neglected children were no more likely to be arrested for a violent crime than their nonabused and nonneglected counterparts. This contrasts sharply with findings for black children . . . who showed significantly increased rates of violent crime arrest [compared to] black children who were not abused or neglected" (Widom and Maxfield, 2001. Diagnoses of antisocial personality disorders are also more prevalent among adults who were abused as children (Luntz & Widom, 1994). As many as three out of four violent juveniles in confinement experienced abuse in the home (DiIulio, 1995:C2). Children raised in abusive environments are crime-prone "because they were raised to be violent, impulsive, self-centered and remorseless by adults who taught these traits by example" (DiIulio, 1995:C2). The obvious policy implication of these findings, as stated bluntly by DiIulio (1995:C1): "remove the children from their homes to other stable settings."

117. See generally, Donnerstein and Linz (1994).

118. Milloy (1991:D3).

119. Milloy (1991:D3).

120. Milloy (1991:D3). Anderson has a somewhat different take on this problem. He notes that these mothers may not know any other way of controlling their children than by resort to violence. He argues that they "love their children dearly" and in effect beat them to make sure they behave decently (Anderson, 1994:83). In any case, they "come up hard," a common term in the ghetto that in this context may have two meanings: their lives are hard, and as a consequence, they are hardened to human feelings. For them, life in the home is a lesson in the use of violence to solve problems or vent frustration.

121. See Anderson (1994); Kotlowitz (1991).

122. Sykes and Matza (1957); Goldstein (1975).

123. Suttles (1968).

124. Even so, the decent people must be able to live by the code of the street when they venture from their homes and mingle with others in public settings. This code, which closely resembles the prison code of conduct, emphasizes toughness and a willingness to use violence to defend or avenge oneself (Anderson, 1994:82).

125. Johnson and Toch (1988:20).

126. Owen (1998:176).

127. For men, see Jacobs (1977), Carroll (1988). For women, see Rierden (1997).

128. Rierden (1997:26).

129. Sykes (1966:101); Toch (1975:6).

130. See Owen (1998).

131. For men, see Lerner (1984:17). For women, see Rierden (1997:32).

132. Seymour (1977:195–96).

133. Cordilia (1983:25–27).

134. Goodstein (1979:253).

135. Goodstein (1979:253).

136. See Glaser (1969) and Toch (1977).

137. Owen (1998:148).

138. See DeRosia (1998); Owen (1998:148).

139. Gendreau, Grant, and Leipciger (1979).

140. Wormith (1984:612–13).

141. Quay (1984:48).

142. See generally, Bonta and Gendreau (1991).

143. Goodstein (1979).

144. Goffman (1961).

145. Goodstein (1979).

146. Thomas and Zingraff (1978) Alpert (1979).

147. Earley (1992:249–50).

148. Thompson (1847/1969:349) [emphasis in original].

149. Coffey (1823:65).

150. Coffey (1823:20–21).

151. Fleisher (1989:22–23).

152. Owen (1998:40).

153. See Toch and Adams (1989:225).

154. Owen (1998:55).

155. MacKenzie, Goodstein, and Blouin (1987:63).

156. Rierden (1997:117).

157. Goodstein (1979); Rierden (1997).

158. See Irwin (1980).

159. Bowker (1980).

160. Quay (1984:48).

161. Toch (1975).

162. Kupers (1999:39).

163. Kupers (1999:55).

164. Kupers (1999:56–57).

165. Kupers (1999:87).

166. Zamble, Porporino, and Kalotay (1984:69–70).

167. Zamble, Porporino, and Kalotay (1984:70).

168. Zamble, Porporino, and Kalotay (1984:81).

169. Quoted in Besozzi (1993:37).

170. Zamble, Porporino, and Kalotay (1984:69–70).

171. See Elgar (1886:6); Anonymous (1871:376); Flanagan (1988); Johnson (1998:245–247). This theme runs through much of Rierden's discussion of female long termers at Niantic Prison. See Rierden (1997).

172. Owen (1998:71).

173. Zamble (1992a:410); see also, Flanagan (1988).

174. Zamble (1992b:13–14).

175. Zamble (1992b:13–14).

176. See Zamble and Porporino (1990:59).

177. Zamble (1992a:423).

178. Zamble (1992b:29).

179. Zamble (1992a:414).

180. Zamble (1992a:415).

181. Zamble (1992b:33).

182. Zamble (1992b:34).

183. Zamble (1992b:20).

184. Zamble (1992b:23).

185. Zamble (1992b:26).

186. Zamble (1992b:22); for further evidence on improved physical health among prisoners, see Bonta and Gendreau (1990:356).

187. Zamble (1992b:22).

188. Toch and Adams (1989:210).

189. Toch and Adams (1989:254).

190. Sykes (1966).

191. See Kassebaum, Ward, and Wilner (1971); Toch (1988); and Rierden (1997). It was apparent in Rierden's study of Niantic Prison for women that as crowding and predatory convict behavior became more common at that institution, including the emergence of a gang culture, the prison became less desirable as a place to live, and the possibility of personal reform became more highly valued.

192. Seymour (1988); Rierden (1997).

193. Toch (1977); Owen (1998).

194. Seymour (1988:268). See also Owen (1998).

195. See Toch (1988).

196. Owen (1998:117).

197. Goodstein and Wright (1989:245).

198. See, for example, Anonymous (1871:78–79 & 94).

199. Johnson and Toch (1988:18).

200. Rierden (1997:9).

201. Rierden (1997:20).

202. See Seymour (1988); Rierden (1997:20).

203. Zamble, Porporino, and Kalotay (1984:80).

204. Conrad (1981).

205. Zamble, Porporino, and Kalotay (1984:136).

206. Gates (1991:68).

207. Gates (1991:68).

208. Sykes (1966).

209. Toch (1975).

210. Wideman (1984:36).

211. Toch (1988:37).

212. Toch (1988:37).

213. See Stotland (1975:3).

214. Toch (1988:37–38).

215. Zamble (1990:34).

216. Bandura (1977:200–202).

217. The self-image of the chronic offender is often inflated because it must protect the person from pervasive and powerful messages from the larger culture that, as a criminal, he or she is a worthless and indeed a profoundly despicable person. An inflated sense of self, in turn, is almost by definition unstable since it has no solid basis in reality. See Baumeister (2001) and Walters (1990).

218. Johnson and Toch (1988:20).

219. Porporino and Zamble (1984:403).

220. Johnson and Toch (1988:20).

221. Toch (1975:326).

REFERENCES

Aichhorn, A. *Wayward Youth: A Psychoanalytic Study of Delinquent Children.* New York: Meridian, 1955.

Allman, W. F. *The Stone Age Present: How Evolution Has Shaped Modern Life—From Sex, Violence, and Language to Emotions, Morals, and Communities.* New York: Simon & Schuster, 1994.

Alpert, G. P. "Patterns of change in prisonization: Longitudinal analysis." *Criminal Justice and Behavior* 6 (3) 1979:159–74.

Anderson, E. "The code of the streets." *Atlantic Monthly* 273 (5) 1994:80–94.

Anonymous. *An Illustrated History and Description of State Prison Life, By One Who Has Been There. Written by a Convict in a Convict's Cell.* Globe Publishing, 1871.

Axelrod, R. *The Evolution of Cooperation.* New York: Basic Books, 1984.

Bandura, A. "Self-efficacy: Toward a unified theory of behavioral change." *Psychological Review* 84 (March 1977):191–215.

Bandura, A. "Human agency in social cognitive theory." *American Psychologist* 44, 1989:1175–1184.

Baumeister, R. F. "Violent pride." *Scientific American* 284 (4) 2001:96–101.

Besozzi, C. "Recidivism: How inmates see it." *Forum on Corrections Research* 5 (3) 1993:35–38.

Blumstein, A. "Prisons." In J. Q Wilson and J. Petersilia (eds.). *Crime.* San Francisco: ICS Press, 1994: 387–420.

Bonta, J., and P. Gendreau. "Reexamining the cruel and unusual punishment of prison life." *Law and Human Behavior* 14 (4) 1990:347–72.

Bonta, J., and P. Gendreau. "Coping with prison." In P. Suedfeld and P. E. Tetlock (eds.). *Psychology and Public Policy.* New York: Hemisphere, 1991:343–54.

Bowker, L. *Prison Victimization.* New York: Elsevier, 1980.

Brennan, P. A., S. A. Mednick, and J. Volavka. "Biomedical factors in crime." In J. Q. Wilson and J. Petersilia (eds.). *Crime.* San Francisco: ICS Press, 1994:65–90.

Brooks, G. *Blacks.* Chicago: Third World Press, 1994.

Bruchac, J. (ed.). *The Light from Another Country: Poetry from American Prisons.* Greenfield Center, NY: Greenfield Review Press, 1984.

Canada, G. *Fist Stick Knife Gun: A Personal History of Violence in America.* Boston: Beacon Press, 1996.

Carroll, L. "Race, ethnicity, and the social order of the prison." In R. Johnson and H. Toch (eds.). *The Pains of Imprisonment.* Prospect Heights, IL: Waveland Press, 1988:181–203.

Clemmer, D. *The Prison Community.* Boston: Christopher Publishing, 1940.

Coffey, W. A. *Inside Out: Or, An Interior View of the New York State Prison; Together with Bibliographic Sketches of the Lives of Several of the Convicts.* New York: Printed for the author, 1823.

Conrad, J. P. "Where there's hope there's life." In D. Fogel and J. Hudson (eds.). *Justice As Fairness.* Cincinnati, OH: Anderson, 1981:3–21.

Cordilia, A. *The Making of an Inmate: Prison as a Way of Life.* Cambridge, MA: Schenkman, 1983.

DeRosia, V. R. *Living Inside Prison Walls: Adjustment Behavior.* Westport, CT: Praeger Publishers, 1998.

Des Pres, T. *The Survivor: An Anatomy of Life in the Death Camps.* New York: Pocket Books, 1977.

DiIulio, J. J. "The plain, ugly truth about welfare: Getting kids out of bad homes is the key to lasting reform." *The Washington Post,* January 15, 1995: Outlook Section C1 & C2.

Ditton, P. M. *Mental Health and Treatment of Inmates and Probationers.* BJS Special Report. Washington, DC: U.S. Department of Justice, Office of Justice Programs, Bureau of Justice Statistics. July 1999.

Donnerstein, E., and D. Linz. "The media." In J. Q. Wilson and J. Petersilia (eds.). *Crime.* San Francisco: ICS Press, 1994:237–64.

Earley, P. *The Hot House: Life Inside Leavenworth.* New York: Bantam Books, 1992.

Elgar, T. (Convict No. 6179) *Convict Life; or, Penitentiary Citizenship in the Illinois State Pen.* Rochester, NY. 1886.

Empey, L. "Implications: A game with no winners." In A. J. Manocchio and J. Dunn. *The Time Game: Two Views of a Prison.* Beverly Hills: Sage, 1982:241–52.

Flanagan, T. J. "Lifers and long-termers: Doing big time." In R. Johnson and H. Toch (eds.). *The Pains of Imprisonment.* Prospect Heights, IL: Waveland Press, 1988:115–45.

Fleischer, M. S. *Warehousing Violence.* Beverly Hills: Sage, 1989.

Foucault, M. *Discipline and Punish: The Birth of the Prison.* New York: Pantheon, 1977.

Freeman, R. B. "The labor market." In J. Q. Wilson and J. Petersilia (eds.). *Crime.* San Francisco: ICS Press, 1994:171–91.

Gates, M. "The excavation." American University: Unpublished manuscript, 1991.

Gendreau, P., B. A. Grant, and M. Leipciger. "Self-esteem, incarceration and recidivism." *Criminal Justice and Behavior* 6 (1) 1979:67–75.

Girslick, L. B. *No Safe Haven: Stories of Woman in Prison.* Boston: Northeastern University Press, 1999.

Glaser, D. *The Effectiveness of a Prison and Parole System.* New York: Bobbs-Merrill, 1969.

Goffman, E. *Asylums.* New York: Anchor Books, 1961.

Goldstein, J. H. *Aggression and Crimes of Violence.* New York: Oxford University Press, 1975.

Goodstein, L. "Inmate adjustment to prison and the transition to community life." *Journal of Research in Crime and Delinquency* 16 (2) 1979:246–72.

Goodstein, L., D. L. Mackenzie, and R. L. Shotland. "Personal control and inmate adjustment to prison." *Criminology* 22 (3) 1984:343–69.

Goodstein, L., and K. N. Wright. "Inmate adjustment to prison." In L. Goodstein and D. L. MacKenzie (eds.). *The American Prison: Issues in Research and Policy.* New York: Plenum Press, 1989:229–51.

Halleck, S. *Psychiatry and the Dilemma of Crime.* New York: Harper & Row, 1967.

Hallinan, J. T. *Going Up The River: Travels in a Prison Nation.* New York: Random House, 2001.

Hannerz, U. *Soulside.* New York: Columbia University Press, 1969.

Harris, J. *They Always Call Us Ladies: Stories from Prison.* New York: Kensington Publishing, 1988.

Hawkins, R., and G. P. Alpert. *American Prison Systems: Punishment and Justice.* Englewood Cliffs, NJ: Prentice-Hall, 1989.

Herrick, E. "The surprising direction of violence in prison." *Corrections Compendium* 14 (6) 1989:1, 4–17.

Herrnstein, R. J. "Criminogenic traits." In J. Q. Wilson and J. Petersilia (eds.). *Crime.* San Francisco: ICS Press, 1994:39–63.

Hirschi, T. "The family." In J. Q. Wilson and J. Petersilia (eds.). *Crime.* San Francisco: ICS Press, 1994:121–40.

Hoffman, M. L. "Is altruism part of human nature?" *Journal of Personality and Social Psychology* 40 1981:121–37.

Hoffman, M. L. "Development of prosocial motivation: Empathy and guilt." In N. Eisenbert (ed.). *The Development of Prosocial Behavior.* New York: Academic Press, 1982:281–313.

Howard, A., and R. A. Scott. "A proposed framework for the analysis of stress in the human organism." *Behavioral Science* 10 (1965):141–60.

Irwin, J. *Prisons in Turmoil.* Boston: Little, Brown, 1980.

Irwin, J., and J. Austin. *It's About Time: America's Imprisonment Binge.* Belmont, CA: Wadsworth, 1994.

Jacobs, J. B. *Stateville: The Penitentiary in Mass Society.* Chicago: University of Chicago Press, 1977.

Johnson, R. *Culture and Crisis in Confinement.* Lexington: Lexington Books, 1976.

Johnson, R. "Crowding and the quality of prison life." In C. Hartjen (ed.). *Correctional Theory and Practice.* Chicago: Nelson-Hall, 1992:139–45.

Johnson, R. *Death Work: A Study of the Modern Execution Process* (Second Edition) Belmont, CA: Wadsworth, 1998.

Johnson, R., and H. Toch. "Introduction." In R. Johnson and H. Toch (eds.). *The Pains of Imprisonment.* Prospect Heights, IL: Waveland Press, 1988:13–21.

Johnson, R., and H. Toch (eds.). *Crime and Punishment: Inside Views.* Los Angeles: Roxbury Publishing, 2000.

Kassebaum, G., D. Ward, and D. Wilner. *Prison Treatment and Parole Survival.* New York: Wiley, 1971.

Katz, J. *Seductions of Crime.* New York: Basic Books, 1988.

Keeley, L. *War Before Civilization.* New York: Oxford University Press, 1995.

Kotlowitz, A. *There Are No Children Here: The Story of Two Boys Growing Up in the Other America.* New York: Anchor Books, 1991.

Kupers, T. A. *Prison Madness: The Mental Health Crisis Behind Bars and What We Must Do About It.* San Francisco, CA: Jossey-Bass Publishers, 1999.

Lerner, S. "Rule of the cruel." *The New Republic* October 15, 1984:17–21.

Lewis, N. "Court cases reveal arms buildup among D.C. youths." *The Washington Post,* January 1, 1995:A1, A24.

Liaison (staff author). "The hardest part is getting out." *Liaison* 10 (10) 1984:4–10.

Lombardo, L. X. "Stress, change, and collective violence in prison." In R. Johnson and H. Toch (eds.). *The Pains of Imprisonment.* Prospect Heights, IL: Waveland Press, 1988:77–93.

Luntz, B. K., and C. S. Widom. "Antisocial personality disorder in abused and neglected children grown up." *American Journal of Psychiatry* 151 (5) 1994:670–74.

Mackenzie, D. L., L. I. Goodstein, and D. C. Blouin. "Personal control and prisoner adjustment: An empirical test of a proposed model." *Journal of Research in Crime and Delinquency* 24 (1) 1987:49–68.

Martin, D. M. & Sussman, P. Y., *Committing Journalism: The Prison Writings of RED HOG.* Norton, 1993.

Maruna, S. *Making Good: How Ex-Convicts Reform and Rebuild Their Lives.* Washington, D.C.: American Psychological Association, 2001.

Mauss, M. *The Gift: Forms and Functions of Exchange in Archaic Societies.* London: Routledge & Kegan Paul, 1969.

McCall, N. *Makes Me Wanna Holler: A Young Black Man in America.* New York: Vintage, 1995.

McLanahan, S., and G. Sandefur. *Growing Up with a Single Parent: What Hurts, What Helps.* Cambridge: Harvard University Press, 1995.

Metzger, D. H. "Life in a microwave." In R. Johnson and H. Toch (eds.). *Crime and Punishment: Inside Views.* Los Angeles: Roxbury Publishing, 2000:138–140.

Miller, W. "Lower class culture as a generating milieu of gang delinquency." *Journal of Social Issues* 14 (3) 1958:5–19.

Milloy, C. "For tragedy of black youths, put blame where it belongs." *The Washington Post,* January 3, 1991:D3.

Montgomery, L. " 'Urban survival' rules at issue in trial." *The Washington Post,* October 26, 1994:A4.

Mueller, J. "Crime is caused by the young and restless." *Wall Street Journal,* March 6, 1985:18.

Nettler, G. *Explaining Crime.* New York: McGraw-Hill, 1984.

Osgood, D. W., E. Gruber, M. A. Archer, and T. M. Newcomb. "Autonomy for inmates: counterculture or cooptation?" *Criminal Justice and Behavior* 12 (1) 1985:71–89.

Owen, B. *"In the Mix": Struggle and Survival in a Women's Prison.* Albany: State University of New York Press, 1998.

Parker, T. *Life After Life: Interviews with Twelve Murderers.* London: Secker and Warburg, 1990.

Pearson, P. *When She Was Bad: Violent Women and the Myth of Innocence.* New York: Viking, 1997.

Porporino, F., and E. Zamble. "Coping with imprisonment." *Canadian Journal of Criminology* 26 (4) 1984:403–21.

Quay, H. C. *Managing Adult Inmates: Classification for Housing and Program Assignments.* College Park, MD: American Correctional Association, 1984.

Rierden, A. *The Farm: A Life Inside a Women's Prison.* Amherst, MA: University of Massachusetts Press, 1997.

Rotter, J. "Generalized expectancies for internal versus external control of reinforcement." *Psychological Monographs* 80 (1966): Whole No. 609.

Samuelson, R. J. " 'Bell curve' ballistics." *The Washington Post,* October 26, 1994:A23.

Schwendinger, H., and J. Schwendinger. "Delinquent stereotypes of probable victims." In M. W. Klein (ed.). *Juvenile Gangs in Context: Theory, Research, and Action.* Englewood Cliffs, NJ: Prentice-Hall, 1967.

Seligman, M.E.P. *Learned Optimism.* New York: Knopf, 1991.

Selye, H. *Stress Without Distress.* New York: Signet, 1975.

Seymour, J. "Environmental sanctuaries for susceptible prisoners." In R. Johnson and H. Toch (eds.). *The Pains of Imprisonment.* Prospect Heights, IL: Waveland Press, 1988:267–84.

Seymour, J. "Niches in prison." In H. Toch. *Living in Prison: The Ecology of*

Survival. New York: Free Press, 1977:179–205.

Smith, D. "Crowding and confinement." In R. Johnson and H. Toch (eds.). *The Pains of Imprisonment.* Prospect Heights, IL: Waveland Press, 1988:45–62.

Staub, E. *The Roots of Evil: The Origins of Genocide and Other Group Violence.* New York: Cambridge University Press, 1989.

Stotland, E. "Self-esteem and stress in police work." In W. H. Kroes and J. J. Hurrell (eds.). *Job Stress and the Police Officer: Identifying Stress Reduction Techniques.* Washington, DC: Government Printing Office, 1975.

Suttles, G. D. *The Social Order of the Slum: Ethnicity and Territory in the Inner City.* Chicago: University of Chicago Press, 1968.

Sykes, G. *The Society of Captives.* New York: Atheneum, 1966.

Sykes, G., and D. Matza. "Techniques of neutralization: A theory of delinquency." *American Sociological Review* 22 (1957):664–70.

Thomas, C., and R. Zingraff. "Structural and social psychological correlates of prisonization." *Criminology* 16 (3) 1978:383–93.

Thompson, G. *Prison Life and Reflections.* New York: Negro Universities Press, 1847/1969.

Toch, H. "The delinquent as poor loser." *Seminars in Psychiatry* 3 (3) 1971:386–99.

Toch, H. *Men in Crisis: Human Breakdowns in Prison.* Chicago: Aldine, 1975.

Toch, H. *Living in Prison: The Ecology of Survival.* New York: Free Press, 1977.

Toch, H. "Studying and reducing stress." In R. Johnson and H. Toch (eds.). *The Pains of Imprisonment.* Prospect Heights, IL: Waveland Press, 1988:25–44.

Toch, H. "An anthropologist in the prison." *Contemporary Psychology* 35 (6) 1990:581.

Toch, H., and K. Adams with J. D. Grant. *Coping: Maladaptation in Prisons.* New Brunswick, NJ: Transaction Publishers, 1989.

Walters, G. D. *The Criminal Lifestyle: Patterns of Serious Criminal Conduct.* Beverly Hills: Sage, 1990.

White, R. W. "Motivation reconsidered: The concept of competence." *Psychological Review* 66 (1959):297–333.

Wideman, J. E. *Brothers and Keepers.* New York: Holt, Rinehart & Winston, 1984.

Widom, C. S. "The cycle of violence." *Research in Brief.* National Institute of Justice (October 1992).

Widom, C. S. and Maxfield, M. G., "An update on the 'cycle of violence.'" *Research in Brief,* Washington, D.C., National Institute of Justice 2001:1–8.

Will, G. "The children's passage of pain." *The Washington Post,* May 1, 1994:C7.

Wilson, J. Q., and R. J. Herrnstein. *Crime and Human Nature.* New York: Simon & Schuster, 1985.

Wooldredge, J. D. "Inmate Experiences and Psychological Well-Being." *Criminal Justice and Behavior* 26 (2) 1999:235–250.

Wormith, J. S. "Attitude and behavior change of correctional clientele: A three-year follow-up." *Criminology* 22 (4) 1984:596–618.

Yochelson, S., and S. E. Samenow. *The Criminal Personality.* 3 Vols. New York: Jason Aronson, 1976.

Zamble, E. "Behavioral and psychological considerations in the success of prison reform." In J. W. Murphy and J. E. Dison (eds.). *Are Prisons Any Better?: Twenty Years of Prison Reform.* Newbury Park, CA: Sage, 1990:129–45.

Zamble, E. "Behavior and adaptation in long-term prison inmates: Descriptive longitudinal results." *Criminal Justice and Behavior* 19 (4) 1992a:409–25.

Zamble, E. "Personal communication relative to coping patterns among long-term prison inmates." (1992b).

Zamble, E., and F. Porporino. *Coping, Behavior and Adaptation in Prison Inmates.* New York: Springer-Verlag, 1988.

Zamble, E., and F. Porporino. "Coping, imprisonment, and rehabilitation: Some data and their implications." *Criminal Justice and Behavior* 17 1990:5–70.

Zamble, E., F. Porporino, and J. Kalotay. *An Analysis of Coping Behaviour in Prison Inmates.* Ministry of the Solicitor General of Canada: Programs Branch User Report, 1984.

5

❖

Prowling the Yard

The Public Culture of the Prison

Prisons readily become grim human warehouses, particularly in the absence of an explicit reform agenda. The modern prison, which as we have noted originated with the penitentiary, is no exception to this observation. "Once the ideal of prisoner reformation is abandoned," which has happened in most maximum-security prisons in this century, "the penitentiary becomes essentially a kind of storage warehouse for society's rejects."[1] The custodial warehouse prison has in fact been described as "the most persistent of any species of prison system."[2] This generic prison type both preceded and survived the penitentiary, and warehousing features persist today in at least some segments of virtually all contemporary prisons.

In the warehouse prisons before the penitentiary, storage involved a regime of undiluted idleness inside the walls and total isolation from family, friends, and others in the free world (see Chapter One). Physical brutality and psychological abuse were common. The procedures followed in twentieth-century warehouse prisons have been more accommodating. These prisons, whether they display specific characteristics of the Big House, the correctional institution, or the contemporary violent prison (see Chapter Three), permit some activity and conviviality among the prisoners, as well as fairly regular personal contact with the outside world in the form of visits and, more recently, furloughs and work-release programs. Such prisons are designated as storage enterprises because the limited activities allowed within them are, in the main, considered to be of little or no demonstrable benefit to the prisoner or society. One might say that they are warehouses more by default than by design: correctional aspirations linger, but no correctional agenda shapes the operation of today's prisons. In the absence of an explicit correctional mission, it is not uncommon for prisoners simply to be housed, clothed, fed, and kept under surveillance.[3]

In its twentieth-century form, the warehouse prison has evolved considerably. What was once a repressive but comparatively safe Big House is now often an unstable and violent social jungle,[4] though as is shown in Chapter Nine, there has been a drop in prison violence produced, in part, by administrative reforms. The twentieth-century warehouse prison has typically featured a smattering of correctional programs, though these are becoming rarer in today's crowded institutions, even as promising advances in treatment programs are noted by researchers and practitioners (see Chapter Ten). In extreme cases, which happily are few in number, our prisons have served *only* to hold and restrain. In such prisons, staff police the prison's periphery, and inmates "dominate the internal polity," with violence a fact of daily prison life.[5]

In all prisons, power is divided in some measure between the staff and the prisoners. The staff man the walls, at a minimum, and maintain a varying degree of order as inmates go through the formal routine of meals, counts, work, recreation, and sometimes correctional programs that the official prison day contains. The threat and occasional use of force are vivid testimony to the staff's power. Outside the formal schedule—on cell block tiers, in recreation areas, on the yard—the inmate body is "ceded a [degree] of self-rule" that may be more or less pronounced in any given prison.[6] Those who exploit this self-rule most visibly and violently are colloquially known as "convicts." They are not to be confused with nondescript inmates who, from the convicts' point of view, comprise a victim pool not unlike that of the general citizenry.[7] In the convict world, toughness and the capacity for violence define power, status, and honor. Here, in the public or mainline culture of the prisoners' prison, the worst of society's rejects create a world in which the prospect and often the reality of violence are facts of everyday life.

The male convict world, which has its symbolic home on the yard of the maximum-security prison, is the subject of this chapter. Two themes are explored. One is the change in the atmosphere of the convict world from one of violence restrained (in the Big House and, to a lesser extent, the correctional institution) to that of violence unleashed and sometimes out of control (in the contemporary violent prison). This is essentially a study in the evolution of the social system of the prison during this century. The second theme concerns the life and adjustment of state-raised convicts. These men have always been the most violent of the convicts. Whereas once they were a fringe element of the convict group, however, they have increasingly come to dominate today's prisons. In this study of the psychology of prison violence, these themes converge; for all that is immature and destructive about adjustment to the pains of prison life, both in inmate conduct and in the staff response, is shown in relief in the contemporary prison world of the state-raised convict. (We discuss the convict world in prisons for women at the end of the chapter, highlighting commonalities—and there are more than one would first suppose—shared by male and female convicts as they go about their daily lives in the prison community.)

THE MALE CONVICT CULTURE OF VIOLENCE

Violence has always been a salient aspect of the convict world. In many of today's prisons, however, the convict culture of violence is unusually pronounced. This was not the case in the Big Houses that dominated the prison scene from the turn of the century until the mid-1960s. There, rigid discipline kept inmate violence under control. Convict violence was also controlled in the penitentiary. In the original nineteenth-century penitentiaries and in twentieth-century Big Houses, the staff maintained a heavy-handed and often violent authority and inmates found their lives closely regulated. Of course, staff control on this order does not necessarily mean that inmates felt secure. It was not uncommon for prisoners to feel vulnerable to abuse by staff.

Crouch and Marquart's account of social control in Texas prisons during most of this century is instructive on this score. Texas featured plantation prisons rather than Big Houses, but their patterns of social control were carefully modeled after those found in Regan's Stateville, a traditional Big House.[8] This was particularly true in Huntsville Prison, the focus of Crouch and Marquart's study. Using *building tenders* (known as BTs) as a kind of inmate militia, officers in Texas's Huntsville Prison could orchestrate a regime of "relentless supervision" and almost total control.[9] If anything, the regime at Huntsville was more physically brutal than that found at Stateville, since the BTs were essentially given a free hand to discipline and control errant inmates as they saw fit:

> Building tenders enjoyed near limitless authority to maintain control. Keeping peace in the tanks [cell blocks] often involved 'set ups,' contrived evidence to injure another for some gain, and terrorism. They openly carried, with staff approval, clubs and knives to protect themselves as well as to threaten and intimidate other inmates.[10]

The BTs, moreover, explicitly understood themselves to be "organizationally sanctioned" agents of the officials, though no written policies authorized their brutal actions.[11] Like the BTs, Texas guards, notably the mounted field officers, used corporal punishment at will to maintain order in the fields, where inmates labored like plantation slaves "under the sun and under the gun" in a situation of virtually complete powerlessness.[12] In contrast, the officers at Stateville were more closely supervised and circumscribed, and the conditions of inmate labor, though hard, were considerably less brutal than found in Texas. Nevertheless, the role played by inmates in social control efforts at both prisons—as informants in Stateville and informants and enforcers in Huntsville—produced comparable climates of rigid discipline and suffocating routine.

Prisoners of Big Houses had less reason to fear one another than they do in today's less controlled prisons. Stateville's guards and Huntsville's BTs were successful in holding down the violence of regular inmates in the cell blocks and in the yard, at least by today's standards.[13] But many prisoners chafed against these controls and others were reduced to numb submission (see Chapter Three). Periodically, those who could not suppress their feelings erupted in emotional explosions. Discussing the rigid discipline at Stateville when it qualified as a Big House, Jacobs notes that "many inmates suffered emotionally and psychologically from this intense supervision. . . . Going 'stir bugs' was an everyday occurrence."[14]

Since inmate violence was relatively uncommon in the Big House, however, this gave the prison a stable and even placid exterior. The high-status convicts were courted by the prison administration and given positions of influence. They were the officers' clerks who could arrange cell transfers and even nightly assignations with "punks" or "queens"; they were also the runners who could move contraband and information around the prison. Troublemakers were routinely "salted away in segregation for as long as a decade."[15] Both the convict elite and the staff had a vested interest in stability and order. The regular inmate was admonished by guard and peer alike to keep his nose clean and do his own time. Congenial or at least stable accommodations of this sort between staff and prisoners are not as much in evidence today, and the social world of the prison has a more unstable and violent climate.[16] As a result, it is considerably harder to do one's own time in our contemporary prisons.

The Big House: Repression and Its Discontents

Stateville penitentiary was a typical Big House from the years of the Depression through the early 1960s. During this time, it was run by Joseph Ragen, an authoritarian warden whose penological philosophy was drawn with little modification from the nineteenth-century notion of the prison as a machine of discipline. This philosophy was implemented, appropriately enough, in the only American prison to embody Bentham's panoptical design, a series of circular tiers described by Foucault as the quintessential rendering of an architecture of power, "a dream building" in which surveillance of dependent and docile bodies is achieved in its ideal form.[17] Fittingly, observed Jacobs,

> Ragen maintained "that if you stress the small things, you will never have to worry about the big ones." Thus, under his fully elaborated system of administration the inmates were subjected to intense supervision under innumerable rules blanketing every aspect of prison life.[18]

As recently as 1960, "the silent system was enforced in the dining room and while marching in lines."[19] "The entire prison" during this era "functioned with Prussian punctuality."[20]

The Big House had few pretensions. It promised, and usually delivered, adequate food, hygiene, and housing. Many of these prisons were formally labeled "correctional institutions," particularly after World War II, but little that could pass for rehabilitation occurred within their walls. The Big House did not aim at transforming the character of its prisoners; yet there was the enduring hope, as in the first congregate penitentiaries, that obedience for its own sake, coupled with regular work, might ensure the conformity of convicts upon their release from prison:

> Ragen reasoned that the strictness of the Stateville regime would coerce the inmate into a conformity that would ultimately produce a respect for the rules. Through obedience to prison rules, the inmate would be resocialized. . . . A cardinal principle . . . [was to] keep every inmate working.[21]

Attributing correctional benefits to bald custodial control perhaps has always been more a rationalization than a rational correctional agenda. In any case, it simply reinforced the legitimacy of the authoritarian regime.

The formal routine of the Big House was often remarkably rigid and even oppressive. Like the penitentiaries that preceded them, the Big Houses were marked by a bell-ringing punctuality that made life there stiff and formal. However, in conjunction with the scheduled and ordered official prison world, "a complex, subtle, informal prisoner world with several subworlds was also operating."[22] This prisoner world had a code of conduct, prescribed social roles, and preferred ways of living. Its norms for correct deportment "pivoted around the convict code," which "could be translated into three rules: Do not inform, do not openly interact or cooperate with the guards or the administration, and do your own time."[23] Prisoners assumed stylized roles that reflected the values of the convict code and "were arranged in a hierarchy of prestige, power, and privilege."[24] The typical mode of adjustment was "to do your own time." This meant, above all,

> avoiding trouble . . . [and] avoiding "hard time." To avoid hard time, prisoners stayed active in sports, hobbies, or reading; secured as many luxuries as possible without bringing on trouble; and formed a group of close friends with whom to share resources and leisure hours and to rely on for help and protection.[25]

The model inmate was the right guy, a convict who stuck by his friends and did his time with a stoic and even exemplary calm. He embodied the notion that

> [t]he rigors of the inmate's world are to be met with a certain self-containment and excessive display of emotion is to be avoided at all costs. The prisoner should speak slowly and deliberately and he should move in the same fashion. Curiosity, anxiety, surprise—all are to be carefully curbed. Even too great a show of humor must be checked since there is the danger of being thought a clown or a buffoon. The prisoner, in short, is urged to "play it cool," to control all affect in a hard silent stoicism which finds its apotheosis in the legendary figure of the cowboy or the gangster.[26]

Yet the informal prisoner world of the Big House was not uniformly populated with right guys who pulled their time like real men. This social role was an ideal rather than a reflection of daily prison living. Victor Nelson, an inmate in a Big House prison, describes the most common type as a boorishly self-centered figure who played the role of the adolescent bad boy at play in the prison:

■ The egocentricity of the average prisoner is revealed in the most startling as well as in the most amusing ways. It is apparent in his brash loudness of voice, his pushing forward of himself and his views at every opportunity. When he is in line, he will crowd and shove his fellows (unless they are bigger than he is); at the table he will reach impolitely across his neighbor's place and grab the biggest or best portions of whatever is in sight; at the table he is inconsiderate and coarse, belching, feeding noisily, and generally revealing the table manners of a healthy pig.[27] ■

It is intriguing to note that Jean Harris paints a similar picture of life in Bedford Hills, a contemporary Big House prison for women. She found "childish egotism" to be the norm. Manners at the dinner table where on a par with those noted by Nelson. "Meals are simple affairs to me," states Harris with characteristic understatement. "I eat in my cell to avoid the prison dining room which has all the ambiance and charm of the Chicago stockyards."[28]

Nelson states emphatically that his porcine contemporaries displayed an "amazing callowness" and indeed were even "infantile" in their daily deportment, which departed sharply from the inmate code:

■ It goes without saying, of course, that in most prisons the admirable part of this code is more honored in the breach than in the observance. Men of high ideals, men with a personal code which is rigorously lived up to, are infinitely more scarce in prison than they are anywhere else.[29] ■

Honor was notable for its absence in culture of the Big House. "There is," writes Nelson a bit wistfully,

■ very little of that "honor among thieves" of which so much has been written. Thieves are, for the most part, pretty treacherous, double-dealing wretches, without a trace of glamour, and very different from the "gentleman thief," "Raffles," and other types beloved of crime-fiction writers and sentimentalists. The average convict, as a matter of fact, however loudly he may assert his adherence to the prison code, usually deems it proper to violate it if he can do so without getting caught and if in so doing he can advance his own interests.[30] ■

Loyalty, too, was scarce among the Big House convicts. "There are," states Nelson, "perhaps fifty or sixty inmates in the population of nine hundred who have any [but the] faintest notion of loyalty to their kind."[31] A fair number of inmates were sufficiently disloyal to become informants, a role that is the antithesis of the right guy and entails flagrant violation of the convict code. Indeed, the prevalence of "rats" in Stateville prison gave substance to Regan's celebrated claim, "Whenever you see three inmates standing together, two of them are mine."

The Big House, though possessed of an orderly social regime, displayed a fairly robust if controlled culture of violence. In a fight, Nelson makes clear, the aim was to win at any cost:

> When the average prisoner has an argument or fight with another inmate, he generally feels called upon to be as vindictive as possible, considering it a sign of weakness and efficacy to shake hands afterwards and make up the peace with his enemy. . . . There is very little good sportsmanship or sense of fair play, it being considered the essence of folly and weakness to give an enemy an even break. The idea is to win, to gain the advantage—no matter how.[32]

Such violence was tolerated and even encouraged by the convict code. The central tenet of the code—that prisoners should "do their own time"—meant that prisoners were to mind their own business when others were being attacked or exploited; this injunction even prohibited victims from invoking the aid of staff. The convict code thus served the interests of the elite and made it easier for them to ride roughshod over the other prisoners.

Prisoners who were not among the convict elite were open game for exploitation, and this included not only hustles and cons but also sexual and other kinds of coercion and violence. Seductions of young convicts would occur in open view; "wolves" would prowl the yard unimpeded by fellow convicts or guards. Nelson recounts the telling case of Dreegan, the undisputed "champion wolf" of Auburn Prison in the thirties:

> Now, whereas most "wolves" have the grace to be more or less discreet in their activity, Dreegan was quite frankly what he was. He went boldly after any young and good-looking inmate whom it was his desire to seduce. That he got a punch in the eye for his pains every so often, and was more than once knifed by boys defending themselves from his vigorous assaults did not disturb Dreegan for very long. He outrageously flattered the objects of his lust; he gave them cigarettes, candy, money, or whatever else he possessed which might serve to break down their powers of resistance. . . . Once the boy had been seduced, if he proved satisfactory, Dreegan would go the whole hog, like a Wall Street broker with a Broadway chorus-girl mistress, and squander all of his possessions on the boy of the moment. In this Dreegan was different from the average "wolf" only in the brazen directness of his conduct.[33]

Violence, ever a threat in these situations—to Dreegan, in this instance, but to unyielding targets in the case of other, less genteel "wolves"—was thoroughly unremarkable in the world of the Big House.

Most of the roles associated with this convict culture involved exploitation that was backed, explicitly or implicitly, by violence.[34] There were also periodic disturbances and riots, sometimes involving tremendous violence.[35] There was often an active market in illicit drugs, which would spur violence among groups to control markets or among individuals to secure drugs to ease their addictions. The presence of drugs, Nelson notes,

> ■ results in a great deal of friction among the prisoners themselves. Various cliques try to get control of the intramural drug trade. There are fights, often bloody and terrible to behold, not only among the professional vendors, but between prison addicts who accuse one another of "holding out" on the secret supply of drugs.[36] ■

Drugs not only corrupted the prisoners; they were also a source of corruption among officers. Poorly paid, the officers would take bribes to smuggle drugs into prison. This would "weaken the defenses of the prison" by reducing the independence and effectiveness of individual officers.[37] Beholden to drug dealers, they would turn a blind eye to all manner of deviance in the prison community.[38] Newspaper accounts and periodic scandals suggest that drug-related corruption, though by no means the norm in our contemporary prisons, may be worse today than during the Big House era.

The Big House was a setting of repressed and controlled behavior. Violence there had a patterned and sometimes even ritualized flavor. One could not wander through the cell blocks knifing people, as reportedly occurs in some prisons today, because one did not wander through the cell blocks at all! But one did carry weapons and sometimes used them, both in self-defense and to intimidate, control, and harm other prisoners. One could also menace and often successfully exploit others through carefully calculated postures and stares. Thus, violence and the threat of violence were key ingredients of prison life, and the capacity to stand up under the pressure this created was the substance of which real men ultimately were made.

The Decline of the Big House

The disciplined routine that both shaped and restrained overt violence in the Big House was periodically put to one side in favor of prison reform efforts, most notably in the self-governance experiments of Osborne and Gill.[39] (These reforms were implemented at the turn of the twentieth century during the heyday of the Big House. They produced an orderly prison, to be sure, but an order based on commitment rather than coercion.) When these reforms were scuttled, usually as a result of social and political forces unrelated to their penological merits, standard discipline was resumed.

The demise of the "repressive but reasonably safe" Big House had many causes.[40] One was the "rise of professional administration."[41] Professional administrators began to enter the prison service as early as the 1930s, though their impact was not fully felt until as late as the 1950s and 60s, with their influence extending through the mid-1970s. Typically, they were committed to the trappings, though not the substance, of rehabilitation.[42] They sought to infuse penal institutions with their own distinctive correctional ambiance.

Often, they did little more than take the discipline out of the Big Houses they inherited.

The management approach of correctional professionals emphasized human relations and sought a relaxed and almost collegial atmosphere. However, nowhere were these changes in prison climate backed by a regime of meaningful programs or opportunities for involvement in prison governance. It would seem that many of these administrators meant to make prisons less oppressive and nothing more, as if a lax prison regime were somehow also a humane one. As a result, reforms undertaken in the name of rehabilitation served to undermine the rigid discipline essential to the operation of the Big House prison, but they did not replace this discipline with a new basis for order. In the context of a correctional treatment climate, discipline appeared punitive and antitherapeutic; yet, in the absence of correctional treatment, there was no reason for inmates to follow the dictates of their keepers.

Another factor in the decline of the Big House was "the intrusion of the courts."[43] Again primarily in the 1960s and 70s, but continuing today in such prison systems as those of Texas and New Mexico, court rulings further restricted the use of authoritarian control strategies. As DiIulio has made clear,

> the doctrinal wall of separation between the judge's chambers and the prison's corridors has crumbled. The courts have intervened on a wide range of prison and jail issues, including crowding, food services, sanitation, health care, due process protections for inmates, and the constitutionality of prison and jail conditions "in their totality."[44]

The discipline of the Big House fell to a court-sanctioned revolt: inmates demanded—and to some extent won—more rights and freedoms, particularly in the areas of expression and association. The holdings in specific cases are not the issue; often these court decisions were "quite modest and even conservative."[45] Judges have been quite cautious in this matter. Even the most liberal reform judges, notes DiIulio, have

> approached institutional penal reform cases in the spirit evoked by these words from a federal circuit court decision handed down in 1988: "Judges are not wardens, but we must act as wardens to the limited extent that unconstitutional prison conditions force us to intervene when those responsible for the conditions have failed to act." Almost without exception, the judges have approached intervention as a necessary evil, not as a positive good.[46]

The larger point, however, is that court rulings gave "legitimacy to inmate protest against authoritarian rule" and hence "provided the ideological basis for a frontal attack upon the entire regime,"[47] an attack that continues, though in muted form, even today. Court holdings have thus contributed substantially to the erosion of custodial control of the prison. As such, they were—and are—resented by most correctional officers and administrators alike.[48]

The advent of professional administration and court intervention had immediate effects on some systems and delayed effects on others. For example,

Texas prisons were able to maintain many of the Big House trappings even into the early 1980s. (In English prisons, the essentials of the Big House were still in place as recently as 1992.)[49] Today, however, the rigid custodial routine that marked the operation of the Big House is a thing of the past in the vast majority of American prisons.[50] Today's prisons are, in the main, more relaxed in their discipline but often more dangerous in their daily operation. The iron hand of the custodian has all too often given way to a "rule of the cruel," with the hard-core convicts now setting the tone of prison life.[51]

Corrections Contained, Violence Unleashed

Most beleaguered prison officials fought to maintain order by resisting rehabilitation and prisoners' rights. Such negative tactics occurred to some degree in all prisons but were not the only means of maintaining order during the increasingly turbulent 1960s and 70s. Officials could have embraced these agendas and created a basis for a civil order in the prison. Correctional programs worth their salt can hold a man's attention and give him something constructive to do with his time. What a correctional system loses in externally imposed discipline can be compensated for by the self-discipline of those who are working for their own reform. Similarly, newly enfranchised inmates could be given a constructive role in shaping the conditions of their confinement, for instance, by means of experiments in self-governance. Again, inmate self-discipline would replace or supplement prison discipline. As a practical matter, however, few correctional programs of any substance emerged in these institutions, nor was there any broadscale attempt to work with inmates to give them some sense of responsibility for the quality of prison life. The promise of corrections—breached almost from the outset—produced a distinctive sense of injustice, and ultimately rage, directed at a prison system that was perceived to be patently hypocritical and manipulative.[52]

Thus, when rules and discipline were played down in most American prisons, ostensibly in the name of correctional treatment and out of respect for rights, what resulted was not a new order but a collapse of the old order. Guard morale and effectiveness fell; predatory behavior among inmates rose; there was a general decline in the conditions of prison life. It is indeed both tragic and ironic that the rehabilitative ideal and prisoners' rights, as implemented in most prisons during this period, "resulted in more violence, worse general living conditions, and fewer programmatic opportunities. The food was worse. There was more fear, more violence, and more sexual assault . . . inmates did more cell time."[53]

Together, relaxed discipline and increased rights reduced some of the pressures of daily life in the typical American prison and made that institution more responsive to individual concerns.[54] The deadening routine of the Big House was gone, for instance, and with it went the "pressure cooker" atmosphere that had made prison life so tense and occasionally explosive. But, as we have noted, these changes also produced a crisis of custodial authority and provided an opportunity for inmates to vent their frustration and anger at the failed correctional system. This crisis of authority and general climate of inmate aggressiveness gave predatory prisoners a free hand to exploit their neighbors. It also set the stage for the emergence of large and often violent gangs and militant groups (which have since proliferated).[55] Explaining rampant gang activity at Stateville during the late 1960s and early 70s, Jacobs observed:

> The abandonment [by the courts] of the "hands-off" doctrine exposed an authoritarian regime to outside accountability, limited the institution's recourse to coercive sanctions and provided the inmates with a legitimate means of expression with which to challenge the system of social control. The rise of professional administration, informed by the rehabilitative ideal and the human relations model of management, led to intrastaff conflict, a decline in the morale of the guard force, and ultimately to the deterioration of the organization's capacity to meet basic control and maintenance goals. It was only in the context of this organizational crisis that the gangs were able to organize, recruit, and achieve dominance.[56]

Similar organizational forces were at work at other prisons.[57] New York prisons, for example, followed a pattern like that of Stateville and the California prisons. Indeed, the infamous Attica riot of 1971 can be traced to failed correctional promises coupled with enhanced inmate freedoms and diminished custodial control. This explosive riot was caused not by the pressures of living in the Big House but, rather, by the pressures that came in the wake of the Big House.[58] Nor did subsequent reforms restore order to the troubled prisons. Sheehan notes that liberal "After Attica" reforms were implemented in New York State prisons between 1971 and 1976 in an effort to create a better correctional treatment climate and to make the institutions more responsive to prisoners' rights.[59] These reforms did in fact make the prisons increasingly less custodial—any traces of the Big House in the New York State prisons of this time were largely obliterated—but they did not make these prisons over into truly correctional institutions. As at Stateville and elsewhere (most notably in California prisons), there was an outraged sense of injustice that could not be contained by a weakened guard force. Again, there was an exploitation of this climate of aggression by the predators. Again, correctional reforms made the prisons considerably more dangerous. The result was, in Sheehan's words, a "breakdown of control."[60]

The growth of the black prisoner population in the 1960s and 70s added a racial element to prison tensions.[61] This was a time when "black rage" had surfaced in social movements in the free world, first in muted form in the civil rights movement, later in more virulent form in the black power movement.[62] Many prisoners drew inspiration from their angriest brethren on the streets, some of whom were subsequently incarcerated for standard felonies but who assumed the status of self-proclaimed political prisoners. The failure of correctional programs took on an almost conspiratorial tone; the larger "system" was rigged against the down-and-outs, the logic ran, and so was the correctional system.[63] Prisoner militancy and black power became synonymous at the outset of what has come to be known as "the prison movement." Clashes between militant black prisoners and the largely white prison authorities became increasingly commonplace. Violence against the staff took on an ominous character:

> Because of the prison movement, many more prisoners openly defied and physically attacked guards than in any period in the history of our prisons. In past eras, violence against guards or other staff members was extremely rare. Also, it was less random. When prisoners attacked guards, it invariably followed some hostile interaction between them. During the prison movement, guards were often randomly selected for attack. Defiance—which was always present, but had been more subtle or covert—became open and bold.[64]

Violence against fellow inmates, formerly "more subtle or covert," also became "open and bold." Militant prisoners were often not the dedicated and selfless revolutionaries they made themselves out to be.[65] More often than not, their commitment, like that of gang members and lone predators, was to violence and survival and not to radical social change.[66] As prisons became less controlled, these prisoners assaulted their peers as well as the staff.

As order yielded to disorder, violence and fear fed upon one another, producing a climate of terror. These forces were shown in relief in Walpole State Prison in Massachusetts in the early 1970s and, a decade later, in Texas prisons. In Walpole, a reform commissioner, riding the crest of legal changes in the rights of inmates, advocated civilian involvement in the monitoring of the prison. The notion that civilians could roam the cell blocks, observing and reporting on the behavior of officers, would have been entirely inconceivable during the Big House era and was a stunning blow to the morale of the line officers. Discredited from above by the commissioner and their warden (who supported this curious venture) and pressured by newly empowered convicts, the authority of the guards was profoundly compromised. The effectiveness of the officer force plummeted. The result was a drop in living conditions (the prison became deplorably dirty) and a rise in violence among inmates and between inmates and staff. Kauffman provides a telling description of the gruesome violence that became the order of the day at Walpole:

> While the inmates were locked in their cells for the night, one inmate began throwing flammable liquid on another inmate who had been asleep in the adjacent cell. For nearly fifteen minutes screams filled the block while the man methodically reached through the bars and doused his terrified quarry. On the undermanned night shift, no officers were in the area, only civilian observers. A frantic effort was made to find someone with keys to open the cells, or at least some fire extinguisher (there were none in the institution). Just as help finally arrived, the inmate tossed lighted matches through the cell door, instantly incinerating his victim and filling the block with smoke.
>
> Four days later an inmate was stabbed twenty times and his body flung from the second tier onto the concrete flats below. More assaults and

attempted murders followed. . . . [T]wo inmates reportedly attempted to hang themselves, four others slashed themselves in an apparent bid to be transferred out of the prison, and one inmate and two officers were assaulted. That night a sizable number of inmates refused to be locked in their cells in [a] dispute over shakedowns. State police were . . . asked to stand by.[67]

"Walpole prison," Kauffman concluded, "was in a state of virtual anarchy."[68] Officer and inmate alike lived in fear.

A similar state of affairs could be found in the Texas prison system following legal reforms undermining its custodial model of social control. The Ruiz decision, handed down in 1972 but resisted by obstinate prison officials for nearly a decade, eventually resulted in the demise of the notorious building tender system, and the imposition of sharp and carefully enforced limits on use of force by officers. Almost immediately, "the highly ordered inmate society began to crumble."[69] The quality of life dropped; dirt and disorder became the norm.[70] Inmate-on-inmate violence was so common that extortion became a kind of cottage industry, replete with the equivalent of service contracts. " 'We had one prison,' a Texas official observed, 'where we found actual written protection policies. $49 a month for complete security, $29 a month for cuts and bruises, that sort of thing.' "[71] Inmates without such protection were left to their own devices. Said one Texas inmate,

> Today there's no more protection without the BTs. You're on your own. You're either gonna survive or perish. No matter which way, it's up to you. . . . You take care of yourself. That's how a convict makes it here.[72]

Once again officers too lived in fear, since in the absence of BTs they had to deal directly with restive and hostile inmates.

Increasingly, violence among inmates took on racial connotations, with formerly repressed black inmates rising to positions of dominance within the prison culture. This reversal of white convict dominance, evident at virtually every prison of this era and continuing today,[73] was particularly salient in the Texas prison system:

> Once the BTs were removed . . . [the] status quo among prisoners changed. Long-repressed racial animosities and hatreds rose to the surface of everyday interactions as minority prisoners began to exert themselves. Blacks, for example, soon dictated television programming and controlled the benches and the domino tables in the dayrooms. Not only did blacks effectively take over in many cellblocks, but they also began to exploit white prisoners.[74]

During this period, the guards in the trenches of our nation's prisons, the vast majority of whom were white, refrained from enforcing the rules in order to avoid conflict; others intervened in aggressive and insensitive ways, including resorting to outright violence and brutality, which served merely

to escalate tensions.[75] Officers with seniority (and presumably the competence to mediate those conflicts properly) elected administrative assignments
or retreated to the towers on the prison walls, far from the dangers of the cell
blocks and the yard.[76] "A general maxim about Walpole," Kauffman observed,
"would have been the greater an officer's experience, the less he had to do
with inmates."[77] This maxim would have applied to many other prisons as
well, notably those in New York, California, and Texas.

   The inexperienced officers running these violent prisons were disproportionately drawn from the ranks of women and minorities, who had been newly
recruited to prison work. These guards entered prisons during a period of turmoil and were resisted by white male officers along with other changes
imposed from outside the prison. In fact, the arrival of female and minority
officers (including, of course, some female minority officers) was seen as part
of the general loss of power to the courts and to central offices of increasingly
bureaucratic prison systems. In the words of one disgruntled officer, mixing
racism and sexism with raw alienation:

■   What will they think of next? They've lowered the standards so anybody
    can get in. First they brought in these minorities; some of them can
    hardly sign their name. Now we've got these women who can't even
    protect themselves. How do they expect us to run a prison? Next thing
    you know, they'll be bringing kids in here to control inmates. We might
    as well give the inmates the keys to the place and go home.[78] ■

Informal accommodations between staff and inmates broke down during
the prisons of this time, in part because seasoned officers were nowhere in evidence. The absence of such officers undermined the various licit and illicit
opportunity systems, noted earlier, that had given stability to the convict culture
of the Big House. With little reason to conform to staff directives or even to
negotiate compromise solutions to problems with the frightened novice officers
manning the key areas of the prison, cell blocks and yards, violence became the
order of the day and the preferred mode of adjustment among the convicts.[79]

   For their part, regular inmates (who now included some prisoners who
would have counted themselves among the convicts of earlier days) assiduously
avoided the public areas of the prison.[80] Many fled to protective custody cells,
which were filled in record numbers.[81] In effect, the prison was given over to
the most predatory convicts, who often prowled the yard in gangs. Gone was
the notion that prisoners should be "right guys" who did their time in the
company of a few "main men" and who respected like-minded "regulars." The
violent convict and his clique of thugs became the leaders of the yard:

    Today the respected public prison figure—the convict or hog—stands
    ready to kill to protect himself, maintains strong loyalties to some small
    group of other convicts (invariably of his own race), and will rob and
    attack or at least tolerate his friends' robbing and attacking other weak
    independents or their foes. He openly and stubbornly opposes the
    administration, even if this results in harsh punishment. Finally, he is

extremely assertive of his masculine sexuality. . . . To circulate in this world, the convict world, one must act like a convict and, with a few exceptions, have some type of affiliation with a powerful racial clique or gang.[82]

If it is true that a society gets the criminals it deserves, it is also true that we get the prisons we deserve. Years of turmoil and violence within our prisons have been met by the larger society with indifference and neglect. Unsurprisingly, we find ourselves the reluctant landlords of prisons that harbor a frightening potential for mean-spirited and unregenerate violence. As Colvin makes clear, the Penitentiary of New Mexico is just such a prison today. The riot at that prison at the close of the violent 1970s, which claimed the lives of thirty-four prisoners and resulted in serious physical injuries for another two hundred inmates, as well as seven of the twelve officers taken hostage, has come to symbolize modern prisons at their worst.[83] Events over the intervening years since that riot serve to confirm New Mexico's image as a tough, violent prison.

We can and often do run prisons that are better, much better, than the Penitentiary at New Mexico (a host of viable prison reforms are explored in the concluding section of this book). But, as Colvin points out, apathy and indecision—and then, frustration and rage—too often guide prison policy. The larger social forces constraining the prison can be formidable, and this, in turn, can leave prison administrators feeling there is little they can do to run a decent prison. An economy with a declining base of working-class jobs (as opposed to low-paying service jobs, which barely provide a living) seems almost to demand warehouse prisons, whose agenda is merely to contain surplus and essentially useless unskilled and unmotivated workers. As the body count rises and the cell blocks become more and more crowded, those prisons are too readily treated like political footballs—courts may confer rights and professionals may promise treatment, but disorder too often overcomes good intentions, yielding grim environments marked by violence and fear. Tales of abuse flourish, but few people outside the prison hear or care. An increasingly punitive public captures the attention of politicians, who lengthen sentences, shorten bottom lines, and call for increasingly spartan prison regimes. Resources shrink, frustrations mount, conditions worsen. Living through this process, Dannie Martin observed: "Somewhere between the closing of our yard and the inexorable tightening-down on small privileges, the prison is evolving from a boring but mellow place to a caldron of fear, hatred, and violence."[84] Under such conditions, staff have low morale, inmates little cohesion, and few people—staff or inmate—treat anyone with simple human compassion. Everyone lives in fear, and rage lurks just beneath the surface of daily prison life. Ultimately, the rage explodes forth, exploiting preexisting breaches in prison security to foment raw anarchy and violent death in the time-honored ritual of the prison riot. Sadly, prison riots have become disturbingly common.[85]

This last point—that riots exploit preexisting weaknesses in the prison security—is mundane but important. Scholars like DiIulio discount the value of studying the social structure of inmate and staff relations (not to mention the larger societal context in which prisons operate), maintaining that prison

problems such as individual and collective violence are *caused* by failures of
prison security.[86] Prisons hold bad people, so the logic runs, and they will
behave badly if we let them. If we run a tight ship, the logic continues, prisons
will run smoothly.

Colvin puts this simplistic view to rest. The Penitentiary of New Mexico
has always been plagued by poor management and lapses in basic security procedures, but relations between staff and inmates were, for much of the prison's
history, quite orderly. For much of the history of the Penitentiary of New
Mexico, staff were willing to accommodate reasonable inmate demands, and
inmates were able to achieve a fairly high level of organization, which they
used to maintain order and stability within the prison community. (Violence
among inmates occurred, of course, but it was sporadic; inmate leaders, out of
self-interest, tried to keep such violence to a minimum. This connection
between inmate cohesion and social order has been noted by others, particularly Gresham Sykes, and is artfully documented by Colvin.) Staff relations
with inmates turned coercive at the Penitentiary of New Mexico over the
course of the 1970s but only after informal sources of order eroded and finally
broke down, mostly along the general lines described by Irwin for other American prisons during this period of turmoil (discussed earlier). The effect of
coercive staff behavior was to divide but not conquer the now-restive convicts.
Instead, heavy-handed approaches by the staff, often featuring violence, were
mirrored within the increasingly fragmented prisoner society. Staff coercion, in
other words, bred coercion among the inmates and, ultimately, between
inmates and staff. Violence, in particular, proved contagious. When invoked by
the staff as a substitute for social control, violence did not produce conformity; it fed on itself, producing more violence in turn. In this explosive context,
failures of security became fatal organizational flaws.

The convict culture of violence, so evident in the Penitentiary of New
Mexico, may be more or less prevalent in any particular prison today. Its coercive power may be supplemented by other types of power available to inmates,
Stojkovic makes clear, most notably that associated with resources (such as
drugs), expertise (jailhouse lawyers and writ writers), and ego building (by
means of ethnic and religious awareness groups).[87] Nevertheless, this culture of
violence is always present in some degree and always shapes the daily life and
adjustment of prisoners. State-raised convicts—men reared on rejection and
abuse in orphanages, detention centers, training schools, and youth prisons—
have come to epitomize this culture of violence.

PRISON VIOLENCE
AND THE STATE-RAISED CONVICT

State-raised convicts have always been bitter and prone to violence. In the Big
House, their violence was held largely in check by discipline. Many of these
prisoners adapted by being cagey and cool—by becoming institutionalized,

and saving their overt violence for their periodic excursions to the free world. Jimmy Dunn, a state-raised convict who served his time during the Big House era, is typical of this class of prisoner:

> ■ I want nothing from the state that they want to give me. All I want is the opportunity to hate them and to destroy everything they stand for and everyone who gets in my way. . . . I'm going to do everything I can, all my life, to beat them, rob them, lie, and con them. I'm going to beat them at their own game. I'll play it like they want it while they've got their eyes on me; but as soon as they turn their backs, or can't see me, I'll kill something that someone thinks is good.[88] ■

Dunn plays the prison game, biding his time until he gets out from under the heel of authority, whereupon he can be the hasty and destructive hedonist he longs to be. It is telling that even his reveries of life in the free world have a violent edge to them. On release, says he,

> ■ I'm going to kill them out there! All that good money from bad women or bad money from good women, it don't make no difference. I'm going to rip-and-tear and have a ball. I'm going to shoot junk, pimp whores, and tear holes in business roofs and live life the way it was meant to be lived. The world's mine and I'm going to kill them dead.[89] ■

State-raised convicts like Dunn are less easily controlled today.[90] Those who, like Dunn, spent their formative years in Big House prisons are also less able to adapt to today's prisons. It is telling that upon his return to confinement in the late 1960s, Dunn found California's prisons, then racked with gang- and other group-related forms of violence, to be unlivable. Out of place in a prison that was so different from the more controlled prisons he had known, Dunn took his life.

It is almost certainly the case that at least some state-raised convicts adapt to today's prisons nonviolently, presumably by becoming institutionalized, much like their predecessors in Big House prisons. Over time, these prisoners, like virtually all prisoners, find themselves better suited to prison life than to life on the outside and are able to get by with less effort and less trouble.[91] State-raised convicts who are serving long terms, for example, often adapt as do the vast majority of lifers, by making the most of the legitimate resources and lifestyles available within the prison community.

It is primarily the aggressive and, if you will, unpacified state-raised convicts who have displayed the tough but accommodating "right guy" as the hero of the prison yard, and it is this group of state-raised convicts that is the subject of our analysis in the remainder of this chapter. They typically come to prison as angry young men; over time, their anger remains unmollified, though it may be punctuated by periods of depression and boredom.[92] Angry, disgruntled, and alienated from the legitimate options such as work and education offered in the prison, these prisoners make their home on the prison yard, where they come to yield considerable—and violence-suffused—power among their fellow prisoners.[93] They have made today's prison a dangerous place for staff and fellow prisoner alike. It is they who, by their violence, intimidate other prisoners and who, again through violence, find themselves embroiled with the custodial staff. They are the prison's bastard children, and this unhappy status brings out the worst in both the prisoners and the prison. They are easily provoked to violence by the stresses of prison life, and in turn they provoke the prison staff to use violence and even brutality to maintain law and order behind bars. Predictably, they find themselves, to quote one of their more famous members, "in the belly of the beast."

Life in the Belly of the Beast

Sociological portraits of the state-raised convict depict him as a man at home in the prison, inured to its abuses and coldly dispensing violence to achieve his selfish ends. He typically moves in predatory cliques, but whether alone or in gangs he is adept at exploiting the weak and defenseless. He finds sexual gratification in the violation of other men; paradoxically, these encounters prove his manliness. He succeeds as a convict because the prison is the only world he knows:

> He was raised in a world where "punks" and "queens" have replaced women, "bonaroos" [specially pressed prison outfits] are the only fashionable clothing, and cigarettes are money. This is a world where disputes are settled with a pipe or a knife, and the individual must form tight cliques for protection. His senses are attuned to iron doors banging, locks turning, shakedowns, and long lines of [uniformed] convicts. He knows how to survive, in fact prosper, in this world, how to get a cell change and a good work assignment, how to score for nutmeg, cough syrup, or other narcotics. More important, he knows hundreds of youths like himself who grew up in the youth prisons and are now in the adult prisons.[94]

State-raised convicts adapt to prison life and even dominate the public culture of the prison, but they are by no means immune to the pains and deprivations of confinement. In fact, many of these men are deeply scarred by a life of imprisonment, and these wounds are apparent in the lives they lead in the prison world.

The most striking thing about state-raised convicts is their facade of adult maturity, their veneer of cool, hard manliness. Yet this demeanor and their sometimes casual use of violence are not badges of strength but tragic testimony to the violence prison has done to them. They were reared in a world where they were susceptible to flagrant abuse. More than other prisoners, they know in their guts what it means to be locked up—to be "helpless and vulnerable" and hence at the "matrix of disaster" while in the arms of the law. In the words of Jack Abbott, in many ways a prototype of the state-raised convict,

■ He who is state-raised—reared by the state from an early age after he is taken from what the state calls a "broken home"—learns over and over

and all the days of his life that people in society can do anything to him
and not be punished by the law. Do anything to him with the full force
of the state behind them.[95] ■

Abbott speaks with some authority in this matter for, sad to say, Abbott's
credentials as a state-raised youth are unimpeachable.[96] His life is a study in
neglect and abuse, in the free world and in the prison.[97] His parents separated
when he was quite young, breaking up what was a turbulent and no doubt
abusive home. He was passed from one foster home to another over a period
of years, during which time he was physically beaten and sexually abused. He
dropped out of school after the sixth grade. Within a year, "he was committed to the Utah State Industrial School for Boys for 'failing to adjust.' He was
twelve years old. He stayed there until his release at age eighteen."[98] His
adjustment never improved. If anything, his lengthy stay in training school—
most juveniles serve short terms—indicates that his adjustment worsened
over time.

Abbott's marginal adjustment to life continued into adulthood. On release,
he developed a drinking problem. He issued fraudulent checks, for which he
was sent to prison. In prison, as a young adult, he appears to have fully cultivated his propensity to violence:

> While serving his court-imposed sentence, Abbott stabbed another
> inmate to death for informing on him. He was convicted and sent back
> to prison with an additional twenty years, but not before throwing a
> water pitcher at the judge and trying to choke one of the jurors.[99]

At one point, Abbott escaped from prison, robbed a bank, and was confined
once again with an additional nineteen years to serve. At this point, his fate was
sealed. He was truly a state-raised man, a product of institutions. "Uncaring and
impersonal, each of these institutions compounded and passed on responsibility for the problem."[100]

A substantial part of "the problem" in Abbott and in other state-raised convicts is chronic defensiveness. Abbott assumes a tough and menacing pose
because he is angry and frightened and because he sees no other way to keep
a hostile and rejecting world at bay. And because this world is almost a caricature of the abusive worlds that spawn the chronic felons who later come to
share adult prisons with him (see Chapter Four), the state-raised convict typically becomes the most impulsive of prison's hasty hedonists, the most cunning
and lethal of its jungle cats.

The state-raised convict's predatory pose has a distinctively adolescent
character—and for good reason. Prison life equates the normal dependency
of childhood with vulnerability and makes adult independence impossible.
Life on these terms is likely to leave the prisoner emotionally stunted, a per-
petual, impulsive adolescent. "You hear a lot about 'arrested adolescence'
nowadays," observes Abbott, "and I believe this concept touches the nub of the
instability of prisoners like myself."[101] The state-raised prisoner, Abbott continues, does not have a chance to mature normally. "As a boy in reform school,

he is punished for being a little boy. In prison, he is punished for trying to be a man." At best, "he is treated as an adolescent in prison."[102]

Abbott's point has been made before, notably by Sing Sing's Warden Lawes, who quotes an English penal authority who observed that "the trouble with the American Reformatory idea"—an idea that shaped many of the prisons that shaped Abbott—"was that it made youths out of adults and adults out of youths, subjecting both to all the odious and cruel oppressions that prevailed in prisons for men steeped in crime and viciousness."[103] More recently, Zamble, Porporino, and Kalotay's research supports Abbott's analysis of the chronic prisoner's adolescent character. "Imprisonment," they found,

> deprives people of the usual experience necessary for the development of coping, and in this way it freezes development at the point when a person enters the institution. Thus, we can see why the behavior of habitual offenders resembles that of adolescents in many ways, e.g., in the dependence on peer groups, emphasis on physical dominance, and [a] generally impulsive behavioral style. It also follows that imprisonment at an early age will have more effect on subsequent behavior than at a later time, since that is when the greater development is normally occurring. Finally, we can also predict that those who have spent the most time in prison will be those who cope most poorly when they are on the outside.[104]

The result for the state-raised convict, in Abbott's words, is that "he lacks experience and, hence, maturity. His judgment is untempered, rash; his emotions are impulsive, raw, unmellowed."[105]

The "raw" emotions of the state-raised convict are not those of the typical adolescent, however. Unlike adolescents in the free world, prison's adolescents have never been taken seriously or cared for as individuals. These prisoners, then, are not only consigned to a lifetime of adolescence, a painful experience in itself, but are also burdened with chronic self-doubt, the often crippling corollary of rejection that reads, "I must be unlovable if I am unloved; I must be bad to be treated badly." Moreover, it is likely that this self-doubt will escalate over time and become personally disabling. A lifetime in prison means emotional and sometimes physical abuse. These experiences produce a legacy of impotent rage (because one is helpless to defend oneself) and ultimately self-hatred (a product of one's sense of shame and contamination). The result, in Abbott's view, is a kind of "prison paranoia" that reduces one's life to a daily struggle to maintain sanity and self-control:

> When I walk past a glass window in the corridor and happen to see my reflection, I get angry on impulse. I feel shame and hatred at such times. When I'm forced by circumstances to be in a crowd of prisoners, it's all I can do to refrain from attack. I feel such hostility, such hatred, I can't help this anger. All these years I have felt it. Paranoid. I can control it. I never seek a confrontation. I have to intentionally gauge my voice in a conversation to cover up the anger I feel, the chaos and pain just beneath

the surface of what we commonly recognize as reality. Paranoia is an illness I contracted in institutions. It is not the reason for my sentences to reform school and prison. It is the effect, not the cause.[106] ■

To my knowledge, Abbott has never been diagnosed as a paranoid psychotic, though this diagnosis is unusually common among prison populations.[107] Yet Abbott is, like all paranoids, profoundly self-centered; his fragile sense of self is always hanging in the balance. His personality is marred by suspicion of others, doubt in himself, and an ugly festering rage and hate that touch virtually everything and everyone in his world. There is no rest for Abbott, no chance to let his defenses down. His image in the mirror is simply a poignant reflection of the continuing struggle he must wage against the pain of the prison world and the hurt he carries within himself.

Prisons thus raise men who are as much at war with themselves as with the world around them. On both fronts they are threatened: internally, with the knowledge of their inadequacy; externally, with the knowledge of their vulnerability. Failure in social encounters, even the slightest hint of defeat, at once exposes their weaknesses to themselves and others. To guard against this, they must avenge even the slightest insult that might cast doubt on their manliness, brook any authority that would curtail their sense of self. To do less, as they see it, is to be demeaned as a man.[108]

The difficulty is that encounters in which such a fragile notion of dignity might be shattered are quite common in prison. Prisoners vie for status and routinely make invidious comparisons among themselves; guards issue and enforce countless orders every day. Under this continuing assault upon their self-esteem—for state-raised convicts, such encounters feel like personal attacks—state-raised convicts readily come to see themselves as innocent victims of an arbitrary world who have no choice but to strike out in their own defense. Their behavior is, for the most part, wildly disproportionate to the objective pressures at hand. Sadly, their justifications for their conduct are transparently false and self-serving to everyone but themselves.

Perhaps the root of the problem with state-raised convicts, and why so many of them appear as pathetic but dangerous adolescents, is that they simply cannot see the world from the other person's point of view. At best, others emerge as pale reflections of their own inner worlds, as persons distorted by the same forces that shaped and ultimately distorted the prisoners themselves. Thus Abbott sees others as contemptible, just as he holds himself in contempt, and as sources of danger, just as he knows the danger within himself. The state-raised youth's dealings with others routinely involve manipulation and deception; that is, he believes, what others deserve and what is required to succeed in life. Yet these stratagems typically fail, at least in one's dealings with other savvy state-raised convicts, and hence one must fall back on violence as the final measure of worth.

Prisoners like Abbott are all the more dangerous, moreover, because the lesson they learn from their redundant interpersonal failures is that violence is in fact their *only* means of becoming men of consequence who are taken seriously. Life is reduced to an either/or proposition: either you or me. As a result, these men have a personal stake in violence, and they protect it jealously. Thus Abbott speaks almost reverently of

> the high esteem we naturally have for violence, force. It is what makes us effective, men whose judgment impinges on others, on the world: Dangerous killers who act alone and without emotion, who act with calculation and principles, to avenge themselves, establish and defend their principles with acts of murder that usually evade prosecution by law; this is the state-raised convicts' conception of manhood, in the highest sense. . . . Here in prison the most respected and honored men among us are those who have killed other men. . . . It is not merely fear, but respect.[109]

One such prisoner bragged to a television reporter about the raw, brutal violence he had used to kill a guard, who had been chosen at random, merely to impress other convicts. He concluded by saying, on camera, "This has just begun for me. I'm only thirty-one years old. I got a lot of bodies to collect yet."[110]

Abbott sees his violence as a dignified—one might say almost solemn—obligation of manhood. This self-serving view is no doubt shared by other convicts and helps them to glorify their explosive tantrums. (If this sounds harsh, remember that Abbott himself traced the "nub" of his character to "arrested adolescence.") This violence does in fact command respect from other prisoners but on the grounds that its authors are the most unrestrained, emotionally immature, and hence dangerous men in the institution. There is even an awareness among the prisoners that this behavior reflects a kind of mental instability not far from Abbott's conception of prison paranoia. In the words of Schroeder, an ex-inmate,

> if you clearly didn't care, if you could convince inmates and guards that you had absolutely nothing to lose and that your countermeasures to even the most trivial provocation would be totally unrestrained and pursued to the utmost of your abilities—then you were given respect and a wide berth, and people looked to you for leadership and advice. "He's crazy," they'd say admiringly, even longingly, when the name came up. "He's just totally, completely insane."[111]

Hence it is that the prisoners who are least equipped for life in the civil world set the tone of adjustment on the prison yard.[112]

The threat of violence, even lethal violence, is a salient norm in the convict world. It begins at the point of entry into the prison, when the young convict must protect himself from the predations of others. But the use of violence to establish one's manly image never stops here, even if one humiliates one's opponents.[113] Violence continues because there is no mechanism within the convict culture that allows prisoners to make peace with one another, to break with the violence of the past and embark on a nonviolent future. Convicts, ever

on the defensive, feel they must draw lines in the prison yard, as it were, demar-
cating that point beyond which others cannot cross for fear of retaliatory violence; to do less is to live without principle or honor in the prison community.[114] The difficulty is that, for many convicts, the very presence of such lines
is an open invitation to test the prisoner's mettle, to see if he will in fact defend
himself. The drawing and crossing of lines of permissible behavior occur endlessly in the prison community, leaving in their wake a history of insult and
retaliation that seems endless. An appreciation for this process may help us
understand how, for example, rape can become a natural accompaniment to a
fight—sexual domination makes the physical domination of the fight seemingly complete:

> A muscular African-American man of average size from the general
> population at a high-security prison tells me that in the holding tank on
> the way to prison he got into a fight with another man, beat him up,
> banged his head on the concrete a few times, and then sodomized him. I
> asked why he had to commit rape after winning the fight. First he tells
> me, with a laugh, it was because he was horny . . . he adds that wasn't
> really it, "It's just that's what you gotta do—if you don't do it, you haven't
> really won the fight."[115]

It may well be that few rape victims avenge themselves, yet one cannot be
sure. It is certainly the case that, as a general matter, past traumas, hurts, and
slights live on in the closed world of the prison, crying out for revenge. Thus
is the theme of a poem, written by Ed Lipman, a prisoner, and aptly entitled
"Because Our Past Lives Every Day."[116] Frank, the protagonist, lives in a world
in which time is a seamless, suffocating web and in which violence lives and
breathes in the prison yard, waiting to pounce on a man to avenge acts he'd
like to leave behind him:

■ They wrapped Big Frank in plaster
   and put him on a bed
   to heal
   & watch
   each approaching stranger
   with dangerous eyes . . .
   The cops assigned
   to guard his door
   can't understand
   that what's become
   the past to them
   can be heard breathing
   softly on The Yard
   thru the eerie quiet
   of this prison hospital
   early in the dawn.

But Frank knows better;
he's learned today
is as much a part
of yesterday as is tomorrow;
and that there are
no innocent bystanders . . . ■

The convict world is populated by men who doubt their worth as human beings and who feel they must constantly find occasions to "prove" themselves. In this world, there is no such thing as an accident, and hence "there are no innocent bystanders." Here, Lipman continues, "paranoia is nothing more than increased awareness."[117] While an apology may often suffice to resolve a conflict among regular inmates,[118] being a convict is, apparently, never having to say you are sorry and certainly never accepting an apology at face value because it is almost certainly a ploy, a trick. For convicts, every insult is premeditated, a planned assault demanding a vengeful response that provides tangible evidence of one's worth. The only proofs of worth that matter in this context are those that entail the subjugation of other men.

The convict world is a world of continuing—and generally escalating— conflict. Aggrieved parties cannot afford to back down, for then they are seen as weak and hence vulnerable to more abuse. Violence in the convict world establishes one's competence as a man who can survive in a human jungle. The ultimate paradox of this world is that only lethal violence can truly assure one's peace of mind:

■ To a prisoner it is an insult to grapple hand-to-hand with anyone. If someone ever strikes him with his hand (another prisoner), he has to kill him with a knife. If he doesn't, he will be fistfighting with him everyday. He might be killed. . . . All violence in prison is geared for murder, nothing else. You can't have someone with ill feelings for you walking around. He could drop a knife in you any day. . . . [Y]ou are not killing in physical self-defense. You're killing someone in order to live respectably in prison. Moral self-defense.[119] ■

As simple and straightforward as this code of violence may be, the notion that, when in doubt, one should hurt or kill one's neighbor produces a bleak and solitary prison "community" in which "most prisoners fear almost every other prisoner around them."[120] In fact, in the convict world,

■ Everyone is afraid. It is not an emotional, psychological fear. It is a practical matter. If you do not threaten someone at the very least someone will threaten you. When you walk across the yard or down the tier to your cell, you stand out like a sore thumb if you do not appear either callously unconcerned or cold and ready to kill. Many times you have to "prey" on someone, or you will be "preyed" on yourself. After so many years, you are not bluffing. No one is.[121] ■

In the convict world, day-to-day relations among prisoners are at best distant and tense, with simple coexistence a major achievement. One is vividly reminded of Sartre's notion of hell as a circumscribed world with "no exit" and hence no escape from people you hold in contempt:

■ You don't comfort one another; you humor one another. You extend that confusion about this reality of one another by lying to one another. You can't stand the sight of each other and yet you are doomed to stand and face one another every moment of every day for years without end. You must bathe together, defecate and urinate together, eat and sleep together, talk together, work together.[122] ■

To be sure, other prisoners may feel less bitter than Abbott, but the quality of their interpersonal relations with fellow prisoners is often much the same (see Chapter Four).

Relations between convicts and staff are, if anything, even worse. (There is no exit here either.) Convicts' perceptions of guards are suffused with resentment. Officers are hacks who comprise a monolithic caste of oppressors; the convicts are their hapless victims. The standard notion that is "us" against "them" does not fully capture the animosity the state-raised convict feels toward his keepers. "Us" against "that" comes closer to the mark:

■ Among themselves, the guards are human. Among themselves, the prisoners are human. Yet between these two the relationship is not human. *It is animal.* Only in reflection—subjective reflection—do they acknowledge sharing a common consciousness. What is that common consciousness? It is the consciousness that we belong to a *common species* of life. But this is not the consciousness of society. It is not humanistic; *it is animalistic.*

What I am saying is that the prisoner is closer to humanity than the guard: because he is *deprived* by the guard. That is why I say that evil exists—not in the prisoner, but in the guard. Intentions play none but an illusory role. *In fact,* the guard is evil. His *society* is demonic. I don't care if he likes the same food I do or the same music—or whatever: this is the illusory role intentions play. Animals can enjoy the same music or food we do.[123] ■

It is almost as if the state-raised convict is impelled into destructive encounters with his keepers. When they treat him in a standard but impersonal way, this is an affront. When they vary their treatment of prisoners, they are revealed as arbitrary tyrants.[124] One senses that guards, by the very exercise of authority, imperil the state-raised convict's tenuous sense of autonomy. The prisoner's only course of action, then, is to rebel and deny the possibility of legitimate prison authority—to "beat the man" by breaking every rule you can, all the while nurturing an unremitting hatred for them and everything they stand for.[125] This stance has both tragic and comic elements, and both are grasped by Abbott:

■ It's impossible. I'm the kind of fool who, facing Caesar and his starving lions, need only retract a statement to walk away scot-free but instead cannot suppress saying "fuck you" to Caesar—knowing full well the consequences. What is more, *I refuse to be martyred;* I don't accept the consequences, and whine all the way to my death. A death, it seems, that I chose.

If I *could* please Caesar, I would, I gladly would. It's a fucked-up world, but it's all I got.[126] ■

The punishment system within the prison that is invoked to handle these degenerating encounters is, as the state-raised convict sees it, by definition a sham, a mockery of any notion of justice.[127] The prisoner knows himself to be helpless before a powerful and malevolent opponent whose goal is to crush one's manhood. Still, he rebels and gets the worst punishments prisons have to offer. This includes, in at least some instances, flagrant acts of brutality.

Abbott, for instance, records a litany of punishments comprised of lengthy solitary confinement, mind-altering drugs, and overt physical violence.[128] These punishments have almost certainly been embellished with time, but the more important point is that in no instance can Abbott see his own role in precipitating these abuses, even though he freely admits to insulting and even attacking "the pigs" at will. Nor can he put himself in the shoes of his punishers or even acknowledge the pain and rage that move them to primitive violence. Always he is utterly innocent; always they are unremittingly brutal. He suffers—and he does suffer—but somehow they only mete out pain. If he errs at all, as Abbott sees things, it is in being too stubbornly faithful to the convict code of manliness even as he nurses his wounds:

■ There is a saying: *The first cut is the deepest.* Do not believe that. The first cut is nothing. You can spit in my face once or twice and it is nothing. You can take something away that belongs to me and I can learn to live without it.

But you cannot spit in my face every day for ten thousand days; you cannot take all that belongs to me, one thing at a time, until you have gotten down to reaching for my eyes, my voice, my hands, my heart. You can't do this and say it is nothing.

I have been made oversensitive—my very *flesh* has been made to suffer sensations and longings I never had before. I have been chopped to pieces by a life of deprivation of sensations; by beatings so frequent I am now a piece of meat and bone; by lies and by drugs that attack my nervous system. I have had my mind turned into steel by the endless smelter of *time* in confinement.

I have been twisted by justice the way other men can be twisted by love.[129] ■

The hurt generated by these encounters seems endless, and still there is no effort on Abbott's part to learn from them, to approach problems differently in the future.

THE PATHOS OF PRISON VIOLENCE

State-raised convicts like Jack Abbott live in a bleak and threatening prison world. Mostly, these men simply endure the various indignities and slights that make up their daily round of prison life. When the opportunity arises, they abuse others in turn, perpetuating the very cycle of violence that has marred their lives. They do not learn new and constructive ways of confronting problems. They bend because they have to and are weakened in the process. In the end, they meet the prison world on its own terms, by suppressing their feelings and acting tough.

Their tough-guy stance is really just a facade. As McCall has observed, drawing on his own prison experience, even the toughest guys on the yard, with rare exceptions, are "really frightened boys, bluffing, trying to mask their fear of the world behind muscular frames."[130] Beneath the hard exterior is a tender core of vulnerability and pain. In Abbott's words,

■ So we can all hold up like good soldiers and harden ourselves in prison. But if you do that for too long, you lose yourself. Because there is something helpless and weak and innocent—something like an infant deep inside us all that really suffers in ways we would never permit an insect to suffer. That is how prison is tearing me up inside. It hurts every day. Every day takes me further from life. And I am not even conscious of how my dissolution is coming about. Therefore, I cannot stop it.[131] ■

But prison officials can and must stop the process of decay. This core of humanity, which state-raised convicts share with other prisoners and with the rest of us, must be preserved and ultimately enriched. Correction means nothing at all if it does not mean preserving humanity, and it is not worth striving for if the humanity we preserve is not that of a mature adult.

Abbott, our poster child for the state-raised convict, is ferociously committed to immaturity. Consequently, he presents himself as a substantial obstacle to the creation of civilized and civilizing prisons. Ironically, though he wishes to reject the prison and everything associated with it, Abbott adopts the lifestyle of the institutions in which he was reared, particularly the prison. As fellow inmate Gary McGivern has noted, Abbott "used his talents to justify a lifestyle as callous in its exchanges as the social institutions about which he wrote."[132] A victim, in prison and out, he felt entitled to victimize others in turn. "He felt it was his 'right' to continue the abuses to which he had been subjected," observed McGivern, but in point of fact "He had no such right."[133] Abbott, it seems, could never comprehend this crucial point.

Abbott was released soon after the publication of his book, though the reasons are unclear. Some contend that he was set free because of his literary talent and because of the support of Norman Mailer, who had become his mentor of sorts. Others contend that Abbott informed on other inmates and was rewarded by the state with early release.[134] In either case, on release, he was imprisoned by his deficiencies and utterly unprepared for life in the free world. In the words of fellow inmate Tommy R. Mason,

■ Abbott emerged from prison a celebrity, yet he remained dependent, no more than a child. Even in walking out of prison he did not 'go free,' because the prison was inside him. The minute he encountered pressure, he reacted with the fury and destructiveness cultivated in that prison.[135] ■

Abbott had described himself in these very terms in his book, as a dangerous man-child, prone to vengeful violence. Within weeks of his release, Abbott killed a waiter in a New York restaurant. The waiter, also an aspiring actor, had insulted Abbott—remember that Abbott is extremely thin-skinned—and Abbott stabbed him, chillingly, using a technique found in Abbott's book, *Life in the Belly of the Beast*. Abbott then fled, taking refuge for a time in the Louisiana oil fields, only to be apprehended, returned to New York, and sentenced to a lengthy prison term.

Some years after his conviction, the widow of Abbott's victim sued to collect damages. Abbott represented himself. At various points in the trial, he berated the widow, claiming her evident feelings of sadness were trumped up to impress the jury and win a healthy settlement. How could Abbott imagine real sadness at the loss of a loved one? No one, after all, had ever expressed sadness about the tragic happenings in his life. At one point, Abbott claimed that his victim was lucky to have been killed by one such as himself, an acknowledged expert with a knife, who could do the job proficiently, with little or no pain. So much for empathy.

It is unlikely Abbott will ever see the free light of day again. Our concern must be not only for Abbott but for the other would-be Abbotts who are working their way through our system. For them, violent convicts like Abbott are heroes, the rest of us villains. As state-raised youths, embarking on a life of prison, they *aspire* to be thugs.[136] We must break this cycle by breaking with violence. As one prison poet observed, "The prison knows how to handle me when I use my right hand in anger but they have to think twice when I use my head."[137] Prison officials must think twice as a matter of policy in their dealings with prisoners. The goal must be to meet the violence of prisoners with empathy and reason and to provide opportunities for mature living that reverse the experiences of failure and rejection upon which the prisoners' violence feeds. The adolescent violence these prisoners engage in—and too often elicit in the staff—has no place in a civilized prison system.

A NOTE ON THE CONVICT
WORLD OF WOMEN'S PRISONS

The convict world in women's prisons shares a number of features with that of men's prisons. Though little has been written about it, prisons for women today are generally more violent and less controlled than in years past, at least in part as a response to legal holdings that changed the balance of power in these prisons as it did in prisons for men.[138] Female convicts, like their male counterparts, are self-proclaimed criminals for whom prison is both a home and a way of life. They have no family outside to speak of, no life in the free world to return to. As one woman put it, "Convicts have always been my family."[139] For better or worse, prison has been her life.

In women's prisons as in men's prisons, the convicts rule the public areas of prison, symbolized by the yard but including the mess hall and other settings where large groups can congregate with relatively little supervision by the staff. Female convicts prize a "convict code," which, in its essentials, is the same as that espoused by male convicts—"do your own time" and resist control by the officials. As one woman convict put it,

■ There are a lot of inmates here, but you have to realize that there are a lot of convicts here too. I don't understand what an inmate is because I have never been an inmate. I have always been a straight-up convict. I don't give a fuck. You tell me what to do and I am not going to do it. The judge sent me here to do my time and that is all I am going to do for you guys. Yeah, I got your W number, I belong to the state, but I am telling you like this, I am coming here to do my time, I am not coming here to program, to do what you want me to do.[140] ■

This women's concerns are virtually indistinguishable from those of male convicts like Jack Abbott, though she may not be as quick to resort to lethal retaliatory violence.

Still, violence is a recurring feature of the female convict world, a world that can be quite shocking to inmates new to the prison world:

■ I had never been to prison before; when a fight would bust out, it would take two to three hours before anyone would get there. I have seen teeth knocked out, I have seen arms broken, I have seen food fights in the dining room, I have seen people being cut.[141] ■

Female convicts may carry shanks; they certainly menace the weaker inmates, those who won't "stand their ground" or fight back (see Chapter Three). Weaker women may be pressured for sex. The pressure is mostly social—few women are raped—but this is true in men's prisons as well. Conover, who found few rapes during his year as an officer at Sing Sing, a men's prison, suggests that, "at least at Sing Sing, sex between (female) officers and inmates is presently more common than forcible sex between inmates. . . ."[142]

To survive in the female convict world, as in the male convict world, one must be street smart and have sharp survival skills. The notion that one must have "juice"—the ability to gets things done through one's contacts with other inmates and with officials—is common in both men's and women's prisons. (This point is central to what prison scholars called the "politician" role; the notion of "juice" in women's prisons is thoughtfully discussed by Owen.)[143] Many female convicts feel the need to join cliques or gangs or at least pair up with another prisoner, just as do many male convicts.[144] (Female families are populated primarily by inmates.)

It appears that women convicts, as a group, do not stand up in opposition to the prison administration as often happens in men's prisons. As one female convict and gang member told Owen,

■ The men will stick together but women seemed to be scared to lose their days, or go to Ad Seg. The women stress on their family stuff and that makes them scared. The women may agree that things need to change but will not come together to do something about it. In 1991, we had a strike, a lay-in, and when the cops started taking people to Ad Seg, everyone gave up.[145] ■

Male convicts may be more cohesive as a group in opposition to the prison administration than are women, but such acts of solidarity, however impressive, are fairly rare in men's prisons. One example would be the collective violence of a prison riot. Riots are certainly more common in men's prisons than in women's prisons and more common in modern prisons than in earlier institutions, but riots in men's prisons are nevertheless comparatively rare events.

Female convicts, like male convicts, create a distinctive subculture of violence within the larger prison culture. Jack Abbott would understand the world of female convicts; female convicts would understand Jack Abbott's world. And certainly the inmates in women's and men's prisons understand the convict worlds that swirl around them in their respective prisons. Most women prisoners, who consider themselves inmates, go to great lengths to avoid the convict world, just as most male prisoners, who consider themselves inmates, studiously avoid the convict world in their prisons as well.

NOTES

1. Stastny and Tyrnauer (1982:25).
2. Stastny and Tyrnauer (1982:25).
3. Cobb (1985).
4. Irwin (1980); Austin and Irwin (2000).
5. Stastny and Tyrnauer (1982:27–28).
6. Stastny and Tyrnauer (1982:27–28).
7. Irwin (1970 & 1980).
8. Crouch and Marquart (1989:39).
9. Crouch and Marquart (1989:41).
10. Crouch and Marquart (1989:88).
11. Crouch and Marquart (1989:105).
12. Crouch and Marquart (1989:71–72).
13. See Crouch and Marquart (1989:46).
14. Jacobs (1977:31 & 44).
15. Jacobs (1977:50).
16. Conrad (1988).
17. Foucault (1977:205).
18. Jacobs (1977:30).
19. Jacobs (1977:44).
20. Jacobs (1977:44).
21. Jacobs (1977:46).
22. Irwin (1980: 11).
23. Irwin (1980:11–12).
24. Irwin (1980:12).
25. Irwin (1980:14).
26. Sykes (1966:101).
27. Nelson (1936:133–34).
28. Harris (1988:16).

29. Nelson (1936:118).

30. Nelson (1936:119).

31. Nelson (1936:130).

32. Nelson (1936:126–27).

33. Nelson (1936:158–59).

34. Bowker (1988:63) draws this observation from Sykes's classic study of Trenton State Prison in the mid-1950s, reminding us that "fully three-fourths of the prisoners he studied played predatory social roles." We need reminding because this is not something Sykes himself emphasized. The implications of this fact for daily prison living are, if anything, played down in Sykes's book, and in most other accounts of the social world of the prison during the Big House era, in favor of a more harmonious "social systems" perspective on prison adjustment.

35. Sykes (1966).

36. Nelson (1936:187–88).

37. Nelson (1936:188).

38. Nelson (1936:188–89).

39. See Murton (1976).

40. Conrad (1988:320).

41. Jacobs (1977:138).

42. Jacobs (1977:138).

43. Jacobs (1977:138).

44. DiIulio (1991:148).

45. Jacobs (1977:107).

46. DiIulio (1991:151).

47. Jacobs (1977:118); see also Rothman and Engel (1983).

48. See, for example, Stojkovic (1995:68).

49. As recently as 1992, British prisons were described as Big Houses marked by spartan and repressive regimes. Since that time, a host of liberal reforms have been introduced, which have produced more relaxed regimes. The relaxation of Big House discipline has produced internal problems, including an increase in violence, much as occurred in America in the late 1960s and on through the early 1980s (see Cavadino and Dignan, 1992; lectures on prison reform by Vivian Stern and Adam Sampson, the Comparative Corrections Institute, sponsored by American University and held at the University of London in the summer of 1994). As in America, part of the problem is that correctional officials do not quite know how to occupy prisoners with considerable amounts of free time on their hands. For a global perspective on these and other issues, see Stern (1998).

50. Aspects of Big House discipline, sometimes augmented by sophisticated modern technology, can be found in so-called supermax or maxi-maxi prisons, reserved for disruptive prisoners, and in short-term boot camp prisons, which are reserved primarily for "young adult offenders convicted of nonviolent crimes who are serving their first prison terms" MacKenzie (1993:21). Facilities such as these are becoming more common, but they are by no means typical American prisons.

51. See Lerner (1984).

52. Irwin (1980).

53. Jacobs (1977:86–87); see also Rothman and Engel (1983).

54. See Jacobs (1983).

55. See Krajick (1980); Fong, Vogel, and Buentello (1992). See also *The Prison Journal* 71 (2) (Fall/Winter 1991), the entire body of which deals with prison gangs. For a discussion of Stateville Prison today as a "gang-entrenched" facility, see Brown (1995:7). Gangs are increasingly prevalent in women's prisons. See, for example, Rierden (1997).

56. Jacobs (1977:138).

57. A parallel process was at work in our public schools during this time and, as is the case in many prisons, continues today. In both settings, order has become *a* dominant (if not *the*) dominant concern, and violence or the threat of violence are facts of daily life. See Toby (1994:152–58).

58. Lombardo (1988).

59. Sheehan (1978).

60. Sheehan (1978:147).

61. Irwin (1980).

62. Grier and Cobbs (1968); Carmichael and Hamilton (1967).

63. See Dorin and Johnson (1978).

64. Irwin (1980: 110).

65. Irwin (1980); Carroll (1974, 1988).

66. Johnson and Dorin (1978). Radical rhetoric, which emphasized the systemic oppression of the poor and the need for organized violence to secure social change, was common in the prisons of the late 1960s and early 70s, but there were few committed revolutionaries. There are many reasons for this (see Irwin, 1980; Carroll, 1988). Perhaps the primary reason is that the stance of the prison revolutionary is flagrantly self-destructive.

The radicalized prisoner, after all, stipulates the existence of a monolithic power structure that is purposely arranged to wreak damage upon him as a helpless member of the underclass. There is . . . the concession of personal impotence in the face of such threats and the view that the only way out is through a violent mass insurrection. While there is, in theory, an army of similarly alienated persons ripe for conscription, most of these potential recruits have suffered at the hands of their fellow convicts and have come to view them with suspicion. To engage in revolutionary action, the prospective militant must develop faith in an unimpressive group of peers, and must then gird himself for what may easily degenerate into a Pyrrhic victory—short-term ascendance following a bloody prison riot. And if our rebel is prisonwise, he may well fear the reign of the inmates and the backlash from guards more than the disturbance itself. (Johnson & Dorin, 1978:45).

67. Kauffman (1988:13).

68. Kauffman (1988: 13).

69. Crouch and Marquart (1989:188).

70. Crouch and Marquart (1989:188).

71. Crouch and Marquart (1989:189).

72. Crouch and Marquart (1989:190).

73. See Jacobs (1977); Carroll (1977); McCall (1995).

74. Crouch and Marquart (1989:192).

75. Colvin (1982 & 1992); Carroll (1988); Crouch and Marquart (1989:175); Kauffman (1988:34).

76. Sheehan (1978:142–43); Cressey (1982:xx); Crouch and Marquart (1989:175).

77. Kauffman (1988:34).

78. Zimmer (1986:59).

79. Colvin (1982:456; & 1992). Analyzing the growth of violence in the New Mexico State Penitentiary over the decade of the 1970s that culminated in a savage riot in 1980, Colvin argues that "removal of legitimate (program) and illegitimate (drug trafficking) opportunities in the prison created a new opportunity structure that produced the 'hero' or 'new breed' role" discussed by Irwin (Colvin, 1982:456).

80. Irwin (1980).

81. Barak (1978); Conrad (1988).

82. Irwin (1980:192–95). Irwin's observations are confirmed in the research of Abdul-Mu'Min (1981) and Colvin (1982 & 1992) and, more recently, Silberman (1995).

83. Colvin (1992:192).

84. Martin and Sussman (1993:145).

85. Useem and Kimball (1989).

86. DiIulio (1991).

87. Stojkovic (1984).

88. Manocchio and Dunn (1982:35).

89. Manocchio and Dunn (1982:238).

90. There is no evidence that the growing influence of state-raised convicts stems from a lower class of criminal confined in today's prison. Prisoners of this type are not statistically more prevalent in today's prisons, nor has there been an increase in the proportion of violent offenders making up prison populations (Colvin, 1982). Instead, they have become a dominant force in today's prisons because today's prisons are less controlled.

91. See Toch and Adams (1989).

92. See, for example, Porporino (1991:6–7).

93. Colvin (1982).

94. Irwin (1970:74).

95. Abbott (1981:12).

96. Many of the more telling and tragic observations made by Abbott about the life of the state-raised youth are confirmed and amplified in the work of Dwight Edgar Abbot (1991).

97. See Nusser (1982).

98. Nusser (1982:560).

99. Nusser (1982:560).

100. Nusser (1982:560).

101. Abbott (1981:13).

102. Abbott (1981:14,15).

103. Lawes (1932:36).

104. Zamble, Porporino, and Kalotay (1984:137).

105. Abbott (1981:15). See also Myers and Levy (1978); Higgins and Thies (1981).

106. Abbott (1981:5).

107. The prison is "rigidly hierarchical and routinized, cold and impersonal" (Johnson, 1976:111). As such, it "parallels the classic paranoid image of conspiratorial control" (Johnson, 1976:111). Psychiatric research reveals that prison attracts a disproportionate number of people with paranoid dispositions and then reinforces their suspicious worldview. Prison also independently creates this disposition. Diagnosis and treatment of prison paranoia are therefore difficult, because the adaptive and maladaptive aspects of paranoid views may be hard to separate (see Thurrell, Halleck, & Johnson, 1965; and Hamburger, 1967).

108. See Abbott (1981:78–79). The facade of many violent persons projects strength and toughness but is ultimately the product of what Baumeister has called "inflated, tenuous and unstable" manifestations of unwarranted self-esteem. "Violent criminals" like Abbott often "describe themselves as special, elite persons who deserve preferential treatment." When they predictably fail to receive such treatment, they feel violated and respond with rage. For a discussion of unstable egotism and violence, see Baumeister (2001).

109. Abbott (1981: 15 & 149–50).

110. Earley (1992:305).

111. Schroeder (1976:23).

112. Harkleroad makes the point that it is the weak-minded—those who react rather than think—that come to dominate the prison world. See Harkleroad (2000:163–4).

113. Abbott (1981:93–94).

114. Earley (1992:186).

115. Kupers (1999:139).

116. See Bruchac (1984: 193).

117. Bruchac (1984:193).

118. See Cooley (1992:36).

119. Abbott (1981:88–89).

120. Abbott (1981:85).

121. Abbott (1981:144).

122. Abbott (1981:102).

123. Abbott (1981:70–71).

124. See Abbott (1981:65–66).

125. See Earley (1992:282–83).

126. Abbott (1981:18).

127. See Abbott (1981:139–40).

128. Abbott (1981:44–45).

129. Abbott (1981:44–45).

130. McCall (1995:209).

131. Abbott (1981:5).

132. McGivern (1982:562).

133. McGivern (1982:562).

134. See Nusser (1982).

135. Mason (1982:564).

136. See Earley (1992:281).

137. Dessus, in Bruchac (1984:86).

138. See Rierden (1997), and Cook and Davies (1999).

139. Owen (1998:55).

140. Owen (1998:177).

141. Owen (1998:66).

142. Conover (2000:263). Of course, sexual coercion may be more common in some prisons than others. One study indicates that fully 22% of male inmates and 7% of female inmates in two maximum security prisons in Nebraska "reported the experience of being pressured or forced into sexual contact in a state prison facility" (Struckman-Johnson, Struckman-Johnson, Rucker, Bumby and Donaldson, 1996: 74). Half of these targets were coerced into anal sex; half of these rape victims, in turn, appear to have been gang raped. (It would seem that one woman in this sample was gang raped by other women.) Many of the targets of sexual abuse were repeatedly pressured for sex by more than one person. Most (80%) reported emotional trauma, including depression and thoughts of suicide. Only one out of four victims reported their victimization to staff, which may explain why officers like Conover view these events as comparatively rare. (Staff were implicated in 18% of the incidents, but it is unclear which ones.) The data are drawn from a questionnaire survey with only a 30% response rate, but these figures are consistent with prior ethnographic research (see Lockwood, 1994). It is troubling to realize that this study took place in "a relatively small, well-managed prison in a rural, sparsely populated state" (Struckman-Johnson, Struckman-Johnson, Rucker, Bumby and Donaldson, 1996:75).

143. Owen (1998:169).

144. See Rierden (1997:32); Owen (1998:73).

145. Owen (1998:74).

REFERENCES

Abbot, D. E. *I Cried, You Didn't Listen: A Survivor's Exposé of the California Youth Authority.* Portland, OR: Feral House, 1991.

Abbott, J. H. *In the Belly of the Beast.* New York: Vintage, 1981.

Abdul-Mu'Min, E. M. *Power and Survival: The Role and Structure of Religious Fellowships, Self-Help Groups and Gangs in a California Prison.* Ann Arbor, MI: University Microfilms International, 1981.

Austin, J., and J. Irwin. *It's About Time: America's Imprisonment Binge.* Belmont, CA: Wadsworth, 2000.

Barak, I. L. *Punishment to Protection: Solitary Confinement in Washington State Penitentiary, 1966–1975.* Ann Arbor, MI: University Microfilms International, 1978.

Baumeister, R. F., "Violent pride," *Scientific American* 284 (4), 2001:96–101.

Bowker, L. H. "Victimizers and victims in American correctional institutions." In R. Johnson and H. Toch (eds.). *The Pains of Imprisonment.* Prospect Heights, IL: Waveland Press 1988:63–76.

Brown, M. "Stateville Correctional Center: A neophyte's view." *The Keeper's Voice* 16 (1) 1995:5–8.

Bruchac, J. (ed.). *The Light from Another Country: Poetry from American Prisons.* New York: Greenfield Review Press, 1984.

Camp, G., and C. Camp. *The Corrections Yearbook.* South Salem, NY: Criminal Justice Institute, 1984.

Carmichael, S., and C. Hamilton. *Black Power.* New York: Random House, 1967.

Carroll, L. *Hacks, Blacks and Cons.* Lexington: Lexington Books, 1974.

Carroll, L. "Race, ethnicity, and the social order of the prison." In R. Johnson and H. Toch (eds.). *The Pains of Imprisonment.* Prospect Heights, IL: Waveland Press, 1988:181–203.

Cavadino M., and J. Dignan. *The Penal System: An Introduction.* London: Sage, 1992.

Cobb, A., Jr. "Home truths about prison overcrowding." *The Annals of the American Academy of Political and Social Science* 478 (March 1985):73–85.

Colvin, M. "The 1980 New Mexico prison riot." *Social Problems* 29 (5) 1982:449–63.

Colvin, M. *The Penitentiary in Crisis: From Accommodation to Riot in New Mexico.* Albany: SUNY Press, 1992.

Conover, T. *Newjack: Guarding Sing Sing.* New York: Random House, 2000.

Conrad, J. P. "What do the undeserving deserve?" In R. Johnson and H. Toch (eds.). *The Pains of Imprisonment.* Prospect Heights, IL: Waveland Press, 1988:313–30.

Cook, S. & Davies, S. (Eds.), *Harsh Punishment: International Experiences of Women's Imprisonment* (Northeastern University Press, 1999).

Cooley, D. "Prison victimization and the informal rules of social control." *Forum on Corrections Research* 4 (3) 1992:31–36.

Cressey, D. R. "Foreword." In F. Cullen and K. E. Gilbert. *Reaffirming Rehabilitation.* Cincinnati, OH: Anderson, 1982.

Crouch, B. M., and J. W. Marquart. *An Appeal to Justice.* Austin: University of Texas Press, 1989.

DiIulio, J. J. *No Escape: The Future of American Corrections.* New York: Basic Books, 1991.

Dorin, D. D., and R. Johnson. "Violence and survival in prison: The case of George Jackson." In J. Inciardi and A. Potheger (eds.). *Violent Crime: Historical and Contemporary Issues.* Beverly Hills, CA: Sage, 1978:125–42.

Earley, P. *The Hot House: Life Inside Leavenworth.* New York: Bantam Books, 1992.

Fitzgerald, M., and J. Sim. *British Prisons.* Oxford: Blackwell, 1982.

Fong, R. S., R. E. Vogel, and S. Buentello. "Prison gang dynamics: A look inside the Texas department of corrections." In P. J. Benekos and A. V. Merlo (eds.). *Corrections: Dilemmas and Directions.* Beverly Hills, CA: Sage, 1992:55–77.

Foucault, M. *Discipline and Punish.* New York: Pantheon, 1977.

Grier, W., and P. Cobbs. *Black Rage.* New York: Basic Books, 1968.

Hamburger, E. "The penitentiary and paranoia." *Correctional Psychiatry and Journal of Social Therapy* 13 (4) 1967:225–30.

Harkleroad, J. W. "Control." In R. Johnson and H. Toch. *Crime and Punishment: Inside Views.* Los Angeles: Roxbury Publishing Company, 2000:161–62.

Harris, J. *They Always Call Us Ladies: Stories from Prison.* New York: Kensington Publishing, 1988.

Higgins, J. P., and A. P. Thies. "Social effectiveness and problem-solving thinking of reformatory inmates." *Journal of Offender Counseling, Services & Rehabilitation* 5(3/4) 1981:93–98.

Irwin, J. *The Felon.* Englewood Cliffs, NJ: Prentice-Hall, 1970.

Irwin, J. *Prisons in Turmoil.* Boston: Little, Brown, 1980.

Irwin, J., and J. Austin. *It's About Time: Imprisonment Binge.* Belmont, CA: Wadsworth, 1994.

Jacobs, J. B. *Stateville: The Penitentiary in Mass Society.* Chicago: University of Chicago Press, 1977.

Jacobs, J. B. "The prisoners' rights movement and its impacts." In J. B. Jacobs. *New Perspectives on Prisons and Imprisonment.* Ithaca, NY: Cornell University Press, 1983:33–60.

Johnson, R. *Culture and Crisis in Confinement.* Lexington: Lexington Books, 1976.

Johnson R., and D. D. Dorin. "Dysfunctional ideology: The black revolutionary in prison." In D. Szabo and S. Katzenelson (eds.). *Offenders and Corrections.* New York: Praeger 1978:31–52.

Kauffman, K. *Prison Officers and Their World.* Cambridge: Harvard University Press, 1988.

Krajick, K. "Profile Texas." *Corrections Magazine* 4 (1) 1978:4–25.

Krajick, K. "At Stateville, the calm is tense." *Corrections Magazine* 6 (3) 1980:6–19.

Kupers, T.A. *Prison Madness: The Mental Health Crisis Behind Bars and What We Must Do About It.* San Francisco, CA: Jossey-Bass Publishers, 1999.

Lawes, L. E. *Twenty Thousand Years in Sing Sing.* New York: Ray Long and Richard R. Smith, 1932.

Lerner, S. "Rule of the cruel." *The New Republic* (October 15, 1984):17–21.

Lockwood, D. "Issues in prison sexual violence." In Brasfield, M.C., Montgomery, R. H., and Lombardo, L. X. (eds), *Prison Violence in America.* (2nd ed.) 1994:97–102.

Lombardo, L. X. "Stress, change, and collective violence in prison." In R. Johnson and H. Toch (eds.). *The Pains of Imprisonment.* Prospect Heights, IL: Waveland Press, 1988:77–93.

MacKenzie, D. L. "Boot camp prisons in 1993." *National Institute of Justice Journal* (November 1993):21–28.

Manocchio, A. J., and J. Dunn. *The Time Game: Two Views of a Prison.* Beverly Hills, CA: Sage, 1982.

Marquart, J. W., and B. M. Crouch. "Judicial reform and prisoner control: The impact of *Ruiz v. Estelle* on a Texas penitentiary." *Law and Society Review* 19 (4) 1985:557–86.

Martin, D. M., and Sussman, P. Y. *Committing Journalism: The Prison Writings of RED HOG.* Norton, 1993.

Mason, T. R. "The epitome of failure: Jack Abbott." *Crime and Delinquency* 28 (4) 1982:557–66. [Note that various inmate writers are featured in this article.]

McCall, N. *Makes Me Wanna Holler: A Young Black Man in America.* New York: Vintage, 1995.

McGivern, G. "The epitome of failure: Jack Abbott." *Crime and Delinquency* 28 (4) 1982:557–66. [Note that various inmate writers are featured in this article.]

Morris, T., and P. Morris. *Pentonville: A Sociological Study of an English Prison.* London: Routledge & Kegan Paul, 1963.

Murton, T. *The Dilemma of Prison Reform.* New York: Holt, Rinehart & Winston, 1976.

Myers, L., and G. W. Levy. "Description and prediction of the intractable inmate." *Journal of Research in Crime and Delinquency* 15 (2) 1978:214–28.

Nelson, V. F. *Prison Days and Nights.* New York: Garden City Publishing, 1936.

Nusser, N. "The epitome of failure: Jack Abbott." *Crime and Delinquency* 28 (4) 1982:557–66. [Note that various inmate writers are featured in this article.]

Owen, B. *"In the Mix": Struggle and Survival in a Women's Prison.* Albany: State University of New York Press, 1998.

Porporino, F. "Differences in response to long-term imprisonment: Implications for the management of long-term offenders." *Research Report No. 10.* Research and Statistics Branch, The Correctional Service of Canada, 1991:1–15.

Rierden, A. *The Farm: A Life Inside a Women's Prison.* Amherst, MA: University of Massachusetts Press, 1997.

Rothman, S., and K. Engel. "Prison violence and the paradox of reform." *The Public Interest* (fall 1983):91–105.

Schroeder, A. *Shaking It Rough.* Garden City, NY: Doubleday, 1976:23.

Sheehan, S. *A Prison and a Prisoner.* Boston: Houghton Mifflin, 1978.

Silberman, M. *A World of Violence: Corrections in America.* Belmont, CA: Wadsworth, 1995.

Stastny, C., and G. Tyrnauer. *Who Rules the Joint?* Lexington: Lexington Books, 1982.

Stern, V. *A Sin Against the Future: Imprisonment in the World*. London: Penguin, 1998.

Stojkovic, S. "Social bases of power and control mechanisms among prisoners in a prison organization." *Justice Quarterly* 1 (4) 1984:511–28.

Stojkovic, S. "Correctional administrators' accounts of their work worlds." *The Howard Journal of Criminal Justice* 34 (1) 1995:64–80.

Struckman-Johnson, C, Struckman-Johnson, D., Rucker, L., Bumby, K. and Donaldson, S. "Sexual coercion reported by men and women in prison." The Journal of Sex Research 33 (1) 1996:67–76.

Sykes, G. *The Society of Captives*. New York: Atheneum, 1966.

Thurrell, R. J., S. L. Halleck, and A. F. Johnson. "Psychosis in prison." *The Journal of Criminology and Police Science* 56 (3) 1965:271–76.

Toby, J. "The schools." In J. Q. Wilson and J. Petersilia (eds.). *Crime*. San Francisco: ICS Press, 1994:141–70.

Toch, H., and K. Adams with J. D. Grant. *Coping: Maladaptation in Prisons*. New Brunswick, NJ: Transaction Publishers, 1989.

Useem, B., and P. Kimball. *States of Siege: U.S. Prison Riots 1971–1986*. New York: Oxford University Press, 1989.

Zamble, E., F. Porporino, and J. Kalotay. *An Analysis of Coping Behavior in Prison Inmates*. Ministry of the Solicitor General of Canada: Programs Branch User Report, 1984.

Zimmer, L. E. *Women Guarding Men*. Chicago: University of Chicago Press, 1986.

6

❖

Living in Prison

The Private Culture of the Prison

L iving well may be the best revenge against social rejection. Each day's
pleasure belies the basic premise of rejection, namely, that the person
ostracized must suffer as a result. Prisoners feel a particularly urgent need
to "reject their rejectors," to live as though the pains of imprisonment are of
no consequence to them.[1] Prisons are monuments to social rejection. Prisoners are nothing in the eyes of the public, and they know it. To cope with the
hurt that would normally accompany ostracism, many prisoners minimize the
pains of confinement, even claiming that prison is easier, better, more accommodating than the outside world. "I can do my time standing on my head,"
goes one common prison refrain. Such assertions promote the view that
tough convicts feel no pain. Where others—regular citizens—would wilt in
prison, convicts blossom and thrive. They are, then, in myth if not in reality,
above punishment.

Among those who count themselves as convicts, the rejection of society
and the adoption of a prison-centered worldview is raised to an article of faith.
"As the years go by and you get older," one convict told Earley,

■ you realize more and more that your life is considered a failure by
society's standards. . . . You are a jailbird. You don't have any money, no
house, no job, no status. In society's eyes you're a worthless piece of shit.
Now, you can buy into what society says and decide you really are a
piece of shit or you can say, "Fuck society, I'll live by my own rules."
That's what I did. I decided to live by my own standards and rules. They

aren't society's but they are mine and that's what I've done. In your society, I may not be anybody, but in here, I am.[2] ■

This attitude may explain why so many male prisoners flaunt big tattoos and even bigger muscles. To the outside world, the flamboyant body art of the prison iron man (weight lifter) marks the convict as "a circus sideshow freak," yet in prison these seeming stigmata are "badges of honor."[3]

The impression made by such prisoners is suitably impressive and even intimidating, at least to newcomers on the prison scene. As one Lompoc prisoner observed, "ink scares new pigs," meaning that tattoos frighten new officers.[4] In this prisoner's view, the effect can prove useful:

■ They think the more ink you have, the longer you been in the joint, and the badder you are. It works. I walk by the office at night with my shirt off when a fish is working, and I can tell he's scared. If new fish cops are scared, they leave us alone.[5] ■

So-called "fish"—newcomers—include new prisoners. They, too, may well find their tattooed neighbors frightening, but they at least have the option of decorating themselves, if you will, using tattoos of their own as camouflage to blend into the prison community. Officers, of course, may sport tattoos, but they can never blend into the prison community.

One sees a related phenomenon in women's prisons, with some of the tougher women—notably the "stud broads"—assuming a defiant and menacing masculinity, an effect generally achieved without tattoos.[6] Pearson describes two cases in point:

. . . [O]ne is African American, tall and broad-shouldered, with gnarled rasta hair and a distinctive mustache. She lopes, moving from her shoulders rather than her hips, projecting an air of supreme self-assurance. The other stud is white, with a brush cut and a goatee. She is shorter, but wiry and muscled, like a marine. There is no point in saying she. These are not women imitating men. . . . They have achieved an almost pure masculinity. Their transformation takes your breath away.[7]

We learn, moreover, that these stud broads have it pretty good. "The girls loved the studs to death, man," one former inmate told Pearson, "'cause they looked like *men!*"[8]

One might fairly conclude from all of this that prisoners, male and female alike, are mocking the conventional world, graphically illustrating how domesticated and weak is the society that must cage its awesome outlaws. Yet, however comforting such beliefs may be, prisoners have little hope of cultivating an enviable lifestyle behind bars. Prisoners do not live well. Nobody envies their lot. For many inmates, prison life is a stage in a theater of survival. In the words of one prisoner,

■ Turning the corner into the prison yard for the first time is like stepping onto the set of a Cecil B. DeMille spectacular where most of the extras are black. Everyone has a yard image. Still there are no plush trimmings, trumpet fanfares or superstars. The only Herculean act performed is survival.[9] ■

If the truth be told, the prison yard features a motley crew of social misfits, some frightening, others frightened, a few merely outlandish; all, after a fashion, a little pathetic. The setting offers limited options. At best, prisoners "choose not a way of life" within their involuntary and largely sterile habitat "but a way to live."[10] Their modest but difficult task is to "create, seemingly from rocklike or diaphanous material, a fabric of life."[11] Simply "living in prison"—getting by from day to day, surviving—may be the only revenge they can take on the prison.[12]

And some prisoners, tragically, are denied even that small pleasure, experiencing psychological breakdowns while confined.[13] Others die behind bars, either at their own hands or at the hands of others.[14] A few, sentenced to die, are executed each year.[15] Most prisoners, of course, are more fortunate. The sentence passes, if not quickly or easily, at least without crisis or trauma.[16] Yet the vast majority of prisoners, as we observed in Chapter Four, grapple ineffectually with their problems and emerge to take up barren and uninviting lives. A few learn something constructive. They live in prison, and subsequently in the free world, in mature and rewarding ways. One might say they have fully avenged themselves, to their benefit and ours.

LIVING IN PRISON

The "fabric of life" most prisoners weave is quite prosaic. It bears little resemblance to the violent and even dramatic convict culture reviewed in the last chapter. The plain fact is that most inmates are not members of the convict culture and do not subscribe to its rules for living. To be sure, they pay lip service to its code and deference to its heroes, but they do not want to live as convicts. They want, instead, to get along without trouble while in prison, and they even hope to go straight upon release.

That most inmates want to do their own time and steer clear of prison after they are released is simply common sense. It is also supported by research. Glaser observed of federal prisoners during the early 1960s, "Our findings from several different types of inquiry indicated that inmates have a predominant interest in adjusting to the demands of the institution and that they have strong noncriminal aspirations."[17] Toch's research, conducted with state prisoners in the mid-1970s, confirms Glaser's point. Though Toch and his associates interviewed prisoners during the peak period of custodial crisis and convict violence (see Chapter Five), the central finding was that today's inmates do indeed want to "live in prison" and make a conventional life for themselves upon release.[18] Zamble, Porporino, and Kalotay, reporting on more recent research with Canadian prisoners, tell us that "examination of subjects' plans for their terms does indicate some attempts to change and improve themselves. Eighty percent said that they had a goal to accomplish during the term, with 75 percent of these specifying either education or job training."[19] Fully half of their sample considered self-improvement to be the main objective of their prison adjustment strategies.[20] Comparable findings are reported for women, who generally stay to themselves in prison and hope to make the most of the time they must serve.[21]

More prisoners may succeed in reforming themselves than first meets the eye. Though most studies tell us that between one-half and three-quarters of ex-prisoners return to crime—that is, they are arrested, though not necessarily sent back to prison, for one or more crimes[22]—it is worth remembering that very few first offenders go to prison. Virtually all ex-prisoners, in other words, were recidivists before they were incarcerated. That from 25 percent to 50 percent of them avoid arrest after release from prison suggests that they either refrained from criminal activity or engaged in criminal activity that was less serious or repetitive than was the case prior to their confinement.[23] Moreover, the fact that most persons arrested for crimes after release from prison are not reconfined—between 30 percent and 40 percent go back to prison[24]—suggests that they, too, engaged in criminal activity that was less serious or repetitive than before their confinement.[25] (There has been a recent increase in parolees returned to prison for technical violations of parole rules, but this says more about our current attitude of punitiveness than about offender behavior.[26])

These partial successes may indicate no more than the effects of aging or discouragement[27] or indeed may reflect the limited ability of law enforcement officers to apprehend criminals.[28] But they may also tell us that some offenders improve themselves while behind bars and hence are able to forge more conventional lives upon release from prison. Research on the impact of life in a comparatively program-rich, medium-security federal prison for men provides data that strongly suggest this possibility;

> When interviewed prior to leaving, 84 percent of the 643 inmates queried reported they had changed for the better. Comparisons of personality test scores and profiles obtained upon entrance and departure showed improvement was much more common than deterioration. A followup study of 1,008 offenders who had been released on the average 3 1/2 years showed that 45 percent had no subsequent arrests, 71 percent had no subsequent convictions and 72 percent had not been returned to prison for any reason.[29]

It is reasonable to conclude that, when given an accommodating correctional milieu, many offenders will make a bona fide effort to use the prison experience to improve themselves and hence to improve their chances for a decent life upon release. (In the last chapter of this book, we consider how maximum-security prisons can be arranged to encourage this result.)

Prisoners who want to live peacefully in prison and go straight upon release are, for the most part, neither voluble nor eloquent in expressing their beliefs. It is quite likely that they overestimate the prevalence and ferocity of the convicts and consider themselves the minority. They are not. The "masses" of inmates have always done their time and avoided "the general prison social activities" dominated by the convicts.[30] This important observation was recently confirmed in an ethnographic study of Leavenworth prison, which revealed that roughly 80 percent of the prisoners "try to avoid trouble and simply do their time as easily as possible."[31] It should be noted that the vast majority of female prisoners—as many as 95 percent—stay to themselves in an effort to avoid trouble.[32] Many of these inmates, to be sure, return to crime on release. They simply avoid prison's dangers but do little to confront and solve the problems that brought them to prison. Yet they are not troublesome prisoners. The mundane world of daily life and adjustment shared by this "silent majority" is and has always been the foundation of stability upon which the prison rests.

Even the convict world, which places a premium on violence, ultimately must reach an accommodation with the masses of inmates who inhabit the institution and the prison officials who run it. Even on the yard there is at least a degree of order to prison life, though in many of today's institutions it is often a "dangerous and tentative order."[33] And it is worth remembering that even convict gang members need some stability in their lives. They are not continuously embroiled in conflict. They also need nurturance now and again, not to mention support for wounded egos.

Violent men and women cannot live by violence alone and have no desire to do so.[34] This means that gangs and other predatory groups must be more than convenient vehicles for exploiting others. To serve the normal human needs of their members, they must also be safe harbors within the lonely and dangerous prison world, providing a kind of extended psychological support system. Jacobs's account of black prison gangs in Stateville prison, for example, underscores their role as a psychological haven of acceptance for prisoners all too familiar with rejection:

> By far the most important function the gangs provide their members at Stateville is psychological support. . . . [Said one gang member,] "[T]hese guys . . . are closer to me than my own family. Anything I do around them is accepted—for stuff that my parents would put me down for, these guys elevate me to a pedestal." Every inmate informant expressed this opinion—that the organizations give to the members a sense of identification, a feeling of belonging, an air of importance. . . . Time and again gang members explained that, whether on the street or in the prison, the gang "allows you to feel like a man": it is a family with which you can identify. Many times young members have soberly stated that the organization is something, the only thing, they would die for.[35]

The supportive function of gangs may be even more pronounced for Latin prisoners. Davidson, for example, has described Chicano prison gangs, which often involve relatives and friends of relatives, as playing the role of a "mother" providing aid for "her child through the long process of enculturation" to prison.[36] Loosely known as "the Family," these gangs offer an unconditionally supportive context in which a man's "machismo" rests assured.[37] Latina prison gangs are quite cohesive as well; their leader is supposed to be tough and even to take a ritual beating when she lets the gang down. Rierden provides a case in point involving the Latin Queens, a gang with a branch at Niantic Prison for Women:

> As an inmate, BeBe has served her punishment. But as a Latin Queen she must face another form of retribution. She approaches two Queens. They're lying on their bunks smoking cigarettes, feeling each second crawl by. "I order you to beat me down," she tells them. They look at her like she is crazy. They resist at first, out of respect, but they know as Latin Queens they have no choice. BeBe is a corona, a reina, a princess-queen. Still, she has dissed the Family by abusing drugs. They owe it to the Family to do what she says. BeBe turns and walks out into the recreation yard. The women follow her until she stops, then they block her from the front and back so the COs can't see. For thirty minutes they smack, slap, punch, slug, and kick her—not severely, but enough to make her feel pain. After it is over she thanks them.[38]

Certainly these gangs are flagrantly criminogenic. They "elevate" people, as Jacobs's informant would have it and as is made clear in the behavior of the Latin Queens, for some fairly primitive behavior and reinforce an almost paranoid view of the world. Nevertheless, these gangs ensure the psychological survival of their members, male or female.[39]

Most prisoners are not members of gangs or other predatory groups, however, and do not try to work out a livable arrangement on the prison yard. Their adjustment reveals that the options for nonviolent and potentially constructive ways of living in prison are more diverse than one would first suppose. Prisons have a uniformly cold and forbidding exterior, giving the impression that life within their walls must be consistently harsh, a continuing war of all against all (or gang against gang) for such scarce commodities as status and respect. These battles are indeed fought by some prisoners, mainly the convicts, though these are not the only battles the convicts fight, as the inner turmoil and loneliness of Jack Abbott and others like him clearly reveal. Moreover, the prison accommodates a wide range of nonviolent lifestyles that are sought, and usually found, by the masses of prisoners who studiously avoid the world of the convicts and who, for the most part, survive prison on their own terms.

The bulk of this chapter is devoted to the ecology of survival in men's prisons, where most of the research has been done. We conclude with a note on the ecology of women's prisons, highlighting the generality of ecological factors in human survival behind bars.

THE ECOLOGY OF PRISON SURVIVAL

To say that prisons support a variety of lifestyles is not to imply that they are in any way inviting. At issue here is not the so-called country club prison. That mythical institution has been likened to the Loch Ness Monster: "[M]any people believe in it," remarks Levinson, "but nobody has ever seen one."[40] Actually, the "arenas that prison provides for action are, in free-world terms, small, poorly equipped, and frequently threatening."[41] Nevertheless, these environments do possess a "remarkable variability."[42] This variability is the product of a transactional process in which the adjustment efforts of prisoners shape and are shaped by prison environments. As researched and codified by Hans Toch, this transactional process reveals seven ecological dimensions that express the preferences and needs of prisoners. These dimensions, according to Toch, are as follows:

1. **Activity** *"A concern about understimulation; a need for maximizing the opportunity to be occupied and to fill time; a need for distraction."*[43] Physical or mental activity, Toch tells us, "can be functional for its own sake—for energy and attention it consumes, for feelings it challenges, for distracting or anesthetizing effects. For such purposes, the nature or content of the activity is irrelevant." Activities that are themselves "meaningful and engrossing," however, offer not just distraction but a degree of personal fulfillment.[44]

2. **Privacy** *"A concern about social and physical overstimulation; a preference for isolation, peace and quiet, absence of environmental irritants such as noise and crowding."*[45] Privacy is in many respects the opposite of activity. "Where activity is a means of enriching experience through self-stimulation, privacy involves *reducing* external stimuli to streamline experience and to make purposive adjustment a simpler task."[46] Privacy-oriented persons are content when they are left alone. States Toch, "The intensely private person lives at peace with himself when he is left to himself. He feels harassed when others demand attention, response or social contact from him."[47] When granted privacy, the main rewards for the prisoner are peace, relaxation and the feeling that the environment is simpler and more easily managed.

3. **Safety** *"A concern about one's physical safety; a preference for social and physical settings that provide protection and that minimize the chances of being attacked."*[48] While privacy-oriented persons seek sanctuary from a wide range of noxious stimuli, safety-oriented people seek sanctuary from a particular type of pressure, that of violence, which they see around them in the prison world and feel within themselves. Persons concerned with safety are apt to label the environment as "tense" or "explosive," characteristics that apply both to themselves and their world. "Violence and its control become," for these inmates, "the main theme of the inner and outer environment."[49]

4. **Emotional feedback** *"A concern about being loved, appreciated and cared for; a desire for intimate relationships that provide emotional sustenance and empathy."*[50] Persons concerned with emotional feedback want "warm" and "responsive" environments populated by "people who care."[51] Prison can be a direct source of emotional feedback, providing inmate friends, concerned staff, or programs that offer the hope of a better future. For

many prisoners, emotional feedback is found in the daily round of talk that helps make bearable the typical prison day:

> ▮ Prison is an oral place. There's not much to look at in a cell, so inmates do a lot of talking. Talking to your neighbor, or the guy locked five cells away, two above, or one below. And when no one else will give any rap, you talk to yourself.
>
> Even in the yard, it's an oral place. Jiving. Joking. Shouting. Laughing. Crying. Often just plain lying. And when there's no one who will listen, you always have yourself.
>
> Inmates will rap about anything, to anyone, to keep the tension off.[52] ▮

The prison can be a mediator between the prisoner and his loved ones outside the walls, facilitating or impeding mail or visits; or it can provide other kinds of contacts with the outside world, such as furloughs. The problem of loneliness in prison, whatever its source, is a problem of inadequate emotional feedback.

5. **Support** *"A concern about reliable, tangible assistance from persons and settings, and about services that facilitate self-advancement and self-improvement."*[53] Some inmates make use of the reintegrative or rehabilitative services available in prison. These are persons who "see themselves having a future and social role, and can thus relate environmental opportunities" like vocational or educational programs "to ends that they prize."[54] Many trace their past failures to deficiencies in their education or training and eagerly embrace prison programs that promise to remedy those deficiencies and afford opportunities for a new life.

6. **Structure** *"A concern about environmental stability and predictability; a preference for consistency, clear-cut rules, orderly and scheduled events and impingements."*[55] An environment affords structure "to the extent to which it furnishes reliable guides for action." Inmates for whom structure is important want a road map of the prison. "Persons concerned with structure have a need to know. . . . The structure person must know where he stands; this knowledge tells him how the outside environment is arranged and what he must do to cope with it."[56]

7. **Freedom** *"A concern about circumscription of one's autonomy; a need for minimal restriction and for maximum opportunity to govern one's own conduct."*[57] The freedom dimension relates authority and dependence in complex and subtle ways. Psychologically speaking, authorities put their subjects in a position of dependency and thus are obligated to protect and serve them as well as to control them. For some men, particularly those raised in inhospitable settings like urban slums and penal institutions, authority figures have operated almost exclusively as sources of control and almost never as sources of protection or nurturance. (Certainly Abbott and other state-raised convicts, male and female, are cases in point.) As a result, these persons are forced to mature without the support and guidance of caring authority figures. Orders issued by a guard thus are presumed to constitute abuse (control for its own sake) or disrespect (treating one like

a child), not an effort to arrange social affairs in an equitable or even responsive manner. An order becomes, then, an occasion to test wills and measure strength, to see who can dominate the other.[58] The process is painful for both parties but particularly for prisoners, who almost always come out on the bottom. Freedom means the ability to maintain a degree of autonomy and yet avoid or minimize these abrasive encounters.

Naturally, inmates vary in terms of their needs and preferences. Older prisoners, for example, often seek privacy; younger offenders are inclined to value freedom and activity. The young and naive are often preoccupied with safety. So, too, the availability of the seven ecological dimensions of prison life is not uniform; a host of demographic and criminal justice variables influence the distribution of ecological concerns.[59] Some institutions are more structured than others or permit more freedom; one facility may offer more support services or be safer than another. Prisons are marked by internal variation as well: the ecological climates of different living quarters, for instance, are not interchangeable. The experiences of a Georgia prisoner are instructive in this regard:

■ Recently I moved from one of [the] violent dormitories to a new unit where I had my own cell. It was like moving out of a junkyard into a Hilton or Holiday Inn: the atmosphere was as different as could be. The noise level went to zero, whereas in the 140-inmate dormitories, the two television sets were always going full blast, as were fifty radios, all on different stations. In the dormitories people talked only about parole, radios, cinnamon rolls—that is, sweet bagels—picture shows, and the like, whereas in the new units there were some conversations about programs, going to college, and other means of self-help. The new units housed only 27 inmates, each in a separate cell, and administration and inmates alike made an effort to keep noise to a minimum. There were, moreover, resources to keep the units well maintained.[60] ■

Of course, cell blocks need not necessarily be superior to dormitories; there are plenty of noisy and dangerous cell blocks in prison. By the same token, there are some prisons in which dormitories are seen as sanctuaries. Lorton Prison, which holds District of Columbia prisoners but is located in Northern Virginia, is a case in point. For many prisoners, the dorms in Lorton offer a niche featuring emotional feedback:

■ Now most of the dormitories in Lorton are like small families. As you walk around, you'll see some of your friends. If they good enough friends of yours, you can get in the dorm with them, the same guys you hung out with on the street.[61] ■

Officers are rarely in evidence in the Lorton dorms.

■ An officer may come into the dormitory and take a look around, but basically he only stay two or three minutes in there. Don't no dormitory hold no officer. Don't no officers stay in no dormitory all day. For no reason.[62] ■

When officers are present, in the dorms and elsewhere in the prison compound, their general attitude is one of laissez-faire: live and let live. Many of the younger inmates like this, because they can do their time as they see fit. For them, the absence of officers connotes freedom. Said one such inmate to a ranking officer, as he refused to get up from his bed, "Judge said I get ten-to-thirty years. He didn't say I got to get out of bed to serve it."[63] The older inmates, however, often feel abandoned in this situation. In the words of one older inmate, "If you read the commitment paper, all it says is 'hold the body.' . . . That's all they care about, to hold my body."[64]

For older prisoners, the absence of officers may also translate into concerns for safety. They report that younger inmates prowl the prison yard in gangs, sometimes invading unprotected dorms. "They wear masks and attack in groups," said one such prisoner.[65] To many older inmates, Lorton offers neither emotional feedback nor freedom but is instead a death trap:

> Almost uniformly the older inmates condemn Lorton Central as a
> "deathtrap." "You can get killed because you have no protection. . . . You
> can't go to a dark room; you can't take a bucket and wash your clothes
> without realizing it's possible you might not come out. It's no such place as
> that you're guaranteed to see tomorrow. You go to bed with a nightmare,
> and the only peace that you ever get is not waking up at all."[66]

The larger point of this discussion is that prison environments—dorms, cells, work areas, even yards—are not stamped from one mold; nor do objectively comparable prison environments have uniform impacts on their inhabitants. One person's niche can be another person's nightmare, as Lorton's dorms so vividly illustrate. There is, in other words, more to prison than the buildings and schedules that mark its official world, and there is more to prison adjustment than a one-way process of people adapting to environments. Always, there is a person–environment transaction in which people and settings interact and shape one another in an ongoing, mutual process.[67] There is, then, the prospect of diverse forms of life and adjustment after one moves beyond the convict world and the prison yard.

Prison Life, Prison Niches

The inmate, confronted with a diversity of prison environments, usually is able to "arrange a microcosm" or "niche" within the larger prison, a world to which he can adapt at least partly on his own terms.[68] Described most broadly, a niche is

> a functional subsetting containing objects, space, resources, people, and
> relationships between people. A niche is perceived as ameliorative; it is
> seen as a potential instrument for the relaxation of stress and the real-
> ization of required ends. It is this quality of niches that stimulates the
> creative process of niche search and niche identification. Niche search is
> usually an explorative process in which a person seeks a specific setting
> because adjustment appears easier there. . . . These settings in prison
> may be work assignments, living units, or programs, and they may feature

any combination among privacy, safety, structure, freedom, support, activity, [and] emotional feedback. . . .[69]

Niches serve as "defenses of the boundaries of self."[70] Though life in a niche "rarely guarantees happiness" or, for that matter, personal reform, it "usually guarantees survival."[71] The prisoner in the process of adapting to prison

> can selectively perceive elements of the prison milieu that either defy his needs or reflect a potential for meeting them. The more salient features of the prison environment—its walls and gates, overlapping security nets, bars and cells, those aspects that have the impact of theater—can fade into psychological insignificance. The inmates attend to a series of invisible subenvironments, with various degrees of movement in or out, population sizes, inmate types, degrees of control and supervision, activities, routines, rules and regulations, behaviors permitted or restrained.[72]

Evidence of these adaptive processes at work can be found in accounts of life in virtually any prison, including the original penitentiaries. Prisoners of these ostensibly monolithic penal environments came to see at least a degree of ecological variability around them. Incoming prisoners of the penitentiaries would be "tested" by peers,[73] news of life inside the prison would travel on a "grapevine",[74] and at least some prisoners were able to secure niches, either in cells or work settings.[75] Prison tiers could be distinguished, at least in a limited way, in terms of social climate,[76] apparently as a function of the supervising officer's style of guarding or of the ethnic or racial composition of the inhabitants.[77] Differential adjustment and survival were features of prison life, even in the most barren of penitentiaries.[78]

One can make the generalization, then, that out of the raw material of the prison—virtually any prison—the prisoner normally fashions a round of life that enhances his ability to negotiate the stresses of prison. The focus of adjustment is on ameliorating those stressors that are of greatest concern to him, variously permitting *activity*—a life in the gym or in which one is otherwise on the run; *privacy*—working in the library or simply spending time alone in one's cell; *safety*—staying close to guards or friends or living in protective custody; *emotional feedback*—preserving one's ties to loved ones, building new ties within the prison with fellow inmates or staff; *support*—a program or activity that offers something of value and hence promises a better future upon release from prison; *structure*—a routine of work and recreation one follows closely so one always knows what is expected or a shop or housing area that is run "by the book"; or *freedom*—a work assignment that requires minimal supervision or a cell block that is run in a relaxed manner.

Prisoners in niches try to live as individuals, not as role types or anonymous members of collectivities. Their goal is to find a routine that meets their basic needs and provides, as much as possible, a "slice of home" in an otherwise alien environment:

> Normally, in the free world, we carry off a surprising number of roles— husband, handyman, father, worker—and we can shape and discard roles.

In prison one's world is more limited. But even though one cannot use the blueprint of one's former life and former roles to construct a way of living in confinement, one uses what is familiar. Though the world of job and street is gone, one of assignment and block can be substituted. Often an inmate creatively alters his space for living to follow old modes as closely as possible.[79]

The gang member from the slums may join the prison chapter of his gang and use it as a niche—to make it possible for him to operate on the yard, to avoid exposure to its dangers, or simply to secure companionship and support. The ubiquitous "street hustler," whether in association with others or alone, may simply take up his hustle once again in the prison, thus following "old modes" of living "as closely as possible" within the constraints of the prison situation. As one prisoner told Susan Sheehan, when asked how he got by in prison, "I hustle, I swag, same as on the street."[80]

A DAY IN THE LIFE

The greater part of Sheehan's book *A Prison and a Prisoner* is an account of the daily life of a self-proclaimed "professional prisoner." The prisoner, whom Sheehan dubbed *George Malinow,* is more adept at prison living than most prisoners. He is able to arrange his affairs to approximate a conventional domestic life and work schedule. This is revealed in a diary kept at Sheehan's request, cataloging "four ordinary days of swagging and spinning out time."[81] Here is one such day in George Malinow's prison life:

■ **6:30 A.M.** Bell rings very loud and long. A certain C.O. [correction officer, or guard] does this (rings bell long) whenever he comes on duty, and I and many other inmates here would like to hit him with a shoe, as he seems to do this on purpose!

God—I hate to get up, I feel so tired!! Serves me right for staying up doing glass painting till 1:55 this morning. But—get up I must and do so. Wash up, shave and get dressed in my work clothes which is green regulation issued pants and shirt and work shoes. Put on water to be boiled for my coffee. Have coffee and 2 do-nuts. Smoke a cigarette and listen to the news, via earphones.

7:15 A.M. Doors open up. I immediately rush off to the mess hall entrance area on the West Side entrance, being I'm one of the first inmates up—no one is near that area at this time of the morning. Terry, a friend of mine (inmate) who works in the kitchen, is there awaiting me. He hands me a large card board box which contains 20 dozen eggs (fresh ones), about 20 pounds of raw bacon, and about 20 pounds macaroni, 20 to 30 oranges, 2 large cans orange juice and one large can of olive oil for cooking. I immediately rush back to my cell, to avoid the other inmates about due to start going to the mess hall for their breakfast.

Hide all said foods items in my cell and my friend Andy's cell. Andy is just at this time up and washing. We joke together about our sudden good windfall from our friend.

7:40 A.M. Andy and I proceed to go to work, the parole-clothing department located at the basement of the Administration Building. Terry stops us to ask us to please get him some shorts, 2 white shirts and black socks. We tell him that we'll give it to him next morning. We reach the check point gate of the Administration Building, get pat frisked and we sign the logbook at the desk to verify at what time we arrived to work. Also left our institutional passes at this check point with the C.O. assigned there, as must be done.

We arrive at the basement parole-clothing area where we work. C.O.s Stevens and Barton are there already. Stevens works the 7:20 to 3:20 shift. Barton does not usually arrive this early because he works the 9:45 to 5:45 shift but today he is working extra early over-time as he has been assigned to drive one of the inmates to an outside hospital for a medical appointment.

The coffee pot is ready as C.O. Stevens always plugs in this pot early as he arrives about 20 minutes to 7, each morning. So Andy, I and Stevens all have coffee and cake. C.O. Barton is busy with the checking of papers for the inmate he is due to take to the hospital so he doesn't join us. We have the radio playing and listening to the local news broadcast. Meanwhile, there are 4 men going home on parole this morning and they just arrived and are getting dressed. Andy and I both help and make certain that all these 4 inmates going home, have all their clothes and personal property packages they may own. They have cups of coffee and relax in casual and happy conversation—about the steaks, drinks and women they'll soon enjoy out there, etc.

Andy and I, both at times, have been asked by many persons—does seeing men talk like this and seeing them go home each day bother us? We don't see it that way as Andy and I, feel very glad to see as many as possible leave any prison as prison represents "hell" in all respects!!

7:50 A.M. All the men due to go home now, leave with C.O. Stevens, to go upstairs to an office where they'll all receive their $40 gate money and whatever's in their inmate account and their release papers. Then C.O. Stevens will escort them out and drive them in the prison van bus to Hopewell jct. station where they will board a bus for N.Y. City. I sorted out all their state issued clothing they turned in to our dept. and also gathered all the earphones they brought to our dept. upon departure. Bagged all state clothes to be sent to State Shop, their final destination.

8:05 a.m. We have an extra relief C.O. to stay with us, as C.O.s Stevens & Barton are out on assignments. Said relief C.O.s name is Officer Dover (works in officers' mess from 10 A.M. onward), who is one of the best natured officers in all respects that I have ever come across. Good sense of humor, always smiling & happy go lucky. Very well mannered, fair and easy to relate with. Should be made a warden.

Andy and I, go to our kitchen room at our basement job area and have another cup of coffee and do-nuts. We relax and talk about general topics on the outside.

8:30 A.M. Another 3 inmates that work with us now arrive to work also. They are Danny, Benno, and Ned.

This morning—we have to take a full inventory of all the stock garments we have and record each item in our general inventory stock so we will know what to order, we are short of. After Danny, Ned, and Benno all have their coffee and buns, all 5 of us get ready to do the inventory.

8:50 A.M. Andy and I, start counting the jackets, slacks, socks, handkerchiefs, belts, shoes and shirts. Danny and Ned start to count the ties, topcoats and the other apparel that the men wear to go out on furloughs, death visits and to courts.

10:35 A.M. We all are caught up on our inventory and go to have coffee again and relax. During all this time of inventory taking, Benno sat at the desk to answer all phone calls of general inquiry and also, made up lists for calling men the next day—that have to be fitted out with civilian clothes for their due release dates soon.

11:05 A.M. Benno starts to prepare the foods that he will cook for our lunch as we are not going to go to the mess hall as there is only franks for lunch. Benno is making steaks, fried onions, French fried potatoes, sauce gravy and sweet green peas for our lunch meal. Benno is an exceptional cook! When he cooks, we all leave the kitchen to be out of his way and also, not to distract him then. One or more of us are available to help him—if he calls us, but most times he does it all by himself.

Of course, he cooks—so all others of us do the cleaning up and wash the pots & dishes.

11:40 A.M. We are just about ready to start eating. We all are in conversation about how good Benno cooked the steaks, the high price of food outside, etc. The radio is playing a late song hit and we all are enjoying the food and are in a good mood.

12:25 P.M. We are done eating—so Andy, Danny and I all take out the dishes, silver ware, pots to the sink area away from the kitchen and wash & dry all. Meantime, Ned swept out kitchen while Benno went to his desk to relax.

12:45 P.M. No inmates to dress this afternoon so Danny and I, recheck all the men due to go home the next morning—on our out going releases sheet. We line up all the clothing outfits and their personal packages containing personal property at the benches where they will get dressed in the morning.

1:15 P.M. We all now sit around the desks and are in conversation about many topics. The parole board's unjust decisions, rehabilitation, politics and prison mismanagement, etc.

2:05 P.M. Phone rings and we have to go to the store house to pick up 6 large cases containing jackets and slacks. Andy, Danny and I, all take a strong push wagon and check out from the check out gate at the administration area, get pat frisked and proceed to go to the store house. Along the way, we stop off at E block, on the East Side, to find out if 2 of the men locking there will be at our Jaycee's meeting tonight? They said they will. We leave for the store house.

We arrive at the store house, load our wagon with all the large cases and pick up a copy of the order-form. We arrive at the front administration check point and again are pat frisked. We start sliding the boxes, one at a time, down the stairs to the basement where we work at. We get all boxes to the rack area. We open all boxes, take out garments and count them. The total checks out correctly. C.O. Stevens signs the receipt form copy and I take it back to the store house civilian clerk. When I return, Andy, Danny, Benno, and Ned are about half way done placing the slacks on the shelfs in their respective sizes, and the jackets on the line racks, in their respective sizes.

I join them in doing this and I sort the jackets. We stop this work at 2:45 P.M. I check and pull out coffee pot plug, stove plug, radio plug and toaster plug. Meanwhile—Andy dumps out all the trash into plastic trash bags due to go out to the dump area, via truck, in the morning. Benno dumps out all water from wash pails in kitchen. Danny washes out coffee pot and prepares it for next morning's use.

2:55 P.M. All of us leave our job area in basement, get pat frisked again at check out gate, pick up our passes and proceed to our cells in C block, all except Ned as he locks in J block.

3:05 P.M. I arrive at my cell, change clothes, wash up and go to the wash room on my gallery's end, to wash out and hang up the clothes I left there to soak yesterday.

3:25 P.M. Returned to cell, put water on for my thermos bottle to make my coffee. Layed down, smoked a cigar and relaxed listening to some soft music via earphones.

4:10 P.M. Got up, made cup of coffee, had a ham and Swiss cheese sandwich. Cleaned up table, brushed teeth and started to get all the necessary materials ready to do my glass painting. Worked on glass painting until lock in.

5:05 P.M. Bell rings—lock in time. Doors close and 2 C.O.s walk by & check the doors & count as they walk past my cell. I continue on working on the glass pictures.

5:25 P.M. C.O. stops at my cell and hands me 8 letters (personal), 2 more business letters and 1 magazine on real estate. C.O. continues on handing out mail to other cells.

Read 3 of these letters which come from the Philippines. One from my sweetheart, one from her sister & the 3rd from her mother. Finish reading all mail and lay down to catch the prison phone bulletin announcements on prison news.

5:55 P.M. Get up, wash up, brush teeth and get all my papers and materials ready for my Jaycees meeting due tonight at the school class building at J block, from 6 to 8:30 P.M.

6:00 P.M. Doors open up. I proceed to block door exit where many other men are waiting to go to different night classes and program classes. The block C.O. checks each one of us out on his master sheet.

I arrive at my Jaycee class room and start writing out on the black board the agenda for tonight's meeting. An outside male Jaycee coordinator arrives and our Jaycee meeting starts. We discuss various project possibilities. One project involves bringing boys from the high schools within a few miles of Green Haven to the prison to see what it is like so that they will never want to commit crimes and will never wind up in prison. We also form committees for each project. Meeting ends at 8:25 P.M. and all of us leave to return to our blocks.

8:35 P.M. Returned to cell. Wash and make cup of coffee & smoke 2 cigarettes. Start to work again on my glass pictures and continue until 10 P.M. I stop to eat a salami & cheese with lettuce & tomato sandwich. Smoke 2 cigarettes and relax on my bed.

I start to think of my sweetheart in the Philippines. What's she doing, etc.? That's rather silly cause since it is a 12 hour difference in time from N.Y. City, it goes without saying it has to be about 10 A.M. there so of course, she can't be sleeping.

10:20 P.M. I start working on my glass pictures again. I accidently spill over the bottle of drawing paint all over my glass and I am angry as hell at myself for my carelessness! Finally get that particular portion on my glass cleaned and I have to re-draw that part of the picture again.

10:55 P.M. The bell rings and that means it's time to lock in for the night. Doors close and the 2 C.O.s again check the doors & take the count. I continue on working on the glass pictures. I feel very tired tonight so I stop working on these pictures at 11:40 P.M. I clean up all paint brushes, table and put away to a safe area, the glass paintings to dry during the night. Have a fast cup of coffee, then wash up, brush teeth and get undressed.

11:55 P.M. Put on only small night lamp, put on phones to catch midnight news. Light up cigarette and listen to the news on phones. Music (Western songs) comes on by some local Poughkeepsie disc jockey and I listen to it until 12:30 A.M.

12:35 A.M. I put out light, pull out phone plug and go to sleep. ■

Malinow's routine is an unusually comfortable one for a maximum-security prisoner and is a testament to his savvy as a "professional." He does seem to live reasonably well if one focuses on the rudimentary material aspects of his existence. Elsewhere in the book, Malinow makes it clear that he was not able to live comfortably when he was young and more rebellious. In those days he worked at less appealing prison jobs and ate his meals in the mess hall. He also had to prove himself to other prisoners, had his share of run-ins with the authorities, and spent a considerable amount of time in segregation. As he aged, he became more modest in his goals and more successful at carving out a life that met his needs. Where once he rebelled against prison authority and raged at the deprivations and hurts he suffered, now a life of "assignment and block" is enough. The larger world of freedom, family, respect, and variety are fading memories that cause little pain. He has been institutionalized, shaped to fit the prison and to live at ease within the girdle of security provided by its walls and routines.[82]

Most prisoners, male or female, do not become institutionalized, however, nor do they live like Malinow. Statistically more typical is the cell block hustler who swags for a living and marks time on the prison yard. This adaptation is common in women's prisons as well, one version of which is sometimes called "canteen pimping":

■ Call it survival
But who is the fittest.
You buy me my cigarettes and
You buy me my deodorant.
Ice Blue Secret is what I use.
And you over there
I'm running low on Ritz Crackers, don't
forget the cheese spread that goes with it.
Canteen Pimpin
Mackin' for the Mustard
Can't wait till Tuesday rolls around,
Brand new crew comes to campus.;
What chu mean "get a job with a pay slot"?
Can't you see I'm loaded down with Kools,
Marlboros, and Camels.
All I gotta do is wear "boxers" and say
I love you.
Going by Lathum now to pick up my Cup O'
Noodles.
Canteen Pimpin
Mackin for the Mustard
By the way Baby, what day do you shop?[83] ■

These prisoners, male and female alike, share with Malinow a basic understanding of "how hard it is to lose one's freedom" and all the pleasures that go with it.[84] They know that monotony is the centerpiece of daily existence in prison. "There's one sure bet around here," states one such prisoner, "nothing changes. You become a creature of habit because every day's program is the same."[85] Malinow's fellow inmates know, too, "how hard it is to endure the daily humiliations of prison life," such as having an inmate number and submitting to constant searches (which may be particularly hard on female offenders).[86] There is, moreover, identity between Malinow's prison life and that of young men (or women) who hustle on the cell blocks, hang out in the yard, and smoke dope at night in the cell blocks (when they can get it), all the while hungering for freedom (both in prison and out) and doing all they can to safely vent the frustrations that build up inside during the normal prison day. The differences between these inmates, male or female, and Malinow are those of particular skills and needs, and thus they move in different prison environments. But all of them have shaped lives in prison more or less on their own terms. They live in prison niches of their own choosing.

PRISON LIFE ON ONE'S OWN TERMS: CHALLENGES AND SOLUTIONS

The fact that there is a diversity of niches that accommodates various lifestyles does not mean that prisoners necessarily find the living arrangements they need. Malinow, for example, was a resourceful inmate who over the years had proven his ability to find a routine to his liking. Less experienced or less competent prisoners, who may be more in need of the oasis Malinow found in the parole-clothing shop, are unlikely to secure these positions. Others, who would prefer the drugs and activity enjoyed by the basketball-playing hustler or gang member, might be afraid to go out into the yard. The prison, like the free world, is more accommodating to some prisoners than to others. More often than not, those who are vulnerable and in need of help are forced to fend for themselves.

The diversity of niches within the prison does not assure a man that his needs will be met. As we noted earlier, one man's niche (for example, a gang in which he feels both autonomous and secure) can be a source of indifference to another man (because the gangs leave him alone) or a source of considerable anxiety (because the presence of gangs introduces, at a minimum, fear and uncertainty into the world of many non–gang members). When the various worlds that operate within prison collide, stress and sometimes conflict are the result. Freedom-oriented inmates, some of whom Malinow mocks for being impetuous youngsters and Abbott admires for being real men, are both a nuisance and a danger to those seeking structure and safety. The freedom to move about the prison and to congregate in one's neighbors' cells (two liberal reforms of the 1960s and 70s) provide occasions for both conviviality with one's friends and exploitation of others—activities that converge, with tragic consequences, in the instance of gang rapes.[87] There is also a perennial though less dramatic conflict when activity- and privacy-oriented prisoners come into contact with one another:

■ You see, down here everybody wants to get familiar with you, and like, myself, I want to just be left alone and do my bit—let the administration leave me alone and in general [be left alone] by the population. I got my little game with my [homemade] jewelry now, and I get my frustrations off with my active sports, and I just want to be left alone, but it is getting to a point now where you can't even play solitaire by yourself. Guys are always bullshitting and hanging around in and around your cell. . . . And these are the type of guys that when you are taking a crap or something, they want to talk to you and they want to know everything you are doing.[88] ■

Under these conditions, otherwise reclusive men are driven to distraction and sometimes to violence.

Niches reflect the diversity of needs of the prisoners who create or stumble upon them or are lucky enough to be formally assigned to them. While it is true that all niches have the psychological connotation of a haven from stress, what constitutes a safe place for a given person may be intensely personal. One inmate of a federal prison maintained that he had to envision a secure world, drawing on his personal life; once the mental image was in place, he could arrange a prison routine that met his needs:

■ The psychological niche may be the first and most difficult to achieve. I imagined the hiding place that I wanted to find. The mental picture that I drew was of an area, surrounded by latticework, under the small back-porch stairs of a house. When I created the niche in my mind that I wanted, the niches that were, in reality, available fell into place: the job in the prison industries, the housing that was the most appropriate, and even the volunteer work that I did with the suicide patients.[89] ■

For this man, and perhaps for most men, "[t]he real niches became the outward manifestations of the internal, personal, and psychological niches."[90]

There is, then, no typical niche, just as there is no typical prisoner. Increasingly, however, niches have one thing in common: they are ways of avoiding the convict culture, of finding shelter from the mainline prison. McCorkle's research on adjustment in a maximum-security prison in Tennessee bears out this point. Fully 300 prisoners filled out questionnaires on prison adjustment. Of that substantial group, over three in four (77.7 percent) indicated that they kept to themselves, living as loners, to avoid victimization. Four of every ten inmates "avoided certain areas of the prison," notably such public areas as the mess hall, housing units other than their own, recreation areas, and the prison yard.[91] While most prisoners in McCorkle's sample were by no means immobilized by fear, "[a] substantial proportion of respondents live with the perception that their personal safety is in constant jeopardy."[92] Cooley's research on prison victimization—featuring interviews "with 117 inmates in five prisons, spanning three security levels in one region" of Canada—provides a similar picture of prison adjustment. At these institutions, "informal rules of social control" emphasized withdrawal from the public world of the prison, expressed in such admonitions as minding one's own business, avoiding the prison economy (which is dominated by the convicts), trusting no one and, when one must engage others, going to considerable lengths to show respect and avoid giving offense.[93] These days, then, the real and often frightening prospect of victimization shapes adjustment. The safest and potentially most rewarding way to live in our threatening prisons is to avoid the predatory world of the convicts and evolve a smaller and more congenial world of one's own.

Convicts are, to be sure, a statistical minority of any prison population, but they are unpredictable and dangerous. These prisoners do not retreat into solitary niches. They move about in the public areas of the prison, often ostentatiously. They seek to deter violence by arming themselves with weapons and lifting weights to beef up their strength. When pressured, they respond with aggression.[94] As we know from Abbott, state-raised convicts often go on the attack to avoid being attacked themselves (see Chapter Five). Consequently, the threat posed by their presence and their periodic predations shapes the adjustments of other prisoners. After all, one knife-wielding convict is not a gang, but he certainly can intimidate others and discourage them from wandering about "his" yard or dining in "his" mess hall. An actual gang of such men is a positive deterrent to venturing far from one's cell block or work area. Scrupulous avoidance of these convicts, Irwin observes, is a goal shared by the vast majority of inmates in today's violent prisons. More than ever, states Irwin,

> prisoners are shying away from public settings and avoiding the activities
> of the convict world. Although they occasionally buy from the racketeers,
> place bets with gamblers, trade commodities with other unaffiliated
> prisoners, or sell contraband on a very small scale, they stay away from the
> rackets and any large-scale economic enterprises. They dissociate
> themselves from the violent cliques and gangs, spend as little time as
> possible in the yard and other public places where gangs hang out, and
> avoid gang members, even though they may have been friends with some
> of them in earlier years. They stick to a few friends whom they meet in
> the cell blocks, at work, through shared interests, in other prisons, or on
> the outside (home boys). With their friends they eat, work, attend
> meetings of various clubs and formal organizations that have abounded in
> the prison, and participate in leisure time activities together. Collectively,
> they have withdrawn from the convict world.[95]

This retreat from the yard may not be a completely honorable one, at least as convicts measure honor, but for most inmates it is workable. "The convicts disrespect those who withdraw," notes Irwin, "but usually ignore them."[96] Of course, being ignored is just what inmates strive for, and it is why they keep to themselves as they go about their daily prison lives.[97]

The first step in arranging a niche away from the convict world is to find a friend or two, or at least an acquaintance one can call upon in a pinch, on the assumption that one cannot afford to be alone and hence easy prey for the tougher convicts. This process of developing protective ties is quite explicitly undertaken by new prisoners:

■ The first thing you needed was allies, and that as quickly as possible. The procedure tended to begin as soon as you were taken from court to the precinct jail, where they gathered the sentenced offenders and handcuffed them two by two for transport to maximum security. You sized up the guy you were handcuffed to and let your instincts do the rest; if he looked like a useful sort, you started up a conversation and established a rapport. You kept this procedure up until you knew enough people to generally cover the territory you were going to run in (e.g., your tier, the exercise yard, your place of work, the gym) and then you chose your friends and chose them carefully, keeping in mind that anything they were involved in would inescapably involve you too. Most of these maneuverings didn't happen as mechanically as this may sound, but the rationale behind them was unavoidably clear and few could afford to ignore the routine. A loner or loser in prison was a goner more often than not.[98] ■

Armed with potential allies, one then constructs a narrow and predictable round of life. This structured existence serves as an antidote to the instability introduced by the violence of the convicts and the sometimes overbearing and even violent control efforts of the staff who do combat with those prisoners. (The "hacks" who do battle with the "cons" are discussed in the next chapter.)

For many inmates, however, allies prove hard to find. Trust, as already noted, is a scarce commodity in prison. Men who are unable to find a reliable "partner" or gain acceptance with a supportive group are left to their own devices in the event that trouble ensues.[99] Because they are unwilling to venture alone into the public prison world, life for many of these solitary inmates virtually begins and ends in the cell. For example, almost four in ten of the Tennessee prisoners (39.5 percent) surveyed by McCorkle reported that they "spent more time in the cell" as an explicit means of avoiding victimization.[100] (Presumably, many of these inmates also avoided public areas of the prison when they *did* leave their cells, but McCorkle's study does not address this matter.) At least one inmate in a Georgia prison has argued that extended cell time is a maxim for prison living. "Certain skills are needed to survive" our dangerous prisons, says he, "the best being the one that enables you to remain in your cell, or on your bunk, 20 to 22 hours a day, year in, year out. It is this ability, above all, that you must acquire if you wish to remain alive and return to the outside."[101] Inside the cell, prisoners like this man find a degree of safety and privacy; alone in their cells, they experience moments of autonomy, however limited and fleeting. Outside the cell they see lurking an intrusive public culture that is at once monotonous and dangerous. For them, then, the cell offers a kind of liberation from prison. The yard and the cell blocks, in contrast, offer only a drab, repetitive, demoralizing routine, which for them epitomizes the constraints of prison life.

Prisoners who log long hours in the cell often describe themselves as alone but not lonely. Paradoxically, when they leave the world they have fashioned in the cell, they may find themselves captive to the lonely crowds that roam the prison world. "Always a lot of fools and crazy people surrounding you," observed Robbie Wideman, "so you ain't never alone but you always lonely."[102] Coping means escape from these lonely and sometimes dangerous crowds:

> ■ Longer I spend in here, the more I back away. Even back away from hangout time with the fellas on the range. I got to find my own space. Even if it's tiny. See in your cell you ain't got nobody else to worry about but your ownself. It's one of the few safe places in here. Course people been offed in they cells. Ain't no place really safe, but least you can be alone, be in your cell with your own stink and your own little bit of stuff and your own thoughts and do. Cause outside your cell ain't nothing going on but the same ole shit. That's what gets to you after a while. Repetition. Same ole, same ole all the time. Same bullshit on the hangout corner. Same slop at breakfast. Same nasty guards. One day just like the other. Same simple cats doing the same dumb numbers. Day in and day out, every day. It gets to you. It surely does.[103] ■

Inmates for whom the cell is a niche are inclined to decorate their cells with care, to fashion them into homes away from home. Said one such inmate, a lifer I interviewed at a Maryland prison,

> ■ I just took a memory and where I could apply it from my house or even my mother's house, and I got something in that cell that reminds me of those things. For instance, the bookshelf reminds me of a wall unit my mother has in her home. The rug on the floor makes me reminisce about the rug in me and my wife's bedroom, the same color pattern and that kind of a thing.[104] ■

Many of these men face long prison terms, including life terms, as we noted in Chapter Four.[105] They know they are going to live in their cells for a considerable time, and they strive to make the cell a living environment.[106] In the words of the Maryland prisoner,

> ■ A lot of people say that when you decorate your cell like that, it means you've moved in permanently. I think in a sense that's true. You wouldn't take the time to do all that if you thought you was going someplace. You want to make it liveable, cause you're going to live there.[107] ■

These same men are inclined to develop jobs that, like their cells, offer them a routine that takes them away from the public culture of the prison. The Maryland prisoner, for example, described his job (as a clerk) as a career that absorbed so much time and energy that he felt removed from daily prison life. For instance, he worked late into the evening on a daily basis, "primarily because I just don't have anything else to do."[108]

Prison, for this man, amounted to cell time or work time. The same can be said for Robbie Wideman. As he makes clear, both cell and work offer a respite from the mainline prison culture:

■ Most of my time away from my cell is in the hospital. My schedule's kind of different from most people's behind me working there. I like my job. Get to be around the nurses, for one thing. You know I dig that. Being around anybody who ain't locked up is a real pleasure, don't care who it is. It's nice too cause in the hospital ain't no guards in my face all day. Sometimes I carry the meals up to the hospital so I can eat in there too. Food ain't no different but it sure do taste better when you ain't sitting with them nuts in the mess hall.[109] ■

For others, the insulation and liberation provided by the cell is achieved through activities that absorb their energy and spirit, transporting them from the confines of the prison. "You know," said one prison poet, "when I'm writing, I'm not in prison."[110] Telander, speaking of a dedicated weight lifter nicknamed Beetle, who had just lifted the equivalent of the "front end of a small car," observed that "for an instant there, Beetle looked as if he were free."[111] Robert B. Smith, a prison poet, writes of the literal liberation— release from prison by court order—sought by prison's writ writers. They work obsessively, devoted to law as if it were an instrument of magic, "more potent than ram's horn," able to breach prison walls with a single phrase or incantation:

■ They search by sunlight, by lamplight,
 by no light,
 knowing the day will, must, come
 when from a sudden page a key
 comes rising, a gold sword from a lake of milk,
 setting them free from the manacles
 that couple them to this desperation, this life[112] ■

More often than not, these writ writers lose their appeals but find a psychological escape in the form of hope. For them, the medium of the law is the message: they can be free within the confines of the prison, psychologically if not physically shorn of "the manacles that couple them to this desperation, this life."

These various inmates adjust by removing themselves from the public prison culture. Yet others, perhaps fewer in number these days, revel in the culture of the prison yard, with its street culture and its communal rhythms of life. Prison poet Raymond Ringo Fernandez, in his "poem for the conguero in D-yard," captures aspects of the public prison culture that are as alien to convicts like Abbott as they are to inmates like Malinow. For Fernandez, the infamous D-yard in Attica, home to a terrible riot and symbol for much of the ferocity of prison life, can at times provide the freedom of a warm summer night in his native Central Park:

■ on warm summer evenings
I hear the tumbao .... [rhythm]
of your blue conga
declamando .... [declaring]
carrying your inspiration
over the wall
like a refreshing
caribbean wind

if it wasn't for
the culturally deprived minds
in the gun towers
i'd swear
I was in central park
chilling out
by the fountain
con un yerbo and a cold.......[with a joint]
can of bud
or
haciendo coro
at un bembe .... [singing in a group]
on a 110th street
where even the children
understand the clave: .... [beat]
.... cla-cla / cla-cla-cla
repica vida conguero .... [alive with bongos]
contratiempo con el tiempo .... [as time passes]
que with each slap
on the congas skin
you bring me closer
to home. . . .■

Fernandez shows us that at least some inmates some of the time—and maybe many inmates at least on occasion—can find slices of home in the very hustle and bustle of music and talk and leisure that are part and parcel of the larger prison culture.

Of course, Malinow wants nothing to do with congo music in the prison yard. He would describe Fernandez's prison yard party as trouble waiting to happen. For him, Fernandez represents "the new element"—mostly urban minority inmates—that is ruining today's prisons. Malinow seeks a niche far from the hostile battlefield Fernandez equates with a congenial urban park. Thus Malinow's routine featured cell activities (mostly writing and hobby-crafts), a job, and a daily routine that was expressly calculated to keep him away from the public areas of the prison. For Malinow, venturing into such areas as the mess hall and the yard meant risking confrontations with guards he didn't know and convicts he didn't want to know. The predictable result of mingling in the convict world was either that one responded to their threats or insults and got into trouble, or one backed down and was further belittled and abused:

It isn't just the uninspiring food and the fact that he can manage to eat well enough on his job and in his cell, it is also the atmosphere of the mess hall that keeps Malinow from going there. Like many experienced inmates at Green Haven, he leads a circumscribed life, avoiding crowds and cutting down on his chances of being hassled by officers and inmates he doesn't know. He dislikes the long walk to the mess hall, the waiting in line, and the possibility he may inadvertently wind up at a table next to some inmates he describes as "the new element," by which he means young black drug addicts. "If one of the new element jumps in line ahead of me or makes a remark about honkies and he knows I've heard it, I'd have to hit him and that would get me into trouble," he said. "I don't need trouble. But I can't let such a remark go by. I'm not from a blue-blooded family, I don't have a million dollars. All I have is my image, how I'm regarded in prison, how I carry myself. Some inmates won't react— you can call their mothers or fathers anything—but from then on they're considered trash, and they're treated accordingly. They'll let a remark go by, and the next thing you know they'll be standing in the yard in front of the TV set and some guy standing behind them will say, `Hey, creep, get out of here,' and they'll have to go. . . ." Malinow rarely goes to the yard. He no longer participates in sports, says he has outgrown idle prison conversations about past and future Cadillacs and women, and considers the yard another place to avoid the new element.[114]

The new element Malinow strives to avoid poses different problems for different prisoners. When Malinow and other, usually older, inmates of contemporary prisons demand a structured and predictable routine, "it is not chaos that they bemoan, it is the prison's failure to control things that need controlling."[115] Malinow, for instance, quite explicitly prizes an ordered prison life and speaks nostalgically about the rigorous and disciplined prisons he has known in his time. Foremost among these is Clinton Prison in upstate New York, a prison that to this day is known for its regimentation:

■ At Clinton, you always knew where you stood. . . . You got up in the morning and went through your daily routine like a robot. You even set yourself a precise schedule for your daily chores, like rinsing out your clothes on Tuesdays and Thursdays from four-thirty to five. . . . Those seven years at Clinton under rigid conditions went by very quickly. . . . Some of the old-timers, men who had been sentenced in the 1920s, when sentences were much longer—thirty to sixty years for first-degree robbery wasn't uncommon—taught me the trick of doing time. They told me never to think of my sentence as a whole but to do one day at a time. They said that if you concentrated on the day you were up, soon the many days and years ahead of you would be behind you. They were right. The seven years went by like three and a half.[116] ■

Jimmy Dunn, a man who served a number of lengthy prison terms in regimented Big Houses, explains the salutary connection between having a routine and taking one day at a time:

■ So I'll get up this morning, like every other morning, and I'll go through the routine, because the routine is what saves me. The days are all the same. Each one exactly like the one preceding it and like the one following it. They're all the same—just a blur—and looking back a year ago when I got this jolt, it seems like only yesterday because yesterday was just like it was a year ago.[117] ■

A structured, circumscribed life need not be an especially barren or lonely one, at least as these terms have meaning in the prison. Years of a robotlike regimentation are preferable to the worse alternative of chronic anxiety about one's reputation or safety. As it happens, Malinow and many of the other prisoners who live highly structured lives off the yard and away from militant groups and gangs have their own networks of support. While one is not showered with spontaneous displays of affection, one is at least provided for on a regular basis:

Within a few minutes [of his arrival at the prison], runners came up to him bringing large bags of groceries and thermoses filled with coffee, compliments of the many friends he had made during his stay [at other prisons]. "I was very appreciative that people thought of me even before I was in the place an hour," he says. "Old-timers know it can be hard in a new prison the first day or two. Sometimes you don't get your personal property immediately, and you don't get to the commissary right away."[118]

There are alternatives to Malinow's comparatively monastic existence that provide structure and predictability, even if his routine is not as sterile as one would suppose. Some inmates join formal prisoner clubs or organizations. These groups, officially sanctioned and closely supervised by prison authorities, are an important aspect of the prison ecology. In some prisons, as many as half of the inmates maintain such affiliations.[119] As Fox observed of the contemporary violent prison, "while an increasing number of prisoners have adopted a hardened posture toward their fellow prisoners and prison officials, many prisoners sought traditional or legitimate solutions to problems of personal and social adjustment in prison."[120] Most of these prisoners, Fox continues, "accept the legitimacy of authority used in their apprehension, conviction, and incarceration."[121] They turn to authorized formal groups to solve adjustment problems because they now have greater rights of association as well as a greater need for shelter against the tempestuous prison yard.

These organizations serve a variety of needs for both prisoners and staff. For prisoners, the diversity of living and program arrangements is supplemented by a host of voluntarily selected group activities relating to cultural awareness, religion, self-help, and various special interests such as community service (for example, through a prison chapter of the Jaycees like the one to which Malinow belonged).[122] Some of these groups serve clearly rehabilitative goals for their members. Given the void many inmates report in their lives, both in the free world and the prison (see Chapter Four), the appeal of these rehabilitative groups would seem to be almost existential, giving meaning and direction to an otherwise empty existence. Other prisoner organizations provide protection to their members or serve as arenas for benign forms of recreation. (A few groups, notably some of the cultural or ethnic awareness organizations, serve as covers for convict gang activities, but they are the exception rather than the rule.) These prisoner groups assure the staff that the prison "masses" now operate to a great extent under their authority and supervision. Officials grant charters to these organizations, approve their activities, and provide the space and administrative support (including security) needed to carry out their various missions. Prisoners are thus more readily served and controlled by virtue of these groups.[123] The "tentative order" Irwin described in today's prisons is in no small part due to the civil relationships that bind these groups and the prison authorities.

Some prisoners have an especially hard time securing a niche in the regular prison population. Younger, inexperienced inmates, for instance, are more vulnerable to prison predators than Malinow and his associates and have fewer avenues of adjustment open to them.[124] Naive white inmates are apt to be particularly vulnerable because, more often than not, black prisoners have assumed positions of dominance in the prison community. Simple civility will mark them as targets. A seasoned white convict at Leavenworth makes this point, with evident contempt for white victims and black victimizers:

■ Most whites fuck up right away when they come into prison, because they try to be friendly. . . . Let's say a white dude is put in a cell with maybe fifteen niggers. If he says hello or even nods to them, then he's already doomed. You see, half of them will think he is just being polite and treating them with respect, but the other half will know he is weak and afraid, because they know that a white man isn't even going to acknowledge them if he's been in prison before, because whites don't speak to niggers in prison. These niggers are going to move on that guy as soon as the hack disappears.[125] ■

Some vulnerable prisoners may be too fearful to join formal prisoner organizations or, having joined one, may find that their fellow Jaycees cannot protect them from predatory convicts. They find that they cannot simply retreat from the public areas of the prison as Malinow and some club members do, because they are actively pursued by aggressors. Often they are friendless, either because they are new to prison or because other inmates avoid them for fear of being targeted by aggressors. (As Schroeder reminds us, in prison one picks one's associates carefully, "keeping in mind that anything they were involved in would inescapably involve you too." The implication is that only prospective victims would gravitate to one another, but, even here, fear keeps would-be supporters apart, each trying to maintain a low profile.) Nor can vulnerable inmates turn to staff. The convict code, which regular inmates respect out of fear, all but precludes a target from enlisting the aid of staff. As

Lockwood has observed, referring to targets of sexual aggression, the prisoner who " 'rats' on those who make aggressive advances to him is a 'sissy,' because he is an object of sexual attention, a 'punk' because he will not fight, and a 'snitch' because he has told a staff member about his problem."[126] He is very much in jeopardy. "Above all, vulnerable inmates learn that no amount of supervision, no physical barriers, can prevent their being the object of threats and advances ranging from simple pleas to physical violence."[127]

For "young and effeminate prisoners," then, "segregation may be their only safe niche."[128] Here, structure serves the need for safety to the virtual exclusion of other living requirements. Inmates who seek what is known as "protective segregation," "protection company," "protection," or simply "PC" are housed

> under conditions similar to those found in disciplinary segregation: they are isolated from the rest of the prison population; they are confined to their cells for all but a small part of the day; they are not able to participate in institutional activities. Indeed, some officials fail to distinguish between disciplinary and protective segregation. As the judge in one case involving sexual assault recently noted, "a threatened inmate can go to the hole."[129]

Only in protection are such men in fact "truly protected from other inmates."[130] Still, they pay a high price for this service:

> In exchange for safety, they sacrificed the freedom of movement that is available to other prisoners, the opportunity to participate in school, and the access to other prison programs. They relinquished their weekly movies and the sports in the yard. In exchange for their safety they lived in quarantine, spending twenty-two hours a day in their cell.[131]

Sadly, the price of safety includes more than discomfort and boredom. For many offenders, living in isolation produces psychological harms as well. In Brodsky's words,

> the PC living experience deprive[s] the inmates of the opportunity to engage in behaviors that allow each of us to define who we are. Without a sense of accomplishment, most people cannot maintain self-esteem. Without interpersonal stimulation, we narrow emotionally. Without the exercise of our emotional and intellectual skills, we become stagnant and lose mastery of ordinary abilities to concentrate and to attend. . . . These constrictions become magnified further in the context of fear and perceived harassment. . . . [As a result,] for up to two-thirds of . . . confined men in the more typical institutions, the PC living experience is harmful in ways that interfere with their mental health and well-being.[132]

And these inmates are likely to remain in quarantine for long periods of time, often for their entire sentence. The reason: they are now visibly labeled as weak and, hence, as fair game for predators. It is for this reason that protective custody has been variously called "an escape hatch with a boomerang" and "a sanctuary from which there is no return."[133]

Yet it is crucial to appreciate that protective custody "is generally liked by its residents," even though it is uncomfortable and sometimes psychologically disabling.[134] These men, unlike the convicts such as Abbott who populate disciplinary segregation, are in all likelihood traumatized by their experiences of victimization and hence in full retreat from the prison world. Victims in prison tend to be drawn disproportionately from among the young and the socially isolated; for all prison victims, but for the young and the isolated in particular, "victimizations that occur in prison are much more 'fear-provoking' than those which occur in the free world."[135] As a result, vulnerable prisoners, for whom the threat if not the reality of victimization is a daily fact of life, have "a preponderant need for safety, and/or a consuming desire for privacy."[136] These concerns are at least minimally satisfied in protective custody, while the convicts' obsession with freedom is flagrantly violated by the same regime. Fearful prisoners prefer "sanctuary in protection to life in a prison population."[137] They "perceive themselves as having made a free and knowledgeable choice" among the range of admittedly unappealing options open to them.[138] While it may seem odd from a free-world perspective, given the harsh realities of life in prison, "one shudders at the fate of these men should the alternative of protection not be available to them."[139]

Niches in Prisons for Women

The process of securing a niche, as well as many of the general contours of what constitutes a niche, are very much the same for female and male prisoners. For women as for men, the adjustment process means learning to read the environment and then to establish a routine that allows one to settle into an acceptable way of life behind bars.

As female inmates "move through the initial processing," observes Owen,

> concerns about their safety, their sexuality, and their ability to "do time" become less pronounced as they gradually adjust to the prison routine, develop their own program for getting through the day, and become acculturated to the prison world. As the weeks and months pass, women start to compose a life inside the walls.[140]

The bottom line, for women and for men, is nicely summed up in the notion that one "composes" or "carves"[141] a life behind prison walls. These adjustments can be understood in ecological terms as offering women as well as men what Owen has insightfully characterized as "some measure of privacy and safety, a range of activity, a satisfying program, a living situation that is fairly comfortable, and a degree of material comforts."[142]

It is significant that the lives prisoners fashion for themselves take place in the private world of the prison, away from the public prison world and especially the prison yard. Owen's observations about women's efforts to avoid the public areas of the prison, most notably the yard, are variations on the same theme that dominates the adjustments of male prisoners: "As the most public place in the prison," notes Owen, "the yard is defined as a place of trouble and with some exceptions, a place to be avoided."[143] Observations made by the women who spoke with Owen reinforce this point:

■ I don't go to the yard. It is messy—the drugs, drinks. The cops search you for no reason. The whole time you are in there, you have to keep your eye out because you never know what is going to happen. A person is likely to throw a syringe at your foot. You can be in the wrong place at the wrong time and you are apt to go to Ad Seg for nothing.

★ ★ ★

. . .[H]ardly anybody goes there because everybody is afraid of the same thing. I just want to stay in my own unit. I am attached to people there and I know them. I feel like it is your own apartment complex—in this hallway we run from this room to that room.

★ ★ ★

I go from here to the library and directly back. Do not pass go, do not collect $200.00, and DO NOT go to jail. I don't fuck around with nothing in the middle. I cannot afford to.[144] ■

Owen's research suggests that "[l]ess than 5 percent of the women interviewed in the survey indicated that they spend their free time on the yard."[145] Though we do not have a comparable survey for men, one is left with the impression that women are at least as likely as men—and perhaps more likely—to remove themselves from the public prison world dominated by the convicts.

In women's prisons, which like men's prisons these days tend to be crowded and often dangerous, privacy is a valued commodity. Life for many women prisoners, like their male counterparts, is restricted to the world of the prison cell. Again, quoting Owen on women in prison: "The dynamics of prison social life are all played out within the confines of this small space."[146] One female prisoner referred to her cell as her "cave"—"let me go back to my cave and stay out of everybody's business."[147] Another reported to Owen that "she climbs up on her bunk and pretends it is a 'condo' away from everybody else."[148] Note how closely these adaptations parallel that of Cobb, a male inmate quoted earlier in this chapter, who lives his solitary prison life perched on the top bunk he calls home in a crowded dormitory. As is true for many men in prison, Owen reports that "Many women walk the track alone or colonize their workspace to find this much-sought-after privacy. . . . Other women told me they wear earphones for their music or radios to block out noise, or lose themselves in a book, hobby, or letter-writing."[149]

A niche allows prisoners to "lose themselves," to quote Owen, by finding a part of themselves—that is, of their selves—in the lives they fashion in the prison. In the women's prison context, Owen captured this theme under the notion of "programming," a notion familiar to students of male prisons as well:

"Programming" is the process of developing a personal accommodation to one's situation of imprisonment. Learning how to "get with the program" is the first step in learning how to do time . . . personal relationships and routine activities offer constructive stimulation and protection from the dangers of the prison environment.[150]

A key feature of one's "program" may be a prison clique or family or gang, or simply a close personal relationship. These affiliations provide comfort and assurance in part because they capture elements of earlier supportive relationships one had (or wished one had) in the outside world.[151] They are an important slice of a real or imagined home that one has drawn from the outside world. Thus, a prison family or a prison gang can replace the family one never had but desperately wanted; a homosexual lover can allow one to "play house" in a way that is familiar enough to be gratifying but different enough to preclude jeopardizing one's intimate free world relationships.

MORE THAN SURVIVAL

Prisons provide stressful and sometimes disabling experiences. There are frightened, vulnerable, lonely inmates who fail to secure protection or support in any form. Cut adrift in a viciously rejecting world, they find no niche, no respite. For them, in the words of prison poet J. A. Hines,

■ There is no escape
   not in dreams
   not in death
   not in dreams of death
   not even in the death of dreams[152] ■

These inmates run a substantial risk of suicide, hoping perhaps to secure the final escape of physical death and the oblivion it seems to promise.[153] Typically, however, confinement is endured without breakdowns or lasting psychological harm. Even in protective custody, an admittedly barren "last-ditch niche," there is life and adjustment.[154] Morale is low, but most prisoners somehow make do in the prison.

The challenge for prison administrators is to translate occasions of stress into opportunities for growth. Persons in niches typically avoid problems, whether they be problems with authorities, fear of peers, anxiety in social situations, or feelings of inadequacy when separated from loved ones. Avoidance is, of course, one aspect of a competent coping strategy: religions have long counseled that one should avoid occasions of sin, and there is merit in this advice. But one cannot avoid all problems, and some methods of avoidance, such as manipulation and deception, are harmful to others. Thus, skills for responsibly circumventing problems must be supplemented with problem-solving skills.

Prisoners who have found a niche are, in a sense, hiding in and from the prison, and they are not likely to come out of hiding unless we offer support and encouragement. The security of the niche, in other words, is unlikely to be given up unless we make the prisoners a better offer. Yet that same sense of security provides an opening for change. As one man observed, the prisoner who is secure in his adjustment evokes confidence in others, who in turn are more likely to see him as a fellow human being who is a worthy candidate for help and support:

■ If you find your niche, the others sense that you feel less threatened and feel less threatened by you. The self-confidence that you gain from feeling secure enables others to have confidence in you. Thus, the staff in particular, because of their heightened ability to do so, and the other inmates, in their more limited and sometimes more profound way, will tend to view you as someone upon whom help will not be wasted. And, because you feel secure in the niche, you are able to accept the help.[155] ■

For this man, and perhaps for most people in prison, "the best help . . . always included letting you know that you were a regular human being" and not a mere criminal or inmate.

The vast majority of prisoners survive confinement in the sense that they make compromises and get by. But corrections must be more than this, must mean more than simply making do. Corrections must mean addressing the problems of confinement with all of the human and environmental resources at our disposal. To do this, relations in the prison world must embody exchanges between and among full-blooded human beings whose aspirations and concerns are taken seriously. Problems in living experienced by the human beings who populate our prisons include those suffered by the convicts as well as by the other prisoners. Among the key actors in the correctional process are the line staff. The adjustments of the line staff and the roles they play in shaping the prison world are the subjects of the next two chapters.

NOTES

1. McCorkle and Korn (1954).

2. Earley (1992:89).

3. Earley (1992:14).

4. Fleisher (1989:122).

5. Fleisher (1989:122).

6. Pearson (1997).

7. Pearson (1997:216).

8. Pearson (1997:216).

9. Washington (1981:9).

10. Seymour (1977:179).

11. Seymour (1977:179).

12. Toch (1977).

13. Toch (1975 & 1992).

14. Bowker (1980); Lester and Danto (1993); Bottoms (1999); Liebling (1999).

15. See Johnson (1998).

16. The relevant research is reviewed in Bonta and Gendreau (1990).

17. Glaser (1964:118).

18. Toch (1977).

19. Zamble, Porporino, and Kalotay (1984:66).

20. Zamble, Porporino, and Kalotay (1984:66 & 67).

21. See, generally, Owen (1998).

22. See Renzema (1988:161) and Beck and Shipley (1989) for recidivism among American ex-prisoners; see Bonta, Lipinski, and Martin (1992) for recidivism among Canadian ex-prisoners. The Beck and Shipley recidivism research reports on a sample of 16,000 prisoners released from confinement in eleven states in 1983 and followed for a three-year period. We learn that "62.5 percent were rearrested for a felony or serious misdemeanor within three years, 46.8 percent were reconvicted, and 41.4 percent returned to prison or jail" (Beck & Shipley, 1989:1). A sizable minority (about 37 percent) were neither rearrested nor reconfined for a felony or a serious misdemeaner. As a group, this cohort of releasees were active criminals *before* confinement, having been "arrested and charged with an average of more than twelve offenses each" (Beck & Shipley, 1989:1). Interestingly, about two-thirds of these prisoners had been confined before; this is about the same confinement rate as displayed after release from prison, suggesting that incarceration had not, on average, increased criminality among this group. Chronic offenders, in particular young chronic offenders, were exceedingly active in crime before and after their imprisonment; fully "94.1 percent of prisoners age eighteen to twenty-four with eleven or more prior arrests were rearrested within three years" (Beck & Shipley, 1989:1). The Beck and Shipley study remains "the best available to approximate the recidivism rate of parolees . . ." (Petersilia, 1999:512).

23. See Nettler (1984).

24. Wallerstedt (1984); Beck and Shipley, (1989:1).

25. See Nettler (1984).

26. Fully 41 percent of California's parole revocations are for technical violations, not new crimes. See Austin and Lawson (1998). For a thoughtful assessment of parole today together with a discussion of promising reforms, see Petersilia (1999).

27. Hoffman and Beck (1984).

28. Bennett (1983:pt. 1).

29. Megargee and Cadow (1980:36).

30. Irwin (1980:14).

31. Earley (1992:44).

32. Owen (1998:181).

33. Irwin (1980:212).

34. Toch (1980).

35. Jacobs (1977:150–53).

36. Davidson (1974:21).

37. Davidson (1974:84).

38. Rierden (1997:125–26).

39. See Carroll (1988).

40. Levinson (1988:242).

41. Seymour (1988:268).

42. Seymour (1988:268).

43. Toch (1977:17).

44. Toch (1977:25).

45. Toch (1977:16).

46. Toch (1977:27).

47. Toch (1977:28).

48. Toch (1977:16).

49. Toch (1977:50).

50. Toch (1977:17).

51. Toch (1977:52).

52. Washington (1981:16).

53. Toch (1977:16).

54. Toch (1977:70).

55. Toch (1977:16).

56. Toch (1977:93).

57. Toch (1977:17).

58. Toch (1977:98).

59. See Toch (1977:123–40).

60. Cobb (1985:74).

61. Blecker (1990:212).

62. Blecker (1990:212).

63. Blecker (1990:244).

64. Blecker (1990:244).

65. Blecker (1990:214–15).

66. Blecker (1990:214–15).

67. See Toch (1977:2).

68. Seymour (1977:180).

69. Seymour (1977:181).

70. Seymour (1977:188).

71. Seymour (1977:188).

72. Seymour (1977:180).

73. Anonymous (1871:60).

74. Anonymous (1871:244).

75. Anonymous (1871:78–79).

76. Anonymous (1871:94).

77. See Coffey (1823:105).

78. See Coffey (1823:116).

79. Seymour (1977:184).

80. Sheehan (1978:95). As Zamble, Porporino, and Kalotay (1984:66) have noted in their research with Canadian prisoners, "despite differences from the outside, the environment in the penitentiary allowed inmates to re-establish on the inside much of the pattern of their outside lives." Leo Carroll has been kind enough to remind me that this observation holds for gang members, who are apt to view at least some of the functions and activities of their gangs in ameliorative terms. That is, gang members are apt to see their gangs as niches (Carroll, personal communication, 1996).

81. Sheehan (1978:96). There are more recent "day in the life" essays available, which confirm the current applicability of Malinow's experience, but none are nearly as detailed as his and it is for this reason that I have retained this entry. The interested reader is invited to consult York (2000) for daily life in a maximum-security prison for men, Redifer (2000) for a high-security prison for women, and Williams (2000) for a minimum-security prison for men.

82. Another example of an inmate providing a case of study of better prison adjustment over time is provided by Johnson (2000).

83. Jamal (1984:146).

84. Sheehan (1978:130–31).

85. York (2000).

86. Sheehan (1978:130–31). See also Metzger (2000:138) for a glimpse of the daily humiliations of prison life for women, which she compares to a microwave oven—prison "destroys you on the inside long before its effects are evident on the outside." It has been argued that searches, in particular, may be more degrading for women because so many women in prison have histories of sexual abuse (Farkas & Rand, 1999).

87. Bowker (1980:4–6).

88. Toch (1977:37).

89. Gates (1991:75).

90. Gates (1991:75).

91. McCorkle (1992:10).

92. McCorkle (1993:87).

93. See Cooley (1992:33–34).

94. See McCorkle (1992:10).

95. Irwin (1980:197).

96. Irwin (1980:202).

97. McCorkle (1992:10).

98. Schroeder (1976:30).

99. See Cooley (1992:34).

100. McCorkle (1992:10).

101. Cobb (1985:74).

102. Wideman (1985:230).

103. Wideman (1984:230).

104. Personal communication (1988).

105. See, generally, Zamble (1992).

106. See, for example, McCall (1995:171).

107. Personal communication (1988).

108. Personal communication (1988).

109. Wideman (1984:232).

110. Klein (1988:15).

111. Telander (1988:4).

112. Smith (1984:298).

113. Fernandez (1984:95).

114. Sheehan (1978:83–85).

115. Seymour (1977:188). Elaborating, Seymour notes, "Older inmates may feel

a particular need for environmental stability, in light of changes in the composition of prison populations. Given a shift
in the inmate subculture, from a
respected coping style of emotional distance and coolness, to one that includes
militancy, confrontation, and testing, new
needs for stability are generated."

116. Sheehan (1978:199 & 205).

117. Manocchio and Dunn (1982:33).

118. Sheehan (1978:238).

119. Fox (1982:141); see also Stojkovic
(1984) and Lin (2000).

120. Fox (1982:88).

121. Fox (1982:106).

122. Fox (1982:141); see also Stojkovic
(1984).

123. Fox (1982:138); see also Stojkovic
(1984).

124. See, for example, McCorkle
(1993:87).

125. Earley (1992:419).

126. Lockwood (1977:215).

127. Lockwood (1977:216).

128. Irwin (1980:202).

129. Lockwood (1977:206); see also
Brodsky (1984).

130. Lockwood (1977:208).

131. Lockwood (1977:208).

132. Brodsky (1984:21); see also Toch
(1975); Burtch and Ericson (1979).

133. Lockwood (1977:211).

134. Lockwood (1977:221).

135. McCorkle (1993:87).

136. Lockwood (1977:223).

137. Lockwood (1977:223).

138. Lockwood (1977:223).

139. Lockwood (1977:223). Though protection may be a niche of sorts under current arrangements, this does not mean that
more accommodating living conditions
cannot be developed to afford protection
cases the privacy and safety they require.

Brodsky (1984) studied one such PC unit
and reported adequate adjustment among
its residents.

140. Owen (1998: 86).

141. It is interesting that the notion of
"carving" an adjustment out of an otherwise impersonal prison world is a theme
applied to men in prison by Seymour,
Toch, myself, and others and to women in
prison by Owen.

142. Owen (1998:117).

143. Owen (1998:109).

144. Owen (1998:110).

145. Owen (1998:181).

146. Owen (1998:89).

147. Owen (1998:110).

148. Owen (1998:95).

149. Owen (1998:95).

150. Owen (1998:97).

151. "Family relationships formed a
foundation for the play family or the
pseudo family. These 'prison families'
reflect significant roles present in family
dynamics in the outside world" (Owen,
1998:120). In women's prisons, families
often are "a primary social unit in the
organization of the prison culture"
(Owen, 1998:120), comparable to male
peer groups and gangs. Younger women
appear more likely to form gangs in prisons, as do younger men (Owen, 1998;
Rierden, 1997).

152. Hines (1984:127).

153. Suicidal behavior is a low-rate phenomenon in all environments. Comparatively speaking, however, suicide is common
in confinement. (For a thoughtful general
review of suicide in confinement, see
Liebling, 1999.) The suicide rate for prison
inmates in the United States is 17.5 per
100,000, which is roughly 50 percent
higher than that of free citizens, for whom
the rate is 11 per 100,000. This figure has
remained constant for fully twenty years
(Bonta & Gendreau, 1990:356). The suicide
rate for jail inmates, for whom the stresses
of transition from free world to confinement are great and the supports in the envi-

ronment few, are anywhere from five to nine times higher than in the free world (see Hayes, 1983; Gibbs, 1988; Hayes & Rowan, 1988). Suicide rates are lower in prison than in jail because prisoners face a less abrupt transition than does the jail inmate (the prisoner comes from a jail rather than the free world), and the prison generally offers a more stable environment than the jail. Self-mutilation, again a low-

rate behavior, occurs among inmates of jails and prisons at an even more disproportionate rate than do suicides (Toch, 1975 & 1992). Once again, rates of self-mutilation are substantially higher in jail than in prison, and for the same reasons.

154. Lockwood (1977:207).

155. Gates (1991: 75–76).

REFERENCES

Anonymous. *An Illustrated History and Description of State Prison Life, By One Who Has Been There. Written by a Convict in a Convict's Cell.* Globe Publishing, 1871.

Austin, J., and R. Lawson. *Assessment of California Parole Violations and Recommended Intermediate Programs and Policies.* San Francisco: National Council on Crime and Delinquency, 1998.

Beck, A. J., and B. E. Shipley. "Recidivism of prisoners released in 1983." Washington, DC: Bureau of Justice Statistics, 1989.

Bennett, R. R. (ed.). *Police At Work: Policy Issues and Analysis.* Beverly Hills, CA: Sage, 1983.

Blecker, R. "Haven or hell? Inside Lorton Central Prison: Experiences of punishment justified." *Stanford University Law Review* 42 (May 1990):1149–249.

Bonta, J., and P. Gendreau. "Reexamining the cruel and unusual punishment of prison life." *Law and Human Behavior* 14 (4) 1990:347–72.

Bonta, J., S. Lipinski, and M. Martin. "Characteristics of federal inmates who recidivate." Ottawa: Statistics Canada, 1992.

Bottoms, A. E. "Interpersonal violence and social order in prisons." In M. Tonry and J. Petersilia. *Prisons.* Chicago: University of Chicago Press, 1999:205–281.

Bowker, L. *Prison Victimization.* New York: Elsevier, 1980.

Brodsky, S. L. "Inmates in protective custody: First data on emotional effects." Presidential Address, Division 18, Annual Meeting of the American Psychological Association, Toronto, Canada, 1984.

Burtch, B. E., and R. V. Ericson. "The silent system: An inquiry into prisoners who suicide and an annotated bibliography." Toronto: University of Toronto Centre of Criminology, 1979.

Carroll, L. "Race, ethnicity, and the social order of the prison." In R. Johnson and H. Toch (eds.). *The Pains of Imprisonment.* Prospect Heights, IL: Waveland Press, 1988:181–203.

Cobb, A., Jr. "Home truths about prison overcrowding." *The Annals of the American Academy of Political and Social Science* 478 (March 1985):73–85.

Coffey, W. A. *Inside Out: Or, An Interior View of the New York State Prison; Together with Bibliographic Sketches of the Lives of Several of the Convicts.* New York: 1823, printed for the author.

Cooley, D. "Prison victimization and the informal rules of social control." *Forum on Corrections Research* 4 (3) 1992:31–36.

Davidson, R. T. *Chicano Prisoners: The Key to San Quentin.* New York: Holt, Rinehart & Winston, 1974.

Earley, P. *The Hot House: Life Inside Leavenworth.* New York: Bantam Books, 1992.

Farkas, M. A., and K. R. L. Rand. "Sex matters: A gender-specific standard for cross-gender searches of inmates." *Women & Criminal Justice* 10 (3) 1999:31–55.

Fernandez, R. R. "Poem for the conguero in D-Yard." In J. Bruchac (ed.). *The Light from Another Country: Poetry from American Prisons.* Greenfield Center, NY: Greenfield Review Press, 1984:95.

Fleischer, M. S. *Warehousing Violence.* Beverly Hills, CA: Sage, 1989.

Fox, J. G. *Organizational and Racial Conflict in Maximum-Security Prisons.* Lexington: Lexington Books, 1982.

Gates, M. "The excavation." Unpublished manuscript. American University, 1991.

Gibbs, J. J. "The first cut is the deepest: Psychological breakdown and survival in the detention setting." In R. Johnson and H. Toch (eds). *The Pains of Imprisonment.* Prospect Heights, IL: Waveland Press, 1988:97–114.

Glaser, D. *The Effectiveness of Prison and Parole Systems.* Indianapolis: Bobbs-Merrill, 1964.

Hayes, L. M. "And darkness closes in . . . A national study of jail suicides." *Criminal Justice and Behavior* 10 (4) 1983: 461–84.

Hayes, L., and J. R. Rowan. *National Study of Jail Suicides: Seven Years Later.* Alexandria, VA: National Center for Institutions and Alternatives, February 1988.

Hines, J. A. "Cancel my subscription." In J. Bruchac (ed.). *The Light from Another Country: Poetry from American Prisons.* Greenfield Center, NY: Greenfield Review Press, 1984:127.

Hoffman, P. B., and J. L. Beck. "Burnout-age at release from prison and recidivism." *Journal of Criminal Justice* 12 (6) 1984:617–23.

Irwin, J. *Prisons in Turmoil.* Boston: Little, Brown, 1980.

Jacobs, J. *Stateville: The Penitentiary in Mass Society.* Chicago: University of Chicago Press, 1977.

Jamal, Y. "Canteen Pimpin'." In J. Bruchac (ed.). *The Light from Another Country: Poetry from American Prisons.* Greenfield Center, NY: Greenfield Review Press, 1984:146.

Johnson, R. *Death Work: A Study of the Modern Execution Process,* 2nd ed. Belmont, CA: Wadsworth, 1998.

Johnson, R. and Toch, H. (Eds.) *Crime and Punishment: Inside Views.* Los Angeles, CA: Publishing Company, 2000.

Klein, R. "Molding a cry and a song: American prisoners as poets." *Commonweal* 115 (1) 1988:14–18.

Lester, D., and B. L. Danto. *Suicide Behind Bars: Prediction and Prevention.* Philadelphia: The Charles Press, 1993.

Levinson, R. "Try softer." In R. Johnson and H. Toch (eds.). *The Pains of Imprisonment.* Prospect Heights, IL: Waveland Press, 1988:241–56.

Liebling, A. "Prison suicide and prisoner coping." In M. Tonry, and J. Petersilia. *Prisons.* Chicago: University of Chicago Press, 1999:283–359.

Lin, A. C. *Reform in the Making: The Implementation of Social Policy in Prison.* Princeton: Princeton University Press, 2000.

Lockwood, D. "Living in protection." In H. Toch. *Living in Prison: The Ecology of Survival.* New York: Free Press, 1977:206–223.

Manocchio, A. J., and J. Dunn. *The Time Game: Two Views of a Prison.* Beverly Hills, CA: Sage, 1982.

McCall, N. *Makes Me Wanna Holler: A Young Black Man in America.* New York: Vintage, 1995.

McCorkle, L. W., Jr., and R. Korn. "Resocialization within walls." *The Annals of the Academy of Political and Social Science* 293 (May 1954):88–98.

McCorkle, R. C. "Institutional violence: How do inmates respond?" *Forum on Corrections Research* 4 (3) 1992:9–11. (This is a summary of McCorkle's "Personal precautions to violence in prison," *Criminal Justice and Behavior* 19 (2) 1992:160–73.)

McCorkle, R. C. "Living on the edge: Fear in a maximum-security prison." *Journal of Offender Rehabilitation* 20 (1/2) 1993:73–91.

Megargee, F. I., and B. Cadow. "The ex-offender and the 'monster' myth." *Federal Probation* 44 (1) 1980:24–37.

Metzger, D. H. "Life in a microwave." In R. Johnson and H. Toch (eds.). *Crime and Punishment: Inside Views.* Los Angeles: Roxbury Publishing, 2000:138–40.

Nettler, G. *Explaining Crime.* New York: McGraw Hill, 1984.

Owen, B. *"In the Mix": Struggle and Survival in a Women's Prison.* Albany: State University of New York Press, 1998.

Pearson, P. *When She Was Bad: Violent Women and the Myth of Innocence.* New York: Viking, 1997.

Petersilia, J. "Parole and prisoner reentry." In M. Tonry and J. Petersilia. *Prisons.* Chicago: University of Chicago Press, 1999:479–529.

Redifer, K. "Big trouble in l'il Chilli'." In R. Johnson and H. Toch (eds.). *Crime and Punishment: Inside Views.* Los Angeles: Roxbury Publishing, 2000:143–46.

Renzema, M. "The stress comes later." In R. Johnson and H. Toch (eds.). *The Pains of Imprisonment.* Prospect Heights, IL: Waveland Press, 1988:147–62.

Rierden, A. *The Farm: A Life Inside a Women's Prison.* Amherst, MA: University of Massachusetts Press, 1997.

Schroeder, A. *Shaking It Rough.* Garden City, NY: Doubleday, 1976.

Seymour, J. "Niches in prison." In H. Toch. *Living in Prison: The Ecology of Survival.* New York: Free Press, 1977:179–205.

Seymour, J. "Environmental sanctuaries for susceptible prisoners." In R. Johnson and H. Toch (eds.). *The Pains of Imprisonment.* Prospect Heights, IL: Waveland Press, 1988:267–84.

Sheehan, S. *A Prison and a Prisoner.* Boston: Houghton Mifflin, 1978.

Smith, R. B. "Jailhouse lawyers." In J. Bruchac (ed.). *The Light from Another Country: Poetry from American Prisons.* Greenfield Center, NY: Greenfield Review Press, 1984:298.

Stojkovic, S. "Social bases of power and control mechanisms among prisoners in a prison organization." *Justice Quarterly* 1 (4) 1984:511–28.

Telander, R. "Sports behind the walls." *Sports Illustrated* 69 (17) 1988:82–96.

Toch, H. *Men in Crisis: Human Breakdowns in Prison.* Chicago: Aldine, 1975.

Toch, H. *Living in Prison: The Ecology of Survival.* New York: Free Press, 1977.

Toch, H. *Violent Men.* Cambridge: Schenkman, 1980.

Toch, H. *Mosaic of Despair: Human Breakdowns in Prison.* Washington, DC: American Psychological Association, 1992.

Wallerstedt, J. F. "Returning to prison." Special Report of the Bureau of Justice Statistics, November 1984 (NCJ-95700).

Washington, J. *A Bright Spot in the Yard: Notes and Stories from a Prison Journal.* Trumansburg, NY: Crossing Press, 1981.

Wideman, J. E. *Brothers and Keepers.* New York: Holt, Rinehart & Winston, 1984.

Williams, R. E. "A weekend with the inmate plumber." In R. Johnson and H. Toch (eds.). *Crime and Punishment: Inside Views.* Los Angeles: Roxbury Publishing, 2000:175–82.

York, M. "Control." In R. Johnson and H. Toch (eds.). *Crime and Punishment: Inside Views.* Los Angeles: Roxbury Publishing, 2000:158–60.

Zamble, E. "Behavior and adaptation in long-term prison inmates: Descriptive longitudinal results." *Criminal Justice and Behavior* 19 (4) 1992:409–425.

Zamble, E., F. Porporino, and J. Kalotay. *An Analysis of Coping Behavior in Prison Inmates.* Ministry of the Solicitor General of Canada, Programs Branch User Report, 1984.

7

❖

To Have and to Hold

The Prison Officer's
Public (Custodial) Agenda

Like the prisoners they supervise, officers adapt to prison life in the context of both public and private worlds. The public world of the prison guard is reflected—and distorted—in images of the officer as a mindless and brutal custodian. Yet this stereotype fits some officers. These officers, dubbed "smug hacks" or "subcultural custodians" by Toch and Klofas,[1] typically account for about a quarter of the guard force. They are custodial officers in the pejorative sense of the term. They seek order at any price, and violence—their own or that of inmate allies—is one of the tools of their trade. Their stance of toughness is exalted in the guard subculture and is the public image (though not the private reality) adopted by most officers. Smug hacks find their counterparts in the convicts of the prison yard. The combative relations that ensue between these groups account for much of the abuse and even brutality that occur in the prison.

The private world of the prison officer is the subject of the next chapter (Chapter Eight). There the focus is on the various ways individual officers take an alienating role and shape it to meet their personal needs as well as those of the inmates under their control. Some officers try to enrich their jobs. They fight alienation by expanding their roles and making them rewarding; they do not succumb to alienation by reducing their work to the bare bones of the custodial role. These men and women are correctional officers in the best sense of the term. Their objective is to provide the human services necessary to make the prison a place where inmates can live as mature adults and perhaps graduate to conventional lives in the free world. They find their counterparts in the many inmates who struggle to carve out niches for themselves in the hope that they can emerge from the prison no worse, and perhaps a little better, than when they went in. Constructive personal relations between these groups account for much of the correctional work that takes place behind prison walls.

THE PRISON GUARD AS HACK

For prison officers, the line between being a figure of authority and an authoritarian figure can be slim. The history of prisons "includes the most arbitrary and sadistic, the most bestial abuses of power of which men—in the guise of debased authority—are capable."[2] Responsibility for such abuses has been placed with the staff, particularly line officers, who can be most readily identified as having trafficked in "debased authority." The resulting image of guards assumes incompetence and brutality.

Accounts by inmates of penitentiaries and Big Houses are replete with references to brutal officers. Some officers, indeed, appear in the eyes of their charges as living caricatures of humanity, as atavisms in action. In the words of an anonymous inmate of Southern Indiana State Penitentiary, writing in the 1860s,

> I heard some one approaching with a shuffling gate, and soon there appeared at the door a short, burly, bow-legged man, with arms dangling nearly to his knees, and having the most villainous countenance it has ever been my misfortune to look upon. You would have known at once that the devil was his master by his unsightly squint and satanic grin. His head was turned slightly to one side as he leered at me from under his shaggy eye-brows. I at once read my fate in his demoniac smile.[3]

If many officers qualify as servants of Satan, a few—a very few—are portrayed as handmaids of humaneness, agents, as it were, of the angels. An inmate of New York State Penitentiary, writing in 1823, had this to say about a ranking officer of the prison, who transcended the evil that surrounded him in the penitentiary:

> In the midst of all the inhumanity of the prison, like a pyramid in the desert, surrounded by nothing but bleakness and ruin, there was one heart that still retained, all the grandeur—all the sincerity—all the elevated sympathy, of our nature. It is to Mr. John Gibson, the Deputy Keeper, that I allude. Upwards of Fifteen years have glided away, since he entered the prison as a Keeper. He has seen every odious picture, in the gallery of depravity;—he has taken the most sickening view of the character of many;—and still he is sympathetic—still he is sensitive—still he is humane. With him, the mere stripedness or texture of a man's garment, makes but little difference; he looks at the heart. Every well meaning convict, finds in him a valuable friend.[4]

Most often, stereotypical views of officers, and indeed of all prison staff members, cast them as uncaring. "From the warden down," observed Nelson, a prisoner in Sing Sing in the 1920s and 30s, "chaplains and all, they're a pretty lousy outfit." The Big House was a creature of discipline, symbolized in the count—inmates would be lined up several times a day and counted to make sure no one was out of place or had escaped. Accordingly, the officers of the Big House were seen as agents of discipline. "All they care about is if the count is right and to have no riots." An orderly, quiet, surface routine was all that mattered. "[O]utside of that, we could all rot to death, and they wouldn't give a fiddler's so-and-so for us."[5]

Prisons today are, in the main, less harsh and depriving than their predecessors of even a generation ago, and guards are better trained and supervised—and also subject to lawsuits for abuse of authority.[6] The discipline imposed on inmates in today's prisons is less extreme and is almost never an end in itself.[7] Routines must be explained and justified. Abuses by officers are less common and tend to occur when the authority of the staff has been directly challenged[8]—and not just any staff. As it happens, challenges to authority are especially provocative for officers who are "more anxious . . . about their security" and, hence, "more likely . . . to react defensively and violently when encountering inmates' resistance or taunts."[9] Such violence is understandable—anyone who has worked in prison will attest to the remarkable abuse heaped on officers by inmates—even when it remains reprehensible. Still, the image of the subhuman and senselessly brutal custodian lives on, as if the modern prison were frozen in time as a relic of the penitentiary or the Big House.

Inmates, for instance, use the symbolic figure of the brutal guard as a rallying point for their public identity as "cons" who despise "hacks," regardless of what their personal experiences with individual prison officers may have been:

> ■ For a prisoner, of course, a guard is possibly the lowest imaginable form of humanoid life, a species somewhere about the level of the gorilla and often rather easily mistaken for one. He's called a bull, a pig, a wethead or a screw, and it's understood he'd rather shoot you than give you the time of day, stick you in the back rather than give you a crust of bread. . . . The intriguing aspect of this view of guards, however, is that no inmate I've ever met came by it through his own experience—at least not initially. It's an opinion a prisoner automatically picks up at the door along with his issue of prison clothes and his government-issued toothbrush, and from that point on he simply looks for incidents to confirm the view. Without having to discuss it, he understands instinctively that such an opinion goes along with his khaki shirt and his cheap boots, that it's wise to establish one's loyalties clearly and that guard-hating is an act which clearly confirms such a loyalty to the inmate cause. It's expressly part of the function of being a prisoner.[10] ■

There is, to be sure, a corresponding stereotype of inmates—the convict as thug—that is embraced by many officers, at least when the officers are nurturing their public identities as tough and unfeeling hacks. "In metaphoric imagery and folklore," states Fleisher,

> convicts have these features: They are hard and emotionless; they are faceless, but have dark, coal-like eyes; they are muscular, very strong, and rather clever; they can sometimes be pleasant, but they are always deceptive and potentially violent; and if one dies, another will be along to take its place. That is a thug.[11]

None of these stereotypes is accurate. The point is that self-righteous convicts like Abbott, working more or less in concert with smug hacks (who don't write books and hence remain nameless), make it their business to provide the incidents of abuse and violence that confirm the stereotypes, in their eyes and in the eyes of others in their groups. The result is a caricature of prison life that deceives and divides some inmates and officers and, it would appear, some of the scholars who have made it their business to study the prison community.

Prison scholars, many of them penologists trained in the social sciences, have been almost as prone as the more hard-boiled convicts to assume, as a matter of course, the incompetence and malevolence of officers and to focus upon unrepresentative incidents. (Violence is almost always only a small part of even a violent person's behavior; to adjudge an officer violent and nothing more is thus a misrepresentation.) It is as though such beliefs were "expressly part of the function" of the penologist's role as well. Certainly this view was not derived from research into the guard's life and adjustment in prison.

The only research that purports to document the inherently negative character of the prison officer focuses not on guards at all but on college students assigned to play this role in a simulated jail populated by other students acting as inmates.[12] However, the students who participated in the "Stanford Prison Experiment," as the study has come to be called, were implicitly encouraged to play out stereotypical conceptions of guard and inmate roles. The student/guards were given no training or guidance. Instead, they were issued uniforms reminiscent of a southern state trooper, complete with silver "Cool Hand Luke" reflective sunglasses and long nightsticks, and then given blanket authorization to run the prison as they saw fit. (Be advised that correctional officers in some states wear slacks and sport coats; officers who come into contact with inmates almost invariably carry no weapons of any kind.) By contrast, the student/inmates wore sacklike dresses. As if this weren't enough, they had bracelets for their ankles and stocking caps for their heads. (Real male inmates sometimes wear unflattering uniforms, but their attire is decidedly masculine in appearance.) Can anyone doubt that the student/guards felt it was appropriate to play the tough-guy role with the emasculated student/inmates over whom they held complete power?

What *is* surprising about this study is that only about one in three of the "guards" did in fact behave abusively. The majority were noted to be fair and even friendly. Interestingly, the decent officers were blamed for perpetuating the negativity of prison. They were alleged to seduce inmates into acceptance of oppressive conditions against which they might otherwise have rebelled. At the same time, the abusive behavior of some student/officers was taken to be prototypical of guard behavior in the real world, as indicative of a pathology built into guarding and into the prison itself. The notion of the guard role as naturally corrupt appears to be widely accepted among penologists. One can gain some comfort from the fact that no one other than the researchers confused the depression shown by the lonely, confused, and frightened student/inmates with the typical inmate's reaction to confinement. In the real prison world, inmate adjustment is quite diverse and, in most cases, oriented to action and denial rather than to passivity and depression (see Chapter Four).

Beyond this study, investigative journalism has resulted in articles that constitute a collage of unmitigated (and usually gratuitous) abuse of the "debased authority" that is seen as the hallmark of prison management. The result is that "much of the material that is available" from prison critics

> presents a stereotypical picture of the guard as a harsh (if not sadistic), power-hungry illiterate—an ignorant, rigid, authoritarian individual who is vigorous only when demanding inmate compliance, when opposing inmate's rights, when criticizing management policies or when scuttling rehabilitation programs. Whereas some prison analysts have described them as thugs, others have viewed them as clones or zombies—an amorphous mass of uniformed automatons, indistinguishable one from the other, performing routine, mundane and mindless tasks which anyone could do, which permit no individual excellence, and require no notable skills.[13]

There is no indication, moreover, that the market for this literature is drying up. Guards have been characterized by John Irwin, a prominent penologist who should know better, as stupid, bigoted hayseeds who can't even learn the byways of their own institution! In Irwin's words,

> guards are more racially prejudiced than the average citizen. . . . Guards' racism takes three forms. First, they do not like, and in fact often hate, nonwhites. . . . Moreover, most white guards believe that nonwhites are inferior. . . . Finally, the guard force, with a rural background and poor education, misunderstand the perspectives or subcultures of most prisoners.[14]

If it is any consolation to the officers, their colleagues among the professional treatment staff fare little better. "It has been my impression," says Irwin, "that the type of staff person who filled the treatment ranks tended to be the less intelligent, less creative, and less ambitious college graduates with B.A.s in the social sciences or social welfare."[15] Irwin concedes that a few good men (and women) may start out in these ranks but contends that they become demoralized and leave. The result, in Irwin's view, is that only the dregs of the college educated stay behind to fill treatment roles in the prison. The impression with which one is left after reading Irwin is that the treatment staff and the guards deserve one another's bad company but that the inmates certainly deserve better!

There is no evidence that guards as a group are distinctively prejudiced or authoritarian or, indeed, share any personality type at all.[16] (Treatment professionals no doubt are also a psychologically heterogeneous group, though I know of no research on this point.) Guards are neither congenital sadists, rabid racists, nor ex-military officers looking for another uniform and more men to boss around. "Most line staff are," in DiIulio's view, "living rebuttals to the popular stereotypes of prisons workers."[17] Unlike many of their fellow citizens, observes DiIulio, line staff separate "the criminal from the crime" and strive to treat inmates even-handedly in terms of their prison adjustment.[18] If the attitudes of officers toward prisoners have anything in common, they are "characterized not by hostility or dislike but rather by despair and disappointment."[19] "It is the fact that prisoners recidivate" observe Morris and Morris, "that the staff find intolerable."[20] Many guards care about recidivism because they view themselves as part of the correctional enterprise. They do more than the "mundane and mindless tasks" associated with custody, and hence recidivism is an indictment of their correctional skills as well as a reflection on the inmates.

Nor must persons who play a guard role inevitably do so in an authoritarian way. The National Guard of Wisconsin, for instance, was able to take over a maximum-security prison during a guard strike and run the institution with a respect for the prisoners' individuality. The inmates responded in kind. In one prisoner's words, "The National Guard came inside and treated us like men and human beings—and we reciprocated."[21] These officers arrived with hostile expectations of criminals—and perhaps with the assumption that they would have to use a heavy-handed authority—but were able to relinquish their stereotypes and evolve a more relaxed style of control after face-to-face contact with the prisoners. This natural experiment, moreover, lasted three weeks, three times longer than the Stanford Prison simulation that supposedly established the pathology of the guard role.

Many real prison guards come to treat inmates as individuals, a fact that is explored in some detail in the next chapter. Suffice it here to say that, like the National Guardsmen assigned to the Wisconsin prison, they start out with false images of inmates but often are quickly disabused of them. This may occur right at the beginning of the officer's career. The following interview excerpt provides a telling case in point:

■ When I started [in 1970], after seeing prison movies, I was scared shitless. I started on a Saturday as a temporary employee. I thought they were criminals and that's it.

Did you find what you expected?

They all looked like people. I couldn't tell them from people on the street. The guy that broke me in in the mess hall was a murderer. You couldn't work for a nicer guy. When I started, the inmates checked everything out in the mess hall to see if things were clean. An inmate broke me in. Inmates trained officers. Really! He told me to stand back and he showed me how and where to frisk. He hit the table top to sound it out. Rap the bars to see if they were solid. Many times when you're running companies, or you're a new officer in a factory, there's an inmate that shows you the right way. On Sunday they let out the wing waiter to mop and clean cells. Now they have four or five at a time. The wing waiter guided you right so there's no confusion. An inmate doesn't want to have any more problems than he has.[22] ∎

Over the years since Lombardo conducted the survey of prison officers from which this excerpt is drawn, the level of order in prison has declined. Entering officers today have, if anything, more reason to be "scared shitless." They must contend with more disorder and less respect than was the case in 1970, the period referred to by Lombardo's interviewee. On the other hand, today's officers are better trained, know more about the diverse human beings who comprise the prison population, and enter the guard force with more confidence in their ability to manage objectively the difficult social world that is the modern prison.

The larger point is this: The keepers and the kept are not necessarily at odds with one another; they are not inevitably locked into oppositional roles. Nor are officers sadists who skulk into prison looking for victims and eager to team up with others of their despicable ilk. It is more accurate to say, in the words of one ex-offender, that many of the officers "simply answered all the want-ads and Corrections gave them a job."[23] As a rule, they know little about what they are getting into, even if they have grown up in such notable prison towns as Auburn, New York, the home of the first congregate penitentiary.[24] According to Lombardo,

> As the naive citizens of Auburn became the guards of the prison
> community, they accepted jobs but did not readily identify with their
> new titles. They quickly learned to identify with and appreciate the
> convicts over whom they would stand guard and learned that convicts
> had to be judged by behavior and not as stereotypes.[25]

As we enter the prison officers' world, the goal is that they too "be judged by behavior and not as stereotypes."

ALIENATION AND ITS CONSEQUENCES

Stereotypes often contain a grain of truth. The problem is that this truth is blown out of proportion; a theme becomes the whole story, a single note a symphony. The grain of truth in the stereotypes of prison guards is that the guard's job is an alienating one.[26] In a number of surveys, for example, roughly two-thirds of the officers sampled indicated that they had second thoughts about their career choice and would rather be in a different job.[27] The average satisfaction score for the officers as a group was "lower than every other occupation category" for which data were available; the list of occupations included a range of "traditional working class occupations."[28] Furthermore, there was evidence that "job satisfaction may be decreasing among correctional officers."[29]

The role of the prison officer is one that is hard to identify with, to see as an extension of one's self, because it can be demeaning, dangerous, and lonely.[30] A case in point is the strip search, an invasive and unpleasant task that must be performed routinely in penal institutions. Conover describes his first strip search:

> He stood naked facing me on a small square of carpet, briefs in his hand. He offered them to me, and I checked them quickly. There was some blood on the seat. "You okay?" I asked. He nodded, and I began directing him through the obligatory motions. But he knew better than I and was always a step ahead.
>
> "Hands through your hair. Pull your ears forward. Mouth open. Put out your tongue, pull out your lips and cheeks." I looked quickly under the tongue. "Arms up." I checked the armpits. "Turn around." He did, and immediately bent over and spread his buttocks so I could see his anus. "Fine, thanks."
>
> I left the booth so he could dress. That was my first strip-frisk, and I hated it. I hated [his] pliant submission. I almost wished he had resisted more, cause me some trouble—I didn't enjoy his servility. I didn't enjoy the visual memory of his anus and dick and the blood in his underwear.[31]

Another problem is the unpredictability of the job, which can switch from monotony to rapid-fire action at any time. As Conover has noted,

> a given day could bring either . . . hair-pulling overwork on a gallery or absolutely nothing to do in a place like the State Shop. I thought of myself as a fairly flexible person, but not knowing what each day would bring was nerve-racking. What were you supposed to do—shut down your brain when you walked into the prison or drink extra coffee and prepare to go into overdrive?[32]

One may get used to such alienating practices but at a cost: stress. Indeed, for most officers, alienation translates into a host of stress-related problems, including the numbing of feelings—so that one can go about one's job without constant emotional discomfort.[33]

A general problem is that officers tend to bring the stresses of prison work home with them, interfering with their personal lives. Conover describes this phenomenon, with a hint of irony:

> After I got home, I went for a run, had a beer with dinner, then helped my two-and-a-half-year-old son get into his pajamas. I was doing well at keeping work off my mind until I noticed his younger sister with her hands on the slats of her crib, looking out. Unnervingly, it reminded me of the same view I had all day long. Like an inmate, she was dependent upon me for everything. These two jobs were very much the same, I thought with disgust.[34]

On another occasion, following a fairly typical shift in which Conover reports that "All day long I was disrespected by criminals," simple disobedience by his young son put him over the edge, to the point where he angrily spanked him—"A use-of-force on my own son, I realized the moment after it happened." Note the use of prison jargon (a use-of-force on my son!), which suggests how pervasive the prison has become as a point of reference for Conover. But the jargon, which implies a certain psychological distance, does not reduce the pain Conover feels, which is considerable:

> There were better ways to handle the situation, I knew, but none that I seemed capable of at the time. I asked him to lie down with me in his bed so I could read him another book, and eventually he did. Then he held on to my arm, kind of tight. I felt like crying into his shirt, breaking down, sobbing for a good hour. I turned my head and read the story.[35]

An aggravating factor for officers is the inability to discuss work problems at home, where the travails of the cell blocks seem out of place and even taboo. If the prison is an example of "dirty work," does one want to bring the dirt home, soiling loved ones? How, for example, does one broach the fact that one might be taken hostage, perhaps raped or killed? Too often, officers keep prison problems inside, where they linger, spoiling moods and often threatening their most valued relationships:

> I didn't want to tell Margot everything I knew or had seen. Back at the Academy, Sergeant Bloom had recommended that we all discuss with our families the possibility of being taken hostage. I didn't want to scare her with that kind of stuff, didn't want to alarm her any more than necessary. And in a different way, I didn't want to sully the kitchen table with the kinds of things I'd seen and heard during the day; it just seemed best to keep it inside.
>
> But inside is a bad place for stress. This is very obvious in retrospect, but wasn't obvious on those nights after we got the kids to bed. I wouldn't volunteer details of my day, and when she tried to update me on her life, often I would just tune her out. I found myself impatient in a way I couldn't explain. I didn't want to hear about the minutiae of her day. There wasn't room in my brain for what seemed like trivialities. Black moods would come from out of nowhere and envelop me. I tried to hide them by acting civil, but "civil" came off as chilly and robotic.[36]

Conover's marriage survived—in part, perhaps, because he served only one year as a correctional officer, with the larger goal of writing a book—but the marriages of many officers do not.[37]

Alienation is a salient feature of the correctional officer's job. Some, usually a minority, respond with violence. The sources of alienation among prison officers and the link between alienation and violence are considered in turn.

Dimensions of Alienation

There are many reasons why the guard's job is alienating. One is that guards are sometimes treated no better than inmates, a fact the officers take to be unjust since they have committed no crimes. Both guards and inmates may be subjected to searches, for instance, upon entering or leaving the prison. (Officers are not subjected to strip searches, though simply conducting such searches is demeaning for officers, as noted earlier.) Both guards and inmates may be publicly "dressed down" and disciplined by superior officers. For officers who live on the prison compound, living quarters are often comparable to those for prisoners. In fact, it wasn't so long ago that the officers' quarters were subjected to the same thorough searches as inmates' cells. If their "rooms" didn't pass muster, the water and electricity might be turned off.[38]

Guards at work share the prison environment with the inmates. Specific work assignments pose many of the same adjustment problems for officers as they do for inmates. Though it may not be obvious, for example, segregation officers are, like their charges, isolated from the rest of the prison, with comparatively little freedom of movement or variety in their daily regime:

> It's confined, this block. It's too small a place. After a while, even the officers start arguing with themselves. It happens every day. Any old thing sets the officers off. Out in [the general prison] population at least you're walking around, you got space out there. Or you have the yard duty or you go on transportation, or hospital detail or something. But down at [segregation]. Where you goin'? Upstairs, downstairs, that's it. We're bangin' into one another.[39]

More generally, when prison conditions are grim, they affect staff as well as inmates. Prison conditions deteriorated dramatically in places like Stateville and Walpole following the demise of prison discipline in the mid-1970s (see Chapter Five). Guards, like the inmates, were directly affected. Kauffman notes that the guards "recognized Walpole for the 'rats' nest, garbage hole' that it was. They had to work daily in the filth, and they hated it."[40]

The similarities between the guards' situation and the inmates' lead many officer to think of themselves merely as "uniformed prisoners." Moreover, guards know that others are tempted to see them in this light; to think of guarding as the kind of job one would naturally fill with men and women of the caliber of uniformed prisoners. This point is made forcefully by Lin,

> Prisoners are not the only ones who 'do time.' Prison staff do so as well, as when they talk about their 'sentence' as the time they've got to do until retirement. Less flippantly, doing time for them is the eight-hour shift, where if they do their job well they can be paralyzed by boredom and if they make a mistake, they can be killed. When they are simply guardians of a human warehouse, their work can seem as pointless as the time the prisoners are doing. And the conditions of their work are exacerbated by their own type of isolation. Though they leave the prison daily, they live among a public that often considers prison staff barely a

step up from the prisoners they guard: whether their neighbors believe that prisons are too easy on prisoners or too brutal toward them, prison staff are an easy target for their scorn and indignation.[41]

From the average citizen's vantage point, far from prison yards and cell blocks, guarding would seem to be a sinecure, a matter of merely watching, opening and closing doors, filing an incident report now and again, and issuing a few orders. If one subscribes fully to the stereotypical image of the guard, one envisions him (or her) indulging in an occasional unprovoked beating. Tower guards do in fact have primitive mandates of this sort; they do simply watch and wait, though they decidedly do not engage in recreational assaults.[42] Ironically, for some officers, the watching and waiting associated with tower duty may offer an experience of solitude that can be, in Conover's words, a "delicious" alternative to the stresses of daily work in the main prison: "The old chair was comfortable, the view stupendous, the feeling of being left alone delicious. I was up there by myself—just me, my guns, my newspaper, and the toilet—working Wallpost 18."[43]

Most officers, in any case, have more substantial and challenging assignments than their colleagues in the prison towers. (Still, tower work offers stresses of its own: "There was nothing much to do," Conover points out, "and yet you had to stay alert. That was the joy and the difficulty of a day in a wall tower. But mostly it was a joy."[44]) All officers within the prison compound carry keys. Knowing when to lock and unlock doors—the supposedly simple-minded work of a "turnkey"—can prove daunting. "Keys were power," states Conover,

> And they were responsibility—because many, many bunglings could be traced back to a set of keys and the person who had been entrusted with them. When to lock and when to unlock was, by one reckoning, what we were here to learn. "You are never wrong, in prison, to lock a gate," a sergeant had reassured us at lineup one day. But it was more complicated than that. Gates had to be unlocked for the prison to function smoothly—and then, at the right moment, to be locked again. Sing Sing was a place of, probably, over two thousand locks, many with the same key. The cardinal sin, the one thing you were never, ever to do, was lose your keys. A lost key could fall into inmates' hands. A lost key was a disaster."[45]

Open the cell at the wrong time, and you—or an inmate or fellow officer—may be violently attacked.

Officers are often called upon to apply abstract rules to a wide variety of concrete situations involving persons who are, for the most part, resentful of authority. On a daily, indeed even minute-to-minute basis, officers are asked to make judgments covering an enormous range of inmate conduct, from the appropriateness of a prisoner's clothing, hair length, and demeanor to patterns of movement, levels of noise in the cells, and any disputes that may arise among inmates or between inmates and staff. Officers must also police the prison for contraband—illicit materials—a category so broad that the New York State prison rule book no longer ennumerates contraband items, but simply states that contraband is "any article that is not authorized by the Superintendent or [his] designee."[46] Most of these decisions involve discretion. No official rule-book can cover all the contingencies.

What does one do, for instance, when an inmate breaks a minor rule, such as the requirement that one's clothing be "presentable" at all times when out of the cell, but the violation occurs in a highly public context such as the mess hall? How about an altercation (short of an actual fight) that takes place in the yard, with hundreds of prisoners watching? Does one intervene at all? If so, what does one do? Many items are permitted on some tiers but not others, due to differing interpretations of what constitutes contraband. Do you follow the norms of the tier you find yourself assigned to or those you have adhered to in the past? Either decision is defensible, which highlights the wisdom of Conover's contention that "The single most interesting word, when it came to the bending and ignoring of rules, was *contraband.*"[47]

Whether defining the subtleties of presentable dress, nonbelligerent conduct, or contraband, or deciding how to handle the less egregious departures from these slippery standards, there are few informal norms to follow, since unguided discretion generally produces a hodgepodge of conflicting interpretations of what is proper policy. In effect, an officer has to make a judgment call, but the formal authority invested in the officer's role makes little or no provision for such ambitious uses of discretion. (An officer may be told to use "common sense" in applying rules, but this injunction is as vague as some of the rules that must be applied.) As a result, the guard often feels left out on a limb, subject to being second-guessed after every decision. "No sooner would an officer become savvy as to which rules were commonly ignored," notes Conover, "than somebody in a white shirt [a superior officer] would appear to shake up his whole understanding of accepted practice."[48] The notion that one is "damned if you do, damned if you don't"—and likely to be thought incompetent in either case—applies with a special urgency to the guard's situation. In the words of one officer,

■ Never mind what the rule book says . . . the fact is that you've got to work it out for yourself. . . . One day this is O.K. and the next day it's not O.K. And the next day . . . well, maybe it's O.K. There are no rules, no regulations for the correctional officer himself. . . . There is no direction and he more or less fends for himself. . . . You're expected to think for yourself in certain situations. If it turns out fine, all's well and good. If you make a decision they expect of you and it doesn't turn out right . . . even if it might not have been the wrong decision but it just didn't work out right . . . then you're an asshole. After a while, if you're called an asshole enough by the inmates, and you're called an asshole enough by the brass and, from what you read in the newspapers, [by] the vocal minority [those fighting for prison reform] . . . well, after a while you begin to feel like one. Who's the asshole? Me for staying, or the guy who left?[49] ■

This officer's concerns are shared by most other officers and even some supervisors; they are a source of serious and sometimes disabling stress.[50] Cheek and Miller analyzing a survey of prison officer stress, report that the typical guard faces a double-bind situation.[51] The problem is precisely the same as that identified by our officer: lack of clear guidelines for guarding, along with lack of autonomy invested in the role, which leaves officers chronically vulnerable to making errors because of factors beyond their control.

The difficulty for officers, then, is not one of being confused over treatment or custodial functions. This confusion exists mainly in the minds of penologists. As Lombardo has made clear,

> From the guard's perspective, prison guard tasks have nothing to do with rehabilitation, just desserts, corrections or punishments. These are issues for the policy planner and program designer—issues that focus upon the inmate's past or attempt to prepare him for the future. For the prison guard going about his day-to-day business, it is the immediate present that matters, life as it is lived and passes *within the prison community;* the outside has little relevance. . . . Faced with a work environment laden with fear, mental tension, uncertainty, isolation, inconsistency and boredom, correction officers are more motivated to develop strategies to cope with these conditions than to pursue management goals.[52]

The problem for officers is one of doing one's custodial job adequately, of knowing what to do so one is not an "asshole."[53] A complicating factor is that each of the officers' audiences within the prison demands something different: administrators look to officers to lead inmates rather than relate to them or otherwise deal with them in interpersonally skillful ways; inmates value inter-personal skills in officers, especially as these relate to problem solving in every-day prison life, and are suspicious of efforts to lead them.[54] Conflicting demands such as these leave many officers feeling alienated from everyone around them and saddled with a palpable fear of failure. Guarding at Sing Sing, states Conover,

> was an experience of living with fear—fear of inmates, as individuals and as a mob, and fear of our own capacity to fuck up. We were sandwiched between two groups: Make a mistake around the white-shirts and you would get in trouble; make a mistake around the inmates and you might get hurt.[55]

It is Cheek and Miller's conclusion that "the officer gets no respect from any-one."[56] As one officer told Stojkovic, "We are the screws no one really cares about."[57] To many officers, it seems that failure—in the eyes of administrators, inmates, or both groups—is virtually unavoidable.

Concerns of this sort may have been muted in the penitentiary and later in the Big House. In those settings, a disciplined regime and harsh punishment kept shows of discontent among the inmates to a minimum; line staff had considerable authority, and staff as a whole exhibited a more united front in opposition to the prisoners. Lewis Lawes, destined to become a famous prison warden, started out as a prison guard in 1905 in Clinton Prison in upstate New York. He recalls the clear role he was given, in an era when, for officers, might made right:

■ "Tread softly and carry a big stick," was my first lesson in penology, on my arrival at Clinton Prison on March 1st, 1905. It was to be followed literally. When I reported for duty that night, I was handed a pair of sneakers and a club. The sneakers, to enable the guard to make his rounds noiselessly, so as not to disturb the sleeping forms within the dark cells, and the club to be used in emergencies should any of those forms become unduly active.[58] ■

Lawes was admonished to wield his club early and often, so as to establish his authority. As he later confessed, "I looked for trouble. I found it soon."[59] Decades later, sitting securely in his warden's chair, Lawes marveled at how normal violence seemed in the yards and cell blocks of the reformatories and prisons of the Big House era, where an officer, in broad daylight and in the middle of the yard, could knock a prisoner out as a disciplinary measure and have the prisoner take it as a perfectly normal state of affairs! In Lawes's words,

■ [I]n order to properly impress the offender, I landed him one on the chin and knocked him out. We worked on him and he was as good as ever in a few moments. The fellow didn't resent my act. He took it for granted.[60] ■

Evidence suggests that Lawes's experience was typical of officers in all prisons run on the Big House model, whether those prisons were of the traditional factory-based or plantation varieties. Crouch and Marquart described the officer subculture of Texas prisons, for example, dating from roughly 1920 through 1970. These prisons were staffed by quintessential hacks who were virtually unrestrained in their authority. Mounted (white) field officers supervising inmates (virtually all black) at work at slave labor in fields and on road gangs were said to epitomize this officer subculture. Crouch and Marquart offer a revealing description of one such officer, as seen through the eyes of an inmate under his dominion:

■ When he raised his head enough so the brim no longer hid his sinister-looking face, I quickly squinted a peek at his eyes. Their icy-blue color contrasted his heavily tanned weathered skin. He seldom blinked, roving his eyes over us. "I'm gonna tell ya'll one time, and one time alone how I'm gonna deal. First off, if airy one uv you tries to run off, I'm gonna kill ya. If airy one uv you 'sputes my word, I'm gonna kill ya. If airy one uv you don' do lak I tell ya, I'm gonna kill ya. If you lay th' hammer down under me [refuse to work], I'm gonna kill ya. And if I jes take a notion to, I'm gonna kill ya."[61] ■

Guards like this were so dominant that they could name and rename inmates at will (based on their physical appearance or attributes as workers) and could command a "highly stylized" etiquette featuring servile submission to their every order. Thus, prisoners demeaned by degrading (and often racist) nicknames would be forced to further demean themselves in order to carry out the most rudimentary functions, such as urinating or smoking a cigarette. "If an inmate wanted to stop for a cigarette, he said, 'Lightin' it up, Boss?' and to urinate, he said, 'Pourin' it out, Boss?' The boss' permission would come as 'Light it' and 'Pour it out.' "[62]

No one questioned the competence of officers like Lawes or his Texas counterparts. Everyone knew who was in control. Concerns about the competence of officers are pronounced in today's prisons, however, where inmates have more autonomy and discipline is more difficult to maintain. Officers are no longer encouraged, or indeed even allowed, to club recalcitrant inmates into submission or even to threaten them with harm. Guards can still punish, but only indirectly, through the issuance of reports that must be reviewed by disciplinary committees. These reports can be rejected by their peers, and though this may not occur often, such rejections of the officer's limited power to punish do occur. In the face of growing due process rights, such rejections are probably occurring at an increasing rate these days. Small wonder that the occupational concerns of contemporary prison guards center on powerlessness: in their dealings with the administration (which many feel has abandoned the rank-and-file officer in the name of inmate rights), as well as in their efforts to control prisoners who claim rights and seek to negotiate the conditions of social control.[63] Nor is it surprising that safety is the next most salient concern.[64] Officers feel vulnerable because they work with increasingly restive and demanding prisoners and, in the main, can expect little support from their superiors in controlling these men. It almost goes without saying that the officer's round of life within the prison community can be an exceedingly lonely one. Perhaps it is to be expected that some officers will express their discontent in behavior that flagrantly contravenes modern penal policy—namely, by being abusive, and sometimes violently abusive, toward the more obstreperous convicts, the offending group that is nearest at hand.

Alienation and Violence

Violence can occur as a function of organizational norms or institutional procedures.[65] When Lawes resorted to his club in Sing Sing prison at the turn of the last century, he was following norms that were central to the functioning of that institution. By his own account, he was not in the least bit alienated. The same holds true for Texas officers throughout most of the twentieth century; their morale was high, in part because they took pride in their effective use of coercion and violence to maintain a high level of order in Texas prisons. The psychology of violence changes when violence is formally prohibited by the institution, as is the case in all modern prisons. Today, when violence occurs on a regular basis, it is the handiwork of alienated officers who feel abandoned or betrayed by the institution and come to feel authorized to make their own rules.

Some alienated officers work on their own as freelance agents of violence, if you will, but most work in a group or with some degree of group support. Group norms supporting violence among the alienated typically emerge because people who feel alienated often band together for reassurance and protection. Life seems simpler and more manageable if it is "us" against "them"; and, indeed in prison, unlike in the free world, "power and authority [are] at stake in nearly every transaction" between officer and inmate.[66] There can be security in polarization: the alienated often go to great lengths to cover for their own, sometimes no matter how reprehensible their behavior. When tension mounts, some staff draw battle lines and dig in for a fight. Some prisoners, especially the convicts like Abbott, see themselves as in the same boat and do likewise. The result is an "implicit combat and warfare model" in which

> staff and clients tend to view each other as enemies and to see their peers as trench-mates. Breaks in client and staff ranks are seen as openings to the enemy. Although a peer may be violent, he is also a comrade-in-arms who deserves protection or silence. Questions of solidarity, of maintaining a common front, become strong concerns. Exaggerations of enemy militance and malevolence become supports for morale.[67]

Staff who adopt a trench-warfare model of prison work do their custodial duties but no more. Few words are wasted, and no back talk is taken. Indeed, these officers keep *any* talking with inmates to a minimum. As Lin has noted, solidarity among control-oriented officers

> is particularly threatened by staff-prisoner communication. Once staff begin to establish a rapport with prisoners by talking to them, acknowledging their side of the story, or resolving problems, accusations that they are not 'backing' each other immediately arise."[68]

At best, then, custodial officers are cool and aloof. At worst, they are looking for trouble in order to prove who's in control. It is as if these officers seek to turn back the clock, to return to the "good old days" of repressive prison control such as those extolled in the Big House.

In this context, the guard's heroes are the "goon squad" officers or other officers formally or informally assigned the duty of physically coercing or even assaulting recalcitrant prisoners.[69] Usually the smuggest of smug hacks, these are the officers who "get the job done" without recourse to such unmanly considerations as tact or persuasion. Bowker's description of goon squad activities highlights the role of force and the image of efficacy these officers project:

> The goon squads are groups of physically powerful correctional officers who "enjoy a good fight" and who are called upon to rush to any area of the prison where it is felt that muscle power will restore the status quo. If a prisoner is ripping up things in his cell and refuses to be quiet, the goon squad may be called and three or four of these correctional officers will forcibly quiet him, administering a number of damaging blows to the head and body. If there is a fight between two prisoners, the goon squad

may break it up. Should a prisoner refuse to report to the hospital when he is ordered to do so, he may be dragged from his cell and deposited in the hospital waiting room. Mentally ill prisoners who are acting out are almost always initially dealt with by goon squads rather than by qualified therapeutic personnel or even by orderlies under the direction of such personnel.[70]

Many prisons today have formal control teams to replace goon squads— variously known as "cell extraction teams," CERT (Crisis Emergency Response Team), or SORT (Special Operations Response Teams)—which are typically more professional and restrained in their use of force.

Some officers no doubt join goon squads or formal control teams for reasons unrelated to alienation or a proclivity for violence. Conrad points out that goon squad officers may see this assignment "as a more interesting job than passing out towels at the shower baths or sitting in a tower."[71] There is little doubt that work on these teams confers status and offers the promise of closure—of showing who is boss. Conover, for example, was honored to join Sing Sing's cell extraction team for a foray into that prison's segregation unit. "We were off," he noted wryly, "to conduct a Nuts and Butts" (a strip search) "with the possible need for Hats and Bats" (helmuts and batons):

> ■ A dozen of us marched purposefully downstairs to the Box. There was action ahead, and I felt suddenly excited to have been included. Despite the ominous tone, and my better instincts, I'd countenanced enough inmate misbehavior and disrespect to feel invigorated by the thought that this is where it all stops. This is where we draw the line. We were going to follow the rules, and we were going to have our way.[72] ■

Whatever their motives for taking the job, the activities of these men are a dramatic reflection of "alienation or an absence of community" with prisoners as well as with their nonviolent fellow officers.[73]

Violence, moreover, is apt to promote or accentuate alienation because it precludes more constructive dealings with inmates and fellow officers. Reflecting on his experience with the cell extraction team, Conover observes:

> ■ It seemed reasonable to believe that we had been sent in to make a statement about who was in charge. And I had to wonder: With the outcome never in doubt, what had we won? What did it do to a man when his work consisted of breaking the spirit of other men? And who had invented this lose-lose game, anyway?[74] ■

Most officers on these teams, it would seem, refuse to see their work as a "lose-lose game." They tend to be fiercely partisan and, over time, come to be deeply committed to violence as a way to solve problems. As a result, "the loyalty of such men is to their own kind, no matter how individually reprehensible they are."[75] Given their attitudes and behavior, "the larger setting is seen as impersonal and threatening."[76] Understandably, the violent officers "feel they have no real stake in the larger community, and they see themselves as having much to lose and little to gain by trying to relate to the world at large."[77] These officers create for themselves a subculture of violence and may go to great lengths to exclude nonviolent officers from their ranks.[78] Perversely, violence may be a source of high morale and even, in the more explicitly punishment-oriented prisons, a route to professional advancement.[79]

Walpole Prison during much of the 1970s provides a vivid illustration of a prison in which alienation ran high and in which a clique of smug hacks—in effect, goon squads—banded together to create a subculture of violence. As Kauffman's research makes clear, officers at Walpole were overwhelmed by the inmate violence that had swamped the prison and were demoralized by their inability to control that violence. They felt fearful and inadequate. "The possibility of serious injury, even death, at the hands of inmates was very real to them."[80] At the root of the problem, in the eyes of the officers, was a weak prison administration. Officers felt abandoned and betrayed by both the warden of Walpole and the state's commissioner of corrections, whose policies sought to placate violent inmates rather than sanction them. At one point, as we have noted, untrained civilian monitors were actually placed throughout Walpole as a kind of United Nations peacekeeping force. The officers felt that the administration was monitoring them rather than the inmates and, in the process, humiliating them and compromising their already limited authority. As one officer told Kauffman, "We're alone. We have only each other. The administration does not give a shit for us."[81]

Officers at Walpole felt they had virtually no powers of formal punishment. This perception stemmed from court rulings, which did in fact limit their authority; but, more centrally, their perceived powerlessness was due to the deeply held belief that the administration would not back them up. As a result, Kauffman's research reveals that many if not most guards at Walpole bypassed the formal punishment system, resorting to petty abuses and illicit sanctions in an effort to harass and control unruly convicts:

■ Guy wants to make a phone call? You can make him wait ten, twenty minutes. Guy wants some writing paper? Tell him you don't have any. Guy wants some matches? You can have a drawer full of matches, "I don't have any matches," you tell him. Just things like that. And they know. . . . And there's the ways that you can screw around with his property when he's not around. . . . One inmate . . . he gave another officer a hard time. . . . This particular inmate loves plants. . . . And he had about . . . two dozen plants. . . . He woke up the next morning and every one of them plants was dead. . . . Say a guy works with the woodworking stuff. Just put a scratch in his furniture or something. He knows how it got there. He knows why it was put there. But there's nothing he can do about it. . . . There's so many ways you can get these guys.[82] ■

Only a minority of officers at Walpole turned to violence with any regularity, though that violence could be quite ferocious. These officers were real "hard asses" in the lingo of Walpole, men "coldly indifferent to inmates and to the violence and sadism around them."[83] In the view of the nonviolent officers at Walpole, these officers were little more than bullies and thugs. "They are just like an inmate," said one fellow officer.[84] "They're the type like Hogan's Heroes," said another, "kick heads and ask questions later."[85] As is generally the case when violence occurs in contravention of official policy, these officers operated primarily on the 3–11 shift, when administrative officials "and other 'outsiders' were gone and the institution was inhabited almost exclusively by inmates and officers."[86] But since they had the tacit support of the shift supervisor, their violence appeared to be authorized and legitimate and served as an example that was followed—or at least not opposed—by other officers. The result: the false impression of "majority support" for officer violence, at least on the evening shift.[87]

For an alienated guard, goon squad member or not, violence is a badge of honor earned in self-defense. To some extent, this is true for all officers at all prisons, at least some of the time. As Conover observed, "A new uniform was a CO's Purple Heart."[88] An officer would be given a new uniform when the old one was bloodied, and this would be a point of pride for the officer in question. As Conover explains, there is so much tension in prison, and so much lingering resentment between officer and inmate, that "violence and the potential for violence became a thrill," at least on occasion, for most officers.[89] "It was the first time in five years that I've been involved in a major incident," one officer told Conover. "And I loved it! I wanted to hit somebody!" As Conover explains,

> There were so many unresolved angry exchanges in Sing Sing, so much that never got settled. How many times had I heard an inmate or an officer say, semi-facetiously, "I'm gonna set if off!" Light a fuse! Start a little chaos! In some warped and exaggerated form, it seemed like the same kind of impulse as getting wild on a Saturday night, letting off steam after a week of tension or boredom."[90]

But some officers, not unlike convicts, feed on violence, and they may do so with the tacit support of their nonviolent colleagues. Indeed, even flagrant violent overreactions may be excused by one's fellow officers. To shoot first and ask questions later makes sense in a battlefield. Prisons in the throes of violence become, like battlefields, totally isolated and isolating worlds. In Kauffman's words, soldiers

> go to war and they say, "Well, I killed this gook and I shot this commie." Officers went to prison and they spoke of maggots killing each other, of inmates bleeding and dying, not men. "What happens here to the inmates does not bother me now in the least. I have no compassion for the inmates as a group. . . . I used to pass out at the sight of blood. Now it doesn't bother me. It's inmate blood."[91]

For many of the officers at Walpole, the prison had become a separate moral realm, to which normal human sentiments and sympathies did not fully or readily apply.[92] They struggled to see inmates not as fellow human beings in distress but as dehumanized creatures beyond the reach of care or compassion. Violence merely shed "inmate blood," over which little sleep was lost.

Numb to the plight of their charges, officers working prisons like Walpole might readily overreact with violence or underreact and, by inaction, leave vulnerable inmates unprotected. Such behaviors are reprehensible; but, under warlike prison conditions, it is only natural that other officers stick by their beleaguered colleagues. At the very least, other officers maintain a discreet silence, because tomorrow they may be the "assholes" in need of protection and support. As Conover put it, speaking from the context of Sing Sing, a more controlled setting than Walpole, "Any day in there I might find myself in a situation where I'd need Officer X to watch my back, to pry a homicidal inmate off of me, at his peril. The logic of the gray wall of silence was instantly clear."[93]

The conditions that create alienation and violence may well foster not only dehumanized views of inmates but also anxiety and self-doubt about one's failure to run a decent prison. All inmates some of the time will appear to guards to be palpably human; some inmates all of the time will command human compassion from officers. Dehumanization is a mechanism of self-defense; but, like all defenses, it is an imperfect one. For most officers there will be, then, at least on occasion, a desperately felt desire to do something, anything, to stem the violence and secure order for the human beings under their authority. Certainly this proved true at Walpole prison:

> Many officers expressed frustration in the interviews over their inability to protect inmates in their charge, even a sense of guilt over deaths or serious injuries they had been unable to prevent. There were officers who felt a personal stake in ensuring the safety of at least some of the inmates. "I can think of some (inmates) up there that if they happen to get hurt or if they were being pushed around (or) something it would affect me greatly. I would do *almost anything* [emphasis added] I could to stop it or make sure that didn't happen again."[94]

Willingness to do *almost anything* can readily extend to include a willingness to tolerate others doing *virtually anything,* assuming that they, like yourself, operate from a presumption of good will—in this case, the desire to secure an orderly prison. And who can confidently question the motives of one's colleagues—or better, in a prison war zone, one's comrades-in-arms? Unsure of the value of their own work, officers are hesitant to judge others—better not to judge and to be immune from judgment in return.

The officers most likely to embrace violence—and to do so with little or no ambivalence—are the "smug hacks," officers who find satisfaction in the exercise of coercive power. Though they typically are a statistical minority of the guard force, they are (smugly) confident that they are the vanguard of the officer force. And they may have good reason for believing this. After all, there are prisons in which they *are* a kind of vanguard, at least for some officers, during periods of turmoil.[95] Even officers who eschew violence will embrace a tough-guy or hard-ass demeanor to help them cope with the stresses of work in a violent prison:

The facade most officers adopt at prisons like Walpole is that of the "Hard Ass," coldly indifferent to inmates and to the violence and sadism around them. "We all change a little bit when we come in the front door for roll call. You put on your cap and assume a different disguise for eight hours a day. . . . You got to kind of knuckle down and be the tough guy." They seek to maintain that "disguise" regardless of the circumstances they are in or the company they are keeping.[96]

More commonly, the smug hacks will merely look like model officers because the style of control one is most likely to see exercised by peers is that associated with the management of inmates in public places like mess halls, gymnasiums, and yards. In these contexts, whether a given prison is violent or calm, guards deal with prisoners en masse and hence are little more than anonymous figures of authority. A formal, distant, tough-minded discipline, sometimes spiced with profanity, bluster, and the implicit threat of violence, is in fact the norm in these contexts.[97] One is also apt to *hear about* a skewed sample of officer-inmate encounters. Those that feature violence, for instance, are the ones that will not only draw attention when they occur but will make up the lore, lovingly retold to novice officers and naive civilians, of "The Embattled Guardian Who Keeps Ferocious Convicts at Bay." Smug hacks may thus come to see themselves as superior officers—as warriors—because they are the men with the nerve to use violence when the chips are down.

The notion that authority means toughness and dominance—the strong coercing the weak—is intuitively appealing to many officers who appear to confuse authoritarian with authoritative uses of their power. (The subject of authoritative correctional officer behavior is covered in the next chapter.) Thus it is that new officers are encouraged to control inmates not by the force of their personalities or the merits of their judgment (that is, by authoritative behavior) but by being aloof, cynical, and intimidating (by authoritarian behavior). That one should cow or deceive convicts to gain compliance— to "mess with their minds" and "keep them off balance"—may seem quite natural to officers who have been schooled in the public version of guard authority.[98]

Crouch and Marquart provide a number of revealing instances of this bogus notion of authority, drawn from their research on Texas prisons. One involved "acting crazy," which "means the guard responds to the inmate in ways quite unrelated to the inmate's question or problem; in this way the inmate is put off and becomes uncertain himself."[99] Alternatively, the officer is admonished to go out of his way to make the prisoner feel ashamed or vulnerable. One method involved

> confronting an unsuspecting inmate with feigned seriousness and asking about something which may make the inmate uncomfortable.
> For example . . . an officer asked an inmate if he was the one who *slumbered* in bed. The inmate paused, looked at the officer, his feet . . . then replied: "I don't know uh—I—maybe—uh—you mean do I sno'?" The officer asked about slumbering again and got a similar reply. The

inmate admitted he did not know what slumber meant and by not knowing appeared inferior to all present and to himself since everyone but he clearly knew the term.[100]

"A more aggressive tactic," Crouch and Marquart continue,

> involves prolonged staring at selected inmates. After a time, the inmate will notice the stare and become increasingly nervous and uncertain. Although the staring is not necessarily prompted by official suspicion of any wrong doing, the inmate does not know this and thus worries about what he has done or what the guard really knows.[101]

The logical outgrowth of the conception of authority underlying these control strategies is to coerce physically (in the extreme, to beat into submission) those who cannot be manipulated or conned into compliance by the officials. One reason is that authoritarian control strategies evoke defensiveness among inmates and, indeed, move inmates to violence against their keepers.[102] Inmate resistance, and particularly violent resistance, in turn sparks more repression on the part of authoritarian officers. Reporting on the behavior of a clique of authoritarian officers not unlike those operating at Walpole, Marquart provides a telling example of escalating strategies of coercion that moved from insulting "verbal assaults" on inmates to more physically abusive "tune-ups," and finally to overtly violent "ass-whippings" and "severe beatings."[103] Inmates who mouthed off or fought back against officers were likely to be punished with the more extreme forms of retaliatory violence.

Primitive uses of authority do not normally reach the extremes observed by Marquart in Texas or Kauffman in Massachusetts. Even officers trapped in violent prisons—and these officers do feel trapped in such prisons[104]—yearn for training and support for more constructive roles. As one Walpole officer exclaimed plaintively, "If there was any other way open to us, we'd take it."[105] Moreover, even in the absence of training, abusive control strategies are often relinquished as officers "mellow" with experience. They learn to control inmates through more constructive "presentations of self," based primarily on an image of competence in solving problems and trustworthiness in personal relationships.[106] Seasoned officers, for example, typically feel less constrained to issue a disciplinary report simply because the prisoner has broken a rule. These officers feel confident in overlooking minor infractions where discretion is the greater part of wisdom or valor.[107] They also feel competent to resolve conflicts informally, drawing upon their experience and their personal relationships with the men under their care.[108] These changes in the officers' use of authority are subtle, however, and are not likely to be obvious in public encounters. The result is that most officers rate their colleagues as more custody-oriented and violence-prone than is actually the case.[109] In effect, then, the smug custodians personify the guard's public role and set the tone for officer behavior in the public areas of the prison, much as the convicts (who are, as Abbott makes clear, also quite smug) determine the public image of the prisoner and the social climate on the prison yard.

Many officers put on a tough facade to appease the smug hacks just as the inmates act tough to keep at a distance those whom they presume to be predatory convicts. This is particularly true in violent prisons, but it is true to some degree in all prisons. What emerges might be called *parallel instances of pluralistic ignorance;* substantial segments of both the guard and inmate populations are putting on a front to impress peers who are doing the very same thing for their benefit! The possibilities for confusion and conflict are many. Small wonder, for example, that many officers feel they are misunderstood and disrespected even by their colleagues[110] and that "interactions with fellow officers heighten stress."[111] Problems are compounded, moreover, because the real hacks and cons of the prison world often gravitate toward one another with violent and sometimes tragic results, since they compete for the same space, often with the same methods. These encounters are relatively uncommon, but they are the stuff of which stereotypes of all officers and inmates are made. It is here that one finds the battles that comprise the prison war, and they are of the making of a small and essentially self-selected sample of officers and inmates.

Organizational Sources of Alienation and Violence

The psychology of warfare in prison is reinforced by official regulations prohibiting staff from developing relationships with inmates. Guards in New York State prisons, for example, are expressly forbidden to

> engage in any conversation, communication, dealing, transaction, association, or relationships with any inmate or former inmate or any visitor, friends or relative of any inmate or former inmate in any manner or form which is not necessary or proper for the discharge of the employee's duties.[112]

These strictures are expressed in the training provided to New York officers at the Training Academy, where students are taught, directly or by inference, to refrain from speaking with inmates! This curious fact emerged during OJT—on-the-job training—where new officers like Conover get their first taste of correctional work after finishing their classroom training:

■ One of the female officers then asked an eminently sensible question: "But are we supposed to talk to them?"

The lieutenant didn't get the question. He apparently didn't know that in the Academy, we had been ordered not to talk to the inmates around us. But the idea of not talking to them here was so preposterous to him that he had a hard time grasping the concept.

"Of course you talk to them!" he finally said. "You'd better talk to them. How else are you going to let them know what to do and hear what they need from you? Oh, yes! The job is all about talking to them. That's really what it's about."

That echoed what Sergeant Bloom, head of the Academy, had told us. And yet it seemed to be a point of pride among Bloom's instructors that training was about *us,* not about *them.* We'd been taught that worrying about inmates' concerns was tantamount to pandering, that it almost demeaned an officer. Let *them* worry about how to communicate with *us* was the more common attitude.[113] ■

Restrictions on communication may not be literally enforced, but they convey a point of view and may "translate into subcultural norms among guards that are counterparts to the 'never talk to a screw' rule of inmates."[114] These norms are espoused by the smug hacks and honored, at least in public encounters, by other officers. This means that officers and inmates meet in public places like the yard as role-players rather than as individuals. Hostility is common and hard to address and resolve since no one admits to sentiments that do not fit their respective tough-guy roles.

Yet, if officers and inmates do not talk openly in their public encounters, they never discover a common ground for order in the prison community. At best, they collude with one another for mutual benefit, with manipulation, deceit, and the threat or use of force as the only means to resolve conflicts of interest. One such collusive relationship involves officers and other officials using "snitches" or "rats" as sources of information about the inmate population. Informants are variously threatened and rewarded to secure their cooperation, and the inmate troublemakers they betray to the staff are punished.[115]

Rats are thought to be an important source of information for the staff, and information in the prison is a key source of power. As one ranking officer at Lompoc observed, "If it weren't for the snitches and the snitches who snitch on snitches, the prison wouldn't be able to run."[116] The supposed prevalence of rats in prison is also a source of humor in some prison circles. Washington, a prisoner and a writer, tells an apocryphal tale on this subject:

■ The last time we tried a hunger strike the warden stormed into the Mess Hall and ordered us to eat. When no one made a move to break our solidarity by eating, the warden dragged a large chalkboard into the middle of the Mess Hall.

"This is your last chance," the warden shouted as he held up a piece of chalk for all to see, then prepared to write. "If you men don't start eating right now," the warden screamed, "I'm going to write the names of every informer, snitch and rat in the prison." Before the chalk touched the board nearly every plate was clean.[117] ■

There is, however, reason to doubt the power and prevalence of prisoners who inform on their peers. In real life, as opposed to fiction or myth, informants often are marginal members of the prison community, so the value of any information they might provide is probably quite limited. And, given the source, if you will, one must question the veracity of some informants, whose motives are not above suspicion. Moreover, many so-called rats are not informants at all. They are men who, by virtue of limited coping competence, have been stigmatized by their peers.[118] The term "rat" thus is often an epithet, not a description of informing behavior. The fact that this degrading and often misleading label is bandied about so casually in prison is one measure of the failure of community within the prison's walls.

The quintessential collusive relationship, often called "corrupt favoritism" in the prison literature,[119] is the antithesis of ratting. Corrupt favoritism pits the prisoner elite against their fellow inmates. It works like this: If the elite "keep the place quiet," they receive special privileges, including immunity from sanction for most rule infractions. The elite are generally free to use whatever methods they choose to preserve the status quo. They protect the good order of the prison because it is in their best interests to do so. Social control becomes an exercise in coercion and violence orchestrated in large measure by the prisoners themselves. The guards' authority is debased more by default than by overt action.

Collusive relationships, particularly of the type involving the prisoner elite, have been common in times past. In the Big House, they involved high-status prisoners, "right guys" who controlled other inmates partly by example and partly by threat.[120] In some contemporary prisons, gangs and other groups of convicts sometimes perform this function, and the impression is that they do so by regular recourse to violence.[121]

Stojkovic has examined patterns of corrupt favoritism in a midwestern prison, highlighting the informal relationships officers develop (for example, with older, more reliable inmates) to aid them in carrying out daily tasks (such as counts) and generally to assist them in maintaining order (by discouraging younger inmates from making trouble, for example). These relationships have a functional side to them in that officers, and perhaps some inmates, have less trouble to worry about. Some aspects of the social order, in other words, may be improved as a function of these arrangements. But Stojkovic's thoughtful work also identifies a tendency of these officers, perhaps *because* their authority is corrupted by these relationships, to shrink back from enforcing rules in dangerous situations—indeed, in precisely those situations one would suppose officers are hired to police. Thus, the officers point out that situations involving sex or drugs are quite dangerous to inmates as well as to officers themselves. As one officer told Stojkovic, speaking about the reluctance to intervene to stop illicit sex or to break up a drug deal, "If I got in the middle of that shit, I would be crazy because I will either get seriously hurt or killed. It would be plain stupid."[122] As a general matter, officers considered themselves wise enough to expressly avoid inmate transactions involving sex or drugs. Though the officers claimed to intervene when weaker inmates were victims of abuse, the claims rang hollow. If one is busy avoiding these situations, how can one draw fine lines distinguishing coercive and noncoercive encounters in an environment in which those distinctions are subtle at best? How can inmates feel secure in such an environment?

In southern prisons, collusive relationships were until quite recently a formal part of the organizational chain of command. Trusted prisoners acted as a kind of deputized force, like an inmate goon squad, with a remarkably free hand in the use of violence. The building tenders of the Texas system are an instructive case in point. Called "BTs," these men operated as a shadow police

force in Texas prisons until late 1981, when, over the objections of prison officials, they were abolished by court order. (The abolition of the BTs is thought
to have contributed significantly to the decline of order noted in some Texas
prisons. See Chapter Five.) These men were, as a rule, older recidivists doing
big time. They were armed (though not with guns, as in some other southern
prisons as recently as the early 1970s) and immune from normal disciplinary
procedures. Formally selected by ranking security officers, these prisoners were
given apprenticeships before assuming the role of the BT. They were even
assigned assistants ("runners") to do the errands and other grunt work that was
beneath the dignity of a full-fledged BT. They proved themselves by maintaining order and by protecting officers from inmate violence. Regular duties
assigned to these quasi-officials called for the threat or use of violence. Thus,
each BT

> learned the script for orienting new inmates in the tank. That is, he noted
> and developed his own version of: "mind your own business" and "keep
> the noise down," "I'll cut you slack the first time and maybe the second,
> but if you screw up again, we'll go down to the wash room and get your
> heart straight."[123]

Under riot conditions, the BTs became a volunteer militia at the disposal
of the staff. The following narrative, which refers to a riot that took place in
the fall of 1981, is a revealing account of their collusive and violence-suffused
relationship with the staff:

> The riot began when inmates . . . started several fires and broke
> windows in the nearby gymnasium by throwing rocks and other debris.
> Within a relatively short period, officers and approximately 150 BTs and
> runners converged in the gymnasium. While the officers were armed
> with riot batons, the BTs had brought clubs and pipes and several
> wielded long wooden toilet brushes. One inmate even passed out
> blackjacks from a paper sack. When all the "troops" were assembled, the
> warden addressed the inmates: "Anyone who don't want to kick ass can
> just go on back to his house (cell)." The inmates cheered in support of
> the warden's declaration and waved their weapons in the air. The door to
> the gymnasium was then opened and officers and inmate elites (who
> identified themselves by wearing red bandannas) attacked the 200 or so
> rioters. . . . Most of the rioting prisoners were injured in some way,
> many quite seriously.[124]

The BT system has been dismantled, though it is possible that some of these
men continue to play violent roles in the informal accommodations linking
staff and inmates in the Texas prisons.

The passing of the BT system produced, for a time, a less orderly prison
regime. Official records revealed an increase in violent attacks of inmates
against one another and against officers. As noted in Chapter Five, the general
quality of life declined dramatically. Paradoxically, the average prisoner did not
feel less secure in these troubled institutions. The explanation for this paradox

is that inmates felt unsafe under the reign of hard-nosed hacks and lawless BTs, just as most inmates feel insecure under any corrupt prison regime. During the transition from an essentially corrupt system to a modern, trained guard force, inmates experienced Texas prisons as dangerous, to be sure, but no more dangerous than during earlier days—the difference was primarily that threat emanated from inmate gangs that had emerged to fill the power vacuum left by the BTs rather than from staff and their inmate henchmen. After a few years of turmoil, the new officer force gained legitimate control of Texas prisons. This they did by learning to wield authority, primarily in the form of cultivating such bureaucratic skills as effective incident report writing (incident reports can land a prisoner in segregation and may even add time to his sentence by removing "good time") and effective and restrained uses of force rather than violence. In today's Texas prisons, most prisoners feel "much safer" than ever before.[125]

CUSTODIAL VIOLENCE IN PERSPECTIVE

Officers must sometimes use force to defend themselves or protect others from harm. The proper response features restraint on the order of the tit-for-tat strategy enunciated in Chapter Four as a feature of mature coping. At Lompoc, a federal prison, the notion of "equal force for equal force" is explicitly endorsed by the officers.[126] The sole object of force is to gain control over the prisoner. Accordingly, Lompoc officers subscribe to the proposition that "once a convict is [under] control, don't use force."[127] Restrained force thus serves to constrain, not to punish or abuse.

The periodic need to use force in prison reminds us that officers must be tough enough, for want of a better word, to fight inmates when the need arises. As one seasoned officer observed, with a hint of irony,

> ■ I think I would make a good convict. I have the qualities you need—toughness, not being afraid of violence. I can handle that. But there is one big difference that separates us. Convicts are predators. They hurt other people. They take advantage of other people. They really only care about themselves. They don't attack the strong, they prey off the weak and helpless in our society and they destroy lives.[128] ■

A good officer, in contrast, is never a predator, "and that is what separates us from them. We don't cross that line."[129]

Regrettably, some officers are—or become—predators. With them, force is used for its own sake, because it is convenient or easy; and that amounts to violence, pure and simple. Violence in service of social control represents a failure of coping, a giving in to alienation. This violence occurs with some regularity in prison, but it is neither as common as suggested by guard stereotypes nor as inevitable as the smug hacks and convicts make it out to be. Guard violence, moreover, is avoidable. Officers can be provided with a range of nonviolent problem-solving skills so that they need not rule by intimidation and threat. As Toch has observed, "Men with more options" when faced with stress and conflict "feel more secure." As a result,

> They are less apt to be trapped into responding to challenges, taunts, baiting, and "tests" of "manhood." They are less likely than some of our present-day staff . . . to play unseemly games with unworthy opponents at everyone else's expense.[130]

Walpole officers provide a revealing, if negative, case study of Toch's proposition. New officer recruits at Walpole, generally sympathetic to the plight of inmates, were routinely posted to the cell blocks, which had been abandoned by seasoned officers in search of safe assignments. These officers were, in Kauffman's words, "left virtually at the mercy of inmates" during a period of almost anarchic violence.[131] The officers were traumatized and, as a result, embittered. "Whatever sympathetic attitudes an officer had held toward inmates on entering the institution were quickly, and permanently, extinguished."[132] For many of these officers, Toch's "unseemly games with unworthy opponents" became the only games in town.

Things could have been different for the Walpole officers, however, given adequate training and deployment. And things are in fact different for most officers in most prisons. Most officers develop constructive, competent ways of carrying out their jobs. Some develop skills and confidence in human relations training, which is increasingly available as part of standard correctional training programs.[133] Many others cultivate these interpersonal skills on the job.[134] Others develop expertise in matters of correctional policy and practice, which makes them on-site bureaucrats who can facilitate problem solving for inmates confronting increasingly bureaucratic correctional systems.[135]

Most officers, whatever the source of their competence, are not impelled to use violence to carry out their jobs, either directly or through collusive relationships. They do not aspire to a berth in the trenches occupied by some of their colleagues. Like most inmates, most guards would rather sit out the prison war. They make an effort to meet alienation head on and to make their jobs worthy of the time and attention they command. In effect, these officers attempt to respond maturely to the challenge of alienation rather than merely sulking or striking out in frustration. These officers, the real correctional officers in our prisons, are the subject of the next chapter.

NOTES

1. Toch and Klofas (1982).

2. Toch (1977a:98).

3. Anonymous (1871:28).

4. Coffey (1823:179).

5. Nelson (1936:25).

6. As one officer told Herberts, "Probably the biggest question asked by people living outside of the prison was, 'Do inmates get beaten?' " His [the officer's] honest

response each time was, "No." Living in a world full of informants, administrators, video cameras, and other electronic surveillance, not to mention the civil liability and hordes of personal lawsuits, those days had passed. . . . The bottom line was that physical confrontations between inmates and staff had to be initiated by the inmate . . . (Herberts, l997:141).

7. Boot camps and supermax prisons are notable exceptions to this observation, but these facilities are by no means typical prisons.

8. Bowker (1980:104); Herberts (1997:141).

9. Kupers (1999:50).

10. Schroeder (1976:151–52).

11. Fleisher (1989:230).

12. See Haney, Banks, and Zimbardo (1981).

13. Ross (1981:3).

14. Irwin (1980:125).

15. Irwin (1980:130).

16. Hawkins (1976:86–87). See also Conover (2000). The officers he trained and worked with were a diverse lot.

17. DiIulio (1991:51).

18. DiIulio (1991:52).

19. Hawkins (1976:87).

20. Morris and Morris (1963:255–56).

21. League of Women Voters of Wisconsin (1981:175).

22. Lombardo (1981:32–33).

23. Schroeder (1976:153).

24. It is commonly thought that people who live in prison towns and who take prison jobs have already been socialized to their roles—and usually to a negative version of those roles—through their association with guards in their families and among their friends. This was not true for the Auburn officers Lombardo studied. "Many officers whose fathers were guards reported that their fathers almost never talked to them about their work, at least until the sons became officers. Then, as

one officer put it, 'That's all we did talk about' " (Lombardo, 1981:23).

25. Lombardo (1981:36).

26. See Seeman (1959).

27. Cullen, Link, Cullen, and Wolfe (1989:97); Toch and Grant (1982:199).

28. Cullen et al. (1989:101).

29. Cullen et al. (1989:97).

30. Poole and Regoli (1981).

31. Conover (2000:78).

32. Conover (2000:79).

33. As a fellow officer told Conover, who had asked him how he dealt with the unpredictability of the job, "I just try to make myself go numb" (Conover, 2000:270). More generally, Cheek and Miller (1983:116) confirm that "correction officers experience considerable stress on the job." (See also Cullen, Link, Wolfe, & Frank 1985.) This stress is associated with "high rates of divorce and serious health problems . . . such as hypertension, ulcers, and heart disease . . . [which] are even higher than those of police officers previously identified as a highly stressed occupational group. Moreover, the corrections officers, like police, perceive many stress-related physical and emotional problems in their fellow workers" (Cheek & Miller, 1983:116). Though the problem has been less thoroughly studied, correctional managers are stressed as well. They feel overworked on their jobs, limited in their authority and control over situations, and unappreciated by those above and below them in the organization (American Correctional Association, 1984:15).

34. Conover (2000:79).

35. Conover (2000:244).

36. Conover (2000:246).

37. See Cheek and Miller (1983); Cullen et al. (1985).

38. Jacobs (1977:40).

39. May (1981a: 13).

40. Kauffman (1988:81).

41. Lin (2000:160).

42. Toch (1981).

43. Conover (2000:157).

44. Conover (2000:157).

45. Conover (2000:80–81).

46. Conover (2000:105).

47. Conover (2000:104).

48. Conover (2000:107).

49. May (1981b:25–26).

50. Research indicates that "Seven out of ten officers agree with statements such as 'we're damned if we do, and damned if we don't.' One out of four hold such alienated views strongly" (Toch & Grant, 1982:199).

51. Cheek and Miller (1983).

52. Lombardo (1981:55 & 165).

53. Poole and Regoli (1980); Willet (1982).

54. See Wahler and Gendreau (1990:265).

55. Conover (2000:95).

56. Cheek and Miller (1983:119).

57. Stojkovic (1990:215).

58. Lawes (1932:12).

59. Lawes (1932:24).

60. Lawes (1932:39).

61. Crouch and Marquart (1989:59).

62. Crouch and Marquart (1989:73).

63. Fox (1982:42–47); see also Fitzgerald and Sim (1982:132) and Kauffman (1988).

64. Fox (1982:51); Kauffman (1988).

65. See Johnson (1986).

66. Conover (2000).

67. Toch (1977b:8).

68. Lin (2000;50).

69. See Marquart (1984) for a description of what amounts to an informal goon squad. See Conover (2000:126–36) for a revealing account of Sing Sing's prestigious "cell extraction team" at work in "the Box," the prison's segregation unit.

70. Bowker (1980:102).

71. John Conrad, personal communication.

72. Conover (2000:131).

73. Toch (1977b:123); Marquart (1984).

74. Conover (2000:135).

75. Toch (1977b: 123); see also Marquart (1984).

76. Toch (1977b:123).

77. Toch (1977b:123).

78. Marquart (1984); Kauffman (1988).

79. See Marquart (1984); Kauffman (1988).

80. Kauffman (1988:123–24).

81. Kauffman (1988:35).

82. Kauffman (1988:66).

83. Kauffman (1988:244).

84. Kauffman (1988:153).

85. Kauffman (1988:139).

86. Kauffman (1988:139), see also Marquart (1984) for a discussion of a similarly situated subculture of officer violence in a Texas prison.

87. Kauffman (1988:140).

88. Conover (2000:274).

89. Conover (2000:275).

90. Conover (2000:276).

91. Kauffman (1988:231), see also Kauffman (1988:238–39).

92. See Kauffman (1988:212). For a more general discussion of the dynamics of dehumanization as it relates to violence, see Johnson (1986).

93. Conover (2000:103–104). The incident Conover describes did not involve violence. His record keeping got another officer in some trouble. Conover was right in what he did, but it became clear to him that he had violated the officer's code of loyalty to one another. "If you were going to survive in jail," he noted, "the goody-goody stuff had to go" (103). See also Farkas (1997) for a discussion of the officer's informal code of conduct, which parallels that of the inmate code discussed in earlier chapters.

94. Kauffman (1988:120).

95. See Marquart (1984); Kauffman (1988).

96. Kauffman (1988:244–45).

97. Crouch and Marquart (1980); Lombardo (1981). Block officers or work assignment officers, who conduct many of their activities away from the gaze of peers and often deal with inmates on a one-to-one basis, may be understanding in their dealings with their men. "In the yard," by contrast, where one deals with prisoners in groups and under the view of one's colleagues or superiors, "displays of understanding are apt to be interpreted as weakness"—by inmate and officer alike (Lombardo, 1981:105–106).

98. Crouch and Marquart (1980:88).

99. Crouch and Marquart (1980:88).

100. Crouch and Marquart (1980:88–89).

101. Crouch and Marquart (1980:89).

102. See Light (1991:258).

103. Marquart (1984).

104. See, for example, Kauffman (1988:240).

105. Kauffman (1988:229).

106. Crouch and Marquart (1980:91); Lombardo (1981:63).

107. Poole and Regoli (1980).

108. Lombardo (1981:74–75).

109. Klofas and Toch (1982); Kauffman (1988:248).

110. Poole and Regoli (1981).

111. Cullen et al. (1985:518).

112. Cited in Toch (1977b:67).

113. Conover (2000:68–69).

114. Toch (1977b:67).

115. See Stojkovic (1986).

116. Fleischer (1989:194).

117. Washington (1981:21).

118. See Johnson (1961).

119. See Sykes (1966).

120. Sykes (1966); Irwin (1980:22–24).

121. Jacobs (1977); Irwin (1980).

122. Stojkovic (1990:225–26).

123. Marquart and Crouch (1984:504).

124. Marquart and Crouch (1984:502).

125. Crouch and Marquart (1989:216).

126. Fleischer (1989:218). See also Herberts (1997:31) for a discussion of limits on the use of force covered in a state prison system, which closely follow those at Lompoc.

127. Fleischer (1989:218).

128. Earley (1992:305–306).

129. Earley (1992:306).

130. Toch (1977b:135).

131. Kauffman (1988:190).

132. Kauffman (1988:194).

133. Frank (1966); Cohen (1979).

134. Johnson (1977 & 1981); Lombardo (1981).

135. See Lombardo (1989).

REFERENCES

American Correctional Association. *Stress Management for Correctional Officers and Their Families.* 1984. Latham, MD: American Correctional Association

Anonymous. *An Illustrated History and Description of State Prison Life, By One Who Has Been There. Written by a Convict in a Convict's Cell.* Globe Publishing, 1871.

Bowker, L. *Prison Victimization.* New York: Elsevier, 1980.

Cheek, F. E., and M. D. S. Miller. "The experience of stress for correction officers: A double-bind theory of correctional stress." *Journal of Criminal Justice* 11 (1983):105–120.

Coffey, W. A. *Inside Out: Or, An Interior View of the New York State Prison; Together with Bibliographic Sketches of the Lives of Several of the Convicts.* New York: Printed for the author, 1823.

Cohen, J. "The correction academy." *Crime & Delinquency* 25 (2) 1979:177–99.

Conover, T. *Newjack: Guarding Sing Sing.* New York: Random House, 2000.

Crouch, B. M., and J. W. Marquart. "On becoming a prison guard." In B. M. Crouch (ed.). *The Keepers: Prison Guards and Contemporary Corrections.* Springfield, IL: Charles C. Thomas, 1980:63–105.

Crouch, B. M., and J. W. Marquart. *An Appeal to Justice.* Austin: University of Texas Press, 1989.

Cullen, F. T., B. G. Link, J. B. Cullen, and N. T. Wolfe. "How satisfying is prison work? A comparative occupational approach." *Journal of Offender Counseling, Services & Rehabilitation* 14 (2) 1989:89–108.

Cullen, F. T., B. G. Link, N. T. Wolfe, and J. Frank. "The social dimensions of correctional officer stress." *Justice Quarterly* 2 (4) 1985:505–533.

DiIulio, J. J. *No Escape: The Future of American Corrections.* New York: Basic Books, 1991.

Earley, P. *The Hot House: Life Inside Leavenworth.* New York: Bantam Books, 1992.

Farkas, M. A. "The Normative Code Among Correctional Officers: An Exploration of Components and Function." *Journal of Crime and Justice* 20 (1) 1997:23–36.

Fitzgerald, M., and J. Sim. *British Prisons.* Oxford: Blackwell, 1982.

Fleischer, M. S. *Warehousing Violence.* Beverly Hills, CA: Sage, 1989.

Fox, J. G. *Organizational and Racial Conflicts in Maximum-Security Prisons.* Lexington: Lexington Books, 1982.

Frank, B. "The emerging professionalism of the correctional officer." *Crime & Delinquency* 12 (3) 1966:272–76.

Haney, C., C. Banks, and P. Zimbardo. "Interpersonal dynamics in a simulated prison." In R. R. Ross (ed.). *Prison Guard/Correctional Officer.* Toronto Canada: Butterworth, 1981:137–68. (Originally published in the *International Journal of Criminology and Penology,* 1973.)

Hawkins, G. *The Prison: Policy and Practice.* Chicago: University of Chicago Press, 1976.

Herberts, S. *6–5: A Different Shade of Blue.* Commack, NY: Kroshka Books, 1997.

Irwin, J. *Prisons in Turmoil.* Boston: Little, Brown, 1980.

Jacobs, J. *Stateville: The Penitentiary in Mass Society.* Chicago: University of Chicago Press, 1977.

Johnson, E. "Sociology of confinement: Assimilation and the prison 'rat.' " *Journal of Criminal Law, Criminology, and Police Science* 51 (1961):228–33.

Johnson, R. "Ameliorating prison stress: Some helping roles for custodial personnel." *International Journal of Criminology and Penology* 5 (3) 1977:263–73.

Johnson, R. "Informal helping networks in prison: The shape of grass-roots correctional intervention." In R. R. Ross (ed.). *Prison Guard/Correctional Officer.* Canada: Butterworth, 1981:105–125. (Originally published in *The Journal of Criminal Justice,* 1979.)

Johnson, R. "Institutions and the promotion of violence." In A. Campbell and J. J. Gibbs (eds). *Violent Transactions: The Limits of Personality.* Oxford: Basil Blackwell, 1986:181–205.

Kauffman, K. *Prison Officers and Their World.* Cambridge, MA: Harvard University Press, 1988.

Klofas, J., and H. Toch. "The guard subculture myth." *Journal of Research in Crime and Delinquency* 19 (2) 1982:238–54.

Kupers, T. A. *Prison Madness: The Mental Health Crisis Behind Bars and What We Must Do About It.* San Francisco: Jossey-Bass, 1999.

Lawes, L. L. *Twenty Thousand Years in Sing Sing.* New York: Ray Long & Richard R. Smith, 1932.

League of Women Voters of Wisconsin. "Changing of the guard: Citizen soldiers in Wisconsin correctional institutions." In R. R. Ross (ed.). *Prison Guard/Correctional Officer.* Toronto, Canada: Butterworth, 1981:169–89. (Originally published by the League of Women Voters of Wisconsin, 1979.)

Light, S. C. "Assaults on prison officers: Interactional themes." *Justice Quarterly* 8 (2) 1991:243–61.

Lin, A. C. *Reform in the Making: The Implementation of Social Policy in Prison.* Princeton: Princeton University Press, 2000.

Lombardo, L. X. *Guards Imprisoned: Correctional Officers at Work.* New York: Elsevier, 1981.

Lombardo, L. X. *Guards Imprisoned: Correctional Officers at Work,* Second Edition. Cincinnati, OH: Anderson Publishing, 1989.

Marquart, J. W. "Prison guards and the use of physical coercion as a mechanism of prisoner control." Paper presented at Annual Meeting of the American Sociological Association, August 1984.

Marquart, J. W., and B. M. Crouch. "Coopting the kept: Using inmates for social control in a southern prison." *Justice Quarterly* 1 (4) 1984:491–509.

May, E. "A day on the job—in prison." In R. R. Ross (ed.). *Prison Guard/Correctional Officer.* Toronto, Canada: Butterworth, 1981a:9–18. (Originally published in *Corrections Magazine,* 1976.)

May, E. "Prison guards in America—the inside story." In R. R. Ross (ed.). *Prison Guard/Correctional Officer.* Toronto, Canada: Butterworth, 1981b:19–40. (Originally published in *Corrections Magazine,* 1976.)

Morris, T., and P. Morris. *Pentonville: A Sociological Study of an English Prison.* London: Routledge & Kegan Paul, 1963.

Nelson, V. F. *Prison Days and Nights.* Garden City, NY: Garden City Publishing, 1936.

Poole, E. D., and R. M. Regoli. "Role stress, custody orientation, and disciplinary actions: A study of prison guards." *Criminology* 18 (2) 1980:215–26.

Poole, E. D., and R. M. Regoli. "Alienation in prison: An examination of the work relations of prison guards." *Criminology* 19 (2) 1981:251–70.

Ross, R. R. "Introduction." In R. R. Ross (ed.). *Prison Guard/Correctional Officer.* Toronto, Canada: Butterworth, 1981:1–5.

Schroeder, A. *Shaking It Rough.* New York: Doubleday, 1976.

Seeman, M. "On the meaning of alienation." *American Sociological Review* 24 (6) 1959:783–90.

Stojkovic, S. "An examination of compliance structures in a prison organization: A study of the types of correctional power." Paper presented at Annual Meeting of ACJS, March 1984.

Stojkovic, S. "Social bases of power and control mechanisms among correctional administrators in a prison organization." *Journal of Criminal Justice* 14 (2) 1986:157–66.

Stojkovic, S. "Accounts of prison work: Corrections officers' portrayals of their work worlds." *Perspectives on Social Problems* 2 (1990):211–30.

Sykes, G. *The Society of Captives.* New York: Atheneum, 1966.

Toch, H. *Living in Prison: The Ecology of Survival.* New York: Free Press, 1977a.

Toch, H. *Police, Prisons, and the Problem of Violence.* DHEW Publication No. (ADM) 76–364, 1977b.

Toch, H. "Is a 'correctional officer' by any other name, a 'screw'?" In R. R. Ross (ed.). *Prison Guard/Correctional Officer.* Toronto, Canada: Butterworth, 1981:87–104. (Originally published in *Criminal Justice Review,* 1978.)

Toch, H., and J. D. Grant. *Reforming Human Services: Change Through Participation*. Beverly Hills, CA: Sage, 1982.

Toch, H., and J. Klofas. "Alienation and desire for job enrichment among correction officers." *Federal Probation* 46 (1982):35–44.

Wahler, C., and P. Gendreau. "Perceived characteristics of effective correctional officers by officers, supervisors, and inmates across three different types of institutions." *Canadian Journal of Criminology* (April 1990):265–77.

Washington, J. *A Bright Spot in the Yard: Notes and Stories from a Prison Journal*. Trumansburg, NY: Crossing Press, 1981.

Willet, T. C. "Report to the commissioner of the correctional service of Canada on a follow-up study of correctional officers and their partners in 1981." Ottowa, Ontario: Correctional Service of Canada, 1982.

8

❖

To Protect and to Serve

The Prison Officer's Private (Correctional) Agenda

Prison officers are, for the most part, an alienated and at times even embittered lot. This is not surprising since they are imprisoned by unflattering stereotypes and have limited autonomy in their work. Yet alienation does not demand a negative or destructive response; officers need not wallow in bitterness and resentment. Many try to come to grips with their situation and find it possible to do something about it.

It is by helping prisoners—by promoting secure and, ideally, responsive prison regimes—that some officers rise above the limitations of their formal custodial role. They use their authority to help inmates cope with prison life; they provide human service rather than custodial repression. They do the best they can with the resources at their disposal to make the prison a better place in which to live and work. In contrast to their merely custodial colleagues, these officers cope maturely with their own problems as well as with the problems experienced by prisoners. They serve, by their helping activities and by example, as true correctional officers.

CORRECTIONAL AUTHORITY: A MATTER OF HUMAN SERVICE

Officers who assume correctional roles are authority figures in the full sense of the term. It is often assumed that authority must have negative connotations—that it exists, particularly in settings like the prison, as a pretext for domination of others. Yet "an essential ingredient of authority," observes Sennett, is possessed by someone "who has strength and uses it to guide others through disciplining them, changing how they act by reference to a higher standard."[1] Guidance, in turn, requires nurturance, a fact we too often deny or distort in our prisons and other social institutions.[2] Punishment administered by authorities, then, must serve a constructive end and be administered by people who care. Punishment can be justified as a proper expression of authority only when it "can be shown to be a good for the wrongdoer," that is to say, when it is "an attempt, by someone who cares, to improve a wayward person."[3]

It is among the ranks of the line officer that we are most likely to find authorities who care enough to work, day in and day out, for the correction of prisoners. And line officers have much to contribute to the well-being of inmates and the correctional mission of the prison. These officers find that to be of real service, however, they must emphasize the constructive side of their jobs or at least de-emphasize the negative, alienating aspects of their work. It is telling that the similarities of situations that make some officers—the hacks—hostile to inmates draw others—the correctional officers—together with inmates in a shared way of life. For correctional officers, being "uniformed prisoners" is an insult that is made into an asset; at least they are, by virtue of their hybrid status in this otherwise rigid caste system, very much a part of life and adjustment in the prison community.

Many officers see correctional work as an intrinsically worthwhile endeavor.[4] They hunger for opportunities to improve the quality of life in the prison community and grasp them when they can. Like most of us, they want to be people who matter. In the prison, the skills that matter are human relations and human services skills. These are the skills that can be used to develop relationships and, hence, to reduce tension, defuse crises, and conduct daily business in a civilized (and potentially civilizing) manner. This point is often obscured by the macho-worship of the smug hack but is nevertheless reaffirmed daily in the successful nonviolent interventions on the part of some officers. As one prison officer observed,

> ■ I am almost ashamed to say it in public, but the key to being a good correctional officer is having a caring attitude. Now that sounds to most staff here as being weak and not very macho. . . . It sounds like you are giving in to the inmates—or at least, that is how the staff interprets it, anyway—but it is not the same at all.[5] ■

To be a professional, this man maintained, means "letting your conscience be your guide" and caring enough about inmates and about yourself to do the job in a responsive way. Violence has no place in such a role, and force is used only as a last resort.

Conover reached the same conclusions during his year as an officer at Sing Sing, based in part on his observations of a fellow officer named Smith. Smith ran a gallery on a cell block, which is the living area for inmates. "Gallery work," Conover tells us, was the essential job of jailing. Forget running a gate or being an escort or doing construction supervision or transportation or manning a wall tower—a good robot might almost do those. The real action was on the gallery looking after inmates. To do this job well you had to be fearless, know how to talk to people, have thick skin and a high tolerance for stress. . . . We were like cops on the beat, the guys who knew the local players, the ones who saw it all.[6]

The gallery officer may well resemble a cop, but it is a cop who follows a community policing role, with a focus on human relations. Once Conover discovered this, he could envision a constructive role for himself:

■ I left work that day happier than I'd been since starting at the Academy. After weeks of hanging out with senior officers who seemed to bring little more to the job than machismo and forbearance, who would say things like "If they're happy, your not doing your job," here was this guy —Smith—who saw gallery work as an art, something you could perform creatively. Interpersonal skills were a big part of it, though nothing like ICP skills the Academy had described to us. Smith melded toughness with an attitude of respect for his inmates. In turn, he was respected back. What he seemed to understand was that at the root of the job was the inevitability of a kind of relationship between us and them–and that the officer played a larger role in determining the nature of that relationship.[7] ■

At the core of that relationship was the simple but essential fact that "Smith succeeded because he viewed the inmates as human beings" and treated them accordingly, maintaining tolerance and a sense of humor.[8]

The human relations perspective of officer work, as opposed to the more machismo-oriented custodial view, appears to resonate especially well among female officers, who began working in men's prisons in the early 1970s. One of San Quentin's female officers assures us, for example, that the presence of women in the guard force produces "a calmer setting" in large measure due to their focus on interpersonal skills rather than physical coercion. The presence of women in the prison trenches, she continues, also

forces male officers not to act as "big, bad and tough" because here they have this little 5'2" 115 lb. woman standing beside them, putting a guy that is 6'4", 230 lbs. in cuffs . . . saying, "Come on now, act right," and not having any problem doing it. Whereas he might have to go in there with 2 or 3 other guys and tackle him down to cuff him. It also forces them to recognize that they can't go home and talk about how bad and mean they are and what a tough day they have had because some little chickie can do the same thing that he is doing.[9]

This officer's observations are borne out by research. Female guards in men's prisons are likely to take a human relations view of the correctional officer job and to prize their interpersonal skills. Though they do not necessarily have a more positive view of inmates and in fact approach the correctional role in a diversity of ways, female officers tend to exert a "softening" influence on the prison environments in which they work, making them more livable and less violent.[10] (The diversity of roles played by female officers is indicated in the finding that women officers tend to hold attitudes that are more punitive than their male peers while at the same time they express more interest in counseling roles.[11]) Though female officers constitute a minority of the overall guard force in most men's prisons, their numbers are growing. This fact augurs well for their careers in the field[12] and for life and adjustment in prisons of the future.

To be sure, human relations are not the exclusive province of women. Long before women worked as officers in men's prisons, Glaser could state with confidence, "There is ample evidence that control can be achieved by staff without a hostile or superior attitude, and that positive leadership and influence is difficult to achieve without at least a minimum of friendliness and respect."[13] Indeed, as Glaser made clear, officers who are fair and friendly—who relate to inmates as fellow human beings—are liked best and obeyed most readily.[14] More recently, Stojkovic has noted that, in the eyes of the officers themselves, "consistency, fairness, and flexibility in the enforcement of rules were what made a good officer," and that "effective officers are able to develop a sense of respect with inmates by being fair and consistent."[15] These officers are open-minded but they are not naive. They know inmates can be quite manipulative. As one officer told Lin, "they have to be incarcerated, but they want everything that they can get." The key, notes Lin, is to deal with inevitable mistrust between inmates and officers "through responsiveness"—by keeping communication lines open.[16]

Male or female officers who cultivate personal relationships with inmates are a critical human resource in conflict-ridden prison environments. "It is not merely the officer's physical presence as an authority figure which serves to check inmates in their conflicts with one another," writes Lombardo,

> but the relationships that develop between an officer and an inmate. A positive relationship allows the inmate to approach the officer when a problem is developing, allowing the officer time to defuse it. Thus one finds a connection between the officer's abilities to maintain order and personal relationships between officers and inmates.[17]

The link between relationships and control even holds during riot situations. At these critical junctures, an officer's familiarity with a prisoner offers the prospect of negotiating life-and-death conflicts. Thus, Guenther and Guenther report that

> officers often emphasized their interest in establishing and maintaining working relationships with inmates . . . for they felt that their ultimate control over inmates during crises was a close function of these associations. The smallest personal knowledge, such as an inmate's name or the job he has in the institution, can be used by an officer to initiate a verbal exchange suggesting trust and a fair settlement.[18]

Research reveals that human service officers have more authority and are more satisfied with their jobs. As Hepburn has observed, "the level of institutional authority appears to be greatest among those guards who also have a less punitive and less custodial orientation, who maintain a lower degree of social distance from inmates, and who express a higher level of job satisfaction."[19] These important findings have been replicated and extended by Hepburn and Knepper in a recent study of custodial and correctional officers in Arizona. The Arizona correctional system "is unique in having a two-track career for correctional officers: one in correctional custody and one in correctional counselling and treatment."[20] Comparing these groups, Hepburn and Knepper state: "We find that job satisfaction is significantly greater among Arizona's more human services-oriented correctional program officers than among the traditional, custody-oriented correctional security officers."[21] Moreover, this seminal study reveals that human service officers experience less role strain than custody officers, even though their job is objectively more complex and therefore more subject to role conflict than is that of their custodial colleagues.

Finally, this body of research supports the key observation that human service officers have greater authority than custodial officers, who tend to see their credibility as a function of the uniforms they wear rather than the services they provide. As a general matter, it would appear that human service officers have more autonomy and, hence, are able to adapt more flexibly to the technical and interpersonal demands of the job than is the case with custodial officers. (Custodial officers appear to confuse flexibility with permissiveness, a cardinal sin in prison. As Conover noted, "permissiveness was a charge that a stupid and unimaginative CO might level against one who was effectively flexible."[22]) It is fair to say that correctional authority—the ability to protect and to serve, and, ultimately, to influence—rests in those officers who develop personal relationships and flexible work strategies rather than with those who play aloof and often rigid custodial roles.

The personal relationships at the heart of correctional authority are valuable because they preserve a civil order behind bars and suggest that problems can be solved in a civilized manner. These relationships also demonstrate respect for the people under one's authority. As one former inmate observed, "the best help that I was offered came in the form that always included letting you know that you were a regular human being."[23] Like all "regular human beings," inmates deserve to be treated within the framework of the Golden Rule, which admonishes us to "Do unto others as we would have them do unto us." Human service officers embody this theme in their work. As one officer told Lin, "You've got to treat inmates as you would like to be treated. Handle their problems just like your own; or think about how you would like to be handled if you did something wrong."[24] Respect for one's basic humanity matters enormously to inmates. Small things, like following through on a promise, prove crucial. In the words of one officer, "Once an officer tells an inmate that he is going to do something, it better get done. To just brush off an inmate, *as though he does not exist,* is the epitome of disrespect" [emphasis added].[25] By and large, prisoners "have had a long history of failure, rejection, and ego deflation"; as a result, they "are especially appreciative of attention, encouragement, and compliments from staff."[26]

When the prison operates as a correctional institution, perhaps the key lesson it teaches prisoners is that they are valuable and unique human beings in their own right, even if they have offended against the society and deserve punishment. Hence it is that

> The common element in the testimonials [of reformed prisoners] is the self-respect that was given to the inmates by the officers whom these men credited as having been rehabilitative influences. This did not mean that the officers were unusually lenient, lax or permissive; it meant only that they treated the men with a personal interest and without pretension or condescension. The officers were friendly in a way that inspired confidence and respect rather than contempt; they were frank, fair and considerate.[27]

The rehabilitated inmates reciprocated, treating officers with respect and consideration. In these relationships we see a bridge, constructed of human ties, that links prisoners to the larger society:

> These [inmates], previously treated as though members of an untouchable caste, were accepted in prison in long periods of daily contact, by persons who were secure and content in respected status groups. Gradually, this contact seems to have given the offenders the ability to identify with persons in socially accepted, conventional groups, and this new self-image replaced that image which caused them to think of themselves as a distinct criminal group rejected by the noncriminal world.[28]

These relationships, and the constructive lives they sometimes help set in motion, are vivid reminders that "conscience rests not on fear but on the more solid emotional foundation of loyalty and gratitude."[29]

Human service and personal relationships would not seem to be the stock in trade of the "typical" guard, but officers can be quite voluble in expressing their preference for these correctional activities. Reporting on a nationwide survey of prison guards conducted for *Corrections Magazine* in the mid-1970s, a turbulent period in American prisons, May observes,

> Many resent what they believe is their too limited role as jailors of America's convicts as well as the lack of encouragement from administration to work more actively with inmates. . . . "You've got to show that he (the officer) is needed," one of them says. "You've got to show that we're doing something that's worthwhile . . . but how in the world can you feel worthwhile if you're just opening and closing doors?"
>
> Everywhere *Corrections Magazine* interviewed officers, they defined the "worthwhile" aspects of their jobs in highly personal anecdotes of inmates they believe they may have helped: Unscrambling administrative snarls for an inmate who may not have received what was due him . . . the isolated success stories of those who "made it on the

street," job assignments they urged for a man who later used the newly learned skill "on the outside."[30]

In these kinds of observations (which recur in many other studies of officers at work), we see alienation countered by a desire for job enrichment. The fact that officers want to develop constructive relationships with inmates, to be agents of human service rather than custodial repression, belies guard stereotypes. Even more enlightening is the distribution of this concern. Research has revealed that "officers are disaffected", but, at the same time, "desire for job enrichment tends to be high," especially among such unlikely groups as older, rural guards.[31] We learn that a " 'human service' orientation increases steadily with seniority": fully 75 percent of the officers with twenty or more years of experience think guards should be involved in providing rehabilitative program services, and 85 percent of this veteran group feel that "it's important . . . to have compassion" for prisoners.[32] (Jurik's research also tells us that "older officers appear to have more optimistic attitudes towards inmates."[33]) Of equal significance, fully two of every three of the younger, urban, less experienced, and more alienated guards still acknowledge the importance of compassion in one's dealings with inmates.[34] These findings have been obtained in research conducted over the last two decades, featuring men only as well as men and women officers, and in medium- as well as maximum-security prisons.[35] Those officers who emphasize human service and compassion, moreover, tend to cope better with the stresses of correctional work and to be more satisfied with their jobs.[36] It would seem that smug hacks—and those who think of them as typical guards—have precious little to be smug about. As Cullen and his associates have noted, this body of research leads to the ironic conclusion

> that the very people used by criminologists to arrive at the image of the brutalized, unhappy prison guard—white, relatively uneducated officers— may be the most satisfied segment of the custodial force, while "newcomers" to the correctional arena such as black and college educated guards may be the least satisfied.[37]

Job enrichment calls for expanded definitions of the guard's job, changing it from a custodial to a human service occupation. This highlights the healthy interdependence of officer and inmate and points to constructive alternatives to the collusive relationships reviewed in Chapter Seven. Just as prisoners want to live in prison in ways that meet their basic needs and hold out the prospect of meaningful activity, guards want to work in prison in ways that satisfy their basic needs and give them a meaningful role to play. "Like inmates," Lombardo tells us,

> officers prefer job assignments that "match" their needs for special kinds of social environments. There is also a discernible tendency for officers who have special motivational concerns to prefer specific job locations. Block jobs, for example, are [more] likely to be associated with activity or the desire to help inmates than with any other need.[38]

Though the link between officer needs and work assignment preferences has not been studied in any detail, this would seem to be a fruitful direction for future research.

We know more about the relationship of officer needs and the guard role, independent of any particular work assignment. The main needs expressed by officers are for activity, autonomy, and a chance to contribute "to the well-being of the inmates or to the overall running of the institution."[39] Thus, officers usually want time to pass in fast and familiar ways, with opportunities to be useful. More often than not, they satisfy these needs by relinquishing a custodial pose and becoming "human service workers dealing with the inmates' personal and institutional adjustment, assisting inmates to cope with the pains of imprisonment."[40] Their search is not just for a comfortable and safe routine—the proverbial rut one assumes guards fall into—but for a constructive work niche. The business of officers who are oriented toward human service is corrections, not custody. They traffic not in debased authority but in human concern, and their helping activities range "from offering advice about routine difficulties in negotiating the prison bureaucracy to nursing the private traumas prison can breed."[41]

THE CORRECTIONAL OFFICER AT WORK

Human service activities undertaken by concerned guards on behalf of prisoners include (1) providing goods and services, (2) acting as referral agents or advocates, and (3) helping with institutional adjustment problems. An officer may specialize in any one of these activities or engage in each of them as the situation requires.[42]

Goods and Services

When prison guards provide such mundane goods and services as food, clothing, shelter, and medication, they are making certain that the prisoners' basic needs are met. Of course, even the most disgruntled hacks are required to provide necessities as a matter of course. However, by providing these goods and services in a regular and responsive manner, officers satisfy a legitimate concern of many prisoners for stability or predictability in their dealings with the prison system.[43] "Above all else," cautioned a seasoned officer, "be consistent. . . . [I]nmates live very structured lives" and do not adjust well to sudden change."[44]

The regular and responsive delivery of goods and services in turn prevents the accumulation of tension among inmates as a consequence of arbitrary and even degrading deprivations. It is nothing less than a gratuitous insult to be forced to go without such basic supplies as soap or toilet paper or to have simple requests for help ignored. Some officers are quick to prevent or redress such problems. They have empathy for the person in the cell and appreciate the significance of the problem-solving role they can play.

■ I often put myself in the inmate's position. If I was locked up and the door was locked up and my only contact with authorities would be the officer walking by, it would be frustrating if I couldn't get him to listen to the problems I have. There is nothing worse than being in need of something and not being able to supply it yourself and having the man who can supply it ignore you: This almost makes me explode inside.[45] ■

Officers who conscientiously deliver basic goods and services are taking care of the routine business of the institution. The result is a minimally habitable environment. They provide other essential services through the enforcement of rules. In the custodial image of prison guards, rule enforcement almost by definition is an exercise in oppression. Yet a prison without rules, or with rules that are enforced in unpredictable ways, is a chaotic, arbitrary, and dangerous place to live.

Even the most service-oriented officer cannot entirely avoid the ambiguity that surrounds prison rules (see Chapter Seven). However, these officers minimize such difficulties by enforcing rules with an eye to improving the quality of life in prison. They seek, often at the request of inmates, to maintain a comparatively clean, quiet, and orderly prison environment, approximating normal domestic life in the cell blocks and normal civil life in the shops and recreation areas.[46] These officers also enforce rules in an effort to promote a sense of basic fairness or justice, to communicate that conflicts are resolved and resources distributed in an equitable manner.[47] Perhaps the most valuable human service function of rule enforcement is security. A New York State prison officer who saw security as a human service rather than a custodial commodity put the matter this way:

■ Security doesn't mean keep them from going over the wall. It means you try to make the guy feel secure, that he's not going to get killed or hurt. You make it so an inmate can sit next to another inmate in the mess hall or auditorium and feel comfortable. So he doesn't have to worry about something happening.[48] ■

Significantly, officers who define their role as a matter of making prisoners "feel secure" hold views of inmates that parallel those of officers who define their role as more explicitly oriented toward human service—who want more directly to help prisoners adjust.[49] By contrast, officers who see correctional work in extrinsic ways, as a means to a paycheck rather than a job with value in itself, hold considerably more negative views of inmates.[50] From the ranks of the extrinsically motivated officers may be recruited the disgruntled hacks discussed in Chapter Seven.

Various goods and services are essential to a civilized prison existence. Officers who provide them, whether they see their work primarily as a matter of security or service, show that they care—for themselves, as self-respecting professionals, and for the inmates who depend on them to maintain a decent standard of life behind bars. In the words of a prison officer,

■ If an inmate hasn't had a change of underwear in two weeks, you should care enough to get him a change of underwear. If he hasn't had a shower in a week, you should care enough to get him a shower. You shouldn't have to wait for someone to tell you to do that or have some regulation tell you.[51] ■

Service provision can, and perhaps should, assume a taken-for-granted connotation to the officer. As one officer observed, a bit crudely,

■ People make this job harder than it is. If an inmate has something coming—his mail, a blanket, whatever—you give it to him. If he don't, you tell him. And most importantly, if an inmate ain't going over the fence or thumping somebody, then you just leave him the fuck alone.[52] ■

Officers maintain that what inmates have coming to them is a blend of regulations tempered by common sense and human decency.[53] No inmate has a right to privacy in prison, for example, either in law or prison policy. Nevertheless, the notion that a prisoner who behaves well should be treated well—which means, in many instances, granted a degree of privacy—is a central tenet of prison wisdom. Officers who commit themselves to the timely delivery of basic goods and services, including such subjective goods as privacy, work on a daily basis to make prisons more responsive living environments. They warrant and often receive the respect and support of the prisoners under their care.

Referrals and Advocacy

Many prison guards act as referral agents and advocates for prisoners. Prisons are cumbersome bureaucracies, and inmates are largely powerless to negotiate directly with the institution on their own behalf. Many inmates therefore turn to the guard for help when the formal bureaucracy fails them. Short of filing legal suits over the daily minutiae of prison life—though a few prisoners do this; suits have been filed over the type of peanut butter available in the prison mess hall—there is nothing else they can do at this juncture. In this context, "the officer [can] aid the inmate in a variety of ways, such as by setting up appointments with counsellors or by calling the correspondence office or commissary to check on the status of an inmate account."[54] Yet assistance of this sort is technically beyond the scope of the officer's formal duties. The officer who undertakes these helping activities may be met with resistance and even abuse from guards and other prison personnel who hew more closely to the custodial line.

Consider the following case. The officer wants to help one man get his prescribed medication, another his proper assignment. Each service is ostensibly simple to perform. Yet to get them done, the officer must battle not only an unresponsive bureaucracy but also fellow guards as well:

■ There's times when a guy's been out of pills, I don't have to do it, I could say piss on you, wait till fill-up day and get them yourself or go over and see the doctor and get them. [But instead] I'll make the trip over and I'll go get them. One or two pills, whatever, to cover the guy for the day. Because I've done it myself, I'm counting out pills or something and I'll drop them on the floor. I could shove it back in the bottle, but I destroy it, and I have to enter it in the book destroyed. There's times when the pharmacy will send over pills that says 28 in a bottle, there's 27, right off the bat I'm one short. So in the course of the week I have to go over and get that extra pill so that we're not short. Especially so that the night shift has got a pill to give the guy. Mainly this man with the sleeping problem and our epileptics. It's mandatory that they have the medication. . . . You go over there to get some pills, they say, "what the fuck you doing over here." "I'm over to check this out." "That's what you got a hospital runner for." "Fuck it, I want to take care of it." . . . Four days ago, an epileptic, way down on the end, had fits, he hadn't been moved yet. So he come up, and he's givin' me static. This is the guy I was telling you, he's a Jew and he called me a Nazi and all this kind of shit. So I said "all right, I'll check into it." So I went over to the hospital, I was over there 2 hours, running this fucking thing down. Come to find out, the only thing that was holding it up was his job classification. You can't put a man on invalid company unless he's a grade four, no job. He can't work, he's medically unfit to work. That was all that was wrong, because they had him marked as a grade one. Grade one, you're going to work. And that was all that was holding it up, and they had to have a written order on it. That the man was changed from one to four; it took me 2 hours to get it. And I got static over that. So the guy will be moving today, everything's kosher.[55] ■

The point here is not the specific goods or services the officer secures. Other examples could have been examined focusing, for example, on interpersonal problems and the need to mobilize the professional treatment staff.[56] What is important in these situations is that the officer acts as an intermediary and advocate—and is sometimes an extraordinarily dedicated and persistent one at that—between the prisoner and some segment of the prison bureaucracy.

Help of this kind is mundane but important. By observing that some guards go out of their way to ensure that legitimate needs are met, inmates find that they are not alone and powerless. They have allies among the correctional officers who support them and give them a degree of control over their prison lives. "A consequence of putting men [and women] in cells and controlling their movements," notes Conover, "is that they can do almost nothing for themselves. For their various needs they are dependent on one person, their gallery officer."[57] The officer, by necessity, finds him or herself in a service role. That role may often be a thankless one ("When grown men are infantilized, most don't take to it nicely"[58]), but the work is clearly important and is, moreover, essential to the smooth running of the institution.

Officers and Inmate Adjustment

Officers commonly attempt to play a direct role in solving inmate problems. And there are, of course, many problems experienced by inmates. It is fair to say that virtually all prisoners, in varying degrees, feel (1) powerless and, therefore, frustrated and resentful; (2) vulnerable and, therefore, anxious and afraid; and (3) alone and, therefore, lonely and depressed. For most inmates, these are difficult but manageable problems. For some, these concerns spark personal crises.[59] Crises become a way of life for a few, whom we think of as psychiatric casualties.[60] For many prisoners, however, the officer is able to recognize problems and crises as they unfold and to play a role in their management.

Consider a scenario encountered by officers. A resentful inmate refuses to leave his cell and threatens harm to anyone who tries to make him. His potential for violence invites attention from the smug hack, who deals out such repressive measures as restraint and segregation, perhaps including the use of physical force. These measures will certainly get the man out of the cell, though the prisoner as well as a few officers may be hurt. Moreover, there are likely to be future problems with this prisoner because custodial measures only accentuate the feelings of powerlessness and vulnerability that underlie his pugnacious stance. The prisoner may also become defensive because he feels alone in the impersonal world of the prison—a shrinking world, as he sees it, of him against the hacks. Custodial measures will only aggravate this problem as well.[61]

In contrast, the officer who is oriented toward human service sees this same volatile situation as one that calls for interpersonal skills and collaborative action. He opts for problem solving rather than problem suppression. His aim is to build trust and to use this as a means to explore nonviolent solutions to the problem:

■ The sergeant called me in and said "go upstairs and move a man downstairs." So right away I assumed that the man was causing some problems because we had all these other officers with us. So we approached the cell, we had about 5 or 6 officers plus the sergeant. The inmate was a young Puerto Rican about 6¢2≤, very, very angry, obviously scared to death. The sergeant says "come on, we'll take you downstairs." He said, "no man, I'm not going to come out, because as soon as I come out you're going to really kick my ass and I don't want anything to do with that." He says "I know I'm going to get hurt but I'm going to take some of you guys with me." . . . I asked if I could speak to him. The sergeant says "yeah, go ahead." So I walked in and said "hey, look, nobody wants to hurt you. I think I understand what your problem is." He says, "what's that?" I said "you're putting yourself under a lot of peer pressure up here. Here you've been spouting off to all the other inmates in the gallery how tough you are. Now you want to prove something. You know and I know that we can take you out of here if we have to, but we don't want to hurt you. And why don't you just come along with me and I'll take you downstairs and nothing's going to happen to you." So after a few moments of saying I was lying to him and everything I guess he really decided what the heck else did he have to lose? He says "you mean to tell me that you are going to take me out of here and nobody else is going to lay a hand on me?" I said "yeah, you got my word. You'll go down to my area and I'll keep you down there and see how you behave yourself." So he agrees to do so. When we walked out of the cell naturally he's waiting for somebody to jump on him and romp around on him a little bit, but to his surprise nobody laid a hand on him.[62] ■

Encounters such as this one produce a host of benefits. They go a long way to undo damage done by less constructive involvements with authority figures:

■ He said "I was scared to death. After all, you come to prison, you hear all kinds of stories."

He said, "I've had a couple of occasions where [guards have] kicked me around a little bit, I thought the same thing was going to happen to me." In fact he made a statement that surprised me the following day. He said, "you know what, I'm afraid of you." I said "why are you afraid of me?" He said "you're too cool." I said "well, did I lie to you?" He said "no, I thought about that." He says "but you're either tough as hell or you got to be crazy." I said "why?" He said "well, you walked in the cell, obviously I was mad enough to hurt somebody." I said "well, I figured if you're going to hurt somebody you're not going to hurt me too bad because I had enough help there to back me up." But I said "I couldn't see you getting hurt from being stupid, and hurting somebody else." So he thought that was pretty good reasoning and we daily built a pretty good relationship.

Did he mention other things that had got him upset and made him act the way he was acting?

Well, he said he was lied to.

By whom?

By other officers. I know another thing that upset him greatly too. I guess when he came in they took some personal property away from him he felt they shouldn't have taken. So I asked him what it was and I found that an officer made a mistake on two items and I got them back for him. So that sort of reassured him that everybody wasn't trying to be unjust to him.[63] ■

Encounters of this nature can also promote long-term personal relation-ships that in turn permit the officer to become a continuing source of advice and support for his formerly rebellious ward:

■ His anger turned into making me more or less a father-image in his behalf. So on a daily basis I talked to this guy, any time he had a problem he'd come to me. . . . I talked to him several times in the yard. He said "what about this peer pressure thing, explain that to me." So I tried to sit down and tell him the term and just what it meant to him and everybody else and he said "gee, that's very interesting, I never looked at it that way." So then we got talking, and we'd sit down and talk about marriage and the problems he'd had with his children and that type of thing. We got along pretty good.[64] ■

Correctional officers have much to offer inmates with all sorts of problems, including those pursued by predatory peers. Officers can, for instance, make it clear that they are "paying special attention" to known aggressors and thereby deter at least some of them.[65] They can also make it clear that they are available to assist potential victims. A prisoner at Attica who personally benefited from this sort of special assistance and surveillance described his experience in the following words:

■ As I came through the Times Square, this officer must have realized that I was terribly green and terribly frightened, because he pulled me aside and talked to me. He said, "You look frightened, and if there's anything that I can do to help, or if you want to talk to me, or you have any problem, tell the officer down there to let you come up. If there's something I can help you with." So apparently, from what I understood later, he called the block and talked to the night officer. So therefore the officers were looking out for me. So they kept an eye on me for four or five days. . . . And then later the hall captain talked with me, because he was always a nice guy. And he seen that I was having a problem. He always managed to make sure that I was alone in my cell, because there they could put two guys in one cell. And unless they got into a desperate situation that they were really filled up, he always left me by myself.[66] ■

Helping fearful inmates is a risky business. Frightened inmates are billed as cowards, and an officer's assistance may inadvertently reinforce this stigmatizing image. Yet the alternative, which is to let them fight and "prove" themselves, is inappropriate and even irresponsible in some cases. On occasion the guard may have no choice but to step in to avert a catastrophe:

■ He was a little guy who was afraid of everything and everybody and then all of a sudden in a day's time he started standing up, which he knew was foolish, but he started standing up to some of the roughest guys in the division. And it just wasn't him. And I was afraid that he was going to get hurt because these guys don't take that kind of stuff. It was a complete reversal.

So it just stood out to you—there's a meek guy acting like a tiger.

And plus it was all in a day's time. One day he was a meek guy and the next day he was on the move and he had just changed like that. . . . The kid was actually serious. He wasn't putting it on. It was actually a serious thing. He actually, if it came right down to it, would have taken these guys on. Regardless of . . . the consequences. This is what I feel anyway, and I knew he would get hurt. . . . So, you know, I had to step in and stop this.[67] ■

Where the officer can do nothing to help, the best advice may be that the inmate seek protective custody. This advice may be gratefully accepted by a frightened and confused prisoner. In the words of one such man,

■ So that was the thing, when the officer came down here one night, I told him what was happening, because I was worried. They wouldn't leave me alone, and they wanted to borrow this and that. And I would give it to them, because I was scared and I didn't want anything to happen. So then this officer came down one night, and he talked to me, and he said, "You know, you should go into protection. I know what's happening and I know that these guys have things that they do to the other inmates, it's happened. And you'll find yourself in real trouble."[68] ■

Loneliness may be the most pervasive and insidious form of prison stress.[69] This problem is particularly acute for those who are abandoned by loved ones or who suffer a death in the family. In cases like this, officers may have to shepherd inmates through periods of enormous stress. Officers who work in cell blocks or in small work areas or shops are the most likely to observe and respond to these crises.[70] The following account given by an industrial shop officer is a case in point:

■ When his grandmother died, he wasn't able to go to the funeral. Now I knew that he couldn't go and he was quite sure that he couldn't, yet he wanted someone to check. So I got ahold of his counselor and we discussed it and I kept the inmate in the office when I did this, so that he would at least know that someone was trying to do something. Then when it was over and he discovered that he couldn't go, the man goes and broke down into tears. And he sat right there and he was crying. And of course the other inmates were going by the office and some of them, you know, had the tendency to snicker a little bit. And just in general conversation with the inmates, I made it plain to them that in my eyes it required some degree of a man to care that much about his family. And I made sure that this particular inmate was there when I said it to kind of reassure him that at least someone in authority didn't consider that crying and concern over a member of the family was childish, was babyish. It was the type of action that one would expect from a sensitive man . . .

I had to keep him busy. I had to keep his mind occupied. But you can't drive a person like that. You have . . . to keep him busy enough to keep his problems off of his mind and at the same time try to communicate to him that . . . you haven't just disregarded him, that you care and you are interested in his problems and what is going on with his family, even though in most cases there is absolutely nothing that I can do about it. All I can do is give him some degree of understanding and try to help him if necessary, try to almost shield him. . . . To give him every hour that you can give him to where he can try to readjust himself with a minimum of pressure.[71] ■

Loneliness in prison is not only a matter of missing family or mourning the death of loved ones. Nor is caring about prisoners restricted to situations of personal crisis. Loneliness also reflects the absence of caring relationships within the prison community. Prisoners feel abandoned, forgotten, consigned to serve "dead time." Yet many officers develop "peculiarly intimate" relationships with at least some prisoners, and in doing so they help them to cope with their loneliness.[72] They have the credentials needed to help prisoners with the many painful personal problems that emerge during their confinement:

■ When I first come to the division I had noticed that he was friendly toward the dudes that was on the floor, the tier boys. And he talked to them with respect, like, you know, "how was your day today, did you do anything interesting?" It was different for a guard to ask inmates these questions. So when I got on the floor I started rapping to him about my main interest, which was cars, and he just happens to be another car freak, and we hit it off really good. And since then he's been a personal friend and not a guard to me. . . . I talk to him about every problem. I go to him before I'll come to a chaplain or to a sergeant or something.

And he's usually pretty helpful?

Very helpful. He's always got a suggestion. I mean it's not like "do this and this and this." He'll give me a suggestion and tell me the alternative, give me another suggestion and tell me another alternative . . .

Do you ever talk to this guy about very personal things, like your wife and your child, or what you think of the future, that type of stuff?

Yeah, almost every night. We have a little chat session every night after lock-in. He stops by my cell. "Hi, how you doing." And we start from there, you know. "Did you get a letter from your wife today?" Because he passes out the mail, he just asks as a joke type thing, you know. And I say "yeah, I got one." "What'd she have to say?" And I tell him this and that, and I won't hold nothing back. If she writes in there that she's having problems with the landlord or something like this, I'll tell it to him, he'll come up with either a suggestion or relate a story that happened to him and his wife, that would possibly help me out of my situation.

So this fellow really treats you as an equal?

Right, he treats me as an individual, man, not as a group inmate. . . . [I]t helps people, I don't know how, but when somebody's concerned about you, you've got the natural instinct to give them something back, whether it's affection or concern. You know, you've got to give them something back. And when you've got a contact like this, when you're concerned about somebody and he's concerned about you back, you've got a relationship going there that brings you above your environment. Brings you to be what you want to be. If you want to be back out in the world, you can put yourself to the point to remember when you were there. And how good it's going to be when you get back out there, not how long it's going to be. . . .[73] ■

The depth of relationships developed between some officers and inmates is a vivid reminder that officers can expand their roles to include the functions of "lay counselors."[74] Their helping efforts confirm the observation that the "successful lay counselor is one who can both provide the individual . . . with the experience of being understood and, at the same time, serve as a model for him to imitate."[75] The vast majority of these officers are untrained for their avocation as lay counselors. Many "play it by ear," fall back on "common sense," and sometimes do no more than "let a guy blow off steam." The quality of the advice they give varies widely. In general, among untrained helpers, "there is a tendency to give the action-oriented solution-type `Ann Landers' response to almost any situation."[76] This is probably true for many untrained correctional officers, who have been dubbed by Toch, with tongue in cheek, as "Meek-but-Sturdy Proletarian Healers of the Disaffected."[77] Still, though the exploration of self at the heart of the counseling process may be shortchanged by many correctional officers, they make an effort to be responsive to the needs of the prisoners. These officers are not "misguided helpers" concerned mostly, even if unconsciously, with helping themselves.[78] They *do* listen. Inmates are given a chance to ventilate their concerns and to explore avenues of adjustment. By their example, these officers serve as both models of mature behavior and agents of personal change.

The skills of the lay counselor are useful in addressing a wide range of problems, including those of a delicate personal nature. These skills may even be applicable with prisoners who are (or are becoming) mentally ill. Mentally disturbed prisoners have been called the number one health problem behind bars and identified as a group that recidivates at an unusually high rate.[79] They are, moreover, a growing problem in corrections, and one that is obvious to line officers:

■ You didn't have to work the galleries long to realize that a large proportion of inmates were mentally ill. The symptoms ranged from the fairly mild— talking to oneself, neglecting to bathe—to the severe: men who didn't know where they were, men who set fire to their own cells, men so depressed they slashed their wrists or tried to hang themselves.[80] ■

It was Conover's contention that "working a gallery was like sharing a crowded urban street with a higher-than-usual number of disturbed street people."[81]

Though the problem is evident, there is no indication that mental health staffs have grown apace or that treatment practices are adequate. In New York State, where Conover worked, it is estimated that 5 percent of inmates (or 3,500 of the state's 70,000 inmates) were profoundly mentally ill and "would be in a psychiatric hospital if they weren't in prison."[82] The New York State prison system had only 1,000 beds available for such cases. Another 10 percent of the New York State prison population—7,000 inmates—"were under the supervision of a psychiatrist" and typically on some form of medication.[83] Prisoners who had mental breakdowns in the cell blocks were sent to Psychiatric Satellite Units, known as PSUs. Their prognosis was grim. "The PSU was a holding tank," states Conover, "not a place where people improved."[84] It was Conover's bleak contention that none of the mentally ill offenders got any better during their time behind bars. There were simply not enough treatment resources. "It took weeks for an inmate in the general population to get an appointment with a therapist, and the wait between appointments, once a relationship had been established, also seemed to be weeks."[85] For these reasons, states Conover, "you just learned to live with the bugs" until one "went off the deep end. . . " Eventually, the prisoner would be medicated and return to the cell blocks, and the process would start all over again.[86]

It is doubtful that more than a handful of prisons will ever have sufficient professional mental health personnel to treat mentally ill prisoners. Prison salaries simply are not competitive with the free-world employment opportunities available to psychiatrists. As a result, psychiatrists are usually available in prisons only on a part-time basis; and, during their limited time, they find themselves saddled with mundane bureaucratic functions that cannot be delegated to others. Only psychiatrists can certify the mental health status of prisoners who need formal psychiatric treatment (or confinement in a hospital for the criminally insane) or who are seeking a furlough or parole. Such functions are important, to be sure, but psychiatrists who do little more than that in effect remain tourists, strangers to the life and culture of the prison. Their potential value in the treatment process is never realized.

Another problem, also related to the low salaries offered in prison, is that psychiatric staffs tend to consist of foreign professionals. Many of these psychiatrists accept prison jobs because they cannot command the free-world salaries of their American counterparts. They often find American prisons to be especially alien work environments. This problem is compounded when they work in prison on a part-time basis, a common practice. The following vignette makes these points with wry humor, though the problem in real life is anything but funny:

> [A]n Indian psychiatrist, who was obviously more familiar with the street argot of Calcutta than that of New York City, asked an inmate to explain the circumstances of his crime. "Me and these cats were sitting in a bar minding our own business," the inmate began.
>
> "We don't talk about cats here, we talk about people," the psychiatrist interrupted.[87]

As a practical matter, we cannot expect that professional psychiatrists will solve the problems of mentally ill prisoners; nor can we rely on counselors, even those formally trained in psychiatric social work. These professionals, though competent to help prisoners—including mentally ill prisoners—with a wide range of adjustment problems, also are in short supply.[88] Disturbed prisoners will have to be managed in ways that capitalize on the lay counseling services of prison officers, which are in more plentiful supply than professional psychiatric services. Interestingly, psychiatry can be understood and practiced in ways that make this proposal quite feasible.

Szasz, for instance, defines psychiatry as

> the study of personal conduct—of clarifying and "explaining" the kinds of games that people play with each other; how they learned these

games; why they like to play them; and so forth. . . . This implies candid recognition that we "treat" . . . not because they are "sick" but rather because: (1) They desire this type of assistance; (2) They have problems in living for which they seek mastery through understanding of the kinds of games which they, and those around them, have been in the habit of playing; and (3) We want and are able to participate in their "education" because this is our professional role.[89]

Szasz's notion of psychiatry as teaching better adjustment games provides a bridge between the counseling activities of correctional officers and more elaborate forms of mental health treatment such as individual or group psychotherapy. Correctional officers, Lombardo states, "learn to interpret and manipulate the rules of 'institutional games'" and therefore can

> participate in the "education of inmates" in the playing of such games. This education should help inmates to cope with the problems of living in confinement in a less destructive, if not more constructive, manner. This task should be part of every correctional worker's professional role.[90]

Lombardo is seconded in this view by Thomas, who reminds us that

> lay people can be as effective as and oftentimes more effective than the professional helper. In our correctional facilities throughout America today, we have a vast reservoir, a natural resource of line staff members who could be trained to complement the efforts of the professional mental health staff.[91]

Helping Networks

Individual prison guards deliver human services to inmates with a wide range of problems. Officers appear to be particularly effective when they collaborate with fellow officers and treatment personnel such as counselors, psychologists, and psychiatrists.[92] This conforms to Bandura's general observation that

> the most beneficial treatments are generally carried out under professional guidance by persons who have intensive contact with the clients and can therefore serve as powerful mediators of change. They are the ones who exercise substantial influence over the very conditions that govern the behavior to be modified. Unless they too alter their practices, any changes, whether produced by professionals or otherwise, may not endure for long.[93]

Collaboration of this sort occurs in prisons, but it is typically informal or *sub rosa*. The assumption, particularly among the correctional officers, is that it does not pay to flout custodial norms.[94]

Members of informal staff groups can describe the benefits of teamwork. A treatment staff member, a counselor referred to as "Mr. G.," observes:

■ I have quite a lot of resources to depend on. One of the reasons is they [officers] know that they can come back to me for . . . help when they have a problem. One of the things I find is that we become a team. I even get called about other counselors' people that won't . . . about the people that won't cooperate up there. And I am saying this to you very honestly and I am not saying it boastfully, just gratefully; my concern is for the men that are here. I am employed because I am to help with correction. And these people [officers] know that by the same token that if they have problems, they can call me and, even if it is not my case, I will go and give them information or try to help the situation.[95] ■

A correctional officer assigned to a shop corroborates Mr. G.'s account. He tells us that

■ Mr. G. and I, we have a working relationship and understanding. It is not an official understanding, but when he does have a man that is assigned to him with a problem—that might have a hard time adjusting or need a little supervision in some areas, such as adjusting to the institution, or perhaps because he is in this particular setting and is away from home and is lonely, or maybe is subject to pressure from his peers within the institution—he sends him to my shop. . . . And up here I take and give the inmates their choice of what they would like to do and I work with them in whatever they choose to do. And in working with him [the man with the problems], I try to keep an eye on his personal [relationships] with each one as I can. . . . And I also tell them that any problems that they have and I can help them with or give advice on, I will help them. And if I don't know the answer, I will find out the answer for them or refer them to the person who has the answer. And it has worked out very well.[96] ■

The payoffs of a team approach can snowball, as friends of team members are inspired to offer their special talents to help with problem-prone inmates. An interview with one such officer (who worked in the cell blocks) was summarized as follows:

■ Mr. G. on occasion asks him to watch some men or to support them and he will do this. And he gave us an example of a guy Mr. G. told him had a problem and had to get into a good program. And this officer went out of his way to recommend to the prisoner that he try to go into the auto maintenance shop. (Apparently the officer had noted that the prisoner had hot rod magazines in his cell.) The officer also knew the auto maintenance man, knew that the shop was small, wouldn't have pressure, and would be a good setting for the prisoner to work in. So the officer personally went to bat for the man. Now apparently the auto maintenance foreman goes out of his way to respond to recommendations from this officer because they are friends and also because this officer gets his car repaired in that shop, so the shop foreman believes that he would only get serious recommendations from him. As it turned out, the prisoner did beautifully in that shop and seemed to be adjusting very well.[97] ■

These teams, whether formally constituted or informally developed over time, expand the pool of services available to prisoners with problems. The immediate result is "more rapid referral, more reliable implementation of treatment plans, more comprehensive follow-up, and the prospect of timely crisis intervention."[98] The long-term result, it is reasonable to suppose, is a perception among inmates of a correctional staff that is making a concerted effort to run a responsive penal institution on their behalf.

HUMAN SERVICE IN PERSPECTIVE

Many officers, often a sizable minority and sometimes even a majority, go out of their way to promote a humane living environment in the prison.[99] They do this by providing a range of human services that reduce stress and encourage mature adjustment among inmates. They play covert correctional roles in an institution that is a monument to custodial repression.

It is worthwhile to ask why officers do this. Helping is not a requirement of the job. Officers get little or no official recognition or support for their helping efforts. In fact, these officers often act in violation of official regulations that ban fraternization with inmates. (Even when official regulations seem to encourage human services, as in some explicitly reform-oriented prisons, officers may be "sanctioned by colleagues and midmanagement security personnel for emphasizing human service.")[100] Many officers who stress human service also feel they are violating an unofficial subcultural code that calls for a tough-minded custodial pose rather than a concerned effort to solve inmate problems (see Chapter Seven). Moreover, treatment staff sometimes see correctional officers as encroaching on their professional turf and, thus, either ignore or discourage the officers' human service activities.[101] Needless to say, some prisoners (the convicts) routinely reject the ministrations of the "screws" no matter how far they depart from guard stereotypes (see Chapter Five). And most prisoners—maybe all prisoners—have led lives so sad and moving that officers may wish that they had remained distant and aloof. Conover's encounter with an inmate he called Delacruz, whose tattoo told a heart-breaking story, is a touching case in point:

■ Delacruz had translated into Spanish from an English translation of Anne Frank's original Dutch. But the gist was still there. It was unmistakable.

When everybody starts hovering over me, I get cross, then sad, and finally end up turning my heart inside out, the bad part on the outside and the good part on the inside, and keep trying to find a way to become what I'd like to become what I'd like to be and what I could be if . . . if only there were no other people in the world.

It was easier to stay incurious as an officer. Under the inmates' surface bluster, their cruelty and selfishness, was almost always something ineffably sad."[102] ■

It should come as no surprise, then, that relatively few officers fly their correctional colors openly. In public encounters, they are custodians; in private, they are correctional officers.[103]

Why, then, do some officers persist in activities that take time and effort, are neither recognized nor rewarded by others, and must be hidden or played down for fear of trouble with administrators, peers, treatment staff, or recalcitrant inmates and which burdens them with a sad wisdom about the lives of the people under their authority? The reason, as alluded to in the beginning of this chapter, is simply this: human service activities make the officer's job richer, more rewarding, and ultimately less stressful.

Correctional officers, it must be remembered, are typically given no role in the formulation of administrative policy. Nor are they asked to do much of consequence in terms of inmate program services. Even their interpersonal relationships with prisoners are supposed to be superficial, as if the officers themselves were merely props for the authority invested in their roles. The result is that many guards feel powerless, vulnerable, and alone. They show the classic symptoms of alienation. In response, some officers reduce their involvements with inmates while others assume a more aggressive custodial pose (see Chapter Seven).

Many officers, however, try to solve the problem of alienation by expanding their roles and making them more substantial and rewarding. These officers discover that in the process of helping inmates and thereby giving them more autonomy, security, and emotional support, they gain the same benefits: more control over their environment; more security in their daily interactions with prisoners; and a sense of community, however inchoate or ill-defined, with at least some of the inmates under their care. (Conover, for example, had relationships with Delacruz and some other inmates, relationships which he found both sobering and rewarding.) In solving inmate adjustment problems, in other words, staff solve their own problems as well.

When inmate problems are averted or resolved, everyone can get on with the business of living and working in prison. Problems that are allowed to linger (in prison, *fester* might be a better word) eventually come home to roost. Officers who neglect their human service obligations are in for trouble. If they are lax in providing the goods and services necessary for an ordered and secure prison life, or if they let personal problems accumulate among the inmates in their care, they are likely to be confronted with a resentful or even explosive population. And if they don't pay for their mistakes, their colleagues will.

Human service officers pride themselves on being responsive to the inmates in their charge. It is critical to note, however, that what constitutes responsive service is not a fixed or set matter. In other words, the correctional officer's role, like the prison in which it is embedded, is not a static entity. Helping activities featuring referral or even informal counseling may be a more or less prominent feature of the officer's role in any given prison system, in part depending on the options open to inmates and the formal roles assigned to staff. Over the last decade or so, inmates in some prison systems have been afforded ready access to telephones and to extended visits. As a result, these inmates are more autonomous; they can address many personal problems on their own by calling home or taking the matter up at a visit. Again, over the last decade or so, in some prison systems, counselors' offices have been moved to the cell blocks, making them more readily available to inmates. The need for officers to serve as referral agents in such systems is reduced.

Auburn Prison provides a telling case in point. In the mid–1970s, when Lombardo first studied the officers at Auburn, inmates had limited access to telephones and to visits, and counselors were housed away from the cell blocks, in distant administrative quarters. Line officers were readily accessible to inmates and, as a result, were often called upon to play an essential intermediary role between inmates with problems and counselors who could authorize special calls or even arrange emergency visits. Some officers expanded their jobs to include the role of informal counselor. By the mid-1980s, when Lombardo conducted a follow-up study of Auburn officers, the situation of the inmates had changed substantially. They had easy access to telephones and to visits; counselors, now housed in the cell blocks, were on-call for the prisoners. As a result, the officers were less often asked to play a referral role. Their informal counseling role proved less in demand as well. To be sure, officers still handled personal problems—60 percent of Lombardo's sample of officers in the follow-up study said they dealt with personal problems on a regular basis, usually encouraging inmates to take up the matter with a counselor or chaplain—but this function was less salient than it had been a decade earlier. And since the helping function was now seen as part of the formal job description of Auburn officers (even, to a degree, helping networks have been formalized at Auburn), the Auburn officers' helping efforts were seen by inmates as less spontaneous and, in some instances, less genuine.[104] Given these factors, the identity of officers was less likely to be tied to helping services.

Other forces operated to change the dynamic of the officer's role at Auburn. Inmates at Auburn, like inmates elsewhere, have more legal rights and, hence, have a basis for demanding accountability from officers. In response, the officer's role at Auburn has become more fully articulated; formal policies and procedures, generated by administrators in consultation with officers, now cover a wide range of job categories and give a more formal structure to officer-inmate relations. Bound by comparatively clear rules and precise job descriptions, the officers at Auburn are a specialized cadre of correctional bureaucrats, ranging from "friskers" to "packers" to disciplinary hearing officers and special operations team officers rather than, as but a decade earlier, a conglomerate of undifferentiated line officers with widely varying interests, skills, and patterns of discretionary decision making.

Officers at Auburn and many other prisons are more professional than in days past. One example of prison officer professionalism is the creation of special operations teams, which are the bureaucratic successors of goon squads in better-run prisons (see Chapter Seven). These teams are comprised of trained officers who are deployed to use controlled force to move recalcitrant inmates, to restrain and disperse crowds, to free hostages, and to break up riots. Unlike in prisons where unofficial goon squads still exist, these professional teams are not authorized to mete out illicit punishments to troublemaking inmates. Another example of prison officer professionalism can be seen in execution teams. In today's prisons, executions are carried out by trained teams of officers whose explicit mission is to conduct executions that are, from the vantage point of officials if not the condemned prisoners, "proper, professional, and dignified."[105]

Security is an increasingly important area of officer accountability in Auburn. If Auburn prisoners in the mid-1980s were more autonomous than their counterparts of a decade earlier, they were also less secure. Auburn in the 1970s was a comparatively nonviolent institution. By the mid-1980s, the forces producing violence in many American prisons were having an impact at Auburn (see Chapter Five). In the words of an officer whose career spanned these changes at Auburn,

■ It's changed a lot. It's more violent. The drugs, the extortion. They steal and take from other guys. It will go on 'til the guy fights back or goes to protective custody. Ten years ago if you had a fight, they'd duke it out and then step back. Now with the peer pressure they'll fight and try to kill each other. Ten years ago a guy might go bughouse. Today he might get a knife. With the availability of drugs and other things they get used to it on the street and with the money around they turn to violence. Fights aren't just personal conflicts any more. They're conflicts over extortion, power conflicts, drugs and other things like that.[106] ■

Violence, now more common and more calculated, poses a considerable threat to officer and inmate alike. As a result, officers at Auburn have been called upon to provide more security-related services. Such services feature "frisks, drug testing and violence prevention" and are aimed primarily at securing physical rather than psychological survival.[107]

The Auburn officers report that fear is a salient theme, but competence at security-related tasks helps them keep fear in check. Significantly, these officers are less alienated than their counterparts of a decade ago. They know what to expect as they carry out their specialized tasks, and they know what is expected of them by inmates and administrators. They are less likely than a decade ago to feel caught in the middle, pressured by conflicting demands from above and below. Tense personal encounters with inmates are less frequent; formal recognition of their accomplishments by administrators is more common. Specialization of function has allowed for the development of specialized skills, in which the officers take great pride. A growing administrative bureaucracy, needed to manage a more differentiated officer force, has opened up avenues for advancement.[108]

One can see in Auburn the evolution of a framework for the correctional role that might unite officers with custodial and human service orientations. This role would focus on professional and accountable delivery of basic goods and services. Services would be construed broadly to include justice, which is operationalized at Auburn in a disciplinary system that features clearly defined procedures, with officers assigned as advisors to inmates during hearings; and security, operationalized at Auburn in a phalanx of officers arrayed in a range of specialized security-related positions, sharing a common concern for protecting inmates from physical harm. The experience at Auburn and elsewhere suggests that, with training, even so-called hacks can be equipped to provide basic security services without resorting to manipulation or violence.[109] Human service–oriented officers, in turn, can develop security-related specializations that allow them to retain a helping function as a corollary of their commitment to inmate safety. (Remember, security is not solely a matter of physical safety; people must feel secure, and this implies supportive or at least nonthreatening relationships with one's keepers.)[110] As at Auburn, referral responsibilities and helping networks could be formalized; officers could become more or less involved in these activities as dictated by job description and personal disposition. Informal problem-solving efforts by officers would remain just that: informal. Officer involvement in such activities would be entirely voluntary.

Reforms of the sort achieved at Auburn require an organizational culture that is committed to "change rather than stability."[111] In the face of a changing environment, Lombardo reminds us, institutions must adapt if they are to function effectively. The legal and political environments in which prisons operate have changed dramatically over the past few decades, posing substantial challenges to the adaptive capacities of prisons. To date, Auburn has responded well because it is a prison in which effective leadership committed to innovation has become part of its institutional culture,[112] and officers there have come to expect change as part of their jobs. Problem solving, a key feature of mature coping, has become a component of the prison's culture. At Auburn, changes emanating from without (for example, as a result of legal decisions) and from within (for example, as a result of inmate or officer demands and expectations) are taken as problems to be solved. As such, they are "perceived as part of the institution's internal environment rather than as threats."[113] The result is adaptive accommodation rather than maladaptive resistance. As we turn to the larger subject of prison reform, the notion of adaptive accommodation—on the part of the prison as well as its prisoners—is one that can fruitfully guide our efforts.

NOTES

1. Sennett (1981:17).

2. Toch (1975 & 1977); Sennett (1981).

3. Hampton (1984:238).

4. See Jurik (1985); Farkas (1999).

5. Earley (1992:269).

6. Conover (2000:219).

7. Conover (2000:91–92).

8. Conover (2000:91–92 & 87).

9. Owen (1985:158).

10. Kissell and Katsampes (1980); Owen (1985).

11. Farkas (1999:503); for studies on the different approaches to the officer role shown by females, see also Jurik (1986); Zimmer (1986).

12. When women first entered men's prisons in the 1970s, they were ostracized by their more custodial male peers. See

Crouch (1985); Jurik (1986); and Zimmer (1986). By today's standards, the ostracism faced by female officers in the 70s would be characterized as sexual harassment; much of this abusive behavior was directly sexual in nature or otherwise created a hostile working environment for women. The impression is that ostracism of female officers is less common these days. In the District of Columbia's Department of Corrections, however, the problem of sexual harassment was endemic at least through the mid-1990s. Reports Locy (1995:A1), "A jury in U.S. District Court yesterday found that the D.C. Department of Corrections engaged in a pattern of sexual harassment against female employees and created a hostile work environment for women." The problem of sexual harassment in D.C. prisons was by all accounts egregious, and "the verdict is believed to be the first time in the country that a governmental agency has been held responsible in a class-action lawsuit of creating and maintaining a sexually hostile work environment" (Locy, 1995:A1). Ideally, the problem of sexual harassment will recede as more women enter the field and the value of their contributions becomes apparent to their male colleagues.

13. Glaser (1969:84–85).

14. Glaser (1969:87).

15. Stojkovic (1984:13 & 19–20).

16. Lin (2000:102).

17. Lombardo (1981:53).

18. Guenther and Guenther (1980:172).

19. Hepburn (1984:584).

20. Hepburn and Knepper (1993:320).

21. Hepburn and Knepper (1993:331).

22. Conover (2000:90).

23. Gates (1991:76).

24. Lin (2000:101–2).

25. Herberts (1997:55).

26. Glaser (1969:92).

27. Glaser (1969:92–93; see also 84).

28. Glaser (1969:94).

29. Lasch (1984:203).

30. May (1981:37–38).

31. Toch and Grant (1982:199–200).

32. Toch and Grant (1982:202).

33. See Jurik (1985:534).

34. Toch and Grant (1982:202).

35. For the latest in this line of research, see Farkas (1999).

36. Cullen, Link, Wolfe, and Frank (1985).

37. Cullen, Link, Cullen, and Wolfe (1989:105).

38. Lombardo (1981:46).

39. Lombardo (1981:46); see also Lasky and Gordon (1986).

40. Lombardo (1981:55).

41. Johnson and Price (1981:352).

42. Lombardo (1988).

43. Lombardo (1981).

44. Herberts (1997:40–41).

45. Jacobs and Retsky (1981:68).

46. Lombardo (1981); Johnson and Price (1981).

47. This goal is summed up in the often-heard statement that officers should be "firm but fair" in their uses of authority. It is also reinforced by grievance mechanisms that permit inmates to have a role in the review of rule enforcement decisions (Rodgers, 1979; Hepburn & Laue, 1980) and in rule enforcement regulations that are clear in themselves and consistently administered (see DiIulio, 1994).

48. Lombardo (1988:293).

49. Jurik (1985).

50. Jurik (1985).

51. Earley (1992:269).

52. Earley (1992:107).

53. See Earley (1992); Lombardo (1981 & 1989); and Glaser (1969).

54. Lombardo (1988:290).

55. Toch (1981a:94–95).

56. See Toch (1981a).

57. Conover (2000:234).

58. Conover (2000:234).

59. Toch (1975); Liebling (1999).

60. Toch, (1982); Kupers (1999).

61. It is for reasons such as these that segregation units, the ultimate custodial milieus, are notoriously tense and explosive. Note that a supermax prison is, in effect, an entire prison given over the segregation. For a thoughtful discussion of the psychology of work in a segregation unit, see Conover's discussion of "working the box." Box is the name given to the segregation unit by officers at Sing Sing Prison in New York (Conover, 2000:127).

62. Toch (1981a:96).

63. Toch (1981a:97).

64. Toch (1981a:96).

65. Lockwood (1980:134).

66. Toch (1977:168).

67. Johnson (1981a:120).

68. Toch (1977:169).

69. Toch (1975); Johnson (1981b).

70. Lombardo (1981).

71. Johnson (1981a:119–20).

72. Webb and Morris (1980:159).

73. Toch (1981a:98–100).

74. Thomas (1975).

75. Thomas (1975:36).

76. Thomas (1975:39).

77. Toch (1981a:333).

78. See Abbey, Holland, and Wortman (1980).

79. Wiehn (1988); Toch (1982); Kupers (1999:87).

80. Conover (2000:138).

81. Conover (2000:138).

82. Conover (2000:138).

83. Conover (2000:138).

84. Conover (2000:142).

85. Conover (2000:142).

86. Conover (2000:138); see generally, Kupers (1999).

87. Sheehan (1978:52).

88. Showalter and Hunsinger (1983); Kupers (1999).

89. Szasz (1961:255).

90. Lombardo (1985:21).

91. Thomas (1975:43).

92. Johnson (1981a).

93. Quoted in Toch (1981b:329).

94. Johnson (1981a).

95. Johnson (1981a:117).

96. Johnson (1981a:117).

97. Johnson (1981a:118). This quotation was edited to make references to the various individuals easier to follow.

98. Johnson (1981a:121).

99. Toch and Grant (1982).

100. See Jurik and Musheno (1986:19).

101. Johnson (1981a: 108–113).

102. Conover (2000:293).

103. The problem, in part, is one of pluralistic ignorance, as noted in Chapter Seven. In some prisons, however, perceptions of guard behavior are more accurate, permitting correctional officers to be more open in their activities (Toch & Grant, 1982:202).

104. Lombardo (1989:86–87).

105. Johnson (1998).

106. Lombardo (1989:166).

107. Lombardo (1989:173 & 211).

108. See generally, Lombardo (1989).

109. In Texas prisons, for example, officers have moved from a largely custodial ethic to one of enforcement of rules in a due process framework in which disciplinary reports have come to replace coercion in daily social control (see Crouch & Marquart, 1989). The federal prison system made this transition some time ago and, indeed, serves as a model of the

bureaucratic management of disciplinary problems (see DiIulio, 1994).

110. Many of the officers interviewed by Lin appeared to share this view. One officer, a former Marine, stated that he was "responsible for the safety of the inmates, [and was] to look after their welfare, and to make sure none of them leave until they are supposed to." (Lin, 2000:101).

111. Lombardo (1989:214).

112. The cultivation of leadership committed to excellence is an important but little-studied feature of the adaptive capabilities of prison organizations. For a seminal work on this topic, directed to scholar and practitioner alike, see Wright (1994).

113. Lombardo (1989:215).

REFERENCES

Abbey, A. A., W. Holland, and C. B. Wortman. "The misguided helper: An analysis of people's responses to their loved ones' crises." In D. G. McGuigan (ed.). *Women's Lives: New Theory, Research and Policy.* Ann Arbor: University of Michigan Press, 1980:257–66.

Conover, T. *Newjack: Guarding Sing Sing.* New York: Random House, 2000.

Crouch, B. M. "Pandora's box: Women guards in men's prisons." *Journal of Criminal Justice* 13 (1985):535–48.

Crouch, B. M., and J. W. Marquart. *An Appeal to Justice.* Austin: University of Texas Press, 1989.

Cullen, F. T., B. G. Link, N. T. Wolfe, and J. Frank. "The social dimensions of correctional officer stress." *Justice Quarterly* 2 (4) 1985:505–533.

Cullen, F. T., B. G. Link, J. B. Cullen, and N. T. Wolfe. "How satisfying is prison work? A comparative occupational approach." *Journal of Offender Counseling, Services & Rehabilitation* 14 (2) 1989:89–108.

DiIulio, J. J. "5270.7 tells the tale." *Federal Prisons Journal* 3 (3) 1994:60–65.

Earley, P. *The Hot House: Life Inside Leavenworth.* New York: Bantam Books, 1992.

Farkas, M. A. "Correctional officer attitudes toward inmates and working with inmates in a 'Get Tough' era." *Journal of Criminal Justice* 27(6) 1999: 495–506.

Gates, M. "The excavation." Unpublished manuscript American University, 1991.

Glaser, D. *The Effectiveness of a Prison and Parole System.* Indianapolis, IN: Bobbs-Merrill, 1969.

Guenther, A. L., and M. Q. Guenther. " Screws vs. thugs." In B. M. Crouch (ed.). *The Keepers: Prison Guards and Contemporary Corrections.* Springfield, IL: Charles C. Thomas, 1980:162–82.

Hampton, J. "The moral education theory of punishment." *Philosophy and Public Affairs* 13 (3) 1984:208–238.

Hepburn, J. R. "The erosion of authority and the perceived legitimacy of inmate social protest: A study of prison guards." *Journal of Criminal Justice* 12 (6) 1984:579–90.

Hepburn, J. R., and P. E. Knepper. "Correctional officers as human service workers: The effect of job satisfaction." *Justice Quarterly* 10 (2) 1993:315–37.

Hepburn, J. R., and J. H. Laue. "Prisoner redress: Analysis of an inmate grievance procedure." *Crime & Delinquency* 26 (2) 1980:162–78.

Herberts, S. *6–5: A Different Shade of Blue.* Commack, NY: Kroshka Books, 1997.

Jacobs, J., and H. G. Retsky. "Prison guard." In R. R. Ross (ed.). *Prison Guard/Correctional Officer.* Toronto, Canada: Butterworth, 1981:55–73. (Originally published in *Urban Life,* 1975.)

Johnson, R. "Informal helping networks in prison: The shape of grass-roots correctional intervention." In R. R. Ross (ed.). *Prison Guard/Correctional Officer.* Toronto, Canada: Butterworth, 1981a:105–25. (Originally published in the *Journal of Criminal Justice,* 1979.)

Johnson, R. *Condemned to Die: Life Under Sentence of Death.* New York: Elsevier, 1981b.

Johnson, R. *Death Work: A Study of the Modern Execution Process.* Belmont, CA: Wadsworth, 1998.

Johnson, R., and S. Price. "The complete correctional officer: Human service and the human environment of prison." *Criminal Justice and Behavior* 8 (3) 1981:343–73.

Jurik, N. C. "Individual and organizational determinants of correctional officer attitudes toward inmates." *Criminology* 23 (3) 1985:523–39.

Jurik, N. C. "Striking a balance: Advancement strategies for women working as correctional officers in men's prisons." *Feminist Studies* 6 (1986). Chicago: Midwestern Sociological Association.

Jurik, N. C., and M. C. Musheno. "The internal crisis of corrections: Professionalization and the work environment." *Justice Quarterly* 3 (4) 1986:457–80.

Kissel, P. J., and P. L. Katsampes. "The impact of women corrections officers on the functioning of institutions housing male inmates." *Journal of Offender Counseling, Services and Rehabilitation* 4 (3) 1980:213–31.

Kupers, T. A. *Prison Madness: The Mental Health Crisis Behind Bars and What We Must Do About It.* San Francisco: Jossey-Bass, 1999.

Lasch, C. *The Minimal Self—Psychic Survival in Troubled Times.* New York: Norton, 1984.

Lasky, G. L., and B. C. Gordon. "Occupational stressors among federal correctional officers working in different security levels." *Criminal Justice and Behavior* 13 (3) 1986:317–27.

Liebling, A. "Prison suicide and prisoner coping." In M. Tonry and J. Petersilia

(eds.). *Prisons.* Chicago: University of Chicago Press, 1999.

Lin, A. C. *Reform in the Making: The Implementation of Social Policy in Prison.* Princeton: Princeton University Press, 2000.

Lockwood, D. *Prison Sexual Violence.* New York: Elsevier, 1980.

Locy, T. "Jury finds harassment in D. C. agency: Corrections conduct leaves the district liable for damages." *The Washington Post* (Wednesday, April 5, 1995): A1 & A16.

Lombardo, L. X. *Guards Imprisoned: Correctional Officers at Work.* New York: Elsevier, 1981.

Lombardo, L. X. "Mental health work in prisons and jails: Inmate adjustment and indigenous correctional personnel." *Criminal Justice and Behavior* 12 (1) 1985:17–28.

Lombardo, L. X. "Alleviating inmate stress: Contributions from correctional officers." In R. Johnson and H. Toch (eds.). *The Pains of Imprisonment.* Prospect Heights, IL: Waveland Press, 1988:285–97.

Lombardo, L. X. *Guards Imprisoned: Correctional Officers at Work.* Cincinnati, OH: Anderson Publishing, 1989.

May, E. "Prison guards in America—The inside story." In R. R. Ross (ed.). *Prison Guard/Correctional Officer.* Toronto, Canada: Butterworth, 1981:19–40. (Originally published in *Corrections Magazine,* 1976.)

Owen, B. A. "Race and gender relations among prison workers." *Crime & Delinquency* 31 (1) 1985:147–59.

Raymond, A. (Director). *Doing Time: Life Inside the Big House.* [Videocassette.] New York: Video Verite, 1991.

Rodgers, B. R. "Inmate grievance procedure design and evaluation: The state of the art." *International Journal of Group Tensions* 1 (4) 1979:75–85.

Sennett, R. *Authority.* New York: Vintage Books, 1981.

Sheehan, S. *A Prison and A Prisoner.* Boston: Houghton Mifflin, 1978.

Showalter, D., and M. Hunsinger. "Social work within a maximum-security setting." In A. A. Roberts (ed.). *Social Work in Juvenile and Criminal Justice Settings.* Springfield, IL: Charles C. Thomas, 1983:257–74.

Stojkovic, S. "An examination of compliance structures in a prison organization: A study of the types of correctional power." Paper presented at Annual Meeting of The Academy of Criminal Justice Sciences, March 1984.

Szasz, T. *The Myth of Mental Illness: Foundations of a Theory of Personal Conduct.* New York: Dell, 1961.

Thomas, A. G. "The Carkhuff training program." In R. E. Hosford and C. S. Moss. *The Crumbling Walls.* Champaign-Urbana: University of Illinois Press, 1975:35–44.

Toch, H. *Men in Crisis: Human Breakdowns in Prison.* Chicago: Aldine, 1975.

Toch, H. *Living in Prison: The Ecology of Survival.* New York: Free Press, 1977.

Toch, H. "Is a 'correctional officer' by any other name, a 'screw'?" In R. R. Ross (ed.). *Prison Guard/Correctional Officer.* Toronto, Canada: Butterworth, 1981a: 87–104. (Originally published in *Criminal Justice Review,* 1978.)

Toch, H. "Psychological treatment of imprisoned offenders." In J. R. Hays,

T. K. Roberts, and K. S. Solway (eds.). *Violence and the Violent Individual.* New York: SP Medical & Scientific Books, 1981b:325–42.

Toch, H. "The disturbed disruptive inmate: Where does the bus stop?" *The Journal of Psychiatry and Law* (Fall 1982):327–49.

Toch, H., and J. D. Grant. *Reforming Human Services: Change Through Participation.* Beverly Hills, CA: Sage, 1982.

Toch, H., and J. Klofas. "Alienation and desire for job enrichment among correctional officers." *Federal Probation* 46 (1982):35–47.

Webb, G. L., and D. G. Morris. "Prison guard conceptions." In B. M. Crouch (ed.). *The Keepers: Prison Guards and Contemporary Corrections.* Springfield, IL: Charles C. Thomas, 1980:150–61.

Wiehn, P. J. "Mentally ill offenders: Prison's first casualties." In R. Johnson and H. Toch (eds.). *The Pains of Imprisonment.* Prospect Heights, IL: Waveland Press, 1988:221–37.

Wright, K. N. *Effective Prison Leadership.* Binghamton, NY: William Neil Publishing, 1994.

Zimmer, L. E. *Women Guarding Men.* Chicago: University of Chicago Press, 1986.

9

Better Living in the Prison Community

Prison Ecology and Prison Reform

At the turn of the twentieth century, a young writer named Hawthorne described his prison experience in a popular article entitled, "Our Barbarous Penal System."[1] Hawthorne was writing about Atlanta Federal Penitentiary, but his point was that prisons, all prisons, were inherently corrupt and cruel. "Penal imprisonment," he observed,

> is an institution of old date, born of barbarism and ignorance, nurtured in filth and darkness, and cruelly administered. It began with the dominion of the strong over the weak, and when the former was recognized as the community, it was called the authority of good over evil.[2]

For Hawthorne, prison reform was impossible, if not absurd. "No one talks of reforming the Black Death," he observed wryly.[3]

Many of today's prison critics share Hawthorne's cynical view. They would have us believe that penal institutions will never serve any constructive purpose. Rehabilitation, they assure us, is dead.[4] We are urged to adapt Gertrude Stein's aphorism to our situation, acknowledge that "a prison is a prison is a prison," and make do with a notoriously unaccommodating institution. Since imprisonment is inevitably painful, the most we can do is lessen the pain. Prison reform amounts to rallying for, of all things, humane warehouses. The difficulty is that warehousing is, at best, a futile undertaking. People simply "are not commodities that can be stored, shelved and retrieved," even if they are permitted to develop an elaborate make-believe world to help them pass the time.[5]

Public opinion on the matter of prison reform is less easily summarized than are the views of prison's scholarly critics. Most Americans seem to favor prisons that offer a combination of punishment and treatment; the view seems to be that criminals should take their medicine (punishment), get well (with the help of education and training), and then get on with their lives.[6] (Interestingly, this view appears to be shared by most correctional officers.[7]) A vocal and influential minority, however, advocates long sentences idled away in grim prisons that offer, at best, the prospect of boring prisoners into submission or scaring them straight.

Politicians resonate to these repressive concerns. As recently as 1994, a session of the Mississippi legislature featured "talk of restoring fear to prisons, of caning, of making prisoners 'smell like a prisoner,' of burning and frying, of returning executions to the county seat and of making Mississippi 'the capital of capital punishment.' "[8] (The death penalty aspirations are those of the governor; there is no indication that the legislature has shirked its duty to make hard time as hard as possible in state of Mississippi.) The difficulty with a baldly punitive approach to crime, at least as it applies to the uses of prisons as distinct from the death penalty, is that inmates must cope maturely with imprisonment if they are to have any hope of going straight upon release. Warehouse prisons, let alone prisons that traffic in what amounts to torture, do not promote coping competence. Instead, such prisons further impair the coping skills of offenders. Sooner or later, and always sooner than most of us would like, these embittered prisoners return to us—and to crime.

The scope and cost of imprisonment in America are growing at a remarkable rate. "State and federal incarceration rates," Blumstein and Beck tell us, "grew by over 200 percent between 1980 and 1996" and continue to grow apace.[9] The latest figures (for fiscal 1998–99) put the total annual adult corrections tab at roughly $29 billion; that covers 1,412 state prisons (at a cost of $26 billion) and 97 federal prisons (at a cost of $3 billion). (This excludes the $6 billion spent on 3,360 local jails and the $4 billion spent on 1,312 juvenile correctional institutions.[10]) During any given year, moreover, the "cost of operating the nation's penal institutions will increase more than $1 billion."[11] The "out-year costs" of running our growing penal archipelago, moreover, will be nothing short of "astronomical."[12] The taxpaying public seems largely oblivious to the economic realities. Indeed, local communities these days compete in so-called prison derbies for the privilege of hosting new prisons, which bring to their communities new jobs and an expanded tax base.[13] For society at large, however, substantial and growing investments in prison are a poor public policy choice.

It is fair to say, with Tonry and Petersilia, that "policy makers have been flying blind, making decisions costing billions of dollars and affecting millions of lives without adequate knowledge"—about presumed reductions in crime rates due to imprisonment (probably small) and unintended negative side effects of imprisonment on prisoners, their families, and society in general (probably large).[14] It should be apparent that putting an expanding portion of budget dollars in prisons takes money away from a host of valuable enterprises such as schools and social services, investments that might well, in the long run, offer better defenses against criminality as well as a generally improved quality of life for the average citizen.[15]

There is an apt saying in public policy, and in life generally, that goes like this: One can pay now or one can pay later, but either way you pay. In the matter of prison reform, this saying is only half right. One pays now *and* one pays later when large numbers of prisoners are allowed to languish in a growing colony of warehouse institutions, eventually to return to haunt us, and all the while draining resources from other key governmental functions. The point is not that we should reform prisons as a bribe to calm restive inmates, as if they were extorting better treatment from a frightened society.[16] We should reform our prisons because *we as a society wish to make our penal institutions effective instruments of punishment.*

Prison reform has at least two connotations these days. On the one hand, reform can mean reducing the size of our prison behemoth. Corollary reforms would have to do with structuring sentencing decisions to assure that only the more serious offenders go to prison, perhaps for longer terms than at present,[17] and with the development of intermediate and other sanctions to take up the slack of a smaller prison system.[18] A full and informed discussion of the proper size of America's penal system is beyond the scope of this book, which focuses on the prison experience and its import rather than on the scale of imprisonment and its significance for public policy.[19] As a general matter, however, it is painfully apparent—no pun intended—that prisons are a prohibitively expensive public policy choice with limited demonstrated effectiveness in reducing crime.[20] As such, prisons should be treated as scarce commodities to be built and deployed only when necessary and certainly not, as is so often the case today, paraded to the public as general purpose cure-alls for criminality.[21]

Our focus is on the second connotation of prison reform, that of improving individual prisons. However many prisons we seek to build and operate, this notion of reform makes it clear that individual prisons should be decent, humane enterprises (see Chapter One). Reformed prisons, following the line of argument developed in this book, must offer spartan but responsive conditions of confinement. The premise is that decent conditions of confinement, which include access to programs, will promote autonomy, security, and relatedness to others and, hence, will allow offenders to shoulder responsibility for their conduct and embark on constructive lives. It stands to reason that, all things being equal, a system comprised of decent prisons, even a bloated system like our current one, is a vast improvement over a system populated with warehouse prisons.

At a minimum, then, prison reform means improving existing prisons, however many prisons there may be in existence, so that they reach or approximate our notion of decency and produce a reasonably effective penal enterprise. As a practical matter, this means that the pains experienced in any given prison must be kept to a minimum. Civilization demands as much, and our prisons are civilized insofar as correctional policy and practice are geared to minimizing the pain of incarceration. But, since prisons will always produce pain, the pains of imprisonment must be coped with maturely. Prison reform thus demands that we acknowledge the pains of prison and, where possible, put them to constructive purposes. We must build our reform agenda, in other words, out of the deprivation and pain that are enduring ingredients of imprisonment. As is shown in this chapter, we can make our *civilized* prisons also *civilizing* prisons, though to date we have only just begun to take up this challenge.

Historically, reformers have failed to come to grips with the pains of imprisonment; they have done little to adapt correctional ideals to prison realities (see Chapter One through Chapter Three). Some reformers have spoken of prison regimes in utopian terms, as disciplined ways of living that would radically improve the characters of their subjects. This is perhaps most clear in the case of the penitentiary,[22] but utopian aspirations lingered in the Big House[23] and in the correctional institution.[24] More recently, prisons have been derided as inherently unnatural environments. In the extreme, they have been described as inherently demeaning total institutions[25] or brutalizing social jungles.[26] For a time, however, the programs offered in these admittedly bleak environments were praised in utopian terms. This contradiction reflected the logic behind the correctional institution. Programs were meant to transform custodial prisons into correctional institutions; when they did not, these programs were expected to be oases that somehow endured in the wasteland of the cell block and yard.[27] Neither reform agenda—utopian prisons or utopian programs—has borne fruit.

We now know that prisons too often have served as warehouses; warehouses do not reform offenders. Treatment programs could improve this situation, but programs do not often thrive in warehouses. Prison treatment programs, moreover, have been more illusory than real. It has been estimated, for instance, that about a $1,000 a year (about $3 a day) is spent on any given prisoner for "inmate programs" (primarily education) and that rehabilitation programs (such as counseling, drug treatment, and cognitive skills training) are extended to a minority of the inmate population—by one estimate, a mere 5 percent.[28] This is typical of the history of prisons. Never has anyone been able to "directly and effectively represent the 'silent majority' of problem inmates, the average person who suffers, the one who wastes away in shooting distance from potentially available resources."[29] Small wonder that we have inherited a legacy of frustration and failure, leavened with periodic violence and even brutality.

But legacies can be changed. Prisons can be seen for what they are, as settings in which the average inmate does indeed suffer. Rehabilitation can be defined as equipping offenders to cope with the pains of imprisonment in mature ways, not wasting away but, rather, growing through the adversity posed by imprisonment (see Chapter Four). This is a sober and workable correctional agenda. By their very nature, penal institutions produce psychological pain;

they provide plenty of stress. Our job is to translate those stresses into occasions for learning rather than invitations to immature and often destructive behavior. In this chapter, we examine how the pains of imprisonment can be harnessed in service of prison reform. The goal is not utopian prison environments or programs. Our goal is to meet the needs of the average prisoner for a livable prison, useful activities, and a chance for a decent life upon release from confinement.

The ultimate goal of prison reform is to produce mature adults who can live in society and cope with the daily problems of life without harming others. Ideally, mature adults also have the capacity to enter into constructive relationships with their fellows. Mature adults honor the minimal obligations of citizenship by not preying upon others.[30] They also strive to be productive citizens, willing and able to work for their keep and to take some responsibility for the well-being of others in the human community.[31] A prison that allows inmates to live within its walls as citizens, and ideally as productive and even caring citizens, provides a rehearsal for mature living in the free world.

Prisoners who are to live in the prison community as citizens must be afforded a safe and lawful existence, one in which it is possible to be neither predator nor prey, criminal nor victim.[32] Most inmates, as we have seen, seek such an existence. They attempt to carve out niches in which to shelter themselves from the violence and exploitation that thrives on the prison yard and in other public areas of the prison (see Chapter Six). Correctional managers must take note of these trends. As Duffee has observed, "managers in complex systems tend to be most effective when they take advantage of the self-direction of organizations rather than fight against it."[33] (It is significant that prison management strategies that work with prisoners' natural proclivities toward autonomy, by affording them some degree of responsibility for the conditions of their daily lives, result in lower levels of disorder.)[34] At the same time, correctional managers must also be leaders; they must have a commitment to excellence in the delivery of correctional services, from basic security to living conditions and programs.[35] Accordingly, correctional policies can dovetail with and encourage the development of constructive niches as pockets of ecological excellence, if you will, building a robust reform agenda from the grass roots of daily life and adjustment in prison. The goal would be to permeate prisons with such niches, so that these institutions are, in effect, communities that are honeycombed with responsive neighborhoods. Terms like *the prison community,* bandied about in the sociological literature on prisons, would have real meaning in such contexts.

None of this will be easy to accomplish. Impediments to changing day-to-day prison policy and practice include limited funds, custodial convenience, and concern for turf.[36] Perversely, simply getting by in the way they always have becomes a mark of competence and a badge of pride for some prison officials. Reforms that fly in the face of these concerns by proposing novel and expensive activities are easily scuttled. In contrast, grassroots reforms that build upon existing trends and stay within existing budgets have a chance of success. The reformer, then, must show practitioners—correctional managers as well as line staff—that "it is possible to rearrange the distribution of currently available resources with the likely result that if we are not doing more with less, at least we are doing more for the same costs."[37] The ecology of adjustment provides an ideal vehicle for reforms that exploit available prison resources.

PRISON ECOLOGY AND PRISON REFORM

The first order of business is to use prison environments, our most available reform resource, in the service of mature adjustment to the stresses of life in prison. One line of reform is to make prisons more "normal," which is to say, more like the free world. A second strategy is to use existing prison environments in a more rational and responsive way. Combinations of these approaches are of course possible.

As a general matter (and with the notable exception of the supermax prison), the direction of penal reform, at least since the demise of the penitentiary, has been to make prisons more normal. For example, prison architecture has evolved over time to allow greater human contact and interaction.[38] The same can be said for the arrangement of internal prison regimes, at least from the penitentiary through to contemporary prisons, as is made apparent in the historical chapters of this book.

From the point of view of mature coping, the benefits of increasingly normal prisons are evident. "The more closely the conditions of imprisonment can begin to approximate those normally seen on the outside," observe Zamble, Porporino, and Kalotay, "the better inmates can learn to survive without resort to criminal behavior."[39] In making prisons more normal—more like the free world—we hope to offer lessons in mature coping that will readily generalize to the conditions of life outside prisons. Clues as to what is normal in a prison environment—other than relaxation of restrictions, as is found most saliently in Dutch prisons—may be found in our analysis of recurring features of prison adjustment. In other words, in the human concerns that guide adjustment, prisoners tell us by their behavior what they feel they must "import" from the free world to make the prison "normal" for them.

Using our review of prisoner adjustment as a guide (Chapter Five and Chapter Six), we can conclude that a normal prison environment must offer, first and foremost, opportunities for the constructive expression of autonomy. A normal prison, then, must offer opportunities for each person to take responsibility for a progressively growing array of choices made within the confines of work, school, and play in the prison community. Such choices make it possible for prisoners to gain, from their own initiative, a sense of security in the world, because they have some control over their fate; and a sense of relatedness to others, because the social world in which they now operate is in some important measure shaped by their interpersonal choices.

Dutch prisons may well be the most normal prisons one can find today, and they appear to bear out these observations. Prisons in The Netherlands operate on a "principle of minimal restrictions."[40] This means that "the prisoner has the same civil rights as any other citizen, unless the realization of these rights is impossible under the necessary conditions of detention."[41] Dutch prisons feature relaxed internal regimes, with prisoners afforded considerable freedom of choice as to what they do, when they do it, and with whom they associate. It is fair to say that Dutch prisons are minimally intrusive and, hence, that the pains of imprisonment are kept to a minimum.[42] The operating premise appears to be that prisons are inherently harmful; reform efforts focus on minimizing the harm by reducing the restrictive conditions of confinement. The ecology of adjustment in these regimes has not been researched, but anecdotal evidence suggests that prisoners do feel relatively autonomous, secure, and related to others around them.[43]

To be sure, the prison community in most penal institutions reflects misguided efforts to secure autonomy, security, and relatedness—through violence, primarily among the convicts, and through retreat into insular niches, primarily among the inmates (see Chapter Five and Chapter Six). This need not remain the case. The urge to be autonomous, secure, and related to others, present in adjustment efforts in prisons from the penitentiaries to contemporary penal institutions, can be guided to better ends. The continuing difficulty is that today's prisons, much like their various predecessors, have in place formal policies and informal practices that actively discourage constructive autonomy.

For example, all inmates currently receive the same goods and services regardless of differences in their behavior. One's meals or clothing or living conditions are the same whether one works or not. Yet it stands to reason that there should be "higher rewards for good behavior and lower benefits for freeloading."[44] To make matters worse, in today's prisons, the convicts often live *better* than more compliant prisoners. By use of threat or violence, the convicts often secure a higher standard of living than their law-abiding inmate counterparts, including ready access to such valued commodities as sex and respect.[45]

It is also the case that "institutional privileges ought to be made at least partly contingent on behavior which is appropriate on the outside, rather than simply on the absence of institutional offenses."[46] In most prisons, inmates may gain privileges simply by avoiding trouble. This is not bad in itself, except that, in many prisons, the absence of rule violations rather than the presence of prosocial behavior is the only route to a better prison life. One consequence of such a reward system is that at least some if not many prisoners, by dint of passivity or deception, are able to live as well as—or, indeed, better than—inmates who strive to improve themselves but occasionally break prison rules. Clearly, inmates who work to rehabilitate themselves should gain the lion's share of privileges, notably better housing and more flexible domestic schedules. These privileges, which amount to affording better neighborhoods and homes to high achievers, should be awarded on the basis of progress in areas that enhance one's capacity to cope with problems in mature ways, from social skills acquisition to education and vocational training.

Along the same lines, "if work assignments were made more meaningful, more realistic and more flexible, they would [reduce] the artificiality of the prison environment" by making one's lot more clearly reflect one's effort.[47] Lompoc Prison provides a case in point. Lompoc has been described as an "industrial penitentiary community."[48] Conformity and hard work pay off at Lompoc. Prisoners can and do live comparatively well at Lompoc; the prison is safe, in part, because prisoners feel they have a stake in the day-to-day quality of prison life and don't want to lose privileges or comforts as a result of misbehavior. For productive and conforming prisoners at Lompoc, behaving like a decent citizen of the prison community translates into "earning a reliable income, having a decent personal lifestyle, and enjoying the social freedom that comes in a peaceful prison community."[49] Reforms of the sort found at Lompoc alter the prison ecology, increasing the likelihood that prisoners will learn some specific lessons in living that are also of value in the free world.

A second type of reform capitalizes on the ecology of prison environments. This approach requires simply that we use existing prison environments in a rational and efficient manner. All prisons have an "ecology of survival"; this ecology can be measured, mapped, and deployed to promote better adjustment.[50] Naturally, to the extent that prison environments are made more normal, ecological matches will be that much more likely to promote mature conduct that has direct relevance to life and adjustment in the free world.

As things stand today, prison policy does not typically produce normal environments. Nor does it draw upon ecological resources in any systematic way. To be sure, officials sometimes make work or housing assignments or arrange recreation or program schedules with the aim of helping prisoners to adjust and perhaps even to pursue personal rehabilitation. But these are the exceptions rather than the rule. More often, assignments and schedules serve custodial needs rather than the adjustment needs of inmates.[51] When the issue of adjustment influences these decisions, the goal is usually to reward conformity or punish infractions rather than to encourage a mature response to the demands of prison life. The result is a self-defeating reward system in which compliant inmates like Malinow are so comfortable they don't want to leave prison (see Chapter Six) and rebellious inmates like Abbott are so bitter and inured to violence they can't be trusted out of segregation (see Chapter Five).

Let me illustrate this point, since it highlights the need to use ecological resources to promote mature adjustment rather than to achieve custodial control. Every prison has some formally designated living environment that features a low-key approach to authority and a relaxed climate. There may also be a host of "perks," such as extra televisions for the block, extended phone privileges, and perhaps even refrigerators in the cells. These settings are generally called "honor blocks" or "privilege blocks," though San Quentin had the perspicacity to christen theirs "Citizens' Row," in recognition that the men there are treated more like citizens and less like prisoners. But hard-core convicts, whose violence is largely a product of authority problems and whose preeminent environmental demand is for freedom from circumscription of their autonomy, are never assigned to units even remotely similar to these. This is true, moreover, even though such settings could be stripped of the material rewards and special privileges that might be construed as incentives for misconduct.

Prisoners who are prone to violence could be assigned to settings that combined the ecological dimensions of freedom and support. It is probable they would live there with fewer incidents and explosions and more chances for learning to manage conflict maturely. Both the prisoners and the staff would be encouraged to resolve conflicts cooperatively instead of resorting to manipulation or force. Relationships, even friendships, would almost certainly develop, gradually undermining stereotypes and building community. Prisoner and staff alike might well come to think of themselves as fellow citizens of the prison community, each with a stake in the well-being of the other. Life in such environments might indeed promote a sense of individual responsibility that would hold up in the free world.

If this scenario sounds unrealistic, it is because only the model inmates of the prison, who can handle regular prison authority situations fairly well, are now permitted to make their home in these more congenial environments. The prevailing idea is that a compliant inmate like Malinow deserves something better than the normal round of prison life. A rebellious inmate like Abbott deserves more punishment. As a consequence, Abbott is assigned to the most repressive cell blocks, gets into trouble, and becomes a regular guest in segregation—where he continues to make trouble for himself and his keepers. (It is increasingly likely that Abbott would be assigned to a supermax prison, where everyone lives in segregation.) Malinow finds what amounts to a comfortable niche but is encouraged simply to lie low and do his time there. Abbott does hard time and is confirmed in his worst beliefs about prison and about himself. Neither is motivated to change or given any incentives or rewards for undertaking the difficult task of personal reform.

Environments that ameliorate stress and promote mature adjustment can become standard features of any prison regime and be made available to most if not all prisoners. The nub of the issue is classification that yields appropriate "person-environment matches."[52] The express purpose of classification is "to determine the personal requirements and assess the needs of individual inmates, and . . . to match requirements and needs with existing correctional resources."[53] The first step is to place people in appropriate environments. Then, constructive activities, from learning to cope with daily adjustment problems to participation in formal correctional programs, must be arranged.

Classification and the Development of Niches

It has been established both theoretically and empirically that classification that relates human and environmental variables can improve prisoner adjustment and prison management, sometimes substantially.[54] There are a number of instruments that can be used in the classification process to provide individual and organizational data that make person-environment matches in ecological terms and, hence, permit us to place inmates—especially the crisis-prone inmates—in niches.[55] These instruments provide "information on which inmates are in distress, what their needs are, what resources they see as available to satisfy needs, what settings best suit their needs, and how they fare in those settings."[56] They allow us to systematically exploit correctional environments but can be expensive and time-consuming to use. Each requires an "ecological mapping" of a prison or prison system, and some correctional departments may be hard-pressed to conduct such an inquiry. However, there are less ambitious options that are likely to produce similar results.

A promising alternative is the Quay classification system, also known as AIMS—Adult Inmate Management System. With this approach, inmates are classified into three groups: "heavies" who prey on or manipulate others (they resemble the convicts discussed in Chapter Five and typified by Abbott); "moderates" who are competent to "do their own time" and willing to leave others in peace (they resemble the main group of inmates discussed in Chapter Six and typified by Malinow); and "lights" who are anxious, dependent, and readily victimized (much like the residual group of protection and high-risk inmates discussed in the closing pages of Chapter Six). The instruments developed by Quay for arriving at these classifications have the virtue of being based on official records and staff observations of prisoner behavior rather than inmate self-reports. (It stands to reason that the wolves of the prison world are not likely to identify themselves on a questionnaire. Some of the more susceptible prisoners may also be less than candid about their shortcomings.) These instruments, moreover, are inexpensive and easy to use. They can be completed by prison staff in the process of carrying out their normal duties.[57]

Using the Quay system, inmates can be assigned to housing and perhaps even program units that segregate predator from prey.[58] The middle or neutral group can be quartered separately but also used to fill out bed or program space throughout the prison since they do not involve themselves in destructive prison games.[59] Interestingly, the "heavies" settle down when the easy victims are removed from their midst; there is a cold war rather than a civil war in these units.[60] Most inmates are able to relax and go about the business of living in prison in a civilized manner. Within the comparatively stable prison worlds produced by this safety-oriented classification process, ecological variation will develop spontaneously to accommodate other kinds of needs. In particular, the natural development of niches and sanctuaries will proceed apace. Information about these ecological developments can be incorporated in subsequent classifications decisions. Thus, prisoners can be assigned to living quarters, for example, that are suitable in terms of both their Quay level and their ecological profile. A "light" inmate with strong privacy and support concerns can be housed with other "light" inmates who have similar or compatible ecological concerns.

In the free world, people develop their own ecological matches (find their own niches) when they select the neighborhoods they live in, the people they associate with, and the activities they pursue. Their capacity to do this is always subject to practical limitations. Nowhere are these limitations more pronounced than in prison, where it is hard to know what different environments are available and often impossible to move from one setting to another. Classification can be used as an aid or even as a substitute for the self-selection process.[61] Classification is particularly effective when it is undertaken by staff teams, who can pool their experiences to make better recommendations. Teamwork often breeds a sense of commitment among staff and, hence, a greater willingness to take inmate concerns into account.[62] When informed and responsive classification decisions are made, the natural diversity of prison environments can be better used to meet the diverse adjustment needs of inmates.

Classification can in fact do more than facilitate self-selection among existing prison environments. Classification permits staff to create special environments—formal enclaves or niches—and to manage them according to the needs and program objectives of their inhabitants. As Weiner has observed,

> we can attain a more flexible system by developing a variety of organizational structures and climates within the confines of a single institutional setting. . . . Different units can also be managed differently. Some institutional units may require tight organizational structure, with rigid rules and no input on the part of inmates regarding their living arrangements. Other living units may be more open and flexible, with fewer rules and more input by inmates regarding decisions affecting them. . . . [I]t seems both feasible and desirable to experiment on the degree to which such settings could be created and to examine the effects such environments might have on reducing stress among inmates and staff and, under certain conditions, providing viable contexts for treatment.[63]

Experiences in the federal prison system, in over half the states (including some jail systems as well) and in such countries as Canada, Holland, Sweden, New Zealand, Australia, Eastern and Central Europe, and South Africa, bear out Weiner's remarks.[64] In these various systems, prisoners are routinely assigned to functional units that differ according to prisoner types, management styles, social norms, and program offerings.

Functional units, according to Levinson, one of the originators of this key correctional innovation, share the following characteristics:

> (a) a relatively small number of offenders—75 to 125; (b) who are housed together—generally throughout the length of their institutional stay; (c) who work in a close, intensive relationship with a multidisciplinary, relatively permanently assigned team of staff members whose offices are located on the unit; (d) with these personnel having decision-making authority for all within-institution aspects of programming and disciplinary actions; and where (e) the placement of an offender in a particular living unit is contingent upon a need for the specific type of treatment program offered.[65]

A prison with a thousand inmates, for example, would be subdivided into roughly ten functional units, with each unit functioning as a small prison with its own social climate and programmatic focus of operation. Prisons that use a unit management system are considerably better organized than other prisons; a high level of organization, in turn, permits responsiveness to the varying needs and concerns of prisons. As a general matter, prisons run on a functional unit model are safer, more humane, and more readily adapted to correctional programming than are traditional, undifferentiated prisons.

Functional unit management offers a flexible approach to the classification and management of different groups. With a functional unit management structure in place, special-risk or special-needs inmates can be readily offered a coherent routine that at once addresses their situation and also integrates them, in varying degrees, into the life of the larger prison. (Note that functional units are never isolation units; they are *in* and *of* the prisons within which they are housed.)

Prisoners with HIV/AIDS provide a case in point. In three states—Alabama, Mississippi, and South Carolina—these inmates are segregated in what amount to isolation units, which are distinctly reminiscent of leper colonies (see Chapter One). This practice has passed muster with the United States Supreme Court.[66] In other states and the federal system, prisoners with HIV/AIDS are mixed in with the general population, either presumptively—as a matter of course—or on a case-by-case basis.[67] Placing infected inmates in the general population is clearly more humane than segregating them in what amounts to punitive isolation, but one danger of this approach is that the prisoners can then be ignored, left to roam the institution on their own, with everyone seemingly ignoring them but keeping them at arm's length. Women at Niantic Prison felt this was the case at that institution and even referred to infected women as a class of lepers:

> Considering that so many women in the program have the virus, it seems absurd not to deal openly with it. But as someone who has returned to Niantic time and again, Patty knows that denial concerning the disease runs deep at the farm and only puts more strain on those infected. Nobody wants to talk about it, as if those infected were the lepers of Niantic.[68]

These perceptions are consistent with the fact that, though AIDS is five times more prevalent among prisoners than among the general U.S. population, only 10 percent of state and federal prisons and 5 percent of city and county jails offer comprehensive HIV-prevention programs.[69] The institutional denial the women sensed at Niantic is apparently widespread.

A functional unit approach would allow correctional administrators to group HIV/AIDS inmates in constructive ways when this is appropriate, arguably reducing the stigma associated with the disease by taking a positive approach to its management. This is true for others with contagious diseases as well.[70] (Doing nothing and saying nothing about HIV/AIDS or any other infectious disease, on the other hand, implies that the sick are untouchables.) In a functional unit for inmates in the advanced stages of HIV infection, unit activities could focus on the medical and psychological problems associated with the disease. Depending on the progression of the disease in individual cases, offenders could be integrated into regular prison program services and activities on a selective basis. For inmates with HIV/AIDS who are asymptomatic, placement in a particular functional unit would be determined by other variables, such as their work or program needs or their style of adjustment. (This is currently the case in most prison systems that use the functional unit model.) In such cases, the unit approach still gives correctional administrators the flexibility to offer some special services (such as unit-based support groups) that are tailored to the unique situation faced by these offenders.

When prisons are "unitized," as is said in correctional circles these days, the results are impressive. Social climate ratings improve; this proves true both "for tougher and for more vulnerable inmates."[71] Particularly worthy of note are reduced rates of violence. Data on violence rates from 1984 through 1989, a period of unitization in a number of systems, shows a startling 50 percent drop in violent deaths in our nation's prisons. This decrease in prison homicides occurred, moreover, in the face of rapid prison population growth. (The prison homicide rate has continued to drop, though less precipitously.[72]) Violence decreases under a functional unit management system because these units, by their very nature, allow for the physical removal of predators from the environments populated by victims and permit individualized management and treatment of aggressive inmates within the functional units to which they are assigned.[73]

Specific success stories in which the use of unit management resulted in dramatic drops in violence and equally dramatic improvements in social climate include Rikers Island in New York, Folsom Prison in California, and, perhaps most notably, Massachusetts's Walpole Prison (now known as Cedar Junction).[74] A report on Walpole in the late 1980s, after the introduction of unit management, concluded that a "10–year history of violence, cost overruns and general administrative turmoil" came to an end once functional unit management was introduced: "The hostile conditions at Walpole have been all but eliminated, and it is a much improved facility in which to live and work. . . . [though] still overcrowded, there is much less violence and fear."[75] Unit management was subsequently adopted at other Massachusetts prisons.[76] It is worth noting that, at least as of 1991, "no system that has adopted unit management has subsequently abandoned it."[77]

One reason for the longevity of unit management is that it receives strong staff support once it is in place. Staff may initially resist this innovation, just as people generally resist any profound change in the way things are done, but they quickly find that functional units are more appropriate to their personal and career needs than traditional prison management approaches. With functional unit management, it is easier for officers to get to know individual inmates and hence to evolve correctional rather than merely custodial roles.[78] (Officer Smith, much admired by Conover—see Chapter Eight—worked on a gallery that was run as a functional unit.[79]) Conflicts between custody and treatment staffs are reduced, since functional units typically develop a healthy collegial climate.[80] Staff with functional units typically give their prisons high marks as working environments,[81] in part because they are given more decision-making authority. Each unit manager is, in effect, a warden; his or her staff are, in effect, high-level administrators of these miniature prison worlds. Since unit staff are more autonomous than their counterparts in regular prisons, they can become effective leaders; as one measure of such leadership, staff can offer more direct and indirect autonomy to the inmates in their care.[82] Finally, there are indications that small but consistent drops in recidivism rates may be a consequence of this organizational reform, independent of the specific correctional programming offered to inmates.[83]

Orientation, Monitoring, and Stress Reduction

Classification and placement in congenial settings is not enough to ensure effective adjustment. Prisoners must be carefully introduced to their new world and monitored in their reactions to it. Even the most accommodating prison environment can be a source of stress, particularly at the outset when the disjuncture between free world and prison world is apt to be great and, for some persons, traumatic.[84] For most prisoners, the initial stress of entering the prison produces social withdrawal and retreat within an emotional shell. This protective reaction, essentially a form of psychological shock, can be easily mistaken for callousness or hostility and used to justify neglectful or even repressive custodial measures. The fact remains, however, that "most stressed persons need and want assistance."[85] Ideally, they should be given task-oriented support that provides reassurance, information, and reinforcement of problem-solving behavior as it applies in the new environment.[86]

Toch has suggested an orientation program for incoming prisoners that would generate constructive anxiety about the prison situation. The newly arrived inmate should feel neither invulnerable ("prison is a snap") nor hopelessly demoralized ("nobody survives this joint"). Instead, common problems and feasible solutions are considered. For example, a prisoner is warned "you might be approached for sex," but advised, "guys who make friends are less likely to be bothered." (This advice could be rendered to female inmates as well.) Advice from selected prisoners may be valuable in this context. Lifers, in particular, would seem able to draw on their personal experiences in prison to help newcomers frame individual adjustment strategies; wisely, they admonish newcomers to "do their own time" and to generally use their time in prison to improve themselves.[87] An overview of prison environments and programs that identifies options in problem-solving gambits is also appropriate. The idea is to apprise newcomers of the problems at hand and the resources at their disposal and then to encourage them to work out plans for reassuring and protecting themmselves. Two goals are thus achieved: (1) The individual's feelings of resourcelessness and vulnerability are reduced; and (2) Inmates as a group begin to see prison as a negotiable set of challenges, to which they might eventually learn to respond in mature and mutually supportive ways.[88]

An effective orientation will help inmates get their feet on the ground and begin to use prison resources to address problems of adjustment, but there is no guarantee that all or even most problems will be handled constructively. Monitoring the placement of individual prisoners and revising assignments as needed are essential to ensuring the viability of person-environment matches. Monitoring will also keep inmates and staff, especially the line officers who are in a position to observe adjustments over time, in continuing and supportive relationships with one another:

> In an ideal prison system, no one would ever send inmates into an environment with which he (the classifier) was not intimately familiar, and where he couldn't personally monitor the consequences of his decisions. All classification would have to be tentative because people and settings change. There would also be routine opportunities for "trial classifications" in which inmates try settings out, and settings try out inmates, and for assignments that are strictly contingent on special conditions (such as peace and quiet, or personal involvement in therapy) in the absence of which they would be voided. . . . [G]uards and other staff would monitor classification. If the classifier is wrong, he must be told he is wrong. Since he may make mistakes, he must learn from them, to avoid endangering the next inmate on the assembly line.[89]

We know from research on pluralistic ignorance that many inmates act tougher than they really are, particularly when they first arrive at a prison. Monitoring will help identify those who were thus incorrectly classified.

As a practical matter, prison officers will be the primary agents of environmental monitoring. The more human service–oriented officers are well suited for this role; some of them will almost certainly expand it to include more ambitious functions. These officers already operate as a kind of indigenous cadre of "environmental engineers." Often they supplement advice and counseling, which make up the grist of human service work, with tangible assistance. In specific terms, they

> alter custodial routines, modulate surveillance and orchestrate assignments for the sole purpose of enhancing adjustment. They do so unsystematically, irregularly, and without a clear sense of the ecological factors being manipulated. The fact that they do so at all, however, suggests that . . . environmental variables can be manipulated naturally and effectively by those familiar with a setting.[90]

Thus, officers need not be limited to a passive role as classification monitors. Nor need they be limited to a haphazard familiarity with the prison ecology. They can be trained to think in ecological terms and even to shape environments. Their task would be not only to monitor placements but, where possible, to improve person-environment matches. Ideally, in recognition of their expanded skills and responsibilities, the correctional officers' role would be invested with more autonomy. Their views on prison ecology and inmate adjustment would be formally taken into account and would influence official decisions pertaining to these matters (for instance, by way of staff classification and assignment teams).[91]

Special training is required to prepare officers for formal roles as environmental agents. Officers must be versed in the ecology of prison and alerted to the possible presence of niches in various locations within their particular facility. They must understand the various "ways in which ecological resources can be cultivated and deployed to reduce stress," ideally by examining their own human service activities and those of fellow staff.[92] Moreover, training should help officers "to see their own experiences and characteristics, as well as those of their inmates, as environmental attributes" that can be used to solve problems.[93]

The training process envisioned here is an active one. General ecological information must be assimilated and applied by officers to specific situations that matter to them. Training that is too general, even if it is otherwise quite thorough, merely frustrates and further alienates officers, who feel unprepared for the challenges they face in their particular prisons and job assignments.[94] The objective of ecological training, by contrast, is to "help staff to think through the implications of available options" and to evolve their own plans for maximizing their effectiveness.[95] Like inmates, they must be introduced to the prison ecology. Hence, the training process parallels the prisoner orientation process, providing information, assurance, and reinforcement of problem-solving behavior. This training satisfies the often-stated desire of officers to develop skills that help them do their jobs right. The ultimate beneficiaries, however, are the inmates; for staff who are equipped to understand and use the prison ecology "can play active roles in providing sanctuaries for inmates in stress" and can serve as models of mature coping under pressure.[96]

Participation, Support, and Community

A supportive prison culture emerges when staff and prisoners work together to make the prison a haven for citizens and not a lair for predator and prey. A supportive prison culture presupposes a classification and management process that, in effect, makes the typical prison environment a niche. It culminates when staff and inmates use these enclaves as arenas for autonomous action and constructive social learning. Niches, in other words, provide a bridge between personal adjustment and personal reform.

In constructive niches, staff and inmates evolve a problem-solving culture instead of merely a shelter from stress. These settings serve as prototypes of responsive or therapeutic prison communities; they also share some of the key attributes of other democratically run prison environments.[97] Inmates and staff cooperate with one another in responsive or therapeutic communities because cooperation serves their individual needs; they quite naturally become altruistic egotists because they partake in a shared and reasonably stable future marked by frequent and durable interpersonal relations (see Chapter Four). An "adult principled moral perspective" can be a predictable product of the "intensive community life" that thrives in such milieus.[98] The reason is that inmates operate in these environments as responsible consumers of correctional services. The give and take of daily community life, in Toch's words, "involves adult-to-adult transactions between prisoners and staff. It requires prisoners to do something to get something."[99] This is never easy, but the process can be profoundly rewarding.

In these environments, prisoners cope maturely; they meet the daily problems of prison life head-on, without manipulation or deception, and with the cooperation and support of other inmates Longer-term adjustment problems can also be broached. Inmates examine their adjustment styles and experiment with new ways of handling stress and resolving conflict.[100] In such environments, Toch notes, "One learns to be prosocial by working with others and to govern oneself through involvement in governance. As one learns, one assists others to learn and is assisted by others in doing so."[101] Prisoners in these environments can be transformed from impulsive adolescents who operate in a dangerous playground to self-governing adults who belong to a small and secure community within the larger prison.[102]

Some level of direct participation in the governance process is an essential element of responsive communities in prison, and it is this feature that promotes a healthy adult autonomy among both staff and inmates. Participation can take many forms and can vary in degree. Depending on skills, interest, and the overall stability of the institution, inmates can be involved, in collaboration with officials, in the governance of the entire institution or a segment of an institution (such as a functional unit). Inmates can be involved, again in conjunction with officials, in specific groups dealing with specific issues, such as orientation, programming, or food service; or prisoners can "individually participate in their own management, sharing critical decisions along the way, and reviewing their progress at key junctures in their careers" with the appropriate officials.[103] Participation brings with it a sense of involvement and commitment. Participants actively engage their environments. They have a stake in the community and a tangible reason to work to improve themselves.

Inmates with HIV/AIDS are a much-maligned and often-marginalized group that might greatly benefit from involvement in responsive prison communities, ideally housed within functional units. These inmates face special challenges and stresses associated with their fateful diagnoses. One would suppose that, if any group needed a constructive niche to help them in their adjustment to prison and indeed to life, it is this group. Their problems are many and the resources available to them in the larger prison, given the fear and loathing their illness may promote, are regrettably few. In a functional unit designed to support these prisoners, for example, community efforts could be focused on managing the disease. The internal regime could be built around efforts to humanize the sometimes painful delivery of medical care, experiment with coping techniques that help the prisoners to face and work through the implications of the illness, and develop self-help groups to foster a climate of relatedness to others. To the extent that these inmates can, as a community, come to grips with their shared problems, they may come to feel that they are living with AIDS rather than dying from it.

Supportive communities, whatever the focus of group involvement, typically flower in relative isolation—in niches rather than in the public areas of the prison. They are intimate arrangements, on the order of neighborhoods rather than cities. To endure, they require support and leadership. "Even the most creative of us," Toch makes clear, "take wing from sure footing. The community catalyzer must provide an accepting, reliable, and supportive milieu (an oasis) before asking clients to take risks."[104] At this juncture, one can engage "higher human needs" than mere survival at any price. "These higher needs include needs for companionship, for recognition, and for creative outlets."[105] These are needs that would seem to beg for expression in correctional programs—our next topic—that hold out the promise of enfranchising the emerging citizens of the prison community.

NOTES

1. Hawthorne (1913).

2. Hawthorne (1913:206).

3. Hawthorne (1913:206).

4. See Alper (1974); Martinson (1974).

5. Toch (1985:59).

6. See, for example, Hawkins and Alpert (1989) and Applegate, Cullen and Fisher (1997) Tonry (1995:9) has summarized the evidence from public opinion surveys on this point:

Although National Opinion Research Center surveys for many years have shown that large majorities of respondents say they believe that sentences are insufficiently harsh, large majorities of Americans also want prisons to rehabilitate offenders. When [a Gallup survey] asked respondents to choose between punishment and rehabilitation as the primary goal of imprisonment, by 48 percent to 38 percent they chose rehabilitation.

A 1991 survey of U.S. legal codes indicates that rehabilitation was the most common formal goal of prisons, affecting forty-one states. Most states sought multiple goals, however, and punishment is becoming an increasingly popular formal goal, especially in the South (see Burton, Dunaway, & Kopache, 1993).

7. See Farkas (1999) for the latest study to confirm that most (71 percent) of officers see value in rehabilitation as well as in tough prison conditions. See, generally, Chapter Eight.

8. Nossiter (1994:1).

9. Blumstein and Beck (1999: 17); see also Blumstein (1994:405).

10. See ACA 2000 and NJADD 2000–2001. See also Stephan (1999:iv).

11. Walsh (1994:A3).

12. Walsh (1994:A3).

13. Walsh (1994:A3). The competition in these prison derbies continues a pace. See Duke (2000).

14. Tonry and Petersilia (1999:7). Though "the national trend for the 1990s is one of rising incarceration and declining crime" (from 1991 to 1998 the rate of incarceration rose by 47 percent and the crime rate declined by 22 percent), there is little evidence that the greater level of incarceration caused the decline in crime (Gainsborough & Maurer, 2000:5). It is interesting to note that

During the national decline in crime from 1991 to 1998, states with the largest increases in incarceration experienced, on average, smaller declines in crime than other states. The "above average" states increased their rate of incarceration by an average of 72% and experienced a 13% decline in crime, while the rate of incarceration in "below average" states rose by 30% and crime rates declined by 17%. (Gainsborough & Maurer, 2000:4)

There are those who maintain that prisons, though indeed expensive, are a bargain because they pay for themselves. The logic is this: A high rate of incarceration keeps many offenders behind bars—this prevents confined criminals from victimizing the public (incapacitation), and it discourages other would-be criminals from committing crimes as well (deterrence). Crime reduction due to incapacitation and deterrence therefore saves vast amounts of money, since crime is believed to exact a heavy economic and social price on individual victims and on the larger society (see, for example, Piehl & DiIulio, 1995). This is, in my view, an area of analysis that requires a series of heroic assumptions, namely, that prisons have sufficient deterrent and incapacitative effects to substantially reduce crime rates, and that such reductions in crime rates will generate real savings for the society that can be said to offset the direct outlays of money undertaken by governmental bodies to build and operate prisons. The work of Blumstein (1994), Forst (1994), and others casts doubt on the value of this line of analysis, at least as it applies to the growth in prisons over the last two decades. In general, it would appear that demographic and socioeconomic forces influence crime rates to a much greater extent than do sentencing policies. See, generally, Tonry and Petersilia (1999).

15. To be sure, prison budgets eat up only a small share of overall state and federal budgets, "[b]ut in terms of growth, prisons are where the action is" (Walsh, 1994:A3). This growth has continued apace and has, moreover, produced a number of anomalies. In the mid-eighties, California spend two and a half times more on higher education than on corrections. By 1994, however, "California's state corrections budget of $3.8 billion was equal to the entire budge for public higher education." Moreover, it has been projected that by 2002, as a result of the continuing prison building boom, corrections will "consume 18 percent of the entire state budget." By contrast, higher education in California's vaunted state colleges and universities are projected to consume less than one percent of the state budget. It is also troubling that "more than half the states spend two times as much on prisons as they do on Aid for Dependent Children." See Merlo (1997:73–4).

16. See Logan and Gaes (1993:258–59).

17. See, for example, Forst (1994:380). At present, as Wilson (1994:499) reminds us, most serious offenders serve less time in prison than they did as recently as the 1940s. One reform strategy would be to send serious offenders to prison for longer terms while sending other offenders, notably low-level drug offenders and lesser property offenders, to community supervision.

18. See, for example, Clear and Braga (1994).

19. See Zimring and Hawkins (1991).

20. See Blumstein (1994) and Tonry and Petersilia (1999:8). More broadly, Tonry (1995:17) reminds us that "For at least twenty-five years, researchers have shown and honest politicians have known that manipulations of penalties have relatively little or no effect on crime rates." The problem is the general weakness of deterrence with respect to run-of-the-mill street criminals, who, as we have noted in Chapter Three, are quite immature and whose "crimes are as impulsive as the rest of their reckless, sad, or pathetic lives" (this quote is drawn from a 1990 White Paper prepared for the English Parliament; see Tonry, 1995:18). It should come as no surprise, then, that "The clear weight of the evidence in every Western country indicates that tough penalties have little effect on crime rates" (Tonry, 1995:19).

21. See Austin and Irwin (2000).

22. See Beaumont and Tocqueville (1833/1964:89).

23. See Jacobs (1977:31).

24. Irwin (1980:47).

25. Goffman (1961).

26. Irwin (1980).

27. Irwin (1980).

28. See Stephan (1995:1); Gendreau and Ross (1980:25).

29. Toch (1981:9).

30. Conrad (1981b:17).

31. Hawkins (1976 & 1983); Erikson (1965).

32. Conrad (1981a:56–62).

33. Duffee (1980:16).

34. See Reisig (1998).

35. See Wright (1994).

36. Hawkins (1976:168). Good theory often fails to get implemented because of practical obstacles to reform. This is a general problem in criminal justice reform and, indeed, one that is encountered in

efforts to change a range of organizations in society. (See Wright, 1994, and Bennett & Bennett, 1982.)

37. Levinson (1988b:241); see also England (1990:63).

38. Atlas and Dunham (1990:55).

39. Zamble, Porporino, and Kalotay (1984:140).

40. Kalmthout and van der Landen (1991:97).

41. Kalmthout and van der Landen (1991:97).

42. See Downes (1988).

43. The anecdotal evidence is comprised of observations drawn from site visits made to penal institutions in Holland in the summers of 1992 and 1994 by myself and, most recently, in the summer of 1999 by Richard Bennett, a colleague and fellow member of the faculty of the Department of Justice, Law and Society of American University.

44. Zamble, Porporino, and Kalotay (1984:141).

45. This was quite apparent in Blecker's account of life in Lorton's dorms and is a theme that runs through much of the ethnographic descriptions of prison life. (See, for example, Blecker, 1990, and Fleisher, 1989.)

46. Zamble, Porporino, and Kalotay (1984:141).

47. Zamble, Porporino, and Kalotay (1984:141).

48. Fleisher (1989:27).

49. Fleisher (1989:27).

50. Toch (1977).

51. Toch (1977); Fitzgerald and Sim (1982:50).

52. Toch (1977:284–85).

53. Toch (1977:286).

54. See Wright, with Harris and Woika (1985); Wright (1991); Toch (1977).

55. These instruments include the following: (1) To measure stress: SCL 90 (Dero-

gatis, Rickels, & Rock, 1976:280) or the well-known MMPI (which, as Derogatis et al. indicate, correlates highly with SCL-90 on stress-related items). Gibbs et al. (1983:38) found the SCL-90 easy to modify for use with a jail population. (2) To assess environmental needs as reflected in individual inmate perceptions: Prison Preference Inventory (Toch, 1977); the Jail Preference Inventory (Gibbs et al., 1983); and the Smith Jail Preference Inventory (Smith, 1984). (3) To pinpoint environmental resources and "organizational climates [that] arise from members' shared experiences in the environment" (Wright, 1991:225): such instruments as the Environmental Quality Scale (Gibbs et al., 1983), any of a variety of the Moos correctional climate scales (for example, Moos, 1974), and Wright's Prison Environment Inventory (Wright, 1985). Most recently, an eight-dimension quality of prison life instrument has been developed and implemented by Logan and applied to a study of three women's prisons (Logan, 1992). This instrument could be readily adapted for use with prisons for men.

56. Gibbs et al. (1983:561).

57. Quay (1984:9–10).

58. See Levinson (1988a).

59. Bohn (1979 & 1980).

60. Bohn (1980).

61. Toch (1981:7).

62. Hepburn and Albonetti (1978).

63. Weiner (1988:304).

64. See Levinson (1991:44); Unit Management Guidelines (1990); Levinson (1998a & 1988b).

65. Levinson (1988b:244–45).

66. The Supreme Court today left intact a lower court's ruling permitting Alabama prisons to "segregate hundreds of HIV positive inmates and keep them from educational programs and even from religious services where they might mix with other prisoners. . . . Alabama was the only state prison system to segregate its HIV positive inmates when the suit was filed [in 1991], but Mississippi and South

Carolina have now adopted similar policies" (Greenhouse, 2000).

67. See, for example, Hammett, Harrold, Gross, and Epstein (1994:59–62); NIC (1997); and Thigpen and Hunter (1998).

68. Rierden (1997:119).

69. Altman (1999).

70. Tuberculosis, including drug-resistant strains, and Hepatitis C are two other contagious diseases that are more common in prison than the free world and that require special management. See NIC (1997) and Thigpen and Hunter (1998).

71. Toch (1981:7); see also Levinson (1988a, 1991 & 1998) and Smith and Fenton (1978).

72. See Herrick (1989); Bottoms (1999:226, Table 4).

73. See Levinson (1991:48).

74. Silberman (1995) reports that the use of functional units in conjunction with the Quay classification system (also known as AIMS—Adult Inmate Management System) reduced violence effectively in "Central Prison," a pseudonym for what appears to be a high-security prison in Pennsylvania.

75. Herrick (1989:8).

76. Herrick (1989:8).

77. Levinson (1991:44). For a time, the South Carolina correctional system dropped function units, for political reasons. They are in the process of reinstituting these units in the maximum-security prisons, with an eye to unitizing (or re-unitizing) the entire system. Personal Communication, Robert Levinson.

78. Levinson (1988b:245); Levinson (1998).

79. Conover (2000:87). I do not know whether Sing Sing formally uses the functional unit system, but Smith's gallery had all the requisite characteristics of a functional unit.

80. See Gerard (1991:34); Pierson (1991:30).

81. Gerard (1991); Levinson (1998).

82. See Levinson (1988a & 1998); Wright (1994).

83. Levinson (1988b:242). These findings reflect a paradox of planned change within penal institutions, namely that "to make a unit completely different from the prison yard may be easier to accomplish than . . . to introduce selective, piece-meal reform" (Toch, 1984:16–17). (Incidentally, Toch points out that this observation applies to "culture building" in other contexts as well.) The reason is that guards and inmates can start fresh in a new unit as a group with shared goals and an open horizon, in effect leaving old resistances and rivalries behind.

84. At entry, inmates are markedly depressed and anxious. "The incidence of severe depression . . . was about 8 times that in the general population, and that for moderate depression was about 5 times the normal rate . . . a substantial number of our subjects had elevated anxiety scores; in fact, 41% had scores above the mean level for the anxiety reaction patients" (Zamble, Porporino, & Kalotay, 1984:72). Comparable findings have emerged from other studies as well (see Zamble and Porporino, 1990; Boothby & Durham, 1999). Symptoms of depression appear to be significantly more prevalent among offenders with a pronounced external locus of control (Reitzel & Harju, 2000:635). As noted in Chapter Four, an external locus of control is generally associated with immature and ineffective coping, which might well make such persons vulnerable to depression under stress.

85. Toch (1988b:26).

86. Janis (1969).

87. See Zamble (1992); Rierden (1997). First-termers, in particular, may be reassured by the presence of inmates in the orientation process (see Hirschorn & Burck, 1977). However, the involvement of inmates must be carefully monitored by staff, who are ultimately responsible for the content and consequences of the orientation process. If staff do not exercise this monitoring obligation in a visible way, novice prisoners may gain the wrong

impression as to who runs the prison. Inmates have considerable subcultural clout, but it is misleading to imply that they run the formal institution as well.

88. Toch (1988b:26–27).

89. Toch (1981:6–7).

90. Seymour (1988:275).

91. Here my aim is to anticipate "organizational-level barriers" to these individual-oriented reforms (see Jurik & Musheno, 1986:19). Simply having good officers who are committed to the notion of human service and responsive to ecological concerns may not be enough to ensure the effective uses of correctional authority. Unless officers are offered training and support for expanded roles and responsibilities, some and perhaps even many of them are apt to get discouraged, becoming pessimistic about helping prisoners and dissatisfied with their jobs (see Jurik & Musheno, 1986:29).

92. Johnson and Price (1981:367).

93. Johnson and Price (1981:367).

94. See Fitzgerald and Sim (1982:128).

95. Toch (1984:14).

96. Johnson and Price (1981:367).

97. Toch (1980:10); Fitzgerald and Sim (1982:117). Most constructive niches were routinely subsumed under the heading "therapeutic community" when the term had rather broad and positive connotations in the prison context. The label remains apt and is still in use, but for my purposes the connotation of therapy is often too narrow. The therapy offered in some therapeutic communities, for example, takes a very heavy-handed approach to help; essentially bogus treatments are more or less forced on offend-ers, who may come to feel violated in the process (see, for example, Silberman's discussion of coercion in some therapeutic communities; Silberman, 1995). Even when helping arrangements in therapeutic communities are benign, they often still occur at the behest of experts, and this downplays our growing concern with facilitating rather than imposing personal change, so that offenders might better take responsibility for their own conduct. The term *responsive community* is meant to capture both the notion of helpfulness at the root of therapy and the notion of responsibility at the root of personal accountability for one's actions. These terms will be used interchangeably in this discussion, since the literature embraces communities that offer therapy as an adjunct to social learning in the community (for example, therapeutic communities for drug or alcohol offenders), as well as communities that offer no formal treatment or therapy but are explicitly organized as staging grounds for social learning (for example, units that involve varying degrees of participatory management, including democratization).

98. Scharf (1978:189); Scharf (1980); Regens and Hobson (1978); Toch (1994a:71).

99. Toch (1994a:71); see also Toch (1994b).

100. Jones (1980); Grant (1980).

101. Toch (1994a:69).

102. One measure of security in these settings is a reduced rate of disorder and victimization. See Reisig (1998).

103. Toch (1994a:69).

104. Toch (1980:10).

105. Toch (1980:11).

REFERENCES

ACA 2000. *Juvenile and Adult Correctional Departments, Institutions, Agencies, and Paroling Authorities.* Lanham, MD: American Correctional Association, 2000.

Alper, B. S. *Prisons Inside-Out: Alternatives in Correctional Reform.* Cambridge: Ballinger, 1974.

Altman, L. "Much more AIDS in prisons than in general population." *The New York Times* (September 1, 1999).

Applegate, B. K., F. T. Cullen, and B. S. Fisher. "Public support for correctional treatment: The continuing appeal of the rehabilitative appeal." *The Prison Journal* 77 (3) 1997:237–258.

Atlas, R. I., and R. G. Dunham. "Changes in prison facilities as a function of correctional philosophy." In J. W. Murphy and J. E. Dison (eds.). *Are Prisons Any Better? Twenty Years of Correctional Reform.* Beverly Hills: Sage, 1990:43–59.

Austin, J., and J. Irwin. *It's About Time: America's Imprisonment Binge.* Belmont, CA: Wadsworth, 2000.

Beaumont, G. D., and A. D. Tocqueville. *On the Penitentiary System in the United States and Its Application in France.* Carbondale: Southern Illinois University Press, 1833/1964.

Bennett, R. R., and S. B. Bennett. "Translating criminological theory into action programs: Theoretical and political considerations." *Criminal Justice Review* 7 (2) 1982:1–8.

Blecker, R. "Haven or Hell? Inside Lorton Central Prison: Experiences of punishment justified." *Stanford University Law Review* 42 (May 1990):1149–249.

Blumstein, A. "Prisons." In J. Q. Wilson and J. Petersilia (eds.). *Crime.* San Francisco: ICS Press, 1994:387–420.

Blumstein, A., and A. J. Beck. "Population growth in U.S. prisons, 1980–1996." In M. Tonry and J. Petersilia (eds.). *Prisons.* Chicago: University of Chicago Press, 1999:17–61.

Bohn, M. J. "Classification of offenders in an institution for young adults." *FCI Research Reports* 10 (1) 1979:1–31.

Bohn, M. J. "Inmate classification and the reduction of institution violence." *Corrections Today* (July/August 1980):48–55.

Boothby, J. L., and T. W. Durham. "Screening for depression in prisoners using the Beck Depression Inventory."

Criminal Justice and Behavior 26 1999:107–124.

Bottoms, A. E. "Interpersonal violence and social order in prisons." In M. Tonry and J. Petersilia (eds.). *Prisons.* Chicago: University of Chicago Press, 1999:205–281.

Burton, V. S., R. G. Dunaway, and R. Kopache. "To punish or rehabilitate? A research note assessing the purposes of state correctional departments as defined by state legal codes." *Journal of Crime and Justice* 16 (1) 1993:177–88.

Clear, T. R., and A. A. Braga. "Community corrections." In J. Q. Wilson and J. Petersilia (eds.). *Crime.* San Francisco: ICS Press, 1994:421–44.

Conover, T. *Newjack: Guarding Sing Sing.* New York: Random House, 2000.

Conrad, J. P. "The state's strongest medicine." In J. P. Conrad. *Justice and Consequences.* Lexington: Lexington Books, 1981a:51–70.

Conrad, J. P. "Where there's hope there's life." In D. Fogel and J. Hudson (eds.). *Justice As Fairness.* Cincinnati, OH: Anderson, 1981b:3–21.

Derogatis, B. R., K. Rickels, and A. F. Rock. "SCI-90 and the MMPI: A step in the validation of a new self-report scale." *British Journal of Psychiatry* 128 (March 1976):280–89.

Downes, D. *Contrasts in Tolerance: Post-War Penal Policy in the Netherlands and England and Wales.* Oxford: Clarendon Press, 1988.

Duffee, D. *Correctional Management.* Englewood Cliffs, NJ: Prentice-Hall, 1980.

Duke, L. "Building a boom behind bars: Prison construction boom transforms small towns." *The Washington Post,* Friday, September 8, 2000:A.

England, D. "Developments in prison administration." In J. W. Murphy and J. E. Dison. *Are Prisons Any Better? Twenty Years of Correctional Reform.* Beverly Hills, CA: Sage, 1990:61–75.

Erikson, E. "Youth: Fidelity and diversity." In E. Erickson (ed.). *The Challenge of Youth.* New York: Doubleday, 1965:1–28.

Farkas, M. A. "Correctional officer attitudes toward inmates and working with inmates in a 'get tough' era." *Journal of Criminal Justice* 27(6) 1999:495–506.

Fitzgerald, M., and J. Sim. *British Prisons.* London: Basil Blackwell, 1982.

Fleischer, M. S. *Warehousing Violence.* Beverly Hills, CA: Sage, 1989.

Forst, B. "Prosecution and sentencing." In J. Q. Wilson and J. Petersilia (eds.). *Crime.* San Francisco: ICS Press, 1994: 363–86.

Gainsborough, J., and M. Maurer. *Diminishing Returns: Crime and Incarceration in the 1990s.* Washington, DC: The Sentencing Project, September 2000.

Gendreau, P., and R. R. Ross. "Effective correctional treatment: Bibliotherapy for cynics." In R. R. Ross and P. Gendreau (eds.). *Effective Correctional Treatment.* Toronto: Butterworth, 1980:3–36.

Gerard, R. E. "The ten commandments of unit management." *Corrections Today* (April 1991):34–36.

Gibbs, J. J., L. A. Maiello, K. S. Kolb, J. Garofalo, F. Adler, and S. R. Costello. *Stress, Setting, and Satisfaction: The Final Report of the Man-Jail Transactions Project.* Rutgers University School of Criminal Justice, 1983.

Goffman, E. *Asylums.* New York: Anchor Books, 1961.

Grant, J. D. "From 'living learning' to 'learning to live': An extension of social therapy." In H. Toch (ed.). *Therapeutic Communities in Corrections.* New York: Praeger, 1980:41–49.

Greenhouse, L. "Supreme Court roundup; Justices allow segregation of inmates with HIV." *The New York Times,* January 19, 2000.

Hammett, T. M., L. Harrold, M. Gross, and J. Epstein. *1992 Update: HIV/AIDS in Correctional Facilities: Issues and Options.* National Institute of Justice, January 1994.

Hawkins, G. *The Prison: Policy and Practice.* Chicago: University of Chicago Press, 1976.

Hawkins, G. "Prison labor and prison industries." In M. Tonry and N. Morris (eds.). *Crime and Justice Annual.* Chicago: University of Chicago Press, 1983:85–181.

Hawkins, R., and G. P. Alpert. *American Prison Systems: Punishment and Justice.* Englewood Cliffs, NJ: Prentice-Hall, 1989.

Hawthorne, J. "Our barbarous penal system." *Hearst's Magazine* (1913):205–212.

Hepburn, J. R., and C. A. Albonetti. "Team classification in state correctional institutions: Its association with inmate and staff attitudes." *Criminal Justice and Behavior* 5 (1) 1978:63–73.

Herrick, E. "The surprising direction of violence in prison." *Corrections Conpendium* 14 (6) 1989:1 & 4–17.

Hirschorn, S. I., and H. D. Burck. "Utilizing inmates as group leaders in the admissions phase of incarceration." *Offender Rehabilitation* 2 (1) 1977:45–52.

Irwin, J. *Prisons in Turmoil.* Boston: Little, Brown, 1980.

Jacobs, J. B. *Stateville: The Penitentiary in Mass Society.* Chicago: University of Chicago Press, 1977.

Janis, I. L. *Stress and Frustration.* New York: Harcourt Brace Jovanovich, 1969.

Johnson, R., and S. Price. "The complete correctional officer: Human service and the human environment of prison." *Criminal Justice and Behavior* 8 (3) 1981:343–73.

Jones, M. "Desirable features of a therapeutic community in a prison." In H. Toch (ed.). *Therapeutic Communities in Corrections.* New York: Praeger, 1980:34–40.

Jurik, N. C., and M. C. Musheno. "The internal crises of corrections: Professionalization and the work environment." *Justice Quarterly* 3 (4) 1986:457–80.

Kalmthout, A. M. V., and D. van der Landen. "Breda Prison, Holland: From water cell to container cell—The state of the Dutch prison." In D. Whitfield (ed.). *The State of the Prisons—200 Years On.* London & New York: Routledge, 1991:88–118.

Levinson, R. B. "Developments in the classification process: Quay's aims approach." *Criminal Justice and Behavior* 15 (1) 1988a:24–38.

Levinson, R. B. "Try softer." In R. Johnson and H. Toch (eds.). *The Pains of Imprisonment*. Prospect Heights, IL: Waveland Press, 1988b:241–56.

Levinson, R. B. "The future of unit management." *Corrections Today* (April 1991):44–48.

Levinson, R. B. *Unit Management in Prisons and Jails*. Latham, MD: American Correctional Association, 1998.

Lin, A. C. *Reform in the Making: The Implementation of Social Policy in Prison*. Princeton: Princeton University Press, 2000.

Logan, C. H. "Well kept: Comparing quality of confinement in private and public prisons." *The Journal of Criminal Law and Criminology* 83 (3) 1992:577–613.

Logan, C. H., and G. G. Gaes. "Meta-analysis and the rehabilitation of punishment." *Justice Quarterly* 10 (2) 1993:245–63.

Martinson, R. "What works? Questions and answers about prison reform." *The Public Interest* (Spring 1974):22–55.

Moos, R. H. *Evaluating Treatment Environments: A Social Ecological Approach*. New York: John Wiley, 1974.

NIC—National Institute of Corrections. *Prison Medical Care: Special Needs Populations and Cost Control*. Longmont, CO: U.S. Department of Justice, 1997.

NJADD 2000–2001. *National Jail and Adult Detention Directory*, Eighth Edition. Lanham, MD: American Correctional Association, 2000.

Nossiter A. "Making hard time harder: States cut jail TV and sports." *The New York Times* (September 17, 1994):1 & 11.

Piehl, A. M. , and J. J. DiIulio. " `Does prison pay?' revisited: Returning to the scene of the crime." *The Brookings Review* 13 (1) 1995:21–25.

Pierson, T. A. "The Missouri experience: One state's success with unit management." *Corrections Today* (April 1991):24–30.

Quay, H. C. *Managing Adult Inmates: Classification for Housing and Program Assignments*. American Correctional Association, 1984.

Regens, J. L., and W. G. Hobson. "Inmate self-government and attitude toward change: An assessment of participation effects." *Evaluation Quarterly* 2 1978:455–79.

Reisig, M. D. "Rates of disorder in higher-custody state prisons: A comparative analysis of managerial practices." *Crime and Delinquency* 44 (2) 1998:229–44.

Reitzel, L. R., and B. L. Harju. "Influence of locus of control and custody level on intake and prison-adjustment depression." *Criminal Justice and Behavior* 27 2000:625–644.

Rierden, A. *The Farm: A Life Inside a Women's Prison*. Amherst, MA: University of Massachusetts Press, 1997.

Scharf, P. "Democratic education and the prevention of delinquency." In *U.S. Department of Health, Education and Welfare, National Institute of Education, School Crime and Disruption: Prevention Models*. Washington, DC: Government Printing Office, 1978.

Scharf, P. "Democracy and justice in a prison therapeutic community." In H. Toch (ed.). *Therapeutic Communities in Corrections*. New York: Praeger, 1980:94–102.

Seymour, J. "Environmental sanctuaries for susceptible prisoners." In R. Johnson and H. Toch (eds.). *The Pains of Imprisonment*. Prospect Heights, IL: Waveland Press, 1988:267–84.

Silberman, M. *A World of Violence: Corrections in America*. Belmont, CA: Wadsworth, 1995.

Smith, D. E. "Local corrections: A profile of inmate concerns." *Criminal Justice and Behavior* 11 (1) 1984:75–99.

Smith, W. A., and C. E. Fenton. "Unit management in a penitentiary: A practical experience." *Federal Probation* 42 (3) 1978:40–46.

Stephan, J. J. *Census of State and Federal Correctional Facilities, 1995.* Washington, DC: U.S. Department of Justice, Office of Justice Programs, Bureau of Justice Statistics, 1999.

Thigpen, M. L., and S. M. Hunter. *Hospice and Palliative Care in Prison: Special Issues in Corrections.* Longmont, CO: U.S. Department of Justice, 1998.

Toch, H. *Living in Prison: The Ecology of Survival.* New York: Free Press, 1977.

Toch, H. "The therapeutic community as community." In H. Toch (ed.). *Therapeutic Communities in Corrections.* New York: Praeger, 1980:3–20.

Toch, H. "A revisionist view of prison reform." *Federal Probation* (1981):3–9.

Toch, H. "Enhancing the quality of survival in prison." Paper delivered at the Symposium on Institutions and Dependent Populations, in the Nelson A. Rockefeller Institute of Government, Albany, NY, April 1984.

Toch, H. "Warehouses for people?" *Annals of the American Academy of Political and Social Science* 478 (March 1985):58–72.

Toch, H. "Rewarding convicted offenders." *Federal Probation* (June 1988a):42–48.

Toch, H. "Studying and reducing stress." In R. Johnson and H. Toch (eds.). *The Pains of Imprisonment.* Prospect Heights, IL: Waveland Press, 1988b:25–44.

Toch, H. "Democratizing prisons." *The Prison Journal* 73 (1) 1994a:62–72.

Toch, H., "Inmate involvement in prison governance." Paper presented at the 12th Annual Conference of the New Jersey Chapter of the American Correctional Association, October 24, 1994(b).

Tonry, M. *Malign Neglect: Race, Crime, and Punishment in America.* New York: Oxford University Press, 1995.

Tonry, M., and J. Petersilia. "American prisons at the beginning of the twenty-first century." In M. Tonry and J. Petersilia (eds.). *Prisons.* Chicago: University of Chicago Press, 1999:1–16.

Unit Management Guidelines. *Achieving Leadership Excellence in Victorian Prisons.* Office of Corrections, Victoria, 1990.

Walsh, E. "Strapped small towns try to lock up prisons: Building boom is seen as economic salvation." *The Washington Post* (December 24, 1994):A3.

Weiner, R. I. "Management strategies to reduce stress in prison: Humanizing correctional environments." In R. Johnson and H. Toch (eds.). *The Pains of Imprisonment.* Prospect Heights, IL: Waveland Press, 1988:299–309.

Wilson, J. Q. "Crime and public policy." In J. Q. Wilson and J. Petersilia (eds.). *Crime.* San Francisco: ICS Press, 1994:489–507.

Wright, K. N. "Developing the prison environment inventory." *Journal of Research in Crime and Delinquency* 22 (1985):257–77.

Wright, K. N. "A study of individual, environmental, and interactive effects in explaining adjustment to prison." *Justice Quarterly* 8 (2) 1991:217–42.

Wright, K. N. *Effective Prison Leadership.* Binghamton, NY: William Neil Publishing, 1994.

Wright, K. N., with J. M. Harris and N. Woika. *Improving Correctional Classification Through a Study of the Placement of Inmates in Environmental Settings.* Final Report, NIJ Grant 83-1J-CX-00 1 1, 1985.

Zamble, E. "Behavior and adaptation in long-term prison inmates: Descriptive longitudinal results." *Criminal Justice and Behavior* 19 (4) 1992:409–425.

Zamble, E., and F. Porporino. "Coping, imprisonment, and rehabilitation." *Criminal Justice and Behavior* 17 1990:53–70.

Zamble, E., F. Porporino, and J. Kalotay. *An Analysis of Coping Behavior in Prison Inmates.* Ministry of the Solicitor General of Canada: Programs Branch User Report, 1984.

Zimring, F. E., and G. Hawkins. *The Scale of Imprisonment.* Chicago: University of Chicago Press, 1991.

10

❖

Better Living in the Free Community

Prison Programs and the Cultivation of Coping Competence

Prisons have had a checkered past when it comes to correctional programs. We reached a low point in the 1970s and 1980s, when it was widely believed—in society and even in the corrections field—that treatment was dead, that "nothing works" and hence that nothing constructive could be done for prisoners. Correctional programs have made something of a comeback over the last decade or so, but the overall picture is still a discouraging one. The typical state prison, for example, offers few programs of substance. To make matters worse, existing programs are often mandatory and of limited appeal to inmates.[1] Most of these programs focus on an inmate's past life and future prospects; they seek to rectify yesterday's problems in order to build a better tomorrow. Too often, however, the struggle for personal survival *today,* in the here-and-now world of the prison, distracts prisoners from the few rehabilitation programs that do exist and might be of benefit to them. To make prison programs more relevant and useful, corrections must (1) operate prisons in which stress remains within manageable limits and is handled maturely, and (2) offer an adequate number of programs that enhance the prisoner's capacity to cope maturely with life stresses, both now in prison and later in the free world. Prisoners live in prison but all hope one day to be released; the vast majority will in fact be released from prison sooner or later. To appeal widely to prisoners, then, programs must hold out the promise of better living in the prison community and, later, in the free community as well.

Reforming criminals is a formidable job. Persistent felons, who are the majority in any prison population, are especially hard to reach. Yet these offenders, Maruna's research shows, typically lack an "enthusiastic commitment to crime." Rather, their criminality is marked by a "ubiquitous feeling of help-lessness," as if they are "doomed to deviance" by a world that is set against them.[2] They are desperately in need of help if they are to maintain hope for a constructive future. As Conrad reminds us,

> a criminal career is a desperate career, a career in which hope must be satisfied by transient "scores," ultimately and inescapably terminated by the successive disasters of apprehension, prosecution, conviction, and incarceration. Anyone experiencing this sequence may well abandon hope of rejoining the conventional society, if he ever had any such aspiration. Most prisons do little to turn the convict from desperation to hope.[3]

Hope is a rare commodity in many of today's prisons. The view that "nothing works" in corrections—a view still held by a some prison practitioners and by many prison critics—permits us to warehouse without pretense and to call it justice.[4]

The notion that "nothing works" originates with Robert Martinson: Based on a survey of studies of correctional programs conducted in 1973, Martinson concluded that "with few and isolated exceptions, the rehabilitative efforts that have been reported so far have had no appreciable effect on recidivism."[5] A similar conclusion was reached a few years later by the Panel on Research on Rehabilitative Techniques convened by the National Academy of Sciences.[6] Why do many programs fail? Many fail (and here I am thinking of standard educational and vocational programs) because they offer too little too late to attract the attention of offenders and to motivate them to change their lives. These programs often seem irrelevant in the prison context. On the one hand, these programs can be notoriously tedious and boring, almost painful in themselves. On the other, the quality of one's prison life normally is unaffected by performance in school or work. To the extent that prisoners participate in such programs and learn something from them, these programs are unlikely, on their own, to remedy the deficits that account for their poor adjustment. They emerge from these programs not as reformed citizens, but as more literate muggers, as robbers who can second as carpenters, or as prostitutes who can quote Shakespeare. Programs that seek to reform offenders, rather than merely tinker with some limited aspect of their behavioral repertoire, fail for different reasons. They attempt too much. Rehabilitative goals are defined in utopian terms, with inmates forced to endure programs that do not address their real concerns.

Group therapy is perhaps the most common form of correctional intervention that aims to reform the person. Braly, an ex-prisoner, has written a novel that touches on the core problem of this method; Manocchio and Dunn, who describe their experiences as therapist and patient, reinforce Braly's observations.[7] In both accounts, the therapist is saddled with a group that has been assigned to him for no other reason than that its members must someday appear before a parole board and claim to be rehabilitated. Undaunted, each therapist asks the group to explore the dynamics of their criminality and, in the process, reveal and examine intimate details from the past. For each therapist, the aim is to elucidate and transform the characters of the reluctant clients; the goal is to produce some semblance of middle-class citizenry. Most of the inmates, however, want no part of the therapeutic agenda. The therapist's middle-class man, they know, will be eaten alive on the yard. So they mock the "hoosiers" who wallow in guilt and self-pity, and they generally subvert the therapeutic process through long silences, diversionary tactics, and caustic humor. Most resent being forced into therapy to secure early release, and make little effort to hide this from the therapist. A cold war ensues. Little that can properly be called therapy takes place.

Note that there are some prisoners in these groups who are willing to explore their personal problems. The treatment climate is ruined, however, by the more numerous malcontents who (quite plausibly) view the entire enterprise as an exercise in coercion that is patently irrelevant to their prison lives. When these therapy groups do take up matters pertaining to prison life, the cynical inmates have nothing to say. Those who talk are seen as stupid (they don't know enough to shut up when officials pump them for information) or untrustworthy (they are "rats" who turn in their fellows to please the staff). The result is that the amenable therapy clients are, at a minimum, ridiculed by their peers. Some of these prisoners may nevertheless persevere and ultimately benefit from the treatment experience, but others may be psychologically harmed by it. The nonamenable prisoners are apt to view the treatment as a waste of time. They will be either untouched or embittered by the experience. It is hardly surprising that overall recidivism rates for the treatment groups would be unimproved, or even made worse, by such correctional programs.

But overall recidivism rates can be misleading. Some rehabilitation programs do indeed work for some offenders under some conditions. The problem is that differential effects are often masked by classification and assignment practices that mix amenable and nonamenable inmates in the same program. As we have just noted, such mixing of offenders contaminates the treatment climate and makes it less likely that the amenable prisoners will benefit from treatment. It also means that the predictable failures of the nonamenable prisoners will be counted as failures of the program, when in point of fact those inmates should not have been there in the first place.[8]

Differential treatment effects have not been considered systematically in correctional practice or research.[9] This omission means that both the impact and the potential of correctional treatment are likely to be understated. Research that takes account of differential treatment effects—that examines the interplay of risk, need, and responsiveness—reveals that programs can reduce recidivism, sometimes substantially, with a range of male and female offenders in a range of penal settings.[10] "At the very least," Gendreau and Ross conclude, following an extensive literature review, "the recent trends in the literature support a grudging acceptance of the renewed possibilities of a potent rehabilitation agenda."[11]

Moreover, ecological factors relating to the inmate's general prison adjustment, which can make or break a treatment regime, have been largely ignored in the treatment area. When person-environment matches in living and working areas reinforce proper program placements, it is reasonable to suppose that the result will be the development, on a large scale, of constructive niches (see Chapter Nine). In these supportive milieus, trust is more readily established. Prisoners may feel secure enough to take the risks necessary to explore delicate matters of adjustment. Fellow participants may serve as helpful colleagues rather than cagey adversaries. Mature coping may become the norm. Under these propitious conditions, differential program effects would be substantially enhanced.

Programs must also be thought of in organizational terms. Their "fit" with a given prison regime is crucial to success or failure. Ignoring organizational dynamics has resulted in what Lin has termed "garish mismanagement" of prison programs, featuring "internecine warfare between staff, outright subversion of programs by prisoners or administrators, untrained staff directed to run a program, or trained staff who are not given the latitude to act." It is fair to say that "One would not expect programs implemented—or misimplemented—in these ways to work."[12]

Prison programs have at least two organizational constituencies: staff and inmates. Maintaining order is the preeminent concern of prison officials, especially correctional officers, who constitute the vast majority of any prison's line personnel. As Lin has reminded us, programs are always suspect in the eyes of security staff, at least at the outset, because they "threaten the sense of order in prisons." That threat is "not so much because [programs] breed disorder, but because they often represent a challenge to established ways of keeping order. They disturb routines, they introduce new ideas, and they do not compensate for the disruption they cause."[13] To work effectively, then, "programs must fit into confinement purposes—must be incorporated into a prison's set of strategies for keeping order." Otherwise, they will be "abandoned or marginalized" by officials and will become, as a result, less useful or appealing to inmates.[14]

Prisoners look at the prison and its programs from their distinctive vantage point. For them, a key consideration is alleviating boredom. Prisoners find themselves with time on their hands, more time than they can readily manage on their own. Naturally, they look around the prison world for ways to fill that time. Programs are one option among many, including exercise, hobbies, clubs, gangs and other groups (for women, prison families), and the various illicit activities available on the prison yard (see Chapters Five and Six). To compete for the attention of prisoners, programs must appeal to their self-interest in direct and immediate ways. "Their participation in programs," Lin's research reveals, "comes not because they have been encouraged by the staff or seen the error of their ways, but because they have decided that they will benefit, in both short- and long-term ways, from being in a program."[15] To capture the attention of prison's captives, Lin continues, programs must "keep prisoners busy, and busy in ways that prisoners believe they benefit from."[16]

Adopting an organizational view of programs suggests that program evaluation may be more complicated than one might first suppose. Ideally, programs should not be evaluated in the abstract or across the board because each program exists in a specific organizational context.[17] Programs, like cell blocks or workshops or yards, do not exist in isolation; they are always part of a larger environment, which in turn has a rich and variable ecology. The meaning and import of prison programs are thus determined by how they are adapted to the prisons in which they are offered and how the prisons incorporate or accommodate the programs they house. Thus, "it is not merely that rehabilitation programs receive different levels of support in different prisons," though this is of course true, "but that they are understood differently in different prisons as well."[18]

When programs are understood differently in different environments, moreover, we can safely assume that the specific interactional dynamics that compose the intervention are different as well. Although it complicates matters enormously, it is wise to remember that programs are not things or commodities that are experienced in the same ways by all people. As Maruna notes,

> the individual client does not experience some undifferentiated 'program,' like behavior therapy or Alcoholics Anonymous (AA). Every individual experiences and interprets unique social interactions within a program setting . . . every intervention or program actually consists of thousands of different micromechanisms of change (e.g., confrontation, learning to trust, and self-reevaluation). Whereas macrolevel research asks, 'Does rehabilitation work?' or 'Does group therapy with offenders work?' this microlevel research starts a few thousand steps back and asks, for instance, 'How do different individuals tend to respond to direct confrontations of their behavior?' By gradually accumulating knowledge about these micromechanisms of change (hence opening the black box), researchers may be able to develop a more theory-driven agenda on effective programming. . . .[19]

Regrettably, we are not at the point where we can point to research that allows us to examine with much precision the micromechanisms of correctional work. (But we are moving in the direction. Mature coping, for example, can be thought of as an underlying theory of personal reform that can guide assessments of differential program effects. Research by Castellano and Soderstrom reveals that mature coping can be reliably measured by a host of instruments sensitive enough to track personal change over time.)[20]

Given the varying ecological, organizational, and interpersonal connotations and forms that can be assumed by programs, it is clear that there is no simple formula for program success, in prison or in the free world.[21] But we do know that communication is key—that is, that communication is a necessary if not sufficient condition for program success, especially in prisons. Communication breaks down the "us versus them" solidarity found in some organizations and in most prisons. Solidarity (in the prison, solidarity reinforces a caste system) is inimical to programs because it generates invidious competition for scarce resources and a climate of mutual hostility. Communication gives "staff an opportunity to talk to and understand the prisoners as individuals."[22] These more personal and less stereotypical interactions help establish a climate that is supportive of serious programs efforts; and programs, when taken seriously, promote more healthy communication among individuals and contribute to the development of an ethic of human service that is apt to spread beyond the program to the larger organization (see Chapter Eight). "As inmates are encouraged to look to structured institutional options to fill their time," notes Lin,

> the staff they look to for assistance are often correctional officers, whom they see every day, rather than teachers or program supervisors, with whom they are less likely to be familiar. Correctional officers, in turn, will informally incorporate this into their job description. Thus an officer is quite likely to explain that he deals with inmates by letting "them know I'm here to help them when I can, and I'll go higher [take the question to a supervisor] if I have to get a question answered.[23]

Fully four in ten of the officers in the prison's studied by Lin "named 'helping inmates' as part of their job description, or simply said that what they liked about the job was 'working with the inmates.' "[24]

Communication promotes teamwork among staff, building mutual respect and support. "The willingness to use communication as a way of resolving conflicts," states Lin, "makes it possible for both programs and custody to be part of the legitimate work of the prison." One reason is that "staff are more likely to be aware of the needs of departments other than their own, and more respectful toward their coworkers." Another is that "each group is secure in its own niche within the prison." Each has a valued role, so "there is no need to anticipate or look for weaknesses in the other's position" or to see every conflict as inevitably a matter of protecting turf.[25] Inmates note such collaborative arrangements among staff and take it as a sign that programs are a genuine good that is offered for their betterment, rather an than empty exercise used to manipulate and control them.[26]

A final point about program implementation in organizational context: Good programs require commitment and follow-through. Just as inmates must be monitored in their adjustments (as we noted in the last chapter), so must programs be monitored in their implementation, that is, in their adaptation to the particular penal environment in which they are embedded. Those who monitor programs, moreover, must understand that they are "fitting a policy to a particular context—not demanding that established practices and beliefs make way for a policy." The result is collaboration. "Policy thus becomes a joint project, incorporating the aims and instruments specified by policymakers, but incorporating as well the preconceptions and the interests of the world in which staff and target groups must operate."[27] The changes we seek in corrections require a process of mutual accommodation—of programs adapting to a given prison's staff and inmates, and of staff and inmates adapting to a given prison's programs. Policymakers, in turn, must build in allowances for this ongoing, interactive implementation process. Change of this sort is not easy, but it is encouraging to note that many wardens are at least open to these possibilities. As it happens, wardens find much of their job satisfaction in the programs and human services their institutions deliver and are inclined, when it is feasible, to downplay custodial approaches.[28]

Martinson later repudiated the simplistic notion that "nothing works", but it is telling that this view ever held sway.[29] The "nothing works" premise, reduced to its essentials, should satisfy no one. It assumes that offenders "are incapable of re-learning or acquiring new behaviors," a belief as untenable as it is self-serving.[30] It is indeed ironic, as Gendreau and Ross observe,

> that while we have often heard the clinical observation that many offenders today seem to avoid responsibility for their behaviors, the fact is that if we persist in the verdict that treatment is unsuccessful then the "nothing works" doctrine also encourages the correctional system to avoid responsibility. By labeling the offender as untreatable we make it apparent to one and all that we cannot be held responsible for his improvement or his deterioration.[31]

A corollary view labels prisons as unregenerate institutions, incapable of anything other than dehumanizing those who enter its walls—a "nothing works" milieu offering "nothing works" programs. We are all off the hook, then, except the prisoners who suffer the consequences of our self-proclaimed impotence.

COLLABORATIVE TRAINING

Though the problems of prisons are serious, as we have seen, they are tractable. The same holds for the problems of prisoners. Robert B. Levinson, a psychologist with years of experience researching rehabilitation programs in prisons, tells us that

> Offenders enter prisons with a variety of deficits. That is, some are socially or morally inept; others are intellectually or vocationally handicapped; some have emotional hang-ups that stem from internal psychological problems and/or have externally generated deficiencies as a consequence of environmental or family circumstances; and still others have a mixture composed of varying proportions of some or even all of these.[32]

These deficits, which collectively express themselves in the immaturity we have examined at some length (see Chapter Four), can often be addressed and resolved by the inmates themselves—with guidance from the staff. "The role of staff," observes Levinson, "is to help prisoners help themselves." It is not the staff's business to cure prisoners of psychological maladies or to overhaul their characters, but rather to "assist them in identifying where their deficits are and encourage them to participate in programs that are designed to help fill in the gaps." At issue is neither involuntary treatment (the hallmark of the rehabilitative ideal) nor calculated punishment (the hallmark of the warehouse prison).

Instead, a *voluntary collaborative training enterprise* is sought. Here, inmates define themselves as amenable to help by seeking the program. They ally themselves with the staff, whose express function is to promote better coping by helping to "train inmates in the use of alternative ways of responding to the pressures of living" in both the prison and the free community.[33]

Staff engaged in collaborative training do not treat disorders or punish indiscretions. The focus of their activities "is not on seeking methods to eliminate 'wrong' behavior," but instead "becomes one of helping prisoners develop a more appropriate repertoire of responses."[34] One of the more potent means of doing this is for staff to practice what they preach, that is, to be living examples of mature behavior under stress. This obligation may be too often honored in the breach. Yet constructive role modeling is quite consistent with how many line officers, the primary staff group with whom inmates come into regular contact, attempt to play their role (see Chapter Eight).

Staff can also draw upon a small but growing body of programs that promote mature behavior in prison. Such programs successfully "develop a more appropriate repertoire of responses" among a fairly wide range of prisoners, "either reducing anti-social behavior in the institution or . . . enhancing the offenders' academic achievement or industrial productivity."[35] Of special interest are those interventions that promote mature responses in the face of interpersonal stress, helping many prisoners to relax under pressure[36] and to relate to others, particularly figures of authority, in a more calm and rational way.[37]

The characteristics of these successful programs conform closely to the notion of collaborative training.[38] They include the following:

1. Successful programs were not imposed on the offenders in authoritarian fashion but involved the offenders in program planning.

2. Successful programs sought to strengthen prosocial behaviors rather than attempting directly to reduce the frequency of inappropriate or anti-social acts. They thus avoided the pitfall of strengthening anti-social behavior by giving it undue attention and avoided generating expectancies for anti-social behavior.[39]

3. Successful programs neutralized the offender's peer group or mobilized them in support of program goals.

Successful programs must, in addition, offer "intensive services" directed at "criminogenic factors" (such as impulsivity) and delivered to "high-risk clients" who are assessed for "responsivity" (or receptivity) to the program and the staff offering it.[40] Low-risk clients, it turns out, often do not need services, and high-risk clients are more likely to benefit from services if they are given in substantial doses. The goal, broadly speaking, is to make conventional living a competitive alternative to a life of crime. Most often, this is done by reinforcing and modeling strategies of conventional living, and by providing sufficient coping skills to allow inmates to adapt effectively in the conventional world. In particular, offenders must be helped to think clearly about problems and to exert self-control.[41]

Broadly speaking, effective programs are characterized by what Gendreau has termed "integrity," meaning that they deliver on their promises in a credible and caring way.[42] To maintain integrity, in turn, programs must have the qualities of formal niches; they need their own space, their own culture or climate, and a degree of independence from the larger prison. (Note that functional unit management provides a ready administrative vehicle for the provision of formal niches for correctional programs.) Offenders, voluntarily involved in meaningful programs that promote a range of prosocial skills, tend to become more constructively autonomous and, as a result, are less likely to recidivate.

Levinson has described the implementation of Norval Morris's "model prison" at the federal prison in Butner, North Carolina.[43] This program of voluntary, facilitated change, housed in functional units, is a prototype of collaborative training.[44] Marked improvements in program participation and prison behavior came in the wake of this reform. These inmates, with help from the staff, coped maturely with imprisonment. There was little violence; candid and constructive efforts at problem solving and relationship building were the norm.[45] Some of these lessons in mature living may have carried over into the free world, resulting in a modest decrease in recidivism.[46] Additionally, the Butner graduates obtained and kept better jobs while on release, stayed out of prison longer than other releasees, and turned to crimes that were, on the whole, less serious than those of other former inmates.[47] If personal reform is a matter of successive approximations of conventional lifestyles in the free world, then the Butner experiment is an important correctional intervention.

Toch has done seminal work on self-management as a means to self-control, particularly in the context of violence among police and criminal populations.[48] The core insight of this work—which is shared with all subsequently developed coping programs, including those with a cognitive focus, to be discussed below—is that people can learn to monitor and control themselves in social environments. They can become "social scientists" in the sense that they learn, with the support of peers in a group context, to objectively observe and then control their own conduct in a range of social situations. As Toch and Grant have observed, "By sharing a review of one's patterned problems with one's peers and then sharing with such peers an accountability strategy for modifying one's pattern, a person can move through cognitive problem solving, to what Maxwell Jones called 'emotional social learning.' "[49] The beneficiaries of such programs are transformed into autonomous actors, persons whose minds are liberated by insight and whose daily behavior is constrained—or better, channeled—by emotional bonds to others.

An explicit focus on developing environments that support mature coping is advocated by Zamble and Porporino. They envision a prison "comprised of a set of modular units" that are, in effect, functional units. In these supportive living environments, programs on coping would predominate. Such programs would

> include training in problem recognition, problem analysis, and weighing and choosing coping alternatives. Because it is clear that inmates need to

learn not only *when* to use certain types of actions but also *how* to use them, there should also be training in a variety of specific coping skills such as negotiation, objectification of situations, and cognitive reevaluation.[50]

Inmates would also be helped to organize time more productively, and, as needed, offered "specific behavioral treatment for alcohol and drug abuse, using an approach consistent with the overall emphasis on coping."[51] Programs would begin at the start of a prisoner's term, when motivation for change is strongest; there would be a concentrated programming effort at the end of the prisoner's term and just after release to facilitate reintegration into the free world.[52] Ideally, functional units, if not the larger prisons in which they are embedded, would reinforce mature coping, operating as " 'total environments' that change coping behavior rather than ones that have no effect or that mostly maintain maladaptive patterns."[53]

COPING: INNOVATIVE AND PROMISING PROGRAMS

A promising innovation that systematically and comprehensively addresses general deficiencies in coping that are common among criminal populations has been undertaken in Canada under the rubric of Cognitive Thinking Skills Program (CTSP), which is the core or foundation of the Living Skills Program (terms I will often use synonymously since there is intentional overlap across modules to facilitate learning). CTSP, and indeed the entire Living Skills Program, focuses on autonomous self-management as an alternative to destructive criminal lifestyles. The various components of Living Skills Program and CTSP "were designed to be available throughout the incarceration period in order to meet the offender's most relevant needs in the process of preparing for reintegration."[54] The aim is to develop coping competence—to promote mature coping so that offenders can adapt constructively to life in prison and in the free community.

As noted, CTSP is the core module of the Living Skills Program. Subsequent modules or programs tackle "living without violence," "family life/parenting skills," "anger/emotional management," "leisure education," and "community integration skills," which include skills relevant to finding and keeping a job and a place to live. It is considered axiomatic in this program that "cognitive inadequacies" are the main sources of criminal deviance.[55] (These inadequacies, in turn, are typically caused by problems in self-control, a key feature of immature coping.)[56] "Offenders with cognitive inadequacies," we learn, "are likely to evidence major difficulties in social adjustment."[57] They are impulsive and tend to act before they think. When they do stop to think, they think poorly. They blame others and fail to see their own impact on others. Their thought processes are variously described as "simplistic and illogical" and "exceptionally shallow, narrow, and rigid."[58] They are egocentric, unable to see the world as others see it or indeed to see others as full-blooded human beings.

Insensitive to others, they misread social situations. They fail to anticipate problems and are unable to foresee solutions. They cannot, if you will, think their way through to a solution of a social problem.

This description of the general patterns of thinking and behavior among criminals is familiar to us from our review of the criminological literature in Chapter Four. The good news is that the Canadian program establishes that many if not most offenders can be *taught to think clearly* and *cope competently* across the range of life situations they will encounter in prison and in the free world.[59] This is not, moreover, a one-way treatment process in which experts act on sick or defective inmates; while the curriculum is a standard one, implementation involves a two-way collaborative process in which staff both *train* offenders and serve as *role models* for clear thinking and mature coping. As noted by the Canadian authorities,

> the individuals chosen as trainers were those who had enough empathic ability to understand what the offender thinks and feels, those who were able to model the kind of effective reasoning and problem solving that they hoped offenders would acquire, and those who were able to communicate a substantial repertoire of socio-cognitive skills concretely and clearly.[60]

Offenders are given opportunities in group sessions to digest and relate program content to their own lives. Experiences in prison—with other inmates and especially with staff—are seen as opportunities to learn and rehearse various facets of mature coping. In point of fact, each staff member within the prison, and not just those directly involved in the program, "must be able to model effective reasoning and problem solving" and hence "must model that which they hope the offender will acquire in the program."[61] To work, then, the prison is treated as a living environment that is staffed by correctional officers (as opposed to custodial officers) and in which mature coping is explicitly encouraged and rewarded.

It is significant to note that, as at Butner, CTSP targeted high-risk and high-need offenders.[62] The methods of education and training are diverse and interesting, including such media and activities as visual aides, puzzles, games, reasoning exercises, role playing, and group discussions.[63] These activities resemble neither traditional treatment methods nor conventional educational approaches. Inmates may, as a result, feel safer and less threatened in these programs.[64] It is clear, in any case, that the offenders were much benefited by participation in CTSP. Based on a series of objective pre- and post-program attitudinal and skill measurement tests, Fabiano, Robinson, and Porporino report that "there is substantial evidence that those offenders who participated in the program increased their levels of cognitive skills and became less criminally oriented in their attitudes."[65] In particular, offenders "became more positive in their attitudes toward the law, courts and police, increased in their social perspective-taking abilities, improved in critical reasoning skills, and showed more capacity for [flexible] thinking."[66]

The participants in CTSP, moreover, perceived themselves to have made substantial strides. The program produced insight, in the sense that the offenders were able to apply the various curricula to their own lives in construct. For example, fully nine out of ten prisoners perceived themselves to improved in the following areas of personal adjustment:

Conversations with friends and others

Controlling anger and other emotions

Handling stress more effectively

Thinking through problems

Preventing jumping to conclusions

Considering others' perspectives and why they react

Patience and tolerance of self and others

Eighty percent of the inmates felt they had improved in the daunting area of "setting goals and planning life more effectively."[67]

Follow-up research with CTSP graduates indicates a statistically significant drop in recidivism, with a 20 percent rearrest rate for the program group and a 30 percent rate for the comparison group.[68] Focussing on high-risk offenders only, the figures are even more impressive: only 18 percent of the high-risk program group recidivated, compared with a 42 percent rate for the high-risk inmates among the comparison group.[69] As the program has been expanded and offered on demand in the Canadian system, results have remained positive but less impressive (the treatment group had a recidivism rate of 44.5% after more than a year in the free world; the control group had a recidivism rate of 50.1%[70]). It may be hard to offer CTSP on a large scale while maintaining program integrity, particularly matching amenable inmates with suitable staff and, further, maintaining a productive "fit" between the program environment and the larger prison's "strategies for keeping order."[71] How many empathic trainers who can model effective problem solving can there be in any one prison system?[72] Can one mount a program that requires intensive and ongoing communication between staff and inmates in every prison in a penal system? Be that as it may, CTSP offers promise as a correctional intervention. It is encouraging that CTSP has been adopted as a central program in the Canadian correctional system and has also been "implemented in the United States, Europe, Australia, and throughout the British Prison system."[73]

Other promising cognitive and behavioral programs exist as well, each with varying approaches to collaborative programming, and each sharing the goal that offenders become more autonomous. Favorable results have been reported for the Cognitive Self-Change Program, developed jointly by the National Institute of Justice and the U.S. Navy,[74] and for the Criminal Violence Program, which is modeled on the Cognitive Self-Change Program.[75] The Delaware Department of Corrections offers a Life Skills Program with a successful track record.[76] Of related interest are programs that deal with drug abuse (discussed later), which could be readily offered in conjunction with, or in addition to, cognitive-behavior programs such as CTSP.

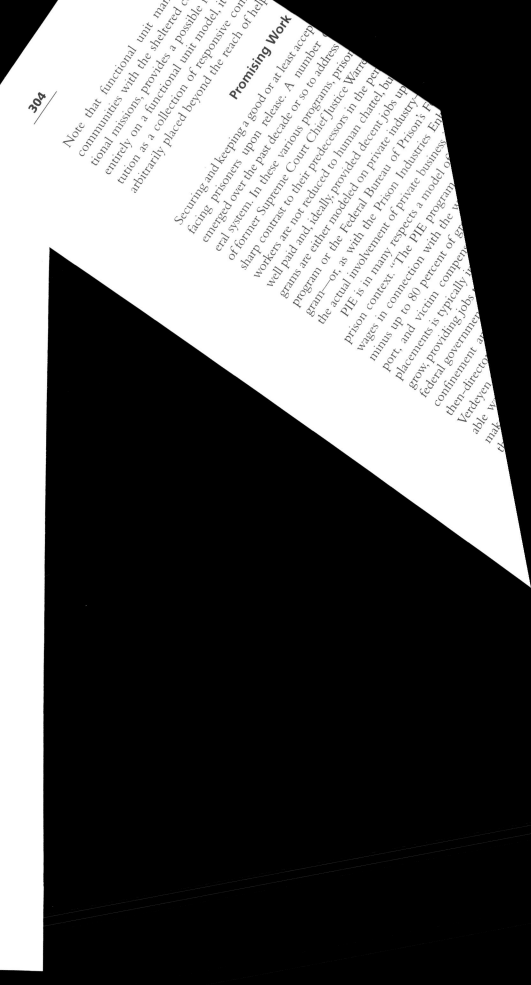

As noted earlier, important advances have been made in helping offenders control anger and aggression. (The most promising efforts, as one would expect, deal with the interplay of anger triggers, self-control, and cognitive style.[77]) Effective programs are also available for drug and alcohol abusers, who can be helped to manage their lives without resorting to these addictive substances. As we noted in Chapter One, drug offenders make up a sizeable segment of a typical prison population. Moreover, roughly two of every three criminals uses drugs regularly in the free world; fully one third of this group uses hard drugs like cocaine or heroin on a daily basis. By the time these offenders enter prisons, whether confined for drug offenses or for other felonies, they are "entrenched in a lifestyle that includes drugs and crime."[78] Often the drugs serve as an anesthetic for the pain and anger that characterize the dead-end lives of so many felons (see Chapter Four). It is of considerable import, then, that there are a number of programs with credible claims to success. (These include Key-Crest, Amity Right Turn, and Triad Drug Treatment, a residential drug treatment program offered by the Federal Bureau of Prisons). This area of research presents difficult measurement problems, and a number of programs that claimed substantial successes have been reevaluated and found wanting (including some reviewed in earlier editions of this book.[79]) It is, however, fair to conclude that drug treatment in prison "combined with aftercare may have dramatic effects, at least in the short run"—that is, for six to eighteen months. Longer term studies have yet to be reported.[80]

To work effectively, collaborative treatment programs must in effect become responsive (and hence therapeutic) communities. This is true independent of the specific content of these programs. The ethos in all such communities is one of self-help through helping others. Relations occur between and among inmates and staff, who function as equals in the program process; destructive stereotypes are shattered by continuing interpersonal contacts. The medium of helping sends an almost tangible message that each and every member of the community is a person of value. This message is profoundly anti-criminogenic. As Staub has observed, "We devalue those we harm and value those we help. As we come to value more highly the people we help and experience the satisfaction inherent in helping, we also come to see ourselves as more caring and helpful."[81] This new sense of oneself as a caring person, once it is firmly in place, readily generalizes to other situations and circumstances. One's self-image as a person who cares, in turn, can provide the basis for a prosocial identity, and can serve as a keen source of motivation to cope maturely in the course of one's life.

It is something of a paradox that these supportive environments, to retain their integrity, must become formal niches that are set apart from the mainline prison. Helping is, of course, an inclusive activity; a formal niche is, by definition, an exclusive undertaking. Yet "it is vital," observe Lipton, Falkin and Wexler, "for a therapeutic community in a prison to have living space and therapeutic areas isolated from the general prison population."[82] In the absence of such isolation, overcrowding or other pressures on the larger prison impinge on the program, destroying its social climate and with it, the ethos of helping.

Note that functional unit management, which readily provides responsive communities with the sheltered context they need to carry out their correctional missions, provides a possible resolution to our paradox. In a prison run entirely on a functional unit model, it is at least possible to envision the institution as a collection of responsive communities. In such a prison, no one is arbitrarily placed beyond the reach of help.

Promising Work Programs

Securing and keeping a good or at least acceptable job is one of the key challenges facing prisoners upon release. A number of promising work programs have emerged over the past decade or so to address this problem, particularly in the federal system. In these various programs, prisons once again become, in the words of former Supreme Court Chief Justice Warren Burger, "factories with fences." In sharp contrast to their predecessors in the penitentiary, however, today's prisoner-workers are not reduced to human chattel, but are typically well fed, well trained, well paid and, ideally, provided decent jobs upon release from prison.[83] Such programs are either modeled on private industry—for example, LEAA's Free Venture program or the Federal Bureau of Prison's Federal Prison Industries (FPI) program—or, as with the Prison Industries Enhancement Program (PIE), "require the actual involvement of private business in correctional industries."[84]

PIE is in many respects a model of free-world work and responsibility in a prison context. "The PIE program requires that the prisoner-workers receive wages in connection with the work they do at the prevailing local wage rate, minus up to 80 percent of gross wages for taxes, room and board, family support, and victim compensation funds."[85] A mechanism for post-release job placements is typically included in these programs. These programs continue to grow, providing jobs to inmates, earnings to companies, tax dollars to state and federal governments, and payments to defray the costs of the prisoner-worker's confinement and to support their families. "It's a win–win situation," PIE's then-director, Robert Verdeyen, claimed in a 1994 interview. Continuing, Verdeyen noted that "Inmates earn self-respect and, in some case, a considerable wage. Taxpayers win because inmates pay taxes from their incomes and make other contributions to the system."[86] Current financial figures indicate that PIE remains very much a win–win situation (a robust 21 million dollars has been paid in taxes by inmate workers since the inception of this program in 1979).[87] As a caveat, however, it should be noted that PIE and related programs employ a growing but still small fraction of any given prison population (the total number of inmates in PIE programs as June 30, 2000, is 3,826.[88]) And it is hard for even the best of these programs to provide the long-term support needed to help offenders establish themselves in conventional careers and go on to become self-supporting citizens.

The Federal Prison Industries program, marketed and best known under the trade name UNICOR, has met with consistent and continuing success. (As noted earlier, the success of this program is at the heart of the decent living conditions found at such federal prisons as Lompoc.) The UNICOR program is a "wholly owned, nonappropriated Government corporation" and is run much like a regular business, except that the goal is not to maximize profits (though the operation is profitable); the goal is to maximize the employment and training of prisoners.[89] UNICOR "was created to provide work for inmates, instill a work ethic for individuals with little past work experience or training, and teach inmates skills so that they will be better prepared to return to the community."[90] The Federal prison system also provides vocational training. A recent controlled study of inmates who worked in UNICOR or received vocational training revealed that these inmates were less likely to violate prison rules (and when they did, to commit less serious rule violations than other inmates), and more likely to be rated as autonomous and responsible by officials. On release, these inmates (male and female) made better adjustments than other inmates. They were more likely to land jobs in the community and to get better-paying jobs than other inmates. Their rates of recidivism were lower than that of controls, and this important finding was described as "both statistically significant and substantively meaningful."[91] A follow up study, involving subjects who were released for between eight and twelve years (a remarkably long period for recidivism research) produced positive results, at least for male inmates.[92] Enhanced autonomy in prison, bred by work and by education for work, carried over to the free world, promoting more mature adjustment there as well.

COLLABORATIVE TRAINING
AND CONTRACTUAL PROGRAMS

A collaborative training model of corrections is quite adaptable. It lends itself most readily to programming under determinate sentencing schemes. Here, prisoners are released on a given date whether or not they participate in programs. They would collaborate with the staff in a purely voluntary manner, with nothing to gain but the benefits of the programs themselves. In this context, the programs—and the inmates—would speak for themselves.

A collaborative training model can also be adapted to indeterminate sentencing schemes. Here, the prospect of a favorable parole decision, and hence early release, would be an incentive to complete a program plan. While prisoners serving an indeterminate sentence might well feel forced to participate in some type of program in order to impress the parole board, they would be able to collaborate freely with staff in the development of the particular program or sequence of programs they chose. This is not an ideal arrangement; some resentments about being coerced into treatment may well linger on among indeterminate-sentence prisoners. But it is better than making inmates enter programs chosen for them unilaterally by the staff. Finally, a collaborative training approach can also be used with program contracts. Prisoners, in collaboration with the staff, would formulate their own correctional programs. By the terms of their particular contracts, they would be promised an early release date or given some other incentive to complete the programs.

As a compromise strategy, offenders can be forced to undergo testing (to assess program needs) and to complete an orientation to the prison's programs (to familiarize themselves with program offerings), but then be free to elect or reject programs of their own volition. Spread before them would be a cafeteria of options, together with some guidance as to which programs might serve them best. Should they elect to take programs, contract terms can then be fashioned. Obligating the authorities to honor these contracts would circumvent the problems caused by coerced change. It would also ensure that programs are provided to interested prisoners by a prison system that is willing to hold itself accountable for delivering on its promises.

Contracts would normally include incentives such as "program time," time taken off one's sentence for completion of programs. Incentives of any kind reserved exclusively for those who take programs may encourage some inmates to take programs for the wrong reasons: to obtain the rewards and not to learn from the programs, with the very real risk that they may ruin the programs for the sincere inmates. Some prisoners may feel compelled to "serve time" in programs, particularly if the incentive is early release. This can be construed to be implicitly coercive.[93] However, unless incentives are excessive and arguably irresistible, so that inmates with no interest in self-improvement flock to programs, they should be viewed as proper uses of rewards. It is reasonable for us to encourage inmates to help themselves and unreasonable to expect them to embark on a major life change without at least some tangible benefits in the offing. Choice in this context may not be entirely free, but some choice is better than no choice at all.[94]

Contracts with program time incentives, when combined with progressive eligibility for placement in less security-oriented institutions, hold open the prospect of major reforms in the allocation of prison populations and resources. Program contracts of this sort would make it possible to (1) shorten sentences and thus reduce overcrowding through the early release of the more motivated and hence more deserving prisoners; and (2) develop comparatively inexpensive "low" or even "no-security" confinement facilities for the bulk of offenders, the majority of whom could be "managed safely in minimum-security institutions" as they go about the business of pursuing their program plans.[95] Of critical importance is the fact that these reforms can be achieved without increasing the risk to the public of increased recidivism.[96]

Contracts that are voluntarily entered into by inmates but binding upon staff offer a rational and fair way to ease prison crowding. They seem, moreover, to be the ideal arrangement in a rehabilitative scheme in which the objective is to promote mature coping. The process of negotiating the contract would itself be an exercise in adult conflict resolution. Here the offender is a bona fide consumer of services rather than a dependent and incompetent recipient of therapeutic or correctional largesse. The prison is transformed from a repository of nonnegotiable treatments or other coercive solutions to problems to a source of services that can be accepted or rejected on their merits. In this context, mature coping means using the services at one's disposal and demanding services when they are absent. Doing the best one can with what is available—while not resorting to violence, deception, or disregard of others—presupposes having done one's best to get what one has coming.

Inmates should have the right to negotiate program contracts that the state is required to honor. Failure of correctional officials to negotiate in good faith or to uphold contracts should result in either monetary damages or early release. Breaches of contracts by inmates would presumably result in the failure to gain whatever skills or knowledge the programs were meant to impart, as well as the forfeiture of any sentence reductions or other tangible benefits associated with the completion of the contract. It is fair to say that "in the long run *the very existence* of a contract system will exert pressure on correctional officials to improve treatment services."[97] It will also reinforce the core notions of mature coping, particularly that violence is a primitive and inappropriate way to solve problems. Men and women "who negotiate their fates," as Fogel has observed "do not have to turn to violence as a method of achieving change."[98] Nor need they use deception or assume a pose of indifference to hide hurt feelings. Instead, a constructive relationship with the correctional authorities provides a vehicle for personal reform.

Scottish Prisons: A Case Study in Correctional Innovation

Prisons in Scotland have implemented many of the innovations we have reviewed relating to the treatment of prisoners as consumers of correctional environments and correctional service. Scottish prisoners are accorded considerable autonomy as a matter of policy. The logic, as explained by John Pearce, Regional Director of the Scottish Prison Service, is that

> if he [the prisoner] is not treated as a Responsible Person whilst in custody, and if he is not given opportunity whilst in prison to exercise some choice over his daily life, then it would be difficult to see how he was being assisted to exercise responsible choice on discharge.[99]

The Scottish penal system regularly surveys the quality of life and work in its institutions, and uses this ecological information to inform a management system whose guiding premise is that the *"actual delivery of service [is] the most important part of the organisation."*[100]

Consumer surveys uncover preferences among prisoners that may differ substantially from those held by bureaucrats removed from the daily ebb and flow of life in the prison. Officials are apt to focus on readily visible features of the prison such as how well it is maintained, how many staff it employs and inmates it holds, the number of programs offered, and so on. In England, this has recently taken the form of a major investment in plumbing, to put toilets in individual cells. (As recently as 1990, most English prisoners "slopped out" each morning because their cells lacked toilets. This had become something of an embarrassment for officials since it gave their prisons a third-world appearance in international correctional circles.) Inmates, in contrast, are apt to focus on the experience of life inside prisons. Though many Scottish prisoners live in cells without toilets, like their English counterparts of a few years ago, when they were surveyed, the installation of in-cell toilets ranked a mere fourth on their priority list. Concerns relating to a productive human environment were paramount. "Overwhelmingly from prisoners was the desire for more and deeper contact with families, for better and more varied opportunities to develop skills and indeed for better relationships and even improved training for staff."[101] It seems entirely likely that similar results would have been obtained among the English prisoners, had they been surveyed as to their consumer preferences.

Scottish inmates, moreover, participate actively in sentence planning, where they in essence contract for services. They have a role in selecting the prison in which they will do time and the manner in which their prison time will be spent. They are assisted in this process by a "Personal Officer," which is to say, a line correctional officer whose job is to help them "work through a series of discussion and assisting papers in order to decide what should be the process and nature of the prisoner's activities through the sentence—that is, to create a Sentence Plan."[102]

Given the aim of treating prisoners as autonomous consumers of correctional services, prison staff are seen as "facilitators in the process of change and personal development."[103] Prison officers, in particular, play a key human service role in the change process. It is, states Pearce, "the ambition shared by Social Work Departments and the Prison Service that prison officers should deliver basic welfare services to prisoners and be supported in this by the professional trained social worker who can then focus on the chronic and more specialist problems of prisoners."[104] Experience in Scotland bears out these ambitions. With training and support, line officers have been "a vital pivot in addressing issues with prisoners ranging from the deeply personal through to the really practical."[105] The deeply personal issues referred to by Pearce have included working in a supportive way with inmates suffering from HIV/AIDS or struggling to end their addiction to drugs. More practical issues have related to running decent units on a daily basis.

The key features of the Scottish Prison Service have been summarized by Pearce in the following five points.

1. That a Prison *Service* is just that—a service—and prisoners are properly a very important part of the customer base.

2. That the prison officer is *the* key worker and with proper support and training is able to deal extremely professionally with the most personal and sensitive areas of a prisoner's life as well as the good order and control tasks.

3. That regimes should reflect the needs of the prisoners to facilitate their better coping at and following release.

4. That bottom up strategic planning [as exemplified in consumer surveys] produces exciting innovation, flexibility and responsiveness and turns the place upside down like no centralised organisation could ever achieve.

5. That glossy, centrally produced programmes usually fall flat on their face.[106]

The first point on the list is crucial. Pearce stresses that "Service Delivery is what is now driving our prisons. We are about not just clean underwear and nice food. We are about the manner in which our inmates interact with each other, interact with us and interact with their families."[107] This focus on service delivery gives great latitude to decision makers in the field, who tailor general management directives to fit the specifics of the ecology of the prisons under consideration. Prison regimes in Scotland and elsewhere, Pearce concludes, can promote better coping through the kinds of collaborative efforts we have reviewed. "I personally believe, after many years experience, that there is much we *can* do with prisoners, *there always was,* the difference these days is that no longer are we doing it *at* them, we are doing it *with* them."[108] It is significant to note that in Scotland, the collaborative, consumer-oriented approach is used across the board, with all types of prisoners and all types of prisons. Even Scotland's version of the supermax prison, reserved for Scotland's most violent and disruptive prisoners, is no exception. Scotland's supermax units offer an instructive contrast to the purely repressive and largely unproductive model of the supermax prison found in America.[109]

PRISONER AS CONSUMERS OF PROGRAM SERVICES

To treat inmates as consumers of program services does not mean to cater to their every whim. But prisoners' preferences matter, since they in effect "purchase" programs with their participation and "boycott" programs through nonparticipation. Consumers in prison, like their counterparts in the free world, should be periodically surveyed to determine their perceptions of both their needs and the means to meet those needs. This, we have noted, is being done in Scottish prisons. Such surveys, again like their counterparts in the free world and in Scottish prisons, should be seen as a guide to program development. Survey results indicate problem areas that should be considered and types of approaches that might most fruitfully address those problems. Guidance should also be obtained from patterns of program selection. On the premise that one cannot make horses, even thirsty horses, drink water on command, programs that prisoners don't want or use should be modified or discarded, while those sought and completed should be retained and used as models for future program development.

There is a virtual absence of specific information on prisoner program preferences, which is itself a telling indication that inmates have not been taken seriously as consumers of correctional services. Still, there are indications of the general direction programs should take, from prior research and from the Scottish prisoner surveys. Broadly speaking, we know that most prisoners feel they need educational and vocational services,[110] and many admit to problems in relationships and deficiencies in self-control.[111] Self-control problems range from concerns about impulsive behavior, including impulsive violence, to concerns about addiction. Additionally, women express a desire for programs that will help them deal with domestic violence, perhaps the leading relationship problem they face; and for programs that will strengthen mother-child ties and generally equip them to be better parents.[112] When offenders, male as well as female, are exposed to programs that deal with cognitive deficiencies, they generally respond with considerable enthusiasm and a dogged willingness to consider new ways of thinking about themselves and the world—the old ways, they know, breed pain and failure. (Note the highly positive subjective appraisals of the Living Skills program, discussed earlier.)

Correctional work cannot operate in a vacuum, however. When prisoners ask for programs, even broad-based programs such as the Life Skills program, they are not just seeking technical assistance. Educational or vocational or social adjustment programs alone will never be enough to reform prisoners. They also need support. To provide relevant and useful support, one must meet inmate "where they're at" developmentally, and then gradually move them toward a proficient level of useful skills.[113] There must also be a system of incentives, such as time reduced from sentences or adequate wages.[114]

The most basic element of the support enterprise is caring. This is true both in prison and out, and independent of the particular program at issue. "To be supported," Toch makes clear, "means to be met halfway. This means being provided not only with the tools to success" in the form of credible programs offered in decent environments, "but also with an expression of human interest."[115] Claude Brown sees the same need among today's "manchildren" of the ghetto, who are working their way toward prison with distressing regularity. "Most of them," Brown tells us, "possess a hunger for guidance and advice so profound it would be too humiliating to express even if they could."[116] One young boy told Brown that "he lost interest in school when the teachers had no obvious interest in instructing him. 'It's all about knowing somebody cares,' he said. 'That's what makes you care.' "[117]

In the prison, caring is expressed by staff "who grease the wheels or who smooth the road when the going gets rocky. It means persons who understand the difficulties of what one is trying to achieve. It means gentle coaxing or firm urging if one's motivation temporarily flags."[118] It also means insulation from destructive peers and, better yet, exposure to "peers who are strongly inclined toward achievement, who can provide mutual assistance and who can help strengthen one's resolves."[119] Program environments, like living and working environments, must become constructive niches—sanctuaries with a purpose—if they are to provide genuine learning experiences. The alternative is to offer programs that do little more than raise expectations but not capabilities, setting prisoners up for failure.[120]

GETTING OUT AND STAYING OUT: TRANSITION SUPPORT

The transition from the prison world to the free world can be difficult. "Even the most repentant, well-meaning, and well-prepared ex-prisoners," states Lin, "face a world that is infinitely more complicated than the isolation and the structure that characterize prison."[121] Complications include a fast-paced life in a world that is alien and unreceptive. The simple fact of imprisonment, moreover, makes it hard for ex-offenders to straighten out their lives. They now have a serious record—computerized and easily accessible to employers and law enforcement authorities—which disqualifies them from voting in many jurisdictions[122] as well as from a host of jobs.[123] Finding a job, *any* job, is difficult, since employers often fear ex-cons. Finding a good job is daunting, in part because ex-prisoners have been out of the job market for so long and typically have few marketable skills.[124] Most ex-cons take the first job they can find, which is generally in the service sector, in fast food restaurants like Burger King. These jobs pay poorly. They also require "customer service"—dealing politely with a wide range of often impatient humanity—which presupposes interpersonal skills many ex-offenders lack.[125] The simple act of taking orders from customers can be difficult for people with a precarious sense of their personal worth.[126]

Problems on the home front are common as well. Many prisoners live on dreams of reunions with loved ones, but often those relationships have been damaged—sometimes beyond repair—by their history of criminality and by the prolonged separation caused by their imprisonment, which precludes normal contact for years on end.[127] Women, in particular, find that they may have to single-handedly recreate the home and the family they left behind, because their familial worlds dissolved in their absence.[128] (Men more often have homes to return to, even if they are less than welcome there.) As with men, the fact of incarceration and the process of prison adjustment make reassimilation difficult. Women, too, have betrayed loved ones; they, too, have lived apart, with relationships often deteriorating as a result. To the extent that a given women has immersed herself in a "prison family" to survive imprisonment, these emotional ties may make it harder for her to reestablish real family ties upon release from prison.[129]

Many ex-offenders, male as well as female, are tired of crime and harbor dreams of a middle class life marked by "a family, a home, a dog, and a white picket fence" as well as a daily existence free of the frustrations and insults so common behind bars. These dreams, Lin notes, are not "blueprints" for life; they are "symbolic images rather than concrete plans."[130] Sadly, these images portray a world that is well out of reach for the vast majority of offenders. Even if releasees make the incomes they expect (Lin reports that ex-offender expect to make about $10.45 per hour), they cannot finance a middle class home or lifestyle. The actual incomes they are likely to make, moreover, will be considerably less than they expect—on average, 60 percent less.[131] In part because of their poor incomes, ex-convicts find daily life in the free world disappointing. Lin's subjects indicated that their days were filled with petty frustrations, including choices that were closed to them because they could not afford them. Nor do they get the respect they craved. Their main feat, prison survival, is a taboo subject in most circles, and indeed was only appreciated by other ex-cons, often a dangerous group to associate with.[132] To make matters worse, ex-convicts know "they have and therefore can survive prison," a setting they may come to view with more than a hint of nostalgia as time passes. In the face of mounting anxiety about frustrations and failures in the free world, the prison may look better all the time, eventually masquerading in their eyes as a curious "mother who provides and protects" her vulnerable dependents.[133] Thus prison, for some, offers an almost comfortable alternative to the struggle to adjust to hostile world. And so, too, may crime develop, if not an allure, at least a practical appeal. "Crime may not be an attractive option," in Lin's words, "[b]ut it is a familiar one" in times of stress.[134] Given the misplaced optimism many offenders express about their criminal exploits—who espects to get caught?—the stage is set for recidivism.[135]

For these many reasons, corrections cannot stop with prison programs, even programs that have an explicit focus on community reintegration (such as the Living Skills program, for example, which includes a sequence on community reintegration skills). Transition-related problems must be directly addressed, and prisoners must be tangibly assisted in their efforts to make the transition back to civilian life. One option is to include within prison programs any of a host of "transfer training techniques" that reinforce the link between mature coping in the prison and mature coping in the community.[136] More ambitiously, programs can come equipped with a "relapse prevention" sequence, featuring supportive supervision in the community[137] (Interestingly, the word recidivism means, literally, to "fall back" or relapse.)[138] Support of this type will reduce the chances that prisoners, upon release, will be unable to get their lives started or will be lured away from the comparatively humdrum existence of a conventional life of decidedly modest proportions.[139]

Securing and keeping a good or at least acceptable job is, as we have noted, one of the key challenges facing prisoners upon release. While promising programs exist (as noted above), many prisoners leave confinement having had little or no correctional treatment relating to work or any other aspect of adjustment to life in the free world. Others are exposed to programs so inadequate and perfunctory as to leave them utterly unprepared to reenter the free community. Thus, many inmates suffer diminished rather than enhanced autonomy as a result of their experiences in confinement. They are, as a consequence, deeply apprehensive on leaving the prison, as fearful of entering our world, the free world, as we are of entering theirs, the prison world. As these inmates see it, they are leaving prison unprepared for a world that is filled with "opportunities for relapse" that threaten to undermine their best coping efforts.[140]

The fears of prisoners facing release cannot be assuaged with a few kind words. Nor will threats help them go straight. The truth is, for many prisoners, their feelings of insecurity and their fears of the free world are justified.[141] They find, on release, that they have not improved their coping competence and there is, indeed, no place for them; continued poor coping in the free world lands them back in prison. As Zamble's research has revealed, poor coping habits retained in prison—or at least, not ameliorated by imprisonment—are replayed in the free world, yielding emotional turmoil that in turn promotes destructive behaviors such as alcohol and drug abuse, undertaken mainly as an escape from the pains of readjustment to life in the free world. This cycle, common among women as well as men, feeds on itself, until it culminates—sometimes quite soon after release—in impulsive acts of crime, followed by arrest and return to prison.[142] Others succeed, but on the most pathetic terms. They may, for example, live for a time with support of relatives or some form of state or federal support, drifting along on the fringes of society, perhaps in and out of crime but never, in any case, a part of the conventional society, and all too often destined for homelessness and an early death on the streets of our cities. (Rita Biggs, a one-time homeless person who described herself as "perfectly impaired," offers a view of incarceration as a break from this dead-end life, though the risk of sinking back into an aimless existence would appear substantial to outside observers.[143])

Today, and no doubt for the foreseeable future, effective correctional programs will be available to only a minority of prisoners. Programs that extend their reach into the community will be even more rare. It is therefore urgent to note that, with or without programming during the course of their confinement, offenders must be given assurances that, on release, they will not be abandoned—as is so often the case today.[144] They must be assured that they will receive not only supervision, but also some support services relative to finding and keeping a job, securing an education, and dealing with emotional and other problems likely to surface during the period of readjustment that awaits them. Supportive follow-up services are essential; even intensive supervision, on its own, has only a minimal effect on recidivism.[145] When support services are routinely provided, and especially when they are provided, in part, by volunteers in the community—whose very presence is a source of hope for apprehensive releasees—recidivism rates drop, sometimes substantially.[146]

In summary, the objective of rehabilitation programs is to create constructive niches where none exist and to enrich those already in existence. Ideally, all inmates should be exposed to niches in which they and their keepers solve the daily problems of prison adjustment in a mature manner, and in which these elementary but vital coping skills are augmented in formal programs. All prisoners, in other words, should be supported in their prison adjustment efforts and offered the opportunity to acquire the social, educational, and vocational skills needed to live a peaceful and ultimately self-sufficient life upon release from confinement. As we have seen, programs exist that promote mature coping—that is, clear thinking about the nature of problems and legitimate solutions to those programs (for example, the Living Skills program), coping without resort to violence or to drug or alcohol addiction (for example, various self-management programs), and living effectively in human communities (for example, various prison therapeutic community programs, whether the focus of such communal living programs is clear thinking, nonviolence, or desistance from drugs or alcohol). Transitional services would extend the reach of programs and support into the community. If prisoners are to maintain hope for a conventional life in the free world, nothing less than a combination of program resources and human support will suffice.

NURTURING HOPE AND REFORMING CRIMINALS

Some prisons operate exclusively as barren human warehouses, and virtually all contemporary prisons lapse into this condition from time to time in at least some of their internal environments. When prisons assume a warehousing function, even one in which pain is minimized, they tax the human spirit and undermine hope. They are vestigial manifestations of the worst features of the historical prison, where storage marked by idleness and isolation comprised the whole of the prison experience. Such prisons may mete out civilized punishments, but they are utterly incapable of civilizing their inhabitants.

When prisons become overcrowded, moreover, the temptation to warehouse inmates as a *matter of policy*—rather than as a failure of policy—is strong. This situation faces all too many of today's penal institutions, where there is a critical absence of commitment among prison leaders to a constructive vision of the prison.[147] For the administrator who must run a prison that is bulging with excess bodies and threatening chaos, custodial concerns are apt to take on an uncommon salience. The administrative agenda will typically be formulated in terms of unit space and musical beds instead of ecology and niches; it will seek containment and control rather than coexistence and coping; it will settle for cell time and surface tranquility rather than program time and the "improvement mess"[148] that often accompanies personal reform.

These compromise goals will serve only to further compromise an environment already in decline. For crowding exaggerates the more primitive side of prison life.[149] Physical conditions are apt to deteriorate; garbage, stench, and noise may become standard features of the daily routine. Even such basic commodities as food and clothing may be in short supply.[150] Social life becomes especially precarious. The simple density of bodies in crowded prisons means that inmates, including state-raised convicts, come into more abrasive public contact with one another. At the same time, the private culture of the prison shrinks as bodies take up the space formerly deployed more flexibly, forcing more and more guards and inmates out of niches and personal roles and into places and roles that are unfamiliar to them. Tension and the potential for violence, including collective violence, become tangible facts of crowded prison life.[151] The need for classification and management strategies that preserve environmental sanctuaries, and for programs that provide constructive activities, becomes urgent.[152] Crowded prisons must be explicitly managed as human ecologies—as places where people spend constructive time rather than where they merely serve time—or they will degenerate, slowly but inexorably, into inhumane warehouses. And it is entirely feasible to preserve a decent human ecology, even in a crowded prison. For "even in times of severely crowded correctional institutions," research and practice reveals that functional unit management "has achieved a high degree of success" and can serve to reduce the ill effects of high population density.[153]

Warehouse prisons may snuff out hope with disheartening regularity, but hope does not necessarily live in more congenial penal environments. It takes more than a secure and responsive prison with decent programs to promote hope. For hope is ultimately the belief that one has "an accepted place in the community," that one has not been abandoned and forgotten but has a chance, however remote, to live once again as a citizen in the free society.[154] As a practical matter, "the reality of this acceptance has to be expressed in the interest and sustained involvement of the community" in the life of the offender and the prison.[155]

If hope is to be preserved, then, the experience of reintegration into the free community must be "an ongoing process rather than an event reserved for those inmates who are about to be released."[156] Constructive relations with one's keepers, whether line staff or treatment staff, are one important source of human bonds that contribute to reintegration; staff members are living embodiments within the prison of the larger community to which most inmates will return.[157] Some peer associations, particularly those that develop in the context of responsive communities or other constructive prison activities, may also promote reintegration; these relations build bridges between adaptation in the prison world and subsequent adaptation in the free community.[158] Community volunteers, too, can do much to promote prosocial attitudes and relationships among prisoners, particularly during the transition to the free world.[159] The critical element in the reintegration process, however, is often the relationships inmates maintain with their family and friends, their significant others in the free community. A number of studies have found "a significant difference in the recidivism rate of prisoners who have had regular, continuing visits from family members as compared to those who did not have visits or had only sporadic visits."[160] This finding, moreover, has stood up over some fifty years of research covering diverse prison populations.[161]

Visits must be facilitated by prison administrators whenever and however possible. Visits matter greatly because prisoners, as Conover reminds us, are all "missing people"—missing from their outside lives. Some, maybe many, are missed by those outside as well. In visits, prisoners and their loved ones reconnect, and often are, consciously or not, doing the work necessary to repair strained relationships and to build a more secure future.

■ It was easy to forget when you worked at Sing Sing that all the inmates there were, essentially, missing from someplace else. Outside the walls, however, they were fathers, sons, brothers, and husbands—mainly of poor people from New York City. In being sent to prison, they had no doubt let people down; some who loved them no longer wanted to see them. But they were missed by many others, and every day of the week these people found their way to the prison via bus, car, train and taxi. They submitted to searches of their person and property and subjected themselves to long waits in order to spend a short time in Sing Sing's Visit Room.

The Visit Room constituted a sort of breach in the wall between the hermetic world of the prison and the universe outside. In it, an inmate could try to reconnect to the real world and prior life, could try to salve the wound of imprisonment. A visitor could contemplate, with more perspective than any prison employee, the effects of incarceration and the prospects of life after it. The Visit Room was about catching up, reconnecting, and looking ahead, about a woman's touch and a child's chatter.[162] ■

Our relations with others, and particularly our family and friends, are the ties that build our self-esteem and bind us to the larger human community. These are "the animating relations with others that sustain us, enrich our lives with meaning, and make life worth living."[163] Human relationships make it possible for men and women to persist in dead-end jobs and to endure lives of quiet desperation, lives that in objective material terms offer meager rewards. Relations with others make the work of mature coping—at home, at work, in the neighborhood, even in the prison—a labor of love rather than a test of endurance. These human connections make real for each individual the core notion that they, as autonomous persons, secure in themselves and in their ties with others, have the power to change themselves and, in both small and large ways, the world around them.

Jesse Jackson artfully explored the theme of personal change in a Christmas Day message to the prisoners of Chicago's Cook County Jail. Though his remarks were given several years ago (in 1994) and tailored to a black audience, it is clear that the message is a universal and contemporary one:

> The key to change is in your mind, in your heart. Malcolm turned a jail cell into a classroom. Racism didn't change for him; the job situation didn't change for him; the police didn't change. Nothing changed but him.

Change must occur within individuals, as Jackson makes clear, but the capacity for change—the will to change—draws on hope. Hope, in turn is rooted in supportive ties to others in the human community. If these ties are absent—if they fail under pressure or never materialize at all—community becomes an empty abstraction, the self an impoverished shell, the future an exercise in narcissism and self-aggrandizement. Life becomes not so much a matter of coping well or badly as maintaining the will to cope at all. At this juncture, conventional life seems pointless and onerous beyond human endurance; crime becomes at once an irresistible temptation to self-indulgence and a poignant expression of anger and despair.[164] It is as if the violence of crime summarizes the violence done to the criminal's life, initiating yet again a sequence of crimes and punishments that reflect and extend that violence and constrict even further the community we all wish to share. Violent crime, increasingly the refuge of hopeless, brutalized children, mirrors the hopelessness and brutality in their lives. It follows, in the wise logic of William Raspberry, Pulitzer-prize-winning columnist for the *Washington Post,* that "Our communities won't be safe *from* our children until we first make them safe, decent and nurturing places *for* our children."[165]

By the same token, our prisons can't be decent and nurturing places unless they are run properly and reserved for those who clearly and unambiguously deserve this fateful sanction. Prisoners can feel abandoned and forgotten by the larger society if they conclude that their very confinement is an injustice. It is wise to recall the admonition of Albert Camus, the distinguished French existentialist, that injustice is a form of violence.[166] For the unjustly confined, even a congenial and responsive prison can be experienced as a human warehouse and as a profound violation of human dignity. Such troubling perceptions may be more common—and more valid—than we in the larger society would care to admit. We noted in Chapter One that our prisons are full to overflowing, bloated with offenders at a rate unmatched elsewhere in the world. A sizable and growing segment of that population is made up of drug offenders and minorities. Many of these offenders feel themselves to be unjustly confined, and a case can be made for the legitimacy of those perceptions.

It is, of course, entirely conceivable that our crowded prisons are filled with people who deserve to be confined and that such a deployment of our limited penal resources is wise. In other words, our crowded prisons could be the result of society's efforts to cope maturely with a difficult crime problem. This is true in principle, but as a practical matter, one has to be skeptical, at the very least. There is, for example, no convincing evidence that our massive use of imprisonment over the last two decades or so has reduced the crime rate in any consistent or substantial way.[167] Moreover, our long-standing tendency to use prison sentences, and sometimes lengthy prison sentences, for lesser property crimes seems patently unwise and out of step with penal trends in other nations in the West.[168] The recent and considerable growth of drug offenders in our prison population, many serving long sentences for what amounts to possession or small-time trafficking, suggests a hysterical response to the social problems that shape patterns of drug use and abuse in our society. The phenomenal growth of the black prison population over the last decade, partly a product of our misguided war on drugs, suggests racist crime control practices.[169] To the extent that we are using prisons as instruments of repression to deal with problems and populations that make us uncomfortable, the case can be made that our penal policy is, indeed, a form of violence. In my terms, such a state of affairs is a classic instance of immature coping in the face of the social stresses produced by crime in modern America.

It is easy to reject this line of argument out of hand. One might readily contend that African Americans experience high rates of confinement because they commit crimes at high rates, including "the kinds of crimes, like homicide, robbery, and aggravated assault, that typically result in prison sentences."[170] Young African-American men are, after all, frisked daily on ghetto streets because they appear to police to be behaving suspiciously, and they are arrested and locked up at high rates for criminal behavior, not simply for being black. But these encounters often involve actual or suspected drug-related behavior rather than standard street crime. It is society's choice to wage an aggressive drug war that in effect targets those who inhabit inner-city streets in contrast to, say, suburban homes or Wall Street offices, two settings that feature deceptively widespread patterns of drug use. Penalties in existing laws, especially federal laws, are such that the drugs of choice in inner cities come in for harsher penalties than the drugs of choice in the surrounding—largely white—communities.[171]

The point is that patterns of police deployment and our ever-growing prison populations are not random events, but rather are a product of policy choices. As Tonry has made clear,

> the rising levels of black incarceration did not just happen; they were the foreseeable effects of deliberate policies. . . . Anyone with knowledge of drug-trafficking patterns and of police arrest policies and incentives could have foreseen that the enemy troops in the War on Drugs would consist largely of young, inner-city minority males.[172]

Different policies would target different groups, resulting in different rates of police contact and, ultimately, in confinement of different groups of offenders. A focus on white-collar crime, for example, would produce a very different prison population. Even a difference in drug enforcement practices as seemingly minor as focusing on powdered cocaine (sniffed in offices and at parties of the professional classes) rather than rock cocaine (that is, crack, smoked on street corners or in abandoned houses in the inner city) would produce different patterns of enforcement, which in turn would yield different patterns of confinement—in this instance, relatively fewer black offenders and more white offenders than is the case today. It should be apparent that political considerations shape policy in this area, making inner-city blacks an easy target of opportunity in what amounts to a selective assault on the drug problem.[173]

And while it is true, as I have argued throughout this book, that prisons can be arranged to help reform offenders, in many cases that help could be more effectively, more cheaply, and more humanely rendered in community settings rather than in prisons.[174] People who deserve prison deserve to be helped while they are there; for them, we must strive to make hard time into constructive time. Prisoners are sent to prison for punishment that, when properly arranged, can prove helpful. Offenders who don't deserve the punishment of prison should not be sent there for punishment or treatment. Those offenders can certainly be offered help, but that help should be provided in the community, not in confinement.

RECONCILIATION

Prisoners spend their sentences apart from the community, but the notion that we can forget them—put them out of sight and out of mind—is an illusion. In a subtle but important existential sense, prisoners are always with us, and we with them. Society penetrates prison walls, shaping many aspects of prison life and adjustment; virtually all offenders return to the community, bringing a little bit of prison life with them in the process. Even those offenders slated to live out their days behind bars remain members of the larger human community, which encompasses both the free society and the society of captives.

Prison reformers, then, must strive to build the human bonds that at once sustain decency in the prison and serve to link the prison to the larger social world of which it is a part.

Yet released prisoners find themselves "in" but not "of" the larger society. Like lepers, we keep ex-prisoners at a distance and avoid them entirely when we can. Even under the best of conditions, ex-offenders face formidable obstacles to reassimilation in the community. Today, released offenders are not exposed to the best of conditions or even to minimally acceptable conditions; they are instead subjected to release policies that are arbitrary and restrictive, producing high rates of revocation and sending releasees back to prison in record numbers. In Petersilia's words,

> Nearly 700,000 parolees are now doing their time on U.S. streets. Most have been released to parole systems that provide few services and impose conditions that almost guarantee their failure. Our monitoring systems[175] are getting better, and public tolerance for failure on parole is decreasing. The result is that a rising tide of parolees is washing back into prison, putting pressure on states to build more prisons, which in turn, takes money away from rehabilitation programs that might have helped offenders while they were in the community. All of this means that parolees will continue to receive fewer services to help them deal with their underlying problems, assuring that recidivism rates and returns to prison remain high and public support for parole remains low.[176]

The underlying problem, in my view, is that ex-convicts suffer from a *presumption of moral contamination* because they have been to prison! There is a cruel irony at work here. We send offenders to prison, warehouse them, then recoil from them because we suppose they have been brutalized by the prison experience we imposed upon them! We can take some comfort in the fact that the majority of prisoners did in fact commit the crimes for which they were punished, though studies of innocent people sent to prison and even to death row provide cautionary tales we ignore at our peril.[177] Be that as it may, we as a society built the prisons that, in the name of justice, render ex-convicts forever suspect. A person can be released from prison, then, but not from the taint of being a prisoner. Instead of marking one's exit from the status "criminal in need of punishment" followed by one's entry into the status "a citizen who has paid has debt to society," release from prison seems to have no positive connotations at all! One simply becomes an ex-convict, with the emphasis on convict.

Imprisonment is an example of a "degradation ceremony," an event that publicly marks prisoners as damaged goods, as outcasts worthy of our hatred and contempt.[178] We convict criminals and incarcerate them with some fanfare. Arrests are visible to neighbors and any onlookers in the vicinity (sometimes including the television viewing public and always including the newspaper reading public); court proceedings are open to the public (and again sometimes to the television viewing public and always to the newspaper reading pubic). Sentences are solemnly intoned in open court, with the convicted offender then whisked off to prison in handcuffs and perhaps leg-irons as well. (Some sense of the enormity of this experience is conveyed in first-hand accounts of crime and punishment.)[179] The person is now, first and foremost, a criminal and a prisoner. Whatever else he or she is or was becomes secondary, if not entirely irrelevant. There is no comparable rite or ritual to mark the transition of offenders back to the status of citizen—no "naturalization ceremony" or "normalization ceremony" that marks and celebrates the termination of their lives as imprisoned criminals and their return to the world as free citizens. We force offenders to skulk out of prison after doing their time. There is little support in the form of guidance or money to help them start their new lives. We don't give any credit—moral credit—for the prison experience. People released from prison have done their time but have not, and indeed perhaps cannot, pay their debt to society. As things stand, that debt lasts a lifetime. There is no effort to reconcile and forgive, to accept time served as a kind of penance, a making of amends for the crime and an effort to build a new future. Instead we watch and wait for people to fail. In a sense the system has succeeded beyond our wildest hopes at the basic task of containment. It captures criminals and won't let them go.[180]

These arrangements are no doubt demoralizing to released prisoners. Many hope to go straight and a fair number succeed, against all odds. We do little to help any of them, and nothing to recognize the considerable achievement of those who do turn their lives around. This is not a case of benign neglect. When we as a society fail to acknowledge a prisoner's reformation, we place that accomplishment in grave doubt. As Maruna has observed,

> Reformation is not something that is visible or objective in the sense it can be 'proven.' It is, instead, a construct that is negotiated through interaction between an individual and significant others . . . Until ex-offenders are formally and symbolically recognized as 'success stories,' their conversion may remain suspect to significant others, and most importantly to themselves. . . . [181]

We urge offenders to change, but when they do, we abandon them—at the very point they might most need encouragement to continue in the often thankless work of personal reformation.[182] We can do better. For persons we can certify as "corrected," we could have a "rehabilitation ceremony" that acknowledges that this is a new human being, not a former offender but an offender no more—a person we allow to start life again with a clean slate. In Maruna's words, "Whatever the requirements" of the rehabilitation ceremony and certification process, "the ultimate reward" for going straight "should be permission to legally move on from the past."[183] If sinners can be born again and forgiven their trespasses, why not offenders?

Some among us may find justice or, better, just desserts in our present, punitive arrangements. Debts must be paid, to be sure, and prisoners, through their suffering, pay dearly for their crimes. But so too must new lives commence, both in prison and, on release, in the free world. Historically, the prison has failed to play a constructive role in the crucial process of reintegration; it has offered punishment, but that punishment, more often than not, has been neither civilized nor civilizing. Too often, the prison has isolated offenders from one another and from the free world. As a result, destructive stereotypes—fostering fear and loathing rather than care and compassion—have flourished in and out of prison. To be sure, the limits of prison as an instrument of reform are substantial, but they are not insurmountable. As we have seen in this book, prison can be a constructive punishment, one that promotes community and citizenship within its walls even as it maintains ties with the community of citizens outside its walls. The knowledge is there; we know how to run decent prisons. What has been lacking is the will to act, to translate humane intentions into humane prisons, and to forgive our wayward neighbors as they come out of prison and struggle to take their place as citizens in the free community.

Today's prisons can, in principle, address the noble goal of the penitentiary—which was meant to fashion its wards into citizens—while categorically rejecting the empty custodial quarantines that have been both the heritage and the legacy of that penal institution. That we might build citizens as we punish offenders has been an enduring aspiration, and one worthy of our best efforts. Each and every one of us, as responsible citizens, has a stake in this endeavor. We may properly dedicate ourselves to the task of prison reform, working to improve ourselves and expand our ranks.

NOTES

1. "Various mandatory programs have already made their way back into the prison system: not only do many states and the federal system require educational standards for prisoners, but federal sentencing policies now require prisoners convicted of drug or drug-related felonies to undergo 40 hours of drug education" (Lin, 2000:156).

2. "The long-term persistent offenders" in Maruna's study of crime desistance "generally said that they are sick of offending, sick of prison, and sick of their position in life. Several talked at length about wanting to go legit or at least doing something different with their lives. . . . Yet, they said that they feel powerless to change their behavior because of drug dependence, poverty, a lack of education or skills, or societal prejudice. They do not want to offend, they said, but feel they have no choice" (Maruna, 2001:74).

3. Conrad (1981b:64).

4. This cynicism allows us to maintain that all we as a society can do is "put prisoners away and hope they stay away" (Lin, 2000:17).

5. Martinson (1974:25).

6. Sechrest, White, and Brown (1979).

7. Braly (1967:90–96); Manocchio and Dunn (1982:109–17).

8. See Grant and Grant (1959).

9. Palmer (1975, 1978, 1991 & 1994).

10. See Andrews et al. (1990); and Kennedy (2000). For women, see Bloom (1999). It is interesting that Bloom, in her consideration of women's programs, uses dimensions of self (empowerment, safety, and connection) that closely resemble those used in this book (autonomy, security, and relatedness to others). Her preferred levels of intervention (cognitive, affective, and behavioral) corrrespond closely to those we have used in this text. One would expect this if one assumes that

humanistic interventions must address the
core concerns of men and women.

11. Gendreau and Ross (1987:351); see
also Cullen (2000).

12. Lin (2000:5).

13. Lin (2000:30).

14. Lin (2000:31).

15. Lin (2000:104).

16. Lin (2000:104).

17. As Lin has in sightfully observed,
"*what* exists must be understood in terms
of *how* it exists. Programs exist in varieties:
varieties of implementation, which result
from variations in the prison context, and
which in practice create programs that
share little but the name. Achieving successful implementation is thus as much
about creating the right context for programming as it is about getting the program's design, incentives, or structure
right: it is about taking the needs of staff
and prisoners seriously and on their own
terms, and about emphasizing—or
promoting—values within the prison that
can provide a 'hook' for appropriate programming" (Lin, 2000:59).

18. Lin (2000:35).

19. Maruna (2001:112).

20. See Castellano and Soderstrom (1997)
and Soderstrom and Castellano (2002).

21. As Lin has thoughtfully observed, "No
magic bullet" or set formula "exists for
implementation. No particular set of values
or incentives is best suited to the successful
implementation of programs, either in
prisons or in general. . . . the successful
implementation of a program can only be
measured in terms of incentives it provides, at any particular time, for staff and
clients to participate in the program, and
in terms of the match between existing
institutional values and the program activities they will justify" (Lin, 2000:128).

22. Lin (2000:52).

23. Lin (2000:52).

24. Lin (2000:52).

25. The quotations in this paragraph are
drawn from Lin (2000:110).

26. Lin (2000:55).

27. (Lin (2000:164).

28. Cullen, Latessa, Kopache, Lombardo,
and Burton (1993).

29. Martinson (1978:4).

30. Gendreau and Ross (1980:5).

31. Gendreau and Ross (1980:27).

32. Levinson (1988:247).

33. Levinson (1988:247).

34. Levinson (1988:247).

35. Ross and McKay (1980: 47–48).

36. Abrams and Siegel (1978); Ellis
(1979); Bleick and Abrams (1984).

37. Bornstein et al. (1979); Golden et al.
(1980); see, generally, Bennett, Rosenbaum
and McCullough (1978).

38. See Ross and McKay (1980:49–50).

39. Behavior that is both severely punished (for example, by parents) and highly
rewarded (for example, by peers) is most
resistant to change. The behavior gains
strength from what is called "punishment
training," which, as explained by Newman
(1978:253), has clear implications for the
management of prisoners. A juvenile gang
member's misbehavior may bring him
immediate rewards, such as status or "rep"
with other gang members. If his parents
find out, he may be severely physically
chastised. Thus he is punished and
rewarded, the net result being the
strengthening of his mischievous gang
behavior. According to punishment
research, subsequent punishment will
merely facilitate this undesirable behavior.

40. See Gendreau (1989); Gaes, et al,
(1999); Kennedy (2000) and Cullen
(2000). Robinson (1996) points out that
the category "high risk" does not always
include the "highest risk" inmates, who
can be stubbornly resistant to change. See
Andrews et al. (1990).

41. See Andrews et al. (1990); Stewart and
Rowe (2000).

42. Gendreau (1989); Gendreau and Goggins (1996). Research on this subject reveals a paradox: program success requires a commitment to process—to making sure the program offers what it is supposed to offer—rather than to outcomes. As Lin has noted, "conditioning support for programs upon their success guarantees that many programs will fail." This is because implementation takes commitment, which will not be forthcoming until success is demonstrated. Without commitment, the program can't get off the ground and hence can't succeed. In Lin's words, "programs that are not implemented successfully will not succeed; and implementing programs successfully demands a level of prior commitment to the program. Implementation requires work: work to discover the values and needs that staff and participants bring to a program, and more work to figure out how these can be balanced with the intentions of policymakers. It requires the wise use of flexibility, for that balance will vary with the history and the institutional arrangements present at a particular site. It demands the willingness to address problems that may not be linked to the introduction of programs themselves. All of this takes time, a minimum commitment of resources, and a certain insulation from threats to the program's existence. And political support is what makes that possible" (Lin, 2000:172).

43. Levinson (1988).

44. Morris (1974).

45. Levinson (1988:251).

46. Note that improvements in the Butner group were measured against a control group of prisoners exposed only to functional units and standard correctional programs in other federal prisons. The original plan for the model prison at Butner included a phased transition into the community, with graduates of the program supervised and supported in the community by the staff who had manned the program in the prison. This part of the plan proved unworkable, for a host of administrative reasons, and was not carried out. It is probable that had this part of the plan been

retained, the reintegration of the prisoners would have occurred with more success.

47. Witte et al. (1983).

48. See, for example, Toch, Grant, and Galvin (1975); Toch (1980); Toch and Adams with Grant (1989); among others.

49. Toch and Grant (1989:222–23).

50. Zamble and Porporino (1990:69).

51. Zamble and Porporino (1990:69).

52. Zamble and Porporino (1990:67).

53. Zamble and Porporino (1990:69–70).

54. Fabiano, Robinson, and Porporino (1991:1). See also Fabiano, Porporino, and Robinson (1991).

55. Fabiano, Robinson, and Porporino (1991:6).

56. Limited self-control impairs cognitive and coping skills; self-control deficits affect more than eight out of ten Canadian felons and are "significantly more common among recidivists" (Stewart & Rowe, 2000:49).

57. Fabiano, Robinson, and Porporino (1991:6).

58. Fabiano, Robinson, and Porporino (1991:5).

59. Fabiano, Robinson, and Porporino (1991:6).

60. Fabiano, Robinson, and Porporino (1991:8).

61. Fabiano, Robinson, and Porporino (1991:10).

62. Fabiano, Robinson, and Porporino (1991:15).

63. Fabiano, Robinson, and Porporino (1991).

64. I am indebted to David Blansky, a former student assistant, for this point.

65. Fabiano, Robinson, and Porporino (1991:17).

66. Fabiano, Robinson, and Porporino, 1991:21).

67. Fabiano, Robinson, and Porporino, 1991:19).

68. Robinson, Grossman, and Porporino, (1991:4).

69. Robinson, Grossman, and Porporino, (1991:8).

70. Gaes, et al. (1999: 379).

71. Lin (2000:31).

72. CTSP tends to work best with violent offenders (a group for whom distortions in thinking may be most pronounced) and with offenders of average or above average intelligence (a group with the cognitive capacity to take the program). As the program is offered on a wide scale basis, more "nonamenable" offenders will be exposed to the regime, presumably reducing success rates (Kennedy, 2000).

73. Gaes, et al. (1999:374).

74. Bush and Bilodeau (1993).

75. Bush (1988); see also Hunter (1993).

76. "An independent evaluation of the Delaware Life Skills Program found that, for the first program cycle, 19 percent of LS [Living Skills] students in the four state prisons reoffended within 1 year after release, compared with 27 percent of a group of inmates that did not participate" (Finn, 1998:2).

77. Serin and Preston (2000:48).

78. NIJ (1989:1).

79. See Lipton, Falkin, and Wexler (1990:23); see also Wexler and Williams (1986). A reanalysis of this body of work on the Stay' N Out program, using multivariate techniques, "showed that treatment volunteers . . . were more likely to recidivate" than the comparison groups. Gaes, et al. (1999:393).

80. Gaes et al. (1999:397.) Many offenders mix alcohol and drugs indiscriminately. Effective programs are available for offenders whose predominant problem is alcohol (see Gendreau & Ross, 1987:384).

81. Staub (1989:277).

82. Lipton, Falkin, and Wexler (1990:28).

83. Hawkins (1976 & 1983); Finn (1998).

84. Hawkins (1983:107).

85. Hawkins (1983:111).

86. Thompson (1994:45).

87. There are presently 41 certified programs with various individual work sites in operation across the nation, employing 3,826 inmates as of June 30, 2000. Since its inception in 1979, PIE has produced substantial earnings—154,890,650 in gross wages; 13,761,635 in money provided to victims' programs; 37,961,635 in money paid to cover prisoners' room and board; 9,105,043 paid out in family support; and 21,034,494 paid in taxes. (See www.correctionalindustries.org).

88. See website for the Correctional Industries Association (www.correctionalindustries.org).

89. Seiter (1994:529).

90. Seiter (1994:528).

91. Saylor and Gaes (1994:538).

92. "Male inmates who had worked in prison industries were 24 percent less likely to recidivate, while those who had participated in either vocational or apprenticeship training were 33 percent less likely to recidivate throughout the follow-up period" (Gaes, et al., 1999:406).

93. Morris (1974).

94. Toch makes this point succinctly. "One established way of promoting inmate participation" in programs, he notes, "is to offer to negotiate contracts in which persons agree to behavior goals whose attainment will be rewarded. It is true that one can point to power imbalances in such contracts between staff and clients who sign them. Limited choice, however, is better than no choice, and volition that is exercised in the absence of constraints or incentives is rarely encountered anywhere" (Toch, 1988:46).

See also Lin (2000:157–8) for a thoughtful discussion of this subject.

95. Austin (1983:575) van den Haag (1981); see also Austin and Irwin (2000).

96. This point is backed by controlled empirical research. One study, conducted in California prisons, involving both vio-

lent and nonviolent offenders, has been summarized as follows:

experimental and control groups . . . differed only on the lengths of their prison terms. The experimentals served six months less time in prison than they would have been expected to serve [× = 31.3 months], while the prison term for the controls was not changed [× = 37.9 months]. . . . Within the first and second years following release to parole, the experimentals and controls did not differ on the likelihood of their being returned to prison either by a court conviction for a new felony or as a result of a parole violation. . . . [Hence,] prison terms can be reduced without affecting recidivism to a significant and practical degree. (Berecochea & Jaman, 1981; summarized in Criminal Justice Abstracts, S 30484, 1982:370–71).

A similar study was conducted by the Wisconsin Department of Health and Social Services (1983), though here the experimental group was composed entirely of nonviolent offenders who were afforded intensive parole supervision upon release from prison. (Given the findings of the California research, the selection and supervision process used in Wisconsin may have been superfluous). Most recently, the expansion of "good time" in Illinois and Oklahoma has resulted in substantial savings accrued from early release without compromising public safety (see Austin & Bolyard, 1993; Irwin & Austin, 1994:172–73; Austin & Irwin, 2000).

97. Cullen and Gilbert (1982:271) [emphasis added].

98. Fogel (1975:206).

99. Pearce (1994:8); see generally, Scottish Prison Service (1990); Frizzel (1996); Scottish Prison Service (2000).

100. Pearce (1994:12); [emphasis in original]; see also Toch (1994:68).

101. Pearce (1994:14).

102. Pearce (1994:10).

103. Pearce (1994:8).

104. Pearce (1994:1).

105. Pearce (1994:8–9).

106. Pearce (1994:17).

107. Pearce (1994:20).

108. Pearce (1994:20).

109. American supermax prisons are in operation in thirty-six states and the Federal Bureau of Prisons. Still, supermax prisons are few in number compared to regular maximum-security prisons, and house less than 2 percent of the American prison population. These institutions, relying on the long-term segregation of prisoners and often featuring continuous camera surveillance, would appear to be high-tech throwbacks to the days of the Big House or even, in some key respects, the solitary version of the earliest penitentiaries. (The Administrative Maximum Facility, for example, in keeping with its maximally sterile name, has been described as offering "hermetic cells" and "a super-controlled environment that enforces a hard-edged solitude to contain the risk of social mixing and violence" among offenders. What is this if not a twentieth-century version of Eastern Penitentiary, reserved exclusively for the clientele of a classic, tough Big House like Alcatraz? See Cline, 1994:B1). Unsurprisingly, administrators of these settings view them as exemplary versions of hard time for hard-core predators, while the prisoners view these institutions as profoundly inhumane (see Haney, 1993; Immarigeon, 1992; Austin & Irwin, 2000).

110. Coffey and Louis (1979); Gaes et al. (1999).

111. Toch (1977); Pearce (1994); Kennedy (2000).

112. Girshick, 1999:138. Girshick estimates that fully 88 percent of the women in her study were victims of domestic violence. "The lack of targeted services to deal with battering," she notes, "is a gaping hole in programming." (Girshick, 1999:150) The centrality of parenting to female inmates is thoughtfully explored in Girshick.

113. Toch (1977:78).

114. Conrad (1981b:65–66).

115. Toch (1977:76) Support-oriented inmates appear to be of the opinion that like-minded peers are rare in prison. Most

demands for support are probably directed to staff, who are presumed to possess competencies not shared by fellow prisoners. These suppositions are borne out by Smith's (1984:75) jail inmate survey, in which prisoners made it clear that they wanted to be left alone by peers, but cared for, protected, and helped by staff and the facility in general, particularly "via program opportunities."

116. Brown (1984:78).

117. Brown (1984:78).

118. Toch (1977:77).

119. Toch (1977:77).

120. Glaser (1975). Wormith (1984:611) notes that "minimal or inadequate training may . . . be antirehabilitative." It raises hopes that can be easily dashed and gives the offender a false sense of efficacy that "can be readily extinguished by disconfirming experiences" (Bandura, 1977:198).

121. Lin (2000:4).

122. See Petersilia (1999:509–511); Love and Kuzma (1996).

123. As Petersilia has observed, "Between 1986 and 1996, state legal codes reveal an increase in restrictions on the rights and opportunities available to released inmates" (1999:509). See Olivares, Burton, and Cullen (1996); Love and Kuzma (1996).

124. The job skills of ex-prisoners tend to be limited. Many had no vocational training at all and others were exposed to programs that were, in varying degrees, out of date (see Murphy, 2000).

125. Lin (2000:140).

126. Maruna (2001).

127. Lin (2000:148).

128. O'Brien (2001:2).

129. O'Brien (2001:14).

130. Lin (2000:145–6).

131. Lin (2000:147–8).

132. Lin (2000:149).

133. Besozzi (1993:38); see also, Duncan (1988); Padron (2000).

134. Lin (2000:150).

135. Lin (2000:141–3).

136. Gendreau (1989).

137. Gendreau (1989); Finn (1998).

138. See Nouwens, Motiuk, and Boe (1993:23).

139. Toch (1977:79–80). Linden and Perry (1982) apply these observations to prison education programs, noting that successful programs are intensive, establish an alternative community within the prison, and offer postrelease services. See also Gaes, et al. (1999), and Stevens (2000).

140. See Besozzi (1993). Inmates approaching release have long been known to experience "gate fever," a constellation of emotions featuring anxiety, depression, irritability, and a host of psychosomatic symptoms of distress. A thoughtful empirical study of this phenomenon has been performed by Castellano and Soderstrom (1997).

141. Feelings of insecurity may be masked by an apparently inflated sense of one's worth, but this facade is often brittle and subject to collapse when difficulties emerge.

142. See Zamble (1993); Howard (2000); O'Brien (2001).

143. Biggs (2000). See, generally, Austin and Irwin (2000).

144. Maruna (2001:114).

145. See NIJ (1993); Clear and Braga (1994); Petersilia (1999).

146. See NIJ (1993); Petersilia (1999:522). Volunteers may also serve to "bring inmates into the community"; as Girshick (1999:180) notes, this can be "an excellent way to break down stereotypes of female prisoners" and presumably male prisoners as well.

147. As Toch (1985:59) has observed, "two disasters" beset corrections in the 1980s: "The advent of (1) unprecedented overcrowding . . . [and] (2) the loss of

faith in correctional rehabilitation." Prisons are even more crowded today, and though the catalog of successful prison programs grows apace, a warehousing stance seems to the primary option that many prisons administrators see as open to them. We can take some consolation in the fact that a number of scholars have identified ways to enrich correctional environments, and hence to avoid warehousing—or at least to minimize its harmful effects (see, for example, Toch, 1985). Innovative, policy-relevant ways to measure crowding and its variation over time are also under development (see Klofas, Stojkovic & Kalinich, 1992). The need for constructive prison leadership to set an agenda for coping with these and other programs is insightfully identified by Wright (1994) and Riveland (1999).

148. As Redl (1980) tells us, people experiencing personal growth often get worse before they get better. They are dealing with problems—at first clumsily and emotionally, later with more poise and self-control—rather than denying problems, suppressing feelings, and doing time. They must be permitted, indeed encouraged, to take risks, fail, and start again.

149. Smith (1988); Fitzgerald and Sim (1982); Toch (1997).

150. Smith (1988); Cobb (1985); Johnson (1992).

151. Smith (1988); Lombardo (1988).

152. Toch (1984).

153. Webster (1991:420). A more modest but also useful organizational reform involves the use of cubicles in dormitories, shops, and classrooms. With proper supervision, these cubicles can serve as a poor man's cell; a group of such cubicles can form the core of a rudimentary functional unit. The point is that functional units and related arrangements provide privacy, which ameliorates the impact of crowding and is "very desirable for the physical and psychological welfare of the inmates as well as from a prison management perspective" (Cox, Paulus & McCain, 1984:1156; see also, Johnson, 1992).

154. Conrad (1981b:66).

155. Conrad (1981b:66).

156. Weiner (1988:306).

157. Glaser (1969).

158. Toch (1980).

159. Andrews et al. (1973 & 1977); Parker and La Cour (1983).

160. Homer (1979:47); Cobean and Power (1978).

161. See Schafer (1978); Burstein (1977).

162. Conover (2000:151).

163. Conrad (1981b:66).

164. Renzema's (1988:160–61) research with parolees makes it clear that "more important than either the stressors in the environment or the discomfort they generated was the respondent's ability to maintain hope. When hope of achieving a satisfactory life through legitimate means failed, trouble followed."

165. Raspberry (1994:A23; 1994:A19).

166. See, for example, Camus's profound essay, "Reflections on the Guillotine" (1969).

167. See Blumstein (1994:416); Tonry and Petersilia (1999).

168. See Lynch (1994:37).

169. See Tonry (1995); Johnson (2000).

170. These grim trends, present in a number of countries, may reflect the "failure of social policies aimed at assuring full participation by members of minority groups in the rewards and satisfactions of life in industrialized democratic countries" (Tonry, 1998:289).

171. See, generally, Reiman (1997); Tonry (1995); Lusane (1991).

172. Tonry (1995:4); Mauer (1992:27).

173. Tonry (1995:39).

174. See Zamble (1992); Clear and Braga (1994); Gendreau, Goggin, and Smith (1996); Gaes, et al. (1999); Cullen (2000)

175. In this context, monitoring systems provide surveillance and sanction rather

than feedback and corrective adjustment, as when an offender's coping is monitored or a program's implementation is monitored.

176. Petersilia (1999:522–3).

177. For a review of this literature, see Schnek, Mayfeld and Duyer (2000).

178. See Garfinkel (1956); see, generally, Garland (1990).

179. See, for example, Majors (2000:42) and Brown (2000).

180. A notable exception to many of these observations is embodied in the work of Travis (2000), who offers an ambitious proposal to facilitate guided reentry into the community. Travis suggests that we frame the process of release in terms of a reentry court, with the judge in charge of the individual's progress. This would require:
- a plan to repay the debt for the offense (time in prison and time for reentry)
- the commitment of family and friends to help achieve the objectives (to prepare for reentry)
- monitoring of participation in prison programs to prepare for release
- the participation of other agencies in the community, such as probation officers, police officers, and drug treatment counselors

The programs the inmate participates in while in prison would be directed at the criminogenic forces at work in his or her life. When the individual has completed all the objectives for release, there would be a formal ceremony in court to welcome him or her back into society, after which more conditions would be set. Those conditions require that the releasee:
- remain drug free
- work to make the community safer (special commendations could be earned here)
- make restitution to the victim(s) and reparation to the community
- continue participation in programs started in prison
- avoid situations that could trigger relapse (gangs, old haunts, etc.)
- make monthly appearances before the judge to see how things are going

Travis (2000) argues persuasively that the benefits of such a system would include: cutting across organizations to meet a common goal (reducing recidivism), holding offenders accountable for their behavior, expanding positive influences for the offender by involving family, allowing a greater opportunity for tailored programming (by making the judge in charge of the treatment plan) and finally, focusing on a plan for reintegration rather than punishment.

I support Travis' focus on post-release supervision and supportive programs, including the idea of a ceremony welcoming the offender back into the community. I reject his contention that "Accepting released offenders into the community without a period of supervised release is morally unsatisfying; they have not yet earned their place at our table" (Travis 2000:2). I would argue that by serving their time in prison, offenders have earned their place at our table. Post-release programming is needed, in no small measure, to rectify problems that have been created or aggravated by imprisonment. It might be more helpful to think of these programs as part of a mutual effort at reconciliation, where offender and society work together to make amends—for hurtful crimes and hurtful punishments—and move forward.

181. Maruna (2001:158).

182. Maruna (2001:114).

183. Maruna (2001:165).

REFERENCES

Abrams, A. I., and L. M. Siegel. "The transcendental meditation program and rehabilitation at Folsom State Prison." *Criminal Justice and Behavior* 5 (1) 1978:3–20.

Andrews, D. A., J. G. Young, J. S. Wormith, C. A. Searle, and M. Kouri. "The attitudinal effects of group discussions between young criminal offenders and community volunteers." *Journal of Community Psychology* 1 (October) 1973:417–22.

Andrews, D. A., J. S. Wormith, D. J. Kennedy, and W. Daigler-Zinn. "The attitudinal effects of structured discussions versus recreation association between young criminal offenders and undergraduate volunteers." *Journal of Community Psychology* 5 (January) 1977:63–71.

Andrews, D. A., I. Zinger, R. D. Hoge, J. Bonta, J. Gendreau, and F. T. Cullen. "Does correctional treatment work? A psychologically informed meta-analysis." *Criminology* 28 1990:369–404.

Austin, J. "Assessing the new generation of prison classification models." *Crime & Delinquency* 29 (4) 1983:561–76.

Austin, J, and M. Bolyard. *The Effectiveness of Shorter Prison Terms*. San Francisco: National Council on Crime and Delinquency, March 1993.

Austin, J. and J. Irwin. *It's About Time: America's Imprisonment Binge*. Belmont, CA: Wadsworth. 2000.

Bandura, A. "Self-efficacy: Toward a unifying theory of behavioral change." *Psychological Review* 84 (2) 1977:191–215.

Bennett, L. A., T. S. Rosenbaum, and W. R. McCullough. *Counseling in Correctional Environments*. New York: Human Services Press, 1978.

Berecochea, J. E., and D. R. Jaman. "Time served in prison and parole outcome: An experimental study." California Department of Corrections, 1981.

Besozzi, C. "Recidivism: How inmates see it." *Forum on Corrections Research* 5 (3) 1993:35–38.

Bleick, C. R., and A. I. Abrams. "The transcendental mediation program and criminal recidivism in California." Unpublished paper, 1984.

Bloom, B. "Gender-responsive programming for women offenders: Guiding principles and practices," *Forum on Corrections Research* 11 (3) Sept. 1999:22–27.

Blumstein, A. "Prisons." In J. Q. Wilson and J. Petersilia (eds.). *Crime*. San Francisco: ICS Press, 1994:387–420.

Biggs, R. L., "Perfectly impaired." In R. Johnson and H. Toch (eds.). *Crime and Punishment: Inside Views*. Los Angeles: Roxbury Publishing Company, 2000:22–33.

Bornstein, P. H. et al. "Interpersonal skills training: evaluation of a program with adult male offenders." *Criminal Justice and Behavior* 6 (2) 1979:119–31.

Braly, M. *On the Yard*. New York: Penguin Books, 1967.

Brown, C. "Manchild in Harlem." *New York Times Magazine* (September 16,) 1984:36–41, 44, 54, 76, 78.

Brown, Mr. (a psuedonym). "There is no justice in Florida." In R. Johnson and H. Toch (eds.). *Crime and Punishment: Inside Views*. Los Angeles: Roxbury Publishing Company, 2000:225–231.

Burstein, J. Q. *Conjugal Visits in Prisons: Psychological and Social Consequences*. Lexington, MA: Lexington Books, 1977.

Bush, J. M. "Violent Offender Program: Review of the First Year." St. Albans, VT: Northwest State Correctional Facility, December 1988.

Bush, J. M., and B. Bilodeau. *Options: A Cognitive Change Program*. NIJ: U.S. Department of Justice, June 1993.

Camus, A. "Reflections on the guillotine." In *Resistance, Rebellion and Death*. New York: Knopf, 1969.

Castellano, T. C. and I. R. Soderstrom. "Self-esteem, depression, and anxiety evidenced by a prison inmate sample: Interrelationships and consequences for prison programming." *The Prison*

Journal 77 (3) September 1997:259–280.

Castellano, T. C. and I. R. Soderstrom. *Developing the Mature Coping Skills of Criminal Offenders: The Impact of Boot Camp Interventions.* Paper presented at the 1997 Annual Meeting of the Academy of Criminal Justice Services.

Clear, T. R., and A. A. Braga. "Community corrections." In J. Q. Wilson and J. Petersilia (eds.). *Crime.* San Francisco: ICS Press, 1994:421–44.

Cline, F. X. "A futuristic prison awaits the hard-core 400." *New York Times* (October 7, 1994):B1 & B10.

Cobb, A. "Home truths about prison overcrowding." *The Annals of the American Academy of Political and Social Science* 478 (March) 1985:73–85.

Cobean, S. C., and P. W. Power. "The role of the family in the rehabilitation of the offender." *International Journal of Offender Therapy and Comparative Criminology* 22 (1) 1978:29–38.

Coffey, O., and C. N. Louis. "Unemployment, crime, and the local jail." *Corrections Today* 41 (2) 1979:36–39.

Conover, T. *Newjack: Guarding Sing Sing.* New York: Random House, 2000.

Conrad, J. P. "Where there's hope there's life." In D. Fogel and J. Hudson (eds.). *Justice As Fairness.* Cincinnati, OH: Anderson, 1981a:3–21.

Conrad, J. P. "The state's strongest medicine." In J. P. Conrad. *Justice and Consequences.* Lexington: Lexington Books, 1981b:51–70.

Cox, V. C., P. B. Paulus, and G. McCain. "Prison crowding research: The relevance for prison housing standards and a general approach regarding crowding phenomena." *American Psychologist* 39 (10) 1984:1148–60.

Cullen, F. T., and P. Gendreau. "Assessing correctional rehabilitation: Policy, practice, and prospects." In *Policies, Processes, and Decisions of the Criminal Justice System, Criminal Justice 2000, Volume 3.* Washington, DC: U.S. Department of Justice, National Institute of Justice. July 2000.

Cullen, F. T., and K. E. Gilbert. *Reaffirming Rehabilitation.* Cincinnati, OH: Anderson, 1982.

Cullen, F. T., E. J. Latessa, R. Kopache, L. X. Lombardo, and V. S. Burton. "Prison wardens' job satisfaction." *The Prison Journal* 73 (2) June 1993:141–161.

Duncan, M. G. "Cradled on the sea: Positive images of prison and theories of punishment." *California Law Review* 76 (6) 1988:1202–47.

Ellis, G. A. *Inside Folsom Prison: Transcendental Meditation and TM-Sidhi Program.* Palm Springs, CA: ETC Publications, 1979.

Enos, S. *Mothering from the Inside: Parenting in a Woman's Prison,* Albany: State University of New York at Albany Press, 2001.

Fabiano, E. A., F. J. Porporino, and D. Robinson. "Canada's cognitive skills program corrects offenders' faulty thinking." *Corrections Today* (August) 1991:102–108.

Fabiano, E. A., D. Robinson, and F. Porporino. *A Preliminary Assessment of the Cognitive Skills Training Program: A Component of Living Skills Programming.* Correctional Service of Canada, 1991.

Finn, P. *Program Focus: Texas' Project RIO (Re-Integration of Offenders).* Washington DC, U.S. Department of Justice, National Institute of Justice. June 1998.

Fitzgerald, M., and J. Sim. *British Prisons.* London: Basil Blackwell, 1982.

Fogel, D. *"We Are the Living Proof": The Justice Model for Corrections.* Cincinnati, OH: Anderson, 1975.

Frizzel, E. W. "Addressing offending behaviour: Lessons from the Scottish experience in developing prisoner programs." Paper presented at the Fourth Commonwealth Correctional Administrators Conference, Brisban, Australia, November, 1996.

Gaes, G. G., T. J. Flanagan L. L. Motiuk and L. Stewart. "Adult correctional treatment." In M. Tonry and J. Petersilia (eds.). *Prisons.* Chicago: University of Chicago Press, 1999:361–426.

Garfinkel, H., "Conditions of successful degradation ceremonies." *The American Journal of Sociology,* 61, 1956:420–24.

Garland, D. *Punishment and Modern Society: A Study in Social Theory.* Chicago: University of Chicago Press, 1990.

Gendreau, P. "Principles of effective intervention." Unpublished paper, November 1989.

Gendreau, P., and R. R. Ross. "Effective correctional treatment: Bibliotherapy for cynics." In R. R. Ross and P. Gendreau. (eds.). *Effective Correctional Treatment.* Toronto: Butterworth, 1980:3–36.

Gendreau, P., and R. R. Ross. "Revivification of rehabilitation: Evidence from the 1980s." *Justice Quarterly* 4 (3) 1987:349–407.

Gendreau, P., C. Goggin, and P. Smith. "The forgotten issue in effective correctional treatment: Program implementation." *International Journal of Offender Therapy and Comparative Criminology, 43 1996: 180–187.*

Girshick, L. B. *No Safe Haven: Stories of Women in Prison.* Boston: Northeastern University Press, 1999.

Glaser, D. *The Effectiveness of a Prison and Parole System.* Indianapolis: Bobbs-Merrill, 1969.

Glaser, D. "Achieving better questions: A half century's progress in correctional research." *Federal Probation* 39 (September 1975):3–9.

Golden, D., C. P. Twentyman, M. Jensen, J. Karan, and J. D. Kloff. "Coping with authority: Social skills training for the complex offender." *Criminal Justice and Behavior* 7 (2) 1980:147–59.

Grant, J. D., and M. Q. Grant. "A group dynamics approach to the treatment of nonconformists in the Navy." *Annals of the American Academy of Political and Social Science* 322 1959:126–35.

Haney, C. "Infamous punishment: The psychological consequences of isolation." *National Prison Project Journal* 8 (2) 1993:3–7.

Hawkins, G. *The Prison: Policy and Practice.* Chicago: University of Chicago Press, 1976.

Hawkins, G. "Prison labor and prison industries." In M. Tonry and N. Morris (eds.). *Crime and Justice Annual.*

Chicago: University of Chicago Press, 1983:85–181.

Homer, E. L. "Inmate-family ties: Desirable but difficult." *Federal Probation* (March) 1979:47–52.

Howard, J. "Freedom within." In R. Johnson and H. Toch (eds.). *Crime and Punishment: Inside Views.* Los Angeles: Roxbury Publishing Company, 2000:69–79.

Hunter, D. "Anger management in the prison: An evaluation." *Forum on Corrections Research* 5 (1) 1993:3–5.

Immarigeon, R. "Marionization of American Prisons." *National Prison Project Journal* 7 (4) 1992:1–5.

Irwin, J., and J. Austin. *It's About Time: America's Imprisonment Binge.* Belmont, CA: Wadsworth, 1994.

Johnson, R. "Crowding and the Quality of Prison Life." In C. Hartjen (ed.). *Correctional Theory and Practice.* Chicago: Nelson-Hall, 1992:139–45.

Johnson, R. "American prisons and the African-American experience: A history of social control and racial oppression," *Corrections Compendium* 25 (9) September 2000: 6–10 & 28–30.

Kennedy, S. M. "Treatment responsivity: Reducing recidivism by enhancing treatment effectiveness." *Forum on Corrections Research* 12 (2) (May) 2000:19–23.

Klofas, J. M., S. Stojkovic, and D. A. Kalinich. "The meaning of correctional crowding: Steps toward an index of severity." *Crime and Delinquency* 38 (2) 1992:171–88.

Levinson, R. B. "Try softer." In R. Johnson and H. Toch (eds.). *The Pains of Imprisonment.* Prospect Heights, IL: Waveland Press, 1988:241–56.

Lin, A. C., *Reform in the Making: The Implementation of Social Policy in Prison.* Princeton: Princeton University Press, 2000.

Linden, R., and L. Perry. "The effectiveness of prison education programs." *Journal of Offender Counseling, Service, & Rehabilitation* 6 (4) 1982:43–57.

Lipton, D. S., G. P. Falkin, and H. K. Wexler. "Correctional drug abuse treatment in the United States: An overview." Paper presented at NIDA Technical Review, Rockville, MD, May 24, 1990.

Lombardo, L. X. "Stress, change, and collective violence in prison." In R. Johnson and H. Toch (eds.). *The Pains of Imprisonment.* Prospect Heights, IL: Waveland Press. 1988:77–93.

Love, M. and S. Kuzma. *Civil Disabilities of Convicted Felons: A State-by-State Survey.* Washington, DC: Office of the Pardon Attorney, 1996

Lusane, C. *Pipe Dream Blues: Racism and the War on Drugs.* Boston. South End Press, 1991.

Lynch, J. P. "Crime in international perspective." In J.Q. Wilson and J. Petersilia (eds.). *Crime.* San Francisco: ICS Press, 1994:11–38

Majors, M. B. "We are all human beings." In R. Johnson, and H. Toch (eds.), *Crime and Punishment: Inside Views.* Los Angeles: Roxbury Publishing Company, 2000:42–47.

Manocchio, A. J., and J. Dunn. *The Time Game: Two Views of a Prison.* Beverly Hills, CA: Sage, 1982.

Martinson, R. "What works? Questions and answers about prison reform." *The Public Interest* (Spring 1974):22–55.

Martinson, R. "Martinson revisited." *Criminal Justice Newsletter* (December 4, 1978):4.

Maruna, S. *Making Good: How Ex-Convicts Reform and Rebuild Their Lives.* Washington, DC: American Psychological Association, 2001.

Morris, N. *The Future of Imprisonment.* Chicago: University of Chicago Press, 1974.

Murphy, G. V. "No one ever asked me, 'why.'" In R. Johnson and H. Toch (eds.), *Crime and Punishment: Inside Views.* Los Angeles: Roxbury Publishing Company, 2000:87–94.

Newman, G. *The Punishment Response.* Philadelphia: Lippincott, 1978.

NIJ—National Institute of Justice. "Research in action: Prison programs for drug involved offenders," October 1989.

NIJ—National Institute of Justice. "What works? A review of the correctional literature on program effectiveness," April 1993.

Nouwens, T., L. Motiuk, and R. Boe. "So you want to know the recidivism rate." *Forum on Corrections Research* 5 (3) 1993:22–26.

O'Brien, P. *Making It in the 'Free World': Women in Transition from Prison.* Albany, NY: State University of New York Press, 2001.

Olivares K., V. Burton, and F. T. Cullen. "The Collateral Consequences of a Felony Conviction: A National Study of State and Legal Codes 10 Years Later." *Federal Probation* 60 1996:10–18.

Padron, E. E. "The long-awaited day of freedom." In R. Johnson and H. Toch (eds.). *Crime and Punishment: Inside Views.* Los Angeles: Roxbury Publishing Company, 2000:196–200.

Palmer, T. "Martinson revisited." *Journal of Research in Crime and Delinquency* 12 (2) 1975:133–52.

Palmer, T. *Correctional Intervention and Research.* Lexington: Lexington Books, 1978.

Palmer, T. "The effectiveness of intervention: Recent trends and current issues." *Crime & Delinquency* 37 (3) 1991:330–46.

Palmer, T. *A Profile of Correctional Effectiveness and New Directions for Research.* Albany: State University of New York Press, 1994.

Parker, J. G., and J. A. La Cour. "Common sense in correctional volunteerism in the institution." In A. A. Roberts (ed.). *Social Work in Juvenile and Criminal Justice Settings.* Springfield, IL: Charles C. Thomas, 1983:275–84.

Pearce, J. (Regional Director of the Scottish Prison Service). Untitled speech to Middle Atlantic States Correctional Association, Killington, VT, May 25, 1994.

Petersilia, J. "Parole and prisoner reentry in the United States." In M. Tonry and

J. Petersilia (eds.). *Prisons.* Chicago: University of Chicago Press, 1999:479–529.

Petersilia, J., and S. Turner. "Comparing intensive and regular supervision for high-risk probationers: Early results from an experiment in California." *Crime & Delinquency* 36 (1) 1990:87–111.

Raspberry, W. "Beyond gun control." *The Washington Post* (August 10, 1994):A19.

Raspberry, W. "Power in the prisons." *The Washington Post* (December 28, 1994):A23.

Redl, F. "The concept of "therapeutic milieu." In H. Toch (ed.). *Therapeutic Communities in Corrections.* New York: Praeger, 1980:21–33.

Reiman, J. *The Rich Get Richer and the Poor Get Prison.* New York: Allyn and Bacon, 1995.

Renzema, M. "The stress comes later." In R. Johnson and H. Toch (eds.). *The Pains of Imprisonment.* Prospect Heights, IL: Waveland Press, 1988:147–62.

Riveland, C. "Prison mangement trends, 1975–2025." In M. Tonry and J. Petersilia (eds.). *Prisons.* Chicago: University of Chicago Press, 1999:163–203.

Robinson, D. "Factors influencing the effectiveness of cognitive skills training." *Forum on Corrections Research* 8 (3) 1996:6–9.

Robinson, D., M. Grossman, and F. Porporino. "Effectiveness of the cognitive skills training program: From pilot to national implementation." Research and Statistics Branch, Correctional Service of Canada: *Research Brief No. B-07,* 1991.

Ross, R. R., and H. B. McKay. "Behavioral approaches to treatment in corrections: Requiem for a panacea." In R. R. Ross and P. Gendreau (eds.). *Effective Correctional Treatment.* Toronto: Butterworth, 1980:37–53.

Saylor, W. G., and G. G. Gaes. "The post-release employment project: Prison work has measurable effects on post-release success." In P. C. Kratcoski (ed.). *Correctional Counseling and Treat-*

ment, Third Edition. Prospect Heights, IL: Waveland Press, 1994:535–42.

Schafer, N. E. "Prison visiting: A background for change." *Federal Probation* 42 (3) 1978:47–50.

Schnek, B., P. Newfeld and J. Duyer. *Actual Innocence: Five Days to Execution and Other Dispatches from the Wrongly Committed.* New York: Doubleday, 2000.

Scottish Prison Service. *Opportunity and Responsibility: Developing New Approaches to the Management of the Long Term Prison System in Scotland.* Crown copyright, May 1990.

Scottish Prison Service, *Intervention and Integration for a Safer Society.* Crown Copyright 2000.

Sechrest, L., S. O. White, and E. D. Brown. *The Rehabilitation of Criminal Offenders: Problems and Prospects.* Washington, DC.: National Academy of Sciences, 1979.

Seiter, R. P. "Federal prison industries: Meeting the challenge of growth." In P. C. Kratcoski (ed.). *Correctional Counseling and Treatment,* Third Edition. Prospect Heights, IL: Waveland Press, 1994:528–34.

Serin, R. C. and D. L. Preston. "Programming for violent offenders." *Forum on Corrections Research* 12 (2) 2000:45–48.

Smith, D. E. "Crowding and confinement." In R. Johnson and H. Toch (eds.). *The Pains of Imprisonment.* Prospect Heights, IL: Waveland Press, 1988:45–62.

Soderstrom, I. R., Castellano T. C., & Figaro, H. R. "Measuring 'mature coping' skills among adult and juvenile offenders: A psychometric assessment of relevant instruments." *Criminal Justice and Behavior* 28 (3) June 2001, 300–328.

Staub, E. *The Roots of Evil: The Origins of Genocide and Other Group Violence.* New York: Cambridge University Press, 1989.

Stewart, L. and R. Rowe. "Problems in self-regulation among adult offenders." *Forum on Corrections Research* 12 (2) 2000:49–52.

Thompson, C. "Luke gets a job." *American Way* 27 (4) 1994:44–46.

Toch, H. *Living in Prison: The Ecology of Survival*. New York: Free Press, 1977.

Toch, H. "The therapeutic community as community." In H. Toch (ed.). *Therapeutic communities in corrections*. New York: Praeger, 1980:3–20.

Toch, H. "Warehouses for people?" *Annals of the American Academy of Political and Social Science* 478 (March) 1985:58–72.

Toch, H. "Rewarding convicted offenders." *Federal Probation* (June 1988):42–48.

Toch, H. "Democratizing prisons." *The Prison Journal* 73 (1) 1994:62–72.

Toch, H., *Corrections: A Humanistic Approach*. Albany, NY: Harrow and Heston, 1997.

Toch, H., J. D. Grant. "Noncoping and maladaptation in confinement." In L. Goodstein and D. L. MacKenzie (eds.). *The American Prison: Issues in Research and Policy*. New York: Plenum Press, 1989:209–27.

Toch, H., and K. Adams with J. D. Grant. *Coping: Maladaptation in Prisons*. New Brunswick, NJ: Transaction Publishers, 1989.

Toch, H., J. D. Grant, and R. Galvin. *Agents of Change: A Study in Police Reform*. Cambridge, MA: Schenkman, 1975.

Tonry, M. *Malign Neglect: Race, Crime, and Punishment in America*. New York: Oxford University Press, 1995.

Tonry, M. "Racial disproportion in U.S. prisons." in Flanagan, T. J., J. W. Marquart and K. G. Adams (eds.). *Incarcerating Criminals: Prisons and Jails in Social and Organizational Context*. New York: Oxford University Press, 1998:287–301.

Tonry, M. and J. Petersilia. "American prisons at the beginning of the twenty-first century." In M. Tonry and J. Petersilia (eds.). *Prisons*. Chicago: University of Chicago Press, 1999:1–16.

Travis, J. "But they all come back: Rethinking prisoner reentry." *Sentencing & Corrections: Issues for the 21st Century*. Washington, DC: U.S. Department of Justice, National Institute of Justice (7) May 2000.

Van Den Haag, E. "Prisons cost too much because they are too secure." *Corrections Magazine* 6 (2) 1980:39–43.

Webster, J. H. "Architectural implications: Designing facilities for effective unit management." *Corrections Today* (April 1991):38–42.

Weiner, R. I. "Management strategies to reduce stress in prison: Humanizing correctional environments." In R. Johnson and H. Toch (eds.). *The Pains of Imprisonment*. Prospect Heights, IL: Waveland Press, 1988:299–309.

Wexler H. K., and R. Williams. "The stay 'n out therapeutic community: Prison treatment for substance abusers." *Journal of Psychoactive Drugs* 18 (3) 1986:221–30.

Witte, A. D., D. F. Woodbury, S. H. Smith, H. Barreto, and R. Beaton. "The effects of a less coercive prison environment and gradual reintegration on postrelease performance: An evaluation of Morris' model of imprisonment as implemented at the Federal Correctional Institution at Butner, N.C." (Mimeo) Federal Bureau of Prisons, June 1983.

Wormith, J. S. "Attitude and behavior change of correctional clientele." *Criminology* 22 (4) 1984:595–618.

Wright, K. N. *Effective Prison Leadership*. Binghamton, NY: William Neil Publishing, 1994.

Zamble, E. "Behavior and adaptation in long-term prison inmates: Descriptive longitudinal results." *Criminal Justice and Behavior* 19 (4) 1992:409–25.

Zamble, E. "Expanding the recidivism inquiry: A look at dynamic factors." *Forum on Corrections Research* 5 (3) 1993:27–30.

Zamble, E., and F. Porporino. "Coping, imprisonment, and rehabilitation: Some data and their implications." *Criminal Justice and Behavior* 17 1990:53–70.

Zamble, E. and V. L. Quinsey. *The Criminal Recidivism Process*. Cambridge: Cambridge University Press, 1997.

Index